WRITING FICTION

Why Do You Need This New Edition?

If you're wondering why you should buy this new edition of *Writing Fiction*, here are 8 good reasons!

❶ Expanded coverage of the writing workshop. The Writer's Workshop section in Chapter 1 will help you start the semester off right by familiarizing you with the expectations and goals of this fundamental part of fiction writing courses.

❷ New selections. More than half of the short stories included in the text are new to this edition, including works by contemporary favorites such as Stuart Dybek, Junot Diaz, Rob Hansen, Sherman Alexie, and many others. Three short stories now appear at the end of each of the chapters on the elements of fiction.

❸ More short-shorts. An ever-popular trend in contemporary American literary culture, this edition features more "short-shorts" than ever before.

❹ New chapter on dialogue. The discussion of dialogue has been expanded into a full chapter to help you master this important tool of the fiction writer.

❺ Refreshed approach to characterization. The discussion of nondialogue methods of characterization has been reorganized to provide a more comprehensive, accessible coverage.

❻ Theme. The discussion of theme has been condensed and incorporated into Chapter 9: Revision. The new organization will encourage you to focus on the particulars of your story and to allow theme to develop naturally.

❼ See revision in action. An early draft of fiction writer Ron Carlson's story "Keith" now accompanies an essay he wrote about revising the story and a final draft of the story, allowing you to trace the evolution of the piece.

❽ New section on comparison in Chapter 2: Showing and Telling. The chapter on comparison has been condensed into the discussion of significant detail in Chapter 2 to provide you with a more straightforward, practical discussion.

PEARSON

WRITING FICTION
A Guide to Narrative Craft

Eighth Edition

JANET BURROWAY
Florida State University

with

ELIZABETH STUCKEY-FRENCH
Florida State University

NED STUCKEY-FRENCH
Florida State University

Longman

Boston   Columbus   Indianapolis   New York   San Francisco   Upper Saddle River
Amsterdam   Cape Town   Dubai   London   Madrid   Milan   Munich   Paris   Montreal   Toronto
Delhi   Mexico City   São Paulo   Sydney   Hong Kong   Seoul   Singapore   Taipei   Tokyo

Senior Editor: Vivian Garcia
Associate Development Editor: Erin Reilly
Executive Marketing Manager: Joyce Nilsen
Production Manager: Jacqueline A. Martin
Project Coordination and Text Design: Elm Street Publishing Services
Electronic Page Makeup: Integra Software Services Pvt. Ltd.
Senior Cover Design Manager/Cover Designer: Nancy Danahy
Cover Image: Bathus (Klossowski de Rola, B.) (1908–2001), *The Street*. 1933. Oil on
  canvas 6'4¾" × 7'10½" (195 × 240 cm). James Thrall Soby Bequest © ARS, NY,
  The Museum of Modern Art, New York, NY, U.S.A./Licensed by SCALA/Art
  Resource, NY.
Senior Manufacturing Buyer: Alfred C. Dorsey
Printer and Binder: RR Donnelley & Sons Company, Crawfordsville
Cover Printer: RR Donnelley & Sons Company, Crawfordsville

For permission to use copyrighted material, grateful acknowledgment is made to the
copyright holders on pp. 401–402, which are hereby made part of this copyright page.

Library of Congress Cataloging-in-Publication Data

Burroway, Janet.
   Writing fiction : a guide to narrative craft / Janet Burroway, Elizabeth Stuckey-
French, Ned Stuckey-French.
      p. cm.
   Includes bibliographical references and index.
   ISBN 978-0-205-75034-4
   1. Fiction—Technique.   2. Fiction—Authorship.   3. Narration (Rhetoric).
   4. Creative writing.   I. Stuckey-French, Elizabeth.   II. Stuckey-French, Ned.
   III. Title.
   PN3355.B79 2009
   808.3–dc22

                                                                    2009031502

7 8 9 10—RRD—15 14 13

Longman
is an imprint of

ISBN-13: 978-0-205-75034-4
ISBN-10:   0-205-75034-6

www.pearsonhighered.com

In loving memory of David Daiches, mentor and friend

CONTENTS

PREFACE

The eighth edition of *Writing Fiction*, like its previous manifestations, attempts to guide the student writer from first impulse to final revision, employing concepts of fiction's elements familiar from literature study, but shifting the perspective toward that of the practicing writer. I wish to address students, however inexperienced, as fellow artists. Students' concerns often include fear, but also have to do with questions of understanding and development of technique.

As experienced instructors are aware, the idea of a text for writing fiction is itself problematic. Unlike such subjects as math and history, where a certain mass of information needs to be organized and conveyed, the writing of fiction is more often a process of trial and error—the learning is perpetual and, paradoxically, the writer needs to know everything at once. If a text is too prescriptive, it's not true to the immense variety of possibilities; if it's too anecdotal, it may be cheering but is unlikely to be of use.

I'm also aware that *Writing Fiction* is used by many instructors in both beginning and advanced writing courses and for students at very different levels of understanding. I've tried, therefore, to make it practical, comprehensive, and flexible, and to keep the focus on the student writer and the process of the writing. My means of doing this is to cover discrete elements in separate chapters, yet to build in each chapter on what has been covered earlier. Focus on the writing process and suggestions for getting started have seemed to me a logical place to begin the book, but I have tried to keep subsequent chapters sufficiently self-contained so that teachers may assign them in any order they prefer. Each chapter follows a similar structure, concluding with three short stories and a selection of writing exercises. Within each chapter, excerpts from other short stories are used in the text to offer quick illustrations of concepts. Boxed quotations from established authors—on topics such as writing from experience, story structure, openings and endings, and revision—offer students a quick and encouraging reminder of key chapter concepts.

New to the Eighth Edition

- **New Selections.** More than half of the short stories included in the text are new to this edition, including works by established contemporary favorites such as Stuart Dybek, Junot Diaz, Ron Hansen, Sherman Alexie, and many others. These stories have been chosen primarily from contemporary American fiction with attention to increased variety in form, mood, and content and emphasis on multicultural representation of authors and experiences.

- **Short-Shorts.** A new attention to "short-shorts," an ever-popular trend in contemporary American literary culture, has allowed us to now include three short stories at the end of each chapter on the elements of fiction.
- **The Writing Workshop.** In response to reviewer requests, our coverage of the writing workshop has been expanded and moved into Chapter 1. This new section will familiarize your students with the expectations and goals of this fundamental part of fiction writing courses.
- **Character and Dialogue.** We have reconceived our coverage of character by expanding our discussion of dialogue into a full chapter and reorganizing our discussion of nondialogue methods of characterization into another full chapter in order to provide a more comprehensive discussion of both topics.
- **Comparison.** The chapter on comparison has been condensed into the discussion of significant detail in Chapter 2 to provide a more straightforward, practical discussion useful to beginning writing students.
- **Theme.** The chapter on theme has been condensed and incorporated into our discussion of revision. Working from the conviction that theme is developed through every element of fiction, we discuss it together with revision, and so encourage beginning writers to focus on the story and allow theme to develop through the use of particulars.
- **Revision.** In the chapter on revision we have added an early draft of fiction writer Ron Carlson's story "Keith," to accompany an essay he wrote about revising the story, and a final draft of the story so that students can trace the evolution of a published piece.

For the seventh edition of *Writing Fiction* I asked my friend, colleague, and fellow fiction writer Elizabeth Stuckey-French to plan and author the revisions, based on many dozens of suggestions from teachers, students, and reviewers. The changes will be found in the readings, the exercises, and the text itself, including many updated references and fresh examples. Elizabeth was aided by her husband, also a colleague at Florida State, and also a writer, Ned Stuckey-French, who joins us in the eighth edition as a co-author. Elizabeth and Ned have made the arduous process a pleasure, for which I'm grateful.

Above all, for the new edition Elizabeth, Ned, and I have kept the exigencies of the creative writing classroom in mind, intending to be catalytic rather than prescriptive, hoping to encourage both students and teachers to feel comfortable with themselves and the writing process.

ACKNOWLEDGMENTS

More than any previous edition, the eighth edition attempts to respond to teachers who use it in the classroom, those who write or e-mail me spontaneously throughout the life of the edition, colleagues in universities and the Associated Writing Programs, and those asked by the publisher to engage in a formal process of review. There is really no appropriate term for these people. A "reviewer" usually makes a take-it-or-leave-it judgment, whereas the reviewers of a text are collaborators in an ongoing attempt to keep the book vital among the changing needs of students, teachers, and the academic zeitgeist. Naturally these teacher/writers tend to nudge the new edition in the direction of their own pedagogical needs and methods, and inevitably some advice conflicts with other. Nevertheless, reviewers are surprisingly often in agreement and often thorough, thoughtful, practical, and inspired.

Many people have helped with the eighth edition of *Writing Fiction*. Thanks go to my students and colleagues in the Writing Program at Florida State University.

I am also grateful to the following writers/teachers who have reviewed this edition: Lawrence Coates, Bowling Green State University; John Holman, Georgia State University; Susan Jackson Rodgers, Kansas State University; Arnie Johnson, Western Michigan University; Barry Lawler, Oregon State University; Jeanne M. Leiby, University of Central Florida; Colleen J. McElroy, University of Washington; Alyce Miller, Indiana University; Keith Lee Morris, Clemson University; Kimme Nuckles, Baker College of Auburn Hills; R. Clay Reynolds, University of Texas at Dallas; Barry Rodman, University of North Texas; Sheryl St. Germain, Iowa State University; Stephen H. Watkins, University of Mary Washington; Charles Waugh, Utah State University; and Betty Wiesepape, University of Texas at Dallas.

We would like to acknowledge the writers Simone Poirier-Bures, Judith Slater, Anne Giles Rimbey, Gerald Shapiro, B. W. Jorgensen, Gordon Johnson, Tobey Kaplan, and Rachel Hall, whose exercises have been adapted from the Associated Writing Programs' publication titled *Pedagogy Papers*. We would also like to acknowledge the writers Robert Olen Butler, Doug Bauer, Lee Smith, Jill McCorkle, Ron Hansen, Tom Batt, Wally Lamb, and Alan Gurganus, whose insightful words from interviews published in the Associated Writing Programs' publication *The Writer's Chronicle* have been quoted in this text. Among the many others who have shared exercises over the years, special thanks go to Nancy Huddleston Packer, John L'Heureux, Alice La Plante, Erin McGraw, Brad Owens, Rick Hillis, Bo Caldwell, Michelle Carter, and Leslee Becker. Some of the exercises were adapted from those appearing in *What If: Writing Exercises for Fiction Writers*, edited by Anne Berneys and Pamela Painter; *Writing Fiction Step by Step* by Josip Novakovich; and *Creating Fiction*, edited by Julie Checkoway.

—J. B.

A Note from the Publisher

The following supplements can be value-packed at no additional cost or at a significant discount with *Writing Fiction*, Eighth Edition. Please contact your Longman representative to arrange a value-pack.

- *A Workshop Guide for Creative Writing* (0-321-09539-1) is a laminated reference tool, including guidelines for criticism, workshop etiquette, and more. Available at no additional cost when packaged with *Writing Fiction*, Eighth Edition.
- *The Longman Journal for Creative Writing* (0-321-09540-5) helps students explore and discover their own writing habits and styles. Available at no additional cost when value-packed with *Writing Fiction*, Eighth Edition.
- **Penguin Discount Program.** A variety of Penguin paperbacks are offered at a significant discount when packaged with *Writing Fiction*, Eighth Edition. To review the complete list of titles available, please visit: http://www.pearsonhighered.com/penguin.
- **Merriam Websters Reader's Handbook: Your Complete Guide to Literary Terms** (0-321-10541-9) includes nearly 2,000 descriptions for every major genre, style, and era of writing. Available at no additional cost when value-packed with *Writing Fiction*, Eighth Edition.

This offer is only available while supplies last.

WRITING FICTION

1

WHATEVER WORKS
The Writing Process

•Get Started

•Keep Going

•A Word About Theme

•Reading as Writers

•About the Writing Workshop

You want to write. Why is it so hard?

There are a few lucky souls for whom the whole process of writing is easy, for whom the smell of fresh paper is better than air, who forget to eat, and who consider the world at large an intrusion on their good time at the keyboard. But you and I are not among them. We are in love with words except when we have to face them. We are caught in a guilty paradox in which we grumble over our lack of time, and when we have the time, we sharpen pencils, check e-mail, or clip the hedges.

Of course, there's also joy. We write for the satisfaction of having wrestled a sentence to the page, for the rush of discovering an image, for the excitement of seeing a character come alive. Even the most successful writers will sincerely say that these pleasures—not money, fame, or glamour—are the real rewards of writing. Fiction writer Alice Munro concedes:

> It may not look like pleasure, because the difficulties can make me
> morose and distracted, but that's what it is—the pleasure of telling the

story I mean to tell as wholly as I can tell it, of finding out in fact what the story is, by working around the different ways of telling it.

Nevertheless, writers may forget what such pleasure feels like when confronting a blank page, like the heroine of Anita Brookner's novel *Look at Me*:

> Sometimes it feels like a physical effort simply to sit down at the desk and pull out the notebook.... Sometimes the effort of putting pen to paper is so great that I literally feel a pain in my head....

It helps to know that most writers share the paradox of at least wanting to do what we most want to do. It also helps to know some of the reasons for our reluctance. Fear of what could emerge on the page, and what it may reveal about our inner lives, can keep us from getting started.

There's another impediment to beginning, expressed by a writer character in Lawrence Durrell's *Alexandria Quartet*. Durrell's Pursewarden broods over the illusory significance of what he is about to write, unwilling to begin in case he spoils it. Many of us do this: The idea, whatever it is, seems so luminous, whole, and fragile, that to begin to write about that idea is to commit it to rubble. "The paradox of writing," says screenwriter Stephen Fischer, "is that you're trying to use words to express what words can't express." Knowing in advance that words will never exactly capture what we mean or intend, we must gingerly and gradually work ourselves into a state of accepting what words can do instead. No matter how many times we find out that what words can do is quite all right, we still shy again from the next beginning. Against this wasteful impulse I have a motto over my desk that reads: "Don't Dread; Do." It's a fine motto, and I contemplated it for several weeks before I began writing this chapter.

The mundane daily habits of writers are apparently fascinating. No author offers to answer questions at the end of a public reading without being asked: *Do you write in the morning or at night? Do you write every day? Do you compose longhand or on a computer?* Sometimes such questions show a reverent interest in the workings of genius. More often, I think, they are a plea for practical help: *Is there something I can do to make this job less horrific? Is there a trick that will unlock my words?*

Get Started

The variety of authors' habits suggests that there is no magic to be found in any particular one. Donald Hall will tell you that he spends a dozen hours a day at his desk, moving back and forth between as many projects. Philip Larkin said that he wrote a poem only every eighteen months or so and never tried to write one that was not a gift. Gail Godwin goes to her workroom every day "because what if the angel came and I wasn't there?" Julia Alvarez begins the day by reading first poetry, then prose, by her favorite writers "to remind me of the quality of writing I am aiming for." The late Andre Dubus recommended to students that they, like Hemingway, stop writing midsentence in order to begin the next day by completing the thought. Dickens could not deal with people when he was working: "The mere consciousness of an engagement will worry a whole day." Thomas Wolfe wrote standing up. Some writers can plop at the kitchen table without clearing the breakfast dishes; others need total seclusion, a beach, a cat, a string quartet.

There is something to be learned from all this, though. The question is not "How do you get it done?" but "How do *you* get it done?" Any discipline or indulgence that actually helps nudge you into position facing the page is acceptable and productive. If jogging after breakfast energizes your mind, then jog before you sit. If you have to pull an all-nighter on a coffee binge, do that. Some schedule, regularity, pattern in your writing day (or night) will always help, but only you can figure out what that pattern is for you.

JOURNAL KEEPING

There are, though, a number of tricks you can teach yourself in order to free the writing self, and the essence of these is to give yourself permission to fail. The best place for such permission is a private place, and for that reason a writer's journal is an essential, likely to be the source of originality, ideas, experimentation, and growth.

A journal is an intimate, a friend that will accept you as you are. Pick a notebook you like the look of, one you feel comfortable with, as you would pick a friend. I find a bound blank book too elegant to live up to, preferring instead a loose-leaf because I write my journal mainly at the computer and can stick anything in at the flip of a three-hole punch. But you can glue scribbled napkins into a spiral, too.

Keep the journal regularly, at least at first. It doesn't matter what you write and it doesn't matter very much how much, but it does matter that you make a steady habit of the writing. Keeping a journal regularly will put you in the habit of observing in words. If you know at dawn that you are committed to writing so many words before dusk, you will half-consciously tell the story of your day to yourself as you live it, finding a phrase to catch whatever catches your eye. When that habit is established, you'll begin to find that whatever invites your attention or sympathy, your anger or curiosity, may be the beginning of invention. *Whoever* catches your attention may be the beginning of a character.

Don't worry about being thorough. Your journal might consist of brief notes and bits of description only you can make sense of. F. Scott Fitzgerald (*The Great Gatsby*) used his journals to keep, among other things, snatches of overheard conversation and potential titles for short stories and novels. Many fiction writers use journals to jot down specific details about people, places, and things they observe and find intriguing. (See exercise 3 at the end of this chapter.) Later, when you're writing fiction and attempting to bring to life a teenager or a city street or a tractor, it's useful to have a bank of striking details in your journal to draw on. Often one or two details about something will be enough to trigger a fuller memory about a place or a person or a situation.

But before the journal-keeping habit is developed, you may find that even a blank journal page has the awesome aspect of a void, and you may need some tricks of permission to let yourself start writing there. The playwright Maria Irene Fornes says that there are two of you: one who wants to write and one who doesn't. The one who wants to write had better keep tricking the one who doesn't. Or another way to think of this conflict is between right brain and left brain—the playful, detail-loving creator, and the linear critic. The critic is an absolutely essential part of the writing process. The trick is to shut him or her up until there is something to criticize.

THE GREAT JAPANESE FILM DIRECTOR AKIRA KUROSAWA said that to be an artist means never to avert your eyes. And that's the hardest thing, because we want to flinch. The artist must go into the white hot center of himself, and our impulse when we get there is to look away and avert our eyes.

ROBERT OLEN BUTLER

FREEWRITING

Freewriting is a technique that allows you to take very literally the notion of getting something down on paper. It can be done whenever you want to write, or just to free up the writing self. The idea is to put

> anything on paper and I mena anything, it doesn't matter as long as it's coming out of your head nad hte ends of your fingers, down ont the page I wonder if;m improving, if this process gets me going better now than it did all those— hoewever many years ago? I know my typing is geting worse, deteriorating even as we speak (are we speaking? to whom? IN what forM? I love it when i hit the caps button by mistake, it makes me wonder whether there isn;t something in the back or bottom of the brain that sez PAY ATTENTION now, which makes me think of a number of things, freud and his slip o tonuge, self-deception, the myriad way it operates in everybody's life, no not everybody's but in my own exp. llike Aunt Ch. mourniong for the dead cats whenevershe hasn't got her way and can't disconnect one kind of sadness from another, I wonder if we ever discon-nect kinds of sadness, if the first homesickness doesn;t operatfor everybody

the same way it does for me, grandma's house the site of it, the grass out the window and the dog rolling a tin pie plate under the willow tree, great heavy hunger in the belly, the empty weight of loss, loss, loss

That's freewriting. Its point is to keep going, and that is the only point. When the critic intrudes and tells you that what you're doing is awful, tell the critic to take a dive, or acknowledge her/him (*typing is getting worse*) and keep writing. If you work on a computer, try dimming the screen so you can't see what you're doing. At times, you might find it liberating to freewrite to music, random or selected. If you freewrite often, pretty soon you'll be bored with writing about how you don't feel like writing (though that is as good a subject as any; the subject is of no importance and neither is the quality of the writing) and you will find your mind and your phrases running on things that interest you. Fine. Freewriting is the literary equivalent of scales at the piano or a short gym workout. All that matters is that you do it. The verbal muscles will develop of their own accord.

Though freewriting is mere technique, it can affect the freedom of the content. Many writers feel themselves to be *an instrument through which*, rather than a *creator of*, and whether you think of this possibility as humble or holy, it is worth finding out what you say when you aren't monitoring yourself. Fiction is written not so much to inform as to find out, and if you force yourself into a mode of informing when you haven't yet found out, you're likely to end up pontificating or lying some other way.

In *Becoming a Writer*, a book that only half-facetiously claims to do what teachers of writing claim cannot be done—to teach genius—Dorothea Brande suggests that the way to begin is not with an idea or a form at all, but with an unlocking of your thoughts on paper. She advises that you rise each day and go directly to your desk (if you have to have coffee, put it in a thermos the night before) and begin writing whatever comes to mind, before you are quite awake, before you have read anything or talked to anyone, before reason has begun to take over from the dream-functioning of your brain. Write for twenty or thirty minutes and then put away what you have written without reading it over. After a week or two of this, pick an additional time during the day when you can salvage a half hour or so to write, and when that time arrives, write, even if you "must climb out over the heads of your friends" to do it. It doesn't matter what you write. What does matter is that you develop the habit of beginning to write the moment you sit down to do so.

I*F you haven't surprised yourself, you haven't written.*

EUDORA WELTY

EXERCISES

The American Dairy Association used to use the tagline "You never outgrow your need for milk." If you're a writer, the same might be said of exercises. Exercises, or prompts as they are sometimes called, can be helpful for all writers. They help you get started, and they can give you focus—whether you are writing in your journal, doing those early morning pages Brande suggests, sneaking in a bit of freewriting during the day, or trying to get to that next scene in a story.

Exercises are a way to tap your unconscious. The process of writing does not proceed clearly and obviously from point A to point B, but if you've been thinking about your story—sleeping on it, puzzling over it, mulling about it, working on a draft—you may well have a solution waiting for you in your unconscious. Stories do not begin with ideas or themes or outlines, so much as with images and obsessions, and they continue to be built by exploring those images and obsessions. Seemingly unrelated prompts can help you break loose that next page. Need to find out what should happen next with Sebastian and Nelly? Here's an exercise: Write two pages about the two of them trying to decide what television show to watch. Pretty soon Sebastian and Nelly are fighting about the remote control, but more than that they're fighting about how Sebastian is remote and always wants control. Nelly is telling him that their relationship has got to change and he's acting like he doesn't have a clue. And you are off and running.

Exercises can be shared. Early in their careers, two young writers, JoAnn Beard and Mary Allen, were splitting a job editing a physics journal at the University of Iowa. One worked one day, one the next. They shared a desk, but were never there at the same time. They decided to start leaving each other a daily writing exercise in the top drawer. "For tomorrow, write a scene that takes place in a car." Or, "Write a scene in which one character is lying." The exercises kept them going, broke the isolation of writing, tapped them into the material they would have written about anyway, and before too terribly long they each had a first book—Allen's *Rooms of Heaven* and Beard's *The Boys of My Youth*.

Gymnasts practice. Pianists practice. Artists sketch. Why shouldn't writers practice? Exercises are a way to exercise your skills, develop them, hone them, make them stronger. The novelist Stanley Elkin talked about sharing an office at the University of Illinois with his friend and fellow writer William H. Gass and being surprised to see Gass practicing sentences on the other side of the room.

Each chapter of *Writing Fiction* will end with some exercises designed to help you get started and move further into the issues discussed along the way. But don't stop there. Go to a bookstore or library and look through exercise collections like *What If? Writing Exercises for Fiction Writers* by Anne Bernays and Pamela Painter. Collect exercises as you might collect possible names for characters or words you like the sound of. Develop your own exercises. Ask writing friends what has worked for them. Note the ones that work for you and vary them and return to them again and again. Exercise. Exercise daily.

THE COMPUTER

I think it's important for a writer to try a pencil from time to time so as not to lose the knack of writing by hand, of jotting at the park or the beach without any source of energy but your own hand and mind.

But for most writers, a computer is a great aid to spontaneity. Freewriting flows more freely on a computer. The knowledge that you can so easily delete makes it easier to quiet the internal critic and put down whatever comes. Turn down the screen or ignore it, stare out the window into middle space. You can follow the thread of your thought without a pause.

However, when you're rereading what you've written, you might want to step away from the screen. Scrolling through your work on a computer screen is not the same as reading it on a printed page—it's too easy to overlook problems. Most writers print out hard copies of their drafts and go over them with pen in hand, taking notes and making changes. This allows them to read more carefully, to easily jump back and skip ahead, to get a better sense of the story's pacing, to notice clunky sentences and weak word choices. Many writers will also read their drafts aloud, either to themselves or to a helpful critic, a process that will make the story's weaknesses even clearer. These revision strategies—and more—will be further discussed in Chapter 9.

Computers are a wonderful tool, but they can't do everything.

THE CRITIC: A CAUTION

The cautionary note that needs to be sounded regarding all the techniques and technology that free you to write is that the critic is absolutely essential afterward. The revising process is continuous and begins as soon as you choose to let your critic in. Freedrafting allows you to create before you criticize, to do the essential play before the essential work. Don't forget the essential work. The computer lets you write a lot because you can so easily cut. Don't forget to do so.

I WANT HARD STORIES, I DEMAND THEM from myself. Hard stories are worth the difficulty. It seems to me the only way I have forgiven anything, understood anything, is through that process of opening up to my own terror and pain and reexamining it, re-creating it in the story, and making it something different, making it meaningful—even if the meaning is only in the act of the telling.

DOROTHY ALLISON

CHOOSING A SUBJECT

Some writers are lucky enough never to be faced with the problem of choosing a subject. The world presents itself to them in terms of conflict, crisis, and resolution. Ideas for stories pop into their heads day after day; their only difficulty is choosing among them. In fact, the habit of mind that produces stories is a habit and can be cultivated, so that the more and the longer you write, the less likely you are to run out of ideas.

But sooner or later you may find yourself faced with the desire (or the deadline necessity) to write a story when your mind is a blank. The sour and untrue impulse crosses your thoughts: Nothing has ever happened to me. The task you face then is to recognize among all the paraphernalia of your mind a situation, idea, perception, or character that you can turn into a story.

Some teachers and critics advise beginning writers to write only from their personal experience, but I feel that this is a misleading and demeaning rule. If your imagination never gets beyond your age group or off campus, never tackles issues larger than dormitory life, then you are severely underestimating the range of your imagination. It is certainly true that you must draw on your own experience (including your experience of the shape of sentences). But the trick is to identify what is interesting, unique, and original in that experience (including your experience of the shape of sentences) that will therefore surprise and attract the reader.

The kind of "writing what you know" that is *least* likely to produce good fiction is trying to tell just exactly what happened to you at such and such a time. Probably all good fiction is "autobiographical" in some way, but the awful or hilarious or tragic thing you went through may offer as many problems as possibilities when you start to turn it into fiction. To the extent you want to capture "what really happened," you remove your focus from what will work as narrative. Young writers, offended by being told that a piece is unconvincing, often defend themselves by declaring that it *really happened*. But credibility in words has almost nothing to do with fact. Aristotle went so far as to say that a "probable impossibility" made a better story than an "improbable possibility," meaning that a skillful author can sell us glass mountains, UFOs, and hobbits, whereas a less skilled writer may not be able to convince us that Mary Lou has a crush on Sam.

A SHORT STORY IS A WRITER'S WAY OF thinking through experience....Journalism aims at accuracy, but fiction's aim is truth. The writer distorts reality in the interest of a larger truth.

JOHN L'HEUREUX

The first step toward using autobiography in fiction is to accept this: Words are not experience. Even the most factual account of a personal experience involves choices and interpretations—your sister's recollection of the same event might be entirely different. If you are writing a memoir or personal essay, then it is important to maintain a basis in fact because, as Annie Dillard says, "that is the convention and the covenant between the nonfiction writer and his reader." But between fiction writer and reader it is the revelation of meaning through the creation of character, the vividness of scene, the effect of action that take priority over ordinary veracity. The test of this other truth is at once spiritual and visceral; its validity has nothing to do with whether such things did, or could, occur. Lorrie Moore says:

> ...[T]he proper relationship of a writer to his or her own life is similar to a cook with a cupboard. What the cook makes from the cupboard is not the same thing as what's in the cupboard....

Dorothy Allison strives to tell "the emotional truth of people's lives, not necessarily the historical truth."

Good. Now: What was it about this experience that made it matter to you? Try writing a *very* brief summary of what happened—no more than a hundred words. What kind of story might this be? Can the raw material of incident, accident, and choice be reshaped, plumped up, pared to the bone, refleshed, differently spiced? You experienced whatever it was chronologically—but is that the best way to bring its meaning out? Perhaps you experienced it over a period of months or years; what are the *fewest* scenes in the *least* amount of time that could contain the action? If "you" are at the center of the action, then "you" must be thoroughly characterized, and that may be difficult. Can you augment some revealing aspect of yourself, change yourself so you are forced to see anew, even make someone else altogether the central character? Use some of the suggestions in this chapter. Try freewriting moments from your memory in no particular order. Or freewrite the last scene first. Describe a place and exaggerate the description: if it's cold, make it murderously cold; if messy, then a disastrous mess. Describe the central character and be at least partly unflattering. All of these are devices to put some distance between you and raw experience so you can begin to shape the different thing that fiction is.

Writer Eudora Welty has suggested writing what you *don't* know about what you know—that is, exploring aspects of experience that remain puzzling or painful. In *Making Shapely Fiction*, Jerome Stern urges a broad interpretation of "writing what you know," recognizing that "the idea of *you* is complex in itself...your self is made of many selves...not only persons you once were, but also persons you have tried to be, persons you have avoided being, and persons you fear you might be." John Gardner, in *The Art of Fiction*, argues that "nothing can be more limiting to the imagination" than the advice that you write about what you know. He suggests instead that you "write the kind of story you know and like best."

This is a useful idea, because the kind of story you know and like best has also taught you something about the way such stories are told, how they are shaped, what kind of surprise, conflict, and change they involve. Many beginning writers who are not yet avid readers have learned from television more than they realize about structure, the way characters behave and talk, how a joke is arranged, how a lie is revealed, and so forth. The trouble is that if you learn fiction from television, or if the kind of story you know and like best is genre fiction—science fiction, fantasy, romance, mystery—you may have learned about technique without having learned anything about the unique contribution you can make to such a story. The result is that you end up writing imitation soap opera or space odyssey, second-rate somebody else instead of first-rate you.

The essential thing is that you write about something you really care about, and the first step is to find out what that is. Playwright Claudia Johnson advises her students to identify their real concerns by making a "menu" of them. Pick the big emotions and make lists in your journal: *What makes you angry? What are you afraid of? What do you want? What hurts?* Or consider the crucial turning points of your life: *What really changed you? Who really changed you?* Those will be the areas to look to for stories, whether or not those stories are autobiographical. Novelist Ron Carlson says, "I always write from my own experiences, whether I've had them or not."

Another journal idea is to jot down the facts of the first seven years of your life under several categories: *Events, People, Your Self, Inner Life, Characteristic Things.* What from those first seven years still occupies your mind? Underline or highlight the items on your page(s) that you aren't done with yet. Those items are clues to your concerns and a possible source of storytelling.

A related device for your journal might be borrowed from the *Pillow Book* of Sei Shonagun. A courtesan in tenth-century Japan, she kept a diary of the goings-on at court and concealed it in her wooden pillow—hence *pillow book.* Sei Shonagun made lists under various categories of specific, often quirky *Things.* This device is capable of endless variety and can reveal yourself to you as you find out what sort of things you want to list: *Things I wish had never been said. Red things. Things more embarrassing than nudity. Things to put off as long as possible. Things to die for. Acid things. Things that last only a day.*

Such devices may be necessary because identifying what we care about is not always easy. We are surrounded by a constant barrage of information, drama, ideas, and judgments offered to us live, printed, and electronically. It is so much easier to know what we ought to think and feel than what we actually do. Worthy authorities constantly exhort us to care about worthy causes, only a few of which really touch us, whereas what we care about at any given moment may seem trivial, self-conscious, or self-serving.

This, I think, is in large part the value of Brande's first exercise, which forces you to write in the intuitively honest period of first light, when the half-sleeping brain is still dealing with its real concerns. Often what seems unworthy is precisely the thing that contains a universal, and by catching it honestly, then stepping back from it, you may achieve the authorial distance that is an essential part of significance. (All you really care about this morning is how you'll look at the dance tonight? This is a trivial obsession that can hit anyone, at any age, anywhere. Write about it as honestly as you can. Now who else might have felt this way? Someone you hate? Someone remote in time from you? Look out: You're on your way to a story.)

FORGET *INSPIRATION*. HABIT IS MORE DEPENDABLE. Habit will sustain you whether you're inspired or not. Habit will help you finish and polish your stories. Inspiration won't. Habit is persistence in practice.

OCTAVIA BUTLER

Eventually you will learn what sort of experience sparks ideas for your sort of story—and you may be astonished at how such experiences accumulate, as if your life were arranging itself to produce material for you. In the meantime, here are a half dozen suggestions for the kind of idea that may be fruitful.

The Dilemma, or Catch-22.   You find yourself facing—or know someone who is facing—a situation that offers no solution. Any action taken would be painful and costly. You have no chance of solving this dilemma in real life, but you're a writer, and it costs nothing to explore it with imaginary people in an imaginary setting, even if the outcome is a tragic one. Some writers use newspaper stories to generate this sort of idea. The situation is there in the bland black and white of this morning's news. But who are these people, and how did they come to be in such a mess? Make it up, think it through.

The Incongruity.   Something comes to your attention that is interesting precisely because you can't figure it out. It doesn't seem to make sense. Someone is breeding pigs in the backyard of a mansion. Who is it? Why is she doing it? Your inventing mind can find the motives and the meanings. An example from my own experience: Once when my phone was out of order, I went out very late at night to make a call from a public phone at a supermarket plaza. At something like two in the morning all the stores were closed but the plaza was not empty. There were three women there, one of them with a baby in a stroller. What were they doing there? It was several years before I figured out a possible answer, and that answer was a short story.

The Connection.   You notice a striking similarity in two events, people, places, or periods that are fundamentally unlike. The more you explore the similarity, the more striking it becomes. My novel *The Buzzards* came from such a connection: The daughter of a famous politician was murdered, and I found myself in the position of comforting the dead girl's fiancé. At the same time I was writing lectures on the Agamemnon of Aeschylus. Two politicians, two murdered daughters—one in ancient Greece and one in contemporary America. The connection would not let go of me until I had thought it through and set it down.

The Memory.   Certain people, places, and events stand out in your memory with an intensity beyond logic. There's no earthly reason you should remember the smell of Aunt K's rouge. It makes no sense that you still flush with shame at the thought of that ball you "borrowed" when you were in fourth grade. But for some reason these things are still vivid in your mind. That vividness can be explored, embellished, given form. Stephen Minot in *Three Genres* wisely advises, though, that if you are going to write from a memory, *it should be a memory more than a year old*. Otherwise you are likely to be unable to distinguish between what happened and what must happen in the story or between what is in your mind and what you have conveyed on the page.

The Transplant.   You find yourself having to deal with a feeling that is either startlingly new to you or else obsessively old. You feel incapable of dealing with it. As a way of distancing yourself from that feeling and gaining some mastery over it, you write about the feeling as precisely as you can, but giving it to an imaginary someone in an imaginary situation. What situation other than your own would produce such a feeling? Who would be caught in that situation? Think it through.

The Revenge.   An injustice has been done, and you are powerless to do anything about it. But you're not really, because you're a writer. Reproduce the situation with another set of characters, in other circumstances or another setting. Cast the outcome to suit yourself. Punish whomever you choose. Even if the story ends in a similar injustice, you have righted the wrong by enlisting your reader's sympathy on the side of right. (Dante was particularly good at this: He put his enemies in the inferno and his friends in paradise.) Remember too that as human beings we are intensely, sometimes obsessively, interested in our boredom, and you can take revenge against the things that bore you by making them absurd or funny on paper.

Keep Going

A story idea may come from any source at any time. You may not know you have an idea until you spot it in the random jottings of your journal. Once you've identified the idea, the process of thinking it through begins and doesn't end until you finish (or abandon) the story. Most writing is done between the mind and the hand, not between the hand and the page. It may take a fairly competent typist about three hours to type a twelve-page story. It may take days or months to write it. It follows that, even when you are writing well, most of the time spent writing is not spent putting words on the page. If the story idea grabs hard hold of you, the process of thinking through may be involuntary, a gift. If not, you need to find the inner stillness that will allow you to develop your characters, get to know them, follow their actions in your mind—and it may take an effort of the will to find such stillness.

The metamorphosis of an idea into a story has many aspects, some deliberate and some mysterious. "Inspiration" is a real thing, a gift from the subconscious to the conscious mind. Still, perhaps influenced by the philosophy (although it was not always the practice) of the Beat authors, some new writers may feel that "forcing" words is aesthetically false—and yet few readers can tell which story "flowed" from the writer's pen and which was set down one hard-won word at a time. Toni Morrison has said that she will frequently rewrite a passage eight times, simply to create the impression of an unbroken, inspired flow; Cynthia Ozick often begins with "simple forcing" until the breakthrough comes, and so bears with the "fear and terror until I've pushed through to joy."

Over and over again, successful writers attest that unless they prepare the conscious mind with the habit of work, the gift does not come. Writing is mind-farming. You have to plow, plant, weed, and hope for growing weather. Why a seed turns into a plant is something you are never going to understand, and the only relevant response to it is gratitude. You may be proud, however, of having plowed.

Many writers besides Dorothea Brande have observed that it is ideal, having turned your story over in your mind, to write the first draft at one sitting, pushing on through the action to the conclusion, no matter how dissatisfied you are with this paragraph, that character, this phrasing, or that incident. There are two advantages to doing this. The first is that you are more likely to produce a coherent draft when you come to the desk in a single frame of mind, with a single vision of the whole, than when you write piecemeal, having altered ideas and moods. The second is that fast writing tends to make for fast pace in the story. It is always easier, later, to add and develop than it is to sharpen the pace. If you are the sort of writer who stays on page one for days, shoving commas around and combing the thesaurus for a word with slightly better connotations, then you should probably force yourself to try this method (more than once). A note of caution, though: If you write a draft at one sitting, it will not be the draft you want to show anyone, so schedule the sitting well in advance of whatever deadline you may have.

It may happen that as you write, the story will take off in some direction totally other than you intended. You thought you knew where you were going and now you don't. You may find that although you are doing precisely what you had in mind, it doesn't work—Brian Moore calls this "the place where the story gets sick," and often found he had to retrace his steps from an unlikely plot turn or unnatural character action. At such times, the story needs more imaginative mulching before it will bear fruit. Or you may find, simply, that your stamina gives out, and that though you have practiced every writerly virtue known, you're stuck. You have writer's block.

"Writer's block" is not so popular a term as it was a few years ago—sometimes writers can be sensitive even to their own clichés. But it may also be that writers began to understand and accept their difficulties. Sometimes the process seems to require working yourself into a muddle and past the muddle to despair. When you're writing, this feels terrible. You sit spinning your wheels, digging deeper and deeper into the mental muck. You decide you are going to trash the whole thing and walk away from it—only you can't, and you keep going back to it like a tongue to an aching tooth. Or you decide you are going to sit there until you bludgeon it into shape—and as long as you sit there it remains recalcitrant. W. H. Auden observed that the hardest part of writing is not knowing whether you are procrastinating or must wait for the words to come.

"What's called writer's block," claims novelist Tom Wolfe, "is almost always ordinary fear." Indeed, whenever I ask a group of writers what they find most difficult, a significant number answer that they feel they aren't good enough, that the empty page intimidates them, that they are in some way afraid. Many complain of their own laziness, but laziness, like money, doesn't really exist except to represent something else—in this case fear, severe self-judgment, or what Natalie Goldberg calls "the cycle of guilt, avoidance, and pressure."

I know a newspaper editor who says that writer's block always represents a lack of information. I thought this inapplicable to fiction until I noticed that I was mainly frustrated when I didn't know enough about my characters, the scene, or the action—when I had not gone to the imaginative depth where information lies.

Encouragement comes from the poet William Stafford, who advised his students always to write to their lowest standard. Somebody always corrected him: "You mean your highest standard." No, he meant your lowest standard. Jean Cocteau's editor gave him the same advice. "The thought of having to produce a masterpiece is giving you writer's cramp. You're paralysed at the sight of a blank sheet of paper. So begin any old way. Write: 'One winter evening…'" In *On Writer's Block: A New Approach to Creativity*, Victoria Nelson points out that "there is an almost mathematical ratio between soaring, grandiose ambition… and severe creative block." More writers prostitute themselves "up" than "down"; more are false in the determination to write great literature than to throw off a romance.

A rough draft is rough; that's its nature. Let it be rough. Think of it as making clay. The molding and the gloss come later.

And remember: Writing is easy. Not writing is hard.

A Word About Theme

The process of discovering, choosing, and revealing the theme of your story begins as early as a first freewrite and continues, probably, beyond publication. The theme is what your story is about and what you think about it, its core and the spin you put on it. John Gardner points out that theme "is not imposed on the story but evoked from within it—initially an intuitive but finally an intellectual act on the part of the writer."

What your story has to say will gradually reveal itself to you and to your reader through every choice you as a writer make—the actions, characters, setting, dialogue, objects, pace, metaphors and symbols, viewpoint, atmosphere, style, even syntax and punctuation, and even in some cases typography.

Because of the comprehensive nature of theme, I have placed the discussion of it in Chapter 9 ("Play It Again, Sam: Revision") after the individual story elements have been addressed. But this is not entirely satisfactory, since each of those elements contributes to the theme as it unfolds. You may want to skip ahead and take a look at that chapter, or you may want to anticipate the issue by asking at every stage of your manuscript: What really interests me about this? How does this (image, character, dialogue, place,...) reveal what I care about? What connections do I see between one image and another? How can I strengthen those connections? Am I saying what I really mean, telling my truth about it?

Reading as Writers

Learning to read as a writer involves focusing on craft, the choices and the techniques of the author. In *On Becoming a Novelist*, John Gardner urges young writers to read "the way a young architect looks at a building, or a medical student watches an operation, both devotedly, hoping to learn from a master, and critically alert for any possible mistake." "Bad poets imitate; good poets steal," was T. S. Eliot's advice.

Ask yourself as you read: What is memorable, effective, moving? Reread, if possible, watching for the techniques that produced those reactions in you. *Why did the author choose to begin at this point? Why did s/he make this choice of imagery, setting, ending? What gives this scene its tension; what makes me feel sympathetic?* You can also learn from stories that don't personally move you— how would you have handled the same material, and what would have changed with that approach? Be greedy from your own viewpoint as an author: *What, from this story, can I learn/imitate/steal?*

About the Writing Workshop

At some point in the process of writing your story, you may find it useful to submit your story to a writing workshop to be critiqued, and if you are enrolled in a fiction-writing class, workshopping your stories may be required. These days nearly every higher learning institution in America offers some form of workshop-based creative writing course or program. The writer's workshop is so commonplace now that it has given rise to a new verb—"to workshop."

To workshop is much more than to discuss. It implies a commitment on the part of everyone concerned to give close attention to work that is embryonic.

The atmosphere of such a group is intense and personal in a way that other college classes are not, since a major text of the course is also the raw effort of its participants. At the same time, unlike the classic model of the artist's atelier or the music conservatory, the instruction is assumed to come largely from the group rather than from a single master of technical expertise. Thus the workshop represents a democratization of both the material for study and its teaching.

Although workshops inevitably vary, a basic pattern has evolved in which twelve to twenty students are led by an instructor who is also a published writer. The students take turns writing and distributing stories, which the others read and critique. What is sought in such a group is mutual goodwill—the desire to make the story under scrutiny the best that it can be—together with an agreed-to toughness on the part of writer and readers.

This sounds simple enough, but as with all democratization, the perceived danger is that the process will flatten out the story's edge and originality, and that the result will be a homogenized "revision by committee." The danger is partly real and deserves attention. Partly, such fear masks protectiveness toward the image—solitary, remote, romantic—of the writer's life.

But those who have taken part in the process tend to champion it. John Gardner asserted that not only could writing be taught but that "writing ability is mainly a product of good teaching supported by a deep-down love of writing." John Irving says of his instructors, "They clearly saved me valuable time . . . [and] time is precious for a young writer." Isabel Allende says, "The process is lonely, but the response connects you with the world."

There are, I think, three questions about the workshop endeavor that have to be asked: Is it good for the most startlingly talented, those who will go on to "become" published professional writers? Is it good for the majority who will not publish but will instead become (as some of my most gifted students have) restaurateurs, photographers, technical writers, high school teachers? And is it good for literature and literacy generally to have students of all fields struggle toward this play and this craft? My answer must in all cases be a vigorous yes. The workshop aids both the vocation and the avocation. Writing is a solitary struggle, and from the beginning, writers have sought relief in the company and understanding of other writers. At its best the workshop provides an intellectual, emotional, and social (and some argue a spiritual) discipline. For the potential professionals there is the important focus on craft; course credit is a form of early pay-for-writing; deadlines help you find the time and discipline to do what you really want to; and above all, the workshop offers attention in an area where attention is hard to command. For those who will not be professional writers, a course in writing fiction can be a valuable part of a liberal arts education, making for better readers, better letters home, better company reports, and better private memoirs. For everyone, the workshop can help develop critical thinking, a respect for craft, and important social skills.

There are also some pitfalls in the process: that students will develop unrealistic expectations of their chances in a chancy profession; that they will dull or provincialize their talents by trying to please the teacher or the group; that they will be buoyed into self-satisfaction by too-lavish praise or that they will be crushed by too-harsh criticism. On the other hand, workshop peers recognize and revere originality, vividness, and truth at least as often as professional critics. Hard work counts for more than anyone but writers realize, and facility with the language can be learned out of obsessive attention to it. The driven desire is no guarantee of talent, but it is an annealing force. And amazing transformations can and do occur in the creative writing class. Sometimes young writers who exhibit only a propensity for cliché and the most hackneyed initial efforts make sudden, breathtaking progress. Sometimes the leap of imaginative capacity is inexplicable, like a sport of nature.

The appropriate atmosphere in which to foster this metamorphosis is a balance constructed of right-brain creative play and left-brain crafted language, and of obligations among readers, writers, and teachers. Of these obligations, a few seem to me worth noting.

HOW WORKSHOPS WORK

The most basic expectation is that the manuscript itself should be professionally presented—that is, double-spaced, with generous margins, proofread for grammar, spelling, and punctuation. In most workshops the content is left entirely to the writer, with no censorship of subject. The reader's obligation is to read the story twice, once for its sense and story, a second time to make marginal comments, observations, suggestions. A summarizing end note is usual and helpful. This should be done with the understanding—on the parts of both writer and reader—that the work at hand is by definition a work in progress. If it were finished, then there would be no reason to bring it into workshop. Workshop readers should school themselves to identify the successes that are in every story: the potential strength, the interesting subject matter, the pleasing shape, or the vivid detail.

It's my experience that the workshop itself proceeds most usefully to the writer if each discussion begins with a critically neutral description and interpretation of the story. This is important because workshopping can descend into a litany of *I like, I don't like*, and it's the responsibility of the first speaker to provide a coherent reading as a basis for discussion. It's often a good idea to begin with a detailed summary of the narrative action—useful because if class members understand the events of the story differently, or are unclear about what happens, this is important information for the author, a signal that she has not revealed what, or all, she meant. The interpretation might then address such questions as: *What kind of story is this? What defining choices do the characters face? What is its conflict-crisis-resolution structure? What is it about? What does it say about what it is about? How sympathetic should the reader feel with the main character? How does its imagery relate to its theme?*

Only after some such questions are addressed should the critique begin to deal with whether the story is successful in its effects. The first speaker should try to close with two or three questions that, in his/her opinion, the story raises, and invite the class to consider these. Most of the questions will be technical: *Is the point of view consistent, are the characters fully drawn, is the imagery vivid and specific?* But now and again it is well to pause and return to more substantive matters: *What's the spirit of this story, what is it trying to say, what does it make me feel?*

THE WRITER'S ROLE

For the writer, the obligations are more emotionally strenuous, but the rewards are great. The hardest part of being a writer in a workshop is to learn this: Be still, be greedy for suggestions, take everything in, and don't defend.

This is difficult because the story under discussion is still new and may feel highly personal. The author has a strong impulse to explain and plead. If the criticism is "This isn't clear," it's hard not to feel "You didn't read it right"—even if you understand that it is not up to the workshop to "get it" but up to the author to be clear. If the reader's complaint is "This isn't credible," it's very hard not to respond "But it really happened!"—even though you know perfectly well that credibility is a different sort of fish than fact, and that autobiography is irrelevant. There is also a self-preservative impulse to keep from changing the core of what you've done: "Don't they realize how much time and effort I've already put in?"

But only the author's attempt at complete receptivity will make the workshop work. The chances are that your first draft really does not say the most meaningful thing inherent in the story, and that most meaningful thing may announce itself sideways, in a detail, within parentheses, an afterthought, a slip. Somebody else may see the design before you do. Sometimes the best advice comes from the most surprising source. The thing you resist the hardest may be exactly what you need.

After the workshop, the writer's obligation alters slightly. It's important to take the written critiques and take them seriously, let them sink in with as good a will as you brought to the workshop. But part of the obligation is also not to let them sink in too far. Reject without regret whatever seems on reflection wrongheaded, dull, destructive, or irrelevant to your vision. It's just as important to be able to discriminate between helpful and unhelpful criticism as it is to be able to write. More often than not, the most useful criticism will simply confirm what you already suspected yourself. So listen to everything and receive all criticism as if it were golden. Then listen to yourself and toss the dross.

(For further discussion of giving and receiving workshop feedback, please see Chapter 9.)

◘ ◘ ◘

Writing Exercises

Keep a journal for two weeks. Decide on a comfortable amount to write daily, and then determine not to let a day slide. To get started, refer to the journal suggestions in this chapter—freewriting, pages 4–5; the Dorothea Brande exercise, page 5; a menu of concerns, page 10; a review of your first seven years, page 10; and a set of *Pillow Book* lists, page 10. At the end of the two weeks, assess your efforts and decide what habit of journal keeping you can develop and stick to. A page a day? A paragraph a day? Three pages a week? Then do it. Probably at least once a day you have a thought worth putting into words, and sometimes it's better to write one sentence a day than to let the habit slide. Like exercise and piano practice, a journal is most useful when it's kept up regularly and frequently. If you pick an hour during which you write each day, no matter how much or how little, you may find yourself looking forward to, and saving things up for, that time.

In addition to keeping a journal, you might try some of these story triggers:

1. Sketch a floor plan of the first house or apartment, or a map of the first neighborhood, you remember. Place an X on the spots in the plan where significant events happened to you—the tree house from which you used to look into the neighbors' window, the kitchen in which you found out that your parents were going to divorce, and so forth. Write a tour of the house as if you were a guide, pointing out its features and its history. If a story starts to emerge from one of the settings, go with it.

2. Identify the kernel of a short story from your experience of one of the following:
   - an early memory
   - an unfounded fear
   - a scar
   - a bad haircut
   - yesterday
   - a sudden change in a relationship
   - the loss of a small object
   - conflict over a lesson you were taught or never taught
   - an experience you still do not fully understand

   Freedraft a passage about it; then write the first page of the story.

3. Take your notebook and go to a place where you can observe people—a library, restaurant, bus station, wherever. Choose a few people and describe them in detail in your notebook. What are they wearing? What are they doing and why do you think they're doing it? If they are talking, can you overhear (or guess) what they're saying? What are they thinking?

Next, choose one character and invent a life for him or her. Write at least two pages. Where does s/he live? Work? What relationships does s/he have? Worries? Fears? Desires? Pleasures? Does this character have a secret? Do you find yourself beginning a story?

4. Have you ever worked as a carpenter, cabdriver, janitor, dentist, bar pianist, waiter, actor, film critic, drummer, teacher, coach, stockbroker, therapist, librarian, or mail carrier? Or maybe you have the inside dope on a job that a close friend or family member has had. Make a list of jobs you've had or of which you have secondhand knowledge of—no matter how odd or how mundane. Now list some incidents that happened at one or another of those jobs, then pick one incident and begin describing it. Don't limit yourself to what actually happened.

5. Everyone in class brings in a photograph, art print, postcard, or advertisement that suggests an intriguing situation. Put all the pictures on a table and have each class member choose one. Write for ten minutes through a pictured character's viewpoint, allowing yourself to discover the thread of a story. In small groups, show the picture, read your writing back to your small group, and together brainstorm possible directions for the story.

2

SEEING IS BELIEVING
Showing and Telling

- *Significant Detail*

- *Comparison*

- *The Active Voice*

- *Prose Rhythm*

- *Mechanics*

Literature offers us feelings for which we do not have to pay. It allows us to love, condemn, condone, hope, dread, and hate without any of the risks those feelings ordinarily involve, for even good feelings—intimacy, power, speed, drunkenness, passion—have consequences, and powerful feelings may risk powerful consequences. Fiction also must contain ideas, which give significance to characters and events. If the ideas are shallow or untrue, the fiction will be correspondingly shallow or untrue. But the ideas must be experienced through or with the characters; they must be felt or the fiction will fail also.

Much nonfiction writing, from editorials to advertising, also tries to persuade us to feel one way rather than another, but nonfiction works largely by means of logic and reasoning. Fiction tries to reproduce the emotional impact of experience. And this is a more difficult task, because unlike the images of film and drama, which directly strike the eye and ear, words are transmitted first to the mind, where they must be translated into images.

In order to move your reader, the standard advice runs, "Show, don't tell." This dictum can be confusing, considering that words are all a writer has to work with. What it means is that your job as a fiction writer is to focus attention not on the words, which are inert, nor on the thoughts these words produce, but through these to felt experience, where the vitality of understanding lies. There are techniques for accomplishing this—for making narrative vivid, moving, and resonant—which can be partly learned and always strengthened.

Significant Detail

In *The Elements of Style*, William Strunk, Jr., writes:

> If those who have studied the art of writing are in accord on any one point, it is on this: the surest way to arouse and hold the attention of the reader is by being specific, definite and concrete. The greatest writers...are effective largely because they deal in particulars and report the details that matter.

Specific, definite, concrete, particular details—these are the life of fiction. Details (as every good liar knows) are the stuff of persuasiveness. Mary is sure that Ed forgot to go pay the gas bill last Tuesday, but Ed says, "I know I went, because this old guy in a knit vest was in front of me in the line, and went on and on about his twin granddaughters"—and it is hard to refute a knit vest and twins even if the furnace doesn't work. John Gardner in *The Art of Fiction* speaks of details as "proofs," rather like those in a geometric theorem or a statistical argument. The novelist, he says, "gives us such details about the streets, stores, weather, politics, and concerns of Cleveland (or wherever the setting is) and such details about the looks, gestures, and experiences of his characters that we cannot help believing that the story he tells us is true."

A detail is "definite" and "concrete" when it appeals to the senses. It should be seen, heard, smelled, tasted, or touched. The most superficial survey of any bookshelf of published fiction will turn up dozens of examples of this principle. Here is a fairly obvious one.

> It was a narrow room, with a rather high ceiling, and crowded from floor to ceiling with goodies. There were rows and rows of hams and sausages of all shapes and colors—white, yellow, red and black; fat and lean and round and long—rows of canned preserves, cocoa and tea, bright translucent glass bottles of honey, marmalade and jam.
>
> I stood enchanted, straining my ears and breathing in the delightful atmosphere and the mixed fragrance of chocolate and smoked fish and earthy truffles. I spoke into the silence, saying: "Good day" in quite a loud voice; I can still remember how my strained, unnatural tones died away in the stillness. No one answered. And my mouth literally began to water like

a spring. One quick, noiseless step and I was beside one of the laden tables. I made one rapturous grab into the nearest glass urn, filled as it chanced with chocolate creams, slipped a fistful into my coat pocket, then reached the door, and in the next second was safely round the corner.

Thomas Mann, *Confessions of Felix Krull, Confidence Man*

The shape of this passage is a tour through the five senses. Mann lets us see: *narrow room, high ceiling, hams, sausages, preserves, cocoa, tea, glass bottles, honey, marmalade, jam.* He lets us smell: *fragrance of chocolate, smoked fish, earthy truffles.* He lets us hear: *"Good day," unnatural tones, stillness.* He lets us taste: *mouth, water like a spring.* He lets us touch: *grab, chocolate creams, slipped, fistful into my coat pocket.* The writing is alive because we do in fact live through our sense perceptions, and Mann takes us past words and through thought to let us perceive the scene in this way.

In this process, a number of ideas not stated reverberate off the sense images, so that we are also aware of a number of generalizations the author might have made but does not need to make; we will make them ourselves. Mann could have had his character "tell" us: *I was quite poor, and I was not used to seeing such a profusion of food, so that although I was very afraid there might be someone in the room and that I might be caught stealing, I couldn't resist taking the risk.*

Such a version would be very flat, and none of that telling is necessary as all these points are "shown." The character's relative poverty is inherent in the tumble of images of sight and smell; if he were used to such displays, his eyes and nose would not dart about as they do. His fear is inherent in the "strained, unnatural tones" and their dying away in the stillness. His desire is in his watering mouth, his fear in the furtive speed of "quick" and "grab" and "slipped."

The points to be made here are two, and they are both important. The first is that the writer must deal in sense detail. The second is that these must be details "that matter." As a writer of fiction you are at constant pains not simply to say what you mean, but to mean more than you say. Much of what you mean will be an abstraction or a judgment—*love requires trust, children can be cruel.* But if you write in abstractions or judgments, you are writing an essay, whereas if you let us use our senses and form our own interpretations, we will be involved as participants in a real way. Much of the pleasure of reading comes from the egotistical sense that we are clever enough to understand. When the author explains to us or interprets for us, we suspect that he or she doesn't think us bright enough to do it for ourselves.

A detail can also matter because it suggests plot development. Chekhov famously said that if a pistol is placed on the mantle in the first act, it must go off in the third. Similarly, when a story offers a new kind of detail or level of specificity it may suggest a change in character or a development of the plot. As you read Teolinda Gersão's "The Red Fox Fur Coat" at the end of this chapter, the narrator will alert you to a heightening of the main character's senses as she goes jogging in the wood, but what does it mean when that character notices "a lizard scurrying through the leaves, an invisible mouse making a twig crack, an acorn falling, [and] a bird landing on a bush"?

A detail is *concrete* if it appeals to one of the five senses; it is *significant* if it also conveys an idea or a judgment or both. *The windowsill was green* is concrete, because we can see it. *The windowsill was shedding flakes of fungus-green paint* is concrete and also significant because it conveys the idea that the paint is old and suggests the judgment that the color is ugly. The second version can also be seen more vividly. (For further discussion of selecting detail, "How Fictional Elements Contribute to Theme," page 347, in Chapter 9.)

Here is a passage from a young writer that fails through lack of appeal to the senses.

> Debbie was a very stubborn and completely independent person and was always doing things her way despite her parents' efforts to get her to conform. Her father was an executive in a dress manufacturing company and was able to afford his family all the luxuries and comforts of life. But Debbie was completely indifferent to her family's affluence.

This passage contains a number of judgments we might or might not share with the author, and she has not convinced us that we do. What constitutes stubbornness? Independence? Indifference? Affluence? Further, since the judgments are supported by generalizations, we have no sense of the individuality of the characters, which alone would bring them to life on the page. What things was she always doing? What efforts did her parents make to get her to conform? What level of executive? What dress manufacturing company? What luxuries and comforts?

> Debbie would wear a tank top to a tea party if she pleased, with fluorescent earrings and ankle-strap sandals.
>
> "Oh, sweetheart," Mrs. Chiddister would stand in the doorway wringing her hands. "It's not *nice*."
>
> "Not who?" Debbie would say, and add a fringed belt.
>
> Mr. Chiddister was Artistic Director of the Boston branch of Cardin and had a high respect for what he called "elegant textures," which ranged from handwoven tweed to gold filigree, and which he willingly offered his daughter. Debbie preferred her laminated wrist bangles.

We have not passed a final judgment on the merits of these characters, but we know a good deal more about them, and we have drawn certain interim conclusions that are our own and not forced on us by the author. Debbie is independent of her parents' values, rather careless of their feelings, energetic, and possibly a tart. Mrs. Chiddister is quite ineffectual. Mr. Chiddister is a snob, though perhaps Debbie's taste is so bad we'll end up on his side.

But maybe that isn't at all what the author had in mind. Perhaps it was more like this version:

One day Debbie brought home a copy of *Ulysses*. Mrs. Strum called it "filth" and threw it across the sunporch. Debbie knelt on the parquet and retrieved her bookmark, which she replaced. "No, it's not," she said.

"You're not so old I can't take a strap to you!" Mr. Strum reminded her.

Mr. Strum was controlling stockholder of Readywear Conglomerates and was proud of treating his family, not only on his salary, but also on his expense account. The summer before, he had justified their company on a trip to Belgium, where they toured the American Cemetery and the torture chambers of Ghent Castle. Entirely ungrateful, Debbie had spent the rest of the trip curled up in the hotel with a shabby copy of some poet.

Now we have a much clearer understanding of *stubbornness, independence, indifference,* and *affluence,* both their natures and the value we are to place on them. This time our judgment is heavily weighed in Debbie's favor—partly because people who read books have a sentimental sympathy with people who read books—but also because we hear hysteria in "filth" and "take a strap to you," whereas Debbie's resistance is quiet and strong. Mr. Strum's attitude toward his expense account suggests that he's corrupt, and his choice of "luxuries" is morbid. The passage does contain two overt judgments, the first being that Debbie was "entirely ungrateful." Notice that by the time we get to this, we're aware that the judgment is Mr. Strum's and that Debbie has little enough to be grateful for. We understand not only what the author says but also that she means the opposite of what she says, and we feel doubly clever to get it; that is the pleasure of irony. Likewise, the judgment that the poet's book is "shabby" shows Mr. Strum's crass materialism toward what we know to be the finer things. At the very end of the passage, we are denied a detail that we might very well be given: *What* poet did Debbie curl up with? Again, by this time we understand that we are being given Mr. Strum's view of the situation and that it's Mr. Strum (not Debbie, not the author, and certainly not us) who wouldn't notice the difference between John Keats and Stanley Kunitz.

One may object that both rewrites of the passage are longer than the original. Doesn't "adding" so much detail make for long writing? The answer is yes and no. No, because in the rewrites we know so much more about the values, activities, lifestyles, attitudes, and personalities of the characters that it would take many times the length of the original to "tell" it all in generalizations. Yes, in the sense that detail requires words, and if you are to realize your characters through detail, then you must be careful to select the details that convey the characteristics essential to our understanding. You can't convey a whole person, or a whole action, or everything there is to be conveyed about a single moment of a single day. You must select the significant.

In fact, the greater significance of realistic details may emerge only as you continue to develop and revise your story, for, as Flannery O'Connor says, "the longer you look at one object, the more of the world you see in it." Certain details "tend to accumulate meaning from the action of the story itself" becoming "symbolic in the way they work," O'Connor notes. "While having their essential place in the literal level of the story, [details] operate in depth as well as on the surface, increasing the story in every direction."

No amount of concrete detail will move us, therefore, unless it also implicitly suggests meaning and value. Following is a passage that fails, not because it lacks detail, but because those details lack significance.

> Terry Landon, a handsome young man of twenty-two, was six foot four and broad-shouldered. He had medium-length thick blond hair and a natural tan, which set off the blue of his intense and friendly long-lashed eyes.

Here we have a good deal of generic sensory information, but we still know very little about Terry. There are so many broad-shouldered twenty-two-year-olds in the world, so many blonds, and so on. This sort of cataloging of characteristics suggests an all-points bulletin: *Male Caucasian, medium height, light hair, last seen wearing gray raincoat.* Such a description may help the police locate a suspect in a crowd, but the assumption is that the identity of the person is not known. As an author you want us to know the character individually and immediately.

The fact is that all our ideas and judgments are formed through our sense perceptions, and daily, moment by moment, we receive information that is not merely sensuous in this way. Four people at a cocktail party may *do* nothing but stand and nibble canapés and may *talk* nothing but politics and the latest films. But you feel perfectly certain that X is furious at Y, who is flirting with Z, who is wounding Q, who is trying to comfort X. You have only your senses to observe with. How do you reach these conclusions? By what gestures, glances, tones, touches, choices of words?

It may be that this constant emphasis on judgment makes the author, and the reader, seem opinionated or self-righteous. "I want to present my characters objectively/neutrally. I'm not making any value judgments. I want the reader to make up his or her own mind." Yet human beings are constantly judging: *How was the film? He seemed friendly. What a boring class! Do you like it here? She's very thin. That's fascinating. I'm so clumsy. You're gorgeous tonight. Life is crazy, isn't it?*

The fact is that when we are not passing such judgments, it's because we are indifferent. Although you may not want to sanctify or damn your characters, you do want us to care about them, and if you refuse to direct our judgment, you may be inviting our indifference. Usually, when you "don't want us to judge," you mean that you want our feelings to be mixed, paradoxical, complex. *She's horribly irritating, but it's not her fault. He's sexy, but there's something cold about it underneath.* If this is what you mean, then you must direct our judgment in both or several directions, not in no direction.

Even a character who doesn't exist except as a type or function will come to life if presented through significant detail, as in this portrait of an aunt in Dorothy Allison's story "Don't Tell Me You Don't Know." Like many of the female relatives the adult narrator mentions, the aunt embodies a powerful, nurturing force that nonetheless failed to protect the narrator from childhood abuse.

My family runs to heavy women, gravy-fed working women, the kind usually seen in pictures taken at mining disasters. Big women, all of my aunts
move under their own power and stalk around telling everybody else what
to do. But Aunt Alma was the prototype, the one I had loved most, starting back when she had given us free meals in the roadhouse she'd run for
awhile.... Once there, we'd be fed on chicken gravy and biscuits, and
Mama would be fed from the well of her sister's love and outrage.

For a character who is a "prototype," we have a remarkably clear image of this
woman. Notice how Allison moves us from generalization toward sharpness of
image, gradually bringing the character into focus. First she has only a size and
gender, then a certain abstract "power" and an appeal to our visual memory of
the grieving, tough women seen in documentary photographs; then a distinct
role as the one who "had given us free meals" when the family hit hard times.
Once in focus as manager of a particular roadhouse, Alma's qualities again
become generalized to the adult women of the family.

The power in them, the strength and the heat!...How could my daddy,
my uncles, ever stand up to them, dare to raise hand or voice to them?
They were a power on the earth.

Finally, the focus narrows to the individual again, whose body has been
formed by the starchy foods that poverty made a necessity and that at least
kept hunger temporarily at bay: "My aunt always made biscuits. What else
stretched so well? Now those starch meals shadowed her loose shoulders and
dimpled her fat white elbows."

The point is not that an author must never express an idea, general quality,
or judgment. But, in order to carry the felt weight of fiction, these abstractions
must be realized through the senses—"I smelled chicken gravy and hot grease,
the close thick scent of love and understanding." Through details these abstract qualities live.

GOOD WRITERS MAY "TELL" ABOUT ALMOST ANYTHING IN fiction
except the characters' feelings. One may tell the reader that the
character went to a private school…or one may tell the reader that
the character hates spaghetti; but with rare exceptions the characters' feelings must be demonstrated: fear, love, excitement, doubt,
embarrassment, despair become real only when they take the form
of events—action (or gesture), dialogue, or physical reaction to
setting. Detail is the lifeblood of fiction.

JOHN GARDNER

WRITING ABOUT EMOTION

Fiction offers feelings for which the reader doesn't pay—and yet to evoke those feelings, it is often necessary to portray sensory details that the reader may have experienced. Simply labeling a character's emotion as love or hatred will have little effect, for such abstraction operates solely on a vague, intellectual level; rather, emotion is the body's physical reaction to information the senses receive. The great Russian director Stanislavski, originator of realistic "Method" acting, urged his students to abandon the clichéd emotive postures of the nineteenth-century stage in favor of emotions evoked by the actor's recollection of sensory details connected with a personal past trauma. By recalling such details as the tingling of fingertips, the smell of singed hair, and the tensing of calf muscles, an emotion such as anger might naturally be induced within the actor's body.

THE PAST IS BEAUTIFUL BECAUSE ONE never realizes an emotion at the time. It expands later, and thus we don't have complete emotions about the present, only about the past.... That is why we dwell on the past, I think.

VIRGINIA WOOLF

Similarly, in written fiction, if the writer depicts the precise physical sensations experienced by the character, a particular emotion may be triggered by the reader's own sense memory. In his story "The Easy Way," author Tom Perrotta describes the moment in which a lottery winner learns of a jealous friend's death: "I stood perfectly still and let the news expand inside of me, like a bubble in my chest that wouldn't rise or pop. I waited for anger or grief to fill the space it opened, but all I felt just then was an unsteadiness in my legs, a faulty connection with the ground." By tracing the physical reaction and staying true to the shock of the moment, Perrotta conveys the initial impact of this loss.

"Get control of emotion by avoiding the *mention* of the emotion," urges John L'Heureux. "To avoid melodrama, aim for a restrained tone rather than an exaggerated one. A scene with hysteria needs more, not less control in the writing: keep the language deflated and rooted in action and sensory detail."

There are further reasons to avoid labeling emotion: emotion is seldom pure. Conflicting feelings often run together; we rarely stop to analyze our passions as we're caught up in them; and the reader may cease to participate when a label is simply given.

FILTERING

John Gardner, in *The Art of Fiction*, points out that in addition to the faults of insufficient detail and excessive use of abstraction, there's a third failure:

> ...the needless filtering of the image through some observing consciousness. The amateur writes: "Turning, she noticed two snakes fighting in among the rocks." Compare: "She turned. In among the rocks, two snakes were fighting..." Generally speaking—though no laws are absolute in fiction—vividness urges that almost every occurrence of such phrases as "she noticed" and "she saw" be suppressed in favor of direct presentation of the thing seen.

The filter is a common fault and often difficult to recognize—although once the principle is grasped, cutting away filters is an easy means to more vivid writing. As a fiction writer you will often be working through "some observing consciousness." Yet when you step back and ask readers to observe the observer—to look *at* rather than *through* the character—you start to tell-not-show and rip us briefly out of the scene. Here, for example, is a student passage quite competent except for the filtering:

> Mrs. Blair made her way to the chair by the window and sank gratefully into it. *She looked out the window and there,* across the street, *she saw* the ivory BMW parked in front of the fire plug once more. *It seemed to her, though,* that something was wrong with it. *She noticed* that it was listing slightly toward the back and side, and *then saw* that the back rim was resting almost on the asphalt.

Remove the filters from this paragraph and we are allowed to stay in Mrs. Blair's consciousness, watching with her eyes, sharing understanding as it unfolds for her:

> Mrs. Blair made her way to the chair by the window and sank gratefully into it. Across the street the ivory BMW was parked in front of the fire plug again. Something was wrong with it, though. It was listing toward the back and side, the back rim resting almost on the asphalt.

A similar filtering occurs when the writer chooses to begin a flashback and mistakenly supposes that the reader is not clever enough to follow this technique without a guiding transition:

> Mrs. Blair *thought back to* the time that she and Henry had owned an ivory car, though it had been a Chevy. *She remembered clearly* that it had a hood shaped like a sugar scoop, and chrome bumpers that stuck out a foot front

and back. And there was that funny time, *she recalled*, when Henry had to change the flat tire on Alligator Alley, and she'd thought the alligators would come up out of the swamp.

Just as the present scene will be more present to the reader without a filter, so we will be taken more thoroughly back to the time of the memory without a filter:

She and Henry had owned an ivory car once, though it had been a Chevy, with a hood shaped like a sugar scoop and chrome bumpers that stuck out a foot front and back. And there was that funny time Henry had to change the flat tire on Alligator Alley, and she'd thought the alligators would come up out of the swamp.

Observe that the pace of the reading is improved by the removal of the fil-ters—at least partly, literally, because one or two lines of type have been removed.

Comparison

Every reader reading is a self-deceiver: We simultaneously "believe" a story and know that it is a fiction, a fabrication. Our belief in the reality of the story may be so strong that it produces physical reactions—tears, trembling, sighs, gasps, a headache. At the same time, as long as the fiction is working for us, we know that our submission is voluntary; that we have, as Samuel Taylor Coleridge pointed out, suspended disbelief. "It's just a movie," says the exas-perated father as he takes his shrieking six-year-old out to the lobby. For the father the fiction is working; for the child it is not.

Simultaneous belief and awareness of illusion are present in both the con-tent and the craft of literature, and what is properly called artistic pleasure derives from the tension of this *is* and *is not*. The content of a plot, for instance, tells us that something happens that does not happen, that people who do not exist behave in such a way, and that the events of life—which we know to be random, unrelated, and unfinished—are necessary, patterned, and come to closure. Pleasure in artistry comes precisely when the illusion rings true without destroying the knowledge that it is an illusion.

In the same way, the techniques of every art offer us the tension of things that are and are not alike. This is true of poetry, in which rhyme is interesting because *tend* sounds like *mend* but not exactly like; it is also true of music, whose interest lies in variations on a theme. And it is the fundamental nature of metaphor, from which literature derives.

Metaphor is the literary device by which we are told that something is, or is like, something that it clearly is not, or is not exactly, like. It is a way of show-ing, because it particularizes the essential nature of one thing by comparing it to another. What a good metaphor does is surprise us with the unlikeness of the two things compared while at the same time convincing us of the truth of the likeness. In the process it may also illuminate the meaning of the story and its theme. A bad metaphor fails to surprise or convince or both—and so fails to illuminate.

TYPES OF METAPHOR AND SIMILE

The simplest distinction between kinds of comparison, and usually the first one grasped by beginning students of literature, is between *metaphor* and *simile*. A simile makes a comparison with the use of *like* or *as*, a metaphor without. Though this distinction is technical, it is not entirely trivial, for a metaphor demands a more literal acceptance. If you say, "A woman is a rose," you ask for an extreme suspension of disbelief, whereas "A woman is like a rose" acknowledges the artifice in the statement.

In both metaphor and simile, the resonance of comparison is in the essential or abstract quality that the two objects share. When a writer speaks of "the eyes of the houses" or "the windows of the soul," the comparison of eyes to windows contains the idea of transmitting vision between the inner and the outer. When we speak of "the king of beasts," we don't mean that a lion wears a crown or sits on a throne (although in children's stories the lion often does precisely that, in order to suggest a primitive physical likeness); we mean that king and lion share abstract qualities of power, position, pride, and bearing.

In both metaphor and simile a physical similarity can yield up a characterizing abstraction. So if "a woman" is either "a rose" or "like a rose," the significance lies not in the physical similarity but in the essential qualities that such similarity implies: slenderness, suppleness, fragrance, beauty, color—and perhaps the hidden threat of thorns.

Every metaphor and simile I have used so far is either a cliché or a dead metaphor (a metaphor so familiar that it has lost its original meaning). Each of them may at one time have surprised by their aptness, but by now each has been used so often that the surprise is gone. I wished to use familiar examples in order to clarify that *resonance of comparison depends on the abstractions conveyed in the likeness of the things compared*. A good metaphor reverberates with the essential; this is the writer's principle of choice.

So Flannery O'Connor, in "A Good Man Is Hard to Find," describes the mother as having "a face as broad and innocent as a cabbage." A soccer ball is roughly the same size and shape as a cabbage; so is a schoolroom globe; so is a street lamp. But if the mother's face had been as broad and innocent as any of these things, she would be a different woman altogether. A cabbage is also rural, heavy, dense, and cheap, and so conveys a whole complex of abstractions about the woman's class and mentality. There is, on the other hand, no innocence in the face of Shrike, in Nathanael West's *Miss Lonelyhearts*, who "buried his triangular face like a hatchet in her neck."

Sometimes the aptness of a comparison is achieved by taking it from an area of reference relevant to the thing compared. In *Dombey and Son*, Charles Dickens describes the ships' instrument maker, Solomon Gills, as having "eyes as red as if they had been small suns looking at you through a fog." The simile suggests a seascape, whereas in *One Flew Over the Cuckoo's Nest*, Ken Kesey's Ruckly, rendered inert by shock therapy, has eyes "all smoked up and gray and deserted inside like blown fuses." But the metaphor may range further from its original, in which case the abstraction conveyed must strike us as strongly and essentially appropriate. William Faulkner's Emily Grierson in "A Rose for Emily" has "haughty black eyes in a face the flesh of which was strained across the temple and about the eyesockets as you imagine a lighthouse-keeper's face ought to look." Miss Emily has no connection with the sea, but the metaphor reminds us not only of her sternness and self-sufficiency, but also that she has isolated herself in a locked house. The same character as an old woman has eyes that "looked like two pieces of coal pressed into a lump of dough," and the image domesticates her, robs her of her light.

Both metaphors and similes can be *extended*, meaning that the writer continues to present aspects of likeness in the things compared.

> There was a white fog...standing all around you like something solid.
> At eight or nine, perhaps, it lifted as a shutter lifts. We had a glimpse of
> the towering multitude of trees, of the immense matted jungle, with the
> blazing little ball of sun hanging over it—all perfectly still—and then the
> shutter came down again, smoothly, as if sliding in greased grooves.
>
> Joseph Conrad, *Heart of Darkness*

Notice that Conrad moves from a generalized image of "something solid" to the specific simile "as a shutter lifts"; reasserts the simile as a metaphor, "then the shutter came down again"; and becomes still more specific in the extension "as if sliding in greased grooves."

Also note that Conrad emphasizes the dumb solidity of the fog by comparing the larger natural image with the smaller manufactured object. This is a technique that contemporary writers have used to effects both comic and profound, as when Frederick Barthelme in *The Brothers* describes a young woman "with a life stretching out in front of her like so many unrented videos" or a man's head "bobbing like an enormous Q-Tip against the little black sky."

In a more usual metaphoric technique, the smaller or more ordinary image is compared with one more significant or intense, as in this example from Louise Erdrich's "Machimanito," where the narrator invokes the names of Anishinabe Indians dead of tuberculosis:

> Their names grew within us, swelled to the brink of our lips, forced our
> eyes open in the middle of the night. We were filled with the water of the
> drowned, cold and black—airless water that lapped against the seal of our

tongues or leaked slowly from the corners of our eyes. Within us, like ice shards, their names bobbed and shifted.

A *conceit*, which can be either metaphor or simile, is a comparison of two things radically and startlingly unlike—in Samuel Johnson's words, "yoked by violence together." A conceit is as far removed as possible from the purely sensuous comparison of "the eyes of the potato." It compares two things that have very little or no immediately apprehensible similarity; and so it is the nature of the conceit to be long. The author must explain to us, sometimes at great length, why these things can be said to be alike. When John Donne compares a flea to the Holy Trinity, the two images have no areas of reference in common, and we don't understand. He must explain to us that the flea, having bitten both the poet and his lover, now has the blood of three souls in its body.

The conceit is more common to poetry than to prose because of the density of its imagery, but it can be used to good effect in fiction. In *The Day of the Locust*, Nathanael West uses a conceit in an insistent devaluation of love. The screenwriter Claude Estee says:

> Love is like a vending machine, eh? Not bad. You insert a coin and press home the lever. There's some mechanical activity inside the bowels of the device. You receive a small sweet, frown at yourself in the dirty mirror, adjust your hat, take a firm grip on your umbrella and walk away, trying to look as though nothing had happened.

"Love is like a vending machine" is a conceit; if the writer didn't explain to us in what way love is like a vending machine, we'd founder trying to figure it out. So he goes on to develop the vending machine in images that suggest not "love" but seamy sex. The last image—"trying to look as though nothing had happened"—has nothing to do with the vending machine; we accept it because by this time we've fused the two ideas in our minds.

Deborah Galyan employs conceit in "The Incredible Appearing Man," in a playfully self-conscious description of the overpowering effect of a new baby's presence.

> A baby transforms you, body and soul. The moment you give birth, your mind is instantaneously filled with Styrofoam peanuts. Your past is trash-compacted to make room for all the peanuts. As the baby grows, you add more peanuts, and the little tin can of your past gets more compressed. But it is still there, underneath all the peanuts. The smashed cans of your past never entirely disappear.

The comparison of a mind and a trash compactor is a conceit because physical or sensuous similarity is not the point. Rather, the similarity is in the abstract idea of material (metal cans or memories) that once loomed large being crushed and all but crowded out by the volume of daily experience.

METAPHORIC FAULTS TO AVOID

Comparison is not a frivolity. It is, on the contrary, the primary business of the brain. Some eighteenth-century philosophers spoke of the human mind as a *tabula rasa*, a blank slate on which sense impressions were recorded, compared, and grouped. Now we're more likely to speak of the mind as a "computer" "storing" and "processing" "data." What both metaphors acknowledge is that comparison is the basis of all learning and all reasoning. When a child burns his hand on the stove and hears his mother say, "It's hot," and then goes toward the radiator and again hears her say, "It's hot," the child learns not to burn his fingers. The implicit real-life comparison is meant to convey a fact, and it teaches a mode of behavior. By contrast, the goal of literary comparison is to convey not a fact but a perception, and thereby to enlarge our scope of understanding. When we speak of "the flames of torment," our impulse is comprehension and compassion.

Nevertheless, metaphor is a dirty word in some critical circles, because of the strain of the pursuit. Clichés, mixed metaphors, and similes that are inept, unapt, obscure, or done to death mar good prose and tax the patience of the most willing reader. If a metaphor is too familiar it operates as an abstraction rather than a particularizing detail. If it is too far-fetched it calls attention to the writer rather than to the meaning and produces a sort of hiccup in the reader's involvement.

There are more *don'ts* than *dos* to list for the writing of metaphor and simile, because every good comparison is its own justification by virtue of being apt and original.

To study good metaphor, read. In the meantime, avoid the following:

> *Cliché* metaphors are metaphors so familiar that they have lost the force of their original meaning. They are inevitably apt comparisons; if they were not, they wouldn't have been repeated often enough to become clichés. But such images fail to surprise, and we blame the writer for this expenditure of energy without a payoff.

Or, to put it a worse way:

> Clichés are *the last word* in bad writing, and *it's a crying shame* to see all you *bright young things* spoiling your *deathless prose* with phrases as *old as the hills*. You must *keep your nose to the grindstone*, because *the sweet smell of success* only comes to those who *march to the beat of a different drummer*.

It's a sad fact that at this stage of literary history, you may not say that eyes are like pools or stars, and you should be very wary of saying that they flood with tears. These have been so often repeated that they've become shorthand for emotions (attractions in the first and second instances, grief in the third) without the felt force of those emotions. Anytime you as writer record an emotion without convincing us to feel that emotion, you introduce a fatal distance between author and reader. Therefore, neither may your characters be hawk-eyed nor eagle-eyed; nor may they have ruby lips or pearly teeth or peaches-and-cream complexions or necks like swans or thighs like hams. Let them not shed single tears or freeze like deer caught in headlights. If you sense—and you may—that the moment calls for the special intensity of metaphor, you may have to sift through a whole stock of clichés that come readily to mind. Or it may be time for freewriting and giving the mind room to play. Sometimes your internal critic may reject as fantastic the comparison that, on second look, proves fresh and apt.

In any case, *pools* and *stars* have become clichés for *eyes* because they capture and manifest something essential about the nature of eyes. As long as eyes continue to contain liquid and light, there will be a new way of saying so.

Cliché can be useful as a device, however, for establishing authorial distance from a character or narrator. If the author tells us that Rome wasn't built in a day, we're likely to think the author has little to contribute to human insight; but if a character says so, in speech or thought, the judgment attaches to the character rather than to the author.

> The door closed and he turned to find the dumpy figure, surmounted by the atrocious hat, coming toward him. "Well," she said, "*you only live once* and paying a little more for it, I at least won't *meet myself coming and going.*"
>
> "Some day I'll start making money..."
>
> "I think you're doing fine," she said, drawing on her gloves. "You've only been out of school a year. *Rome wasn't built in a day.*"
>
> Flannery O'Connor, "Everything That Rises Must Converge"
> (italics added)

Far-fetched metaphors are the opposite of clichés: They surprise but are not apt. As the dead metaphor *far-fetched* suggests, the mind must travel too far to carry back the likeness, and too much is lost on the way. When such a comparison does work, we speak laudatorily of a "leap of the imagination." But when it does not, what we face is in effect a failed conceit: The explanation of what is alike about these two things does not convince. Very good writers in the search for originality sometimes fetch too far. Ernest Hemingway's talent was not for metaphor, and on the rare occasions that he used a metaphor, he was likely to strain. In this passage from *A Farewell to Arms*, the protagonist has escaped a firing squad and is fleeing the war.

> You had lost your cars and your men as a floorwalker loses the stock of his department in a fire. There was, however, no insurance. You were out of it now. You had no more obligation. If they shot floorwalkers after a fire in the department store because they spoke with an accent they had always had, then certainly the floorwalkers would not be expected to return when

the store opened again for business. They might seek other employment;
if there was any other employment and the police did not get them.

Well, this doesn't work. We may be willing to see the likeness between stock
lost in a department store fire and men and cars lost in a military retreat; but
"they" *don't* shoot floorwalkers as the Italian military shot defeated line officers.
And although a foreign accent might be a disadvantage in a foreign war, it's hard
to see how a floorwalker could be killed because of one, although it might make
it hard for him to get hired in the first place, if.... The mind twists trying to find
any illuminating or essential logic in the comparison of a soldier to a floorwalker,
and fails, so that the protagonist's situation is trivialized in the attempt.

Mixed metaphors are so called because they ask us to compare the original
image with things from two or more different areas of reference: *As you walk
the path of life, don't founder on the reefs of ignorance.* Life can be a path or a sea,
but it cannot be both at the same time. The point of the metaphor is to fuse
two images in a single tension. The mind is adamantly unwilling to fuse three.

Separate metaphors or similes too close together, especially if they come
from areas of reference very different in value or tone, disturb in the same way
the mixed metaphor does. The mind doesn't leap; it staggers.

> They fought like rats in a Brooklyn sewer. Nevertheless her presence was
> the axiom of his heart's geometry, and when she was away you would see
> him walking up and down the street dragging his cane along the picket
> fence like an idle boy's stick.

Any of these metaphors or similes might be acceptable by itself, but rats,
axioms, and boys' sticks connote three different areas and tones, and two
sentences cannot contain them all. Pointed in too many directions, a reader's
attention follows none.

Obscure and *overdone metaphors* falter because the author has misjudged the
difficulty of the comparison. The result is either confusion or an insult to the
reader's intelligence. In the case of obscurity, a similarity in the author's mind
isn't getting onto the page. One student described the spines on a prickly pear
cactus as being "slender as a fat man's fingers." I was completely confused by this.
Was it ironic, that the spines weren't slender at all? Ah no, he said, hadn't I noticed how startling it was when someone with a fleshy body had bony fingers and
toes? The trouble here was that the author knew what he meant but had left out
the essential abstraction in the comparison, the startling quality of the contrast:
"the spines of the fleshy prickly pear, like slender fingers on a fat man."

In this case, the simile was underexplained. It's probably a more common
impulse—we're so anxious to make sure the reader gets it—to explain the
obvious. In the novel *Raw Silk*, I had the narrator describe quarrels with her
husband, "which I used to face with my dukes up in high confidence that we'd
soon clear the air. The air can't be cleared now. We live in marital Los Angeles. This is the air—polluted, poisoned." A critic friend pointed out to me that

anybody who didn't know about L.A. smog wouldn't get it anyway, and that all the last two words did was ram the comparison down the reader's throat. He was right. "The air can't be cleared now. We live in marital Los Angeles. This is the air." The rewrite is much stronger because it neither explains nor exaggerates; and the reader enjoys supplying the metaphoric link.

Metaphors using *topical references*, including brand names, esoteric objects, or celebrity names, can work as long as a sense of the connection is given; don't rely for effect on knowledge that the reader may not have. To write, "The sisters looked like the Dixie Chicks" is to make the trio do your job; and if the reader happens to be a Beethoven buff, or Hungarian, or reading your story twenty years from now, there may be no way of knowing what the reference refers to. "They had the blindingly blond, in-your-face exuberance of the Dixie Chicks" will convey the sense even for someone who doesn't watch country music cable. Likewise, "She was as beautiful as Theda Bara" may not mean much to you, whereas if I say, "She had the saucer eyes and satin hair of Theda Bara," the comparison will "show," and you'll get it, close enough.

The Active Voice

If your prose is to be vigorous as well as vivid, if your characters are "come to life," you must make use of the active voice. The active voice occurs when the subject of a sentence performs the action described by the verb of that sentence: *She spilled the milk.* When the passive voice is used, the object of the active verb becomes the subject of the passive verb: *The milk was spilled by her.* The subject is acted upon rather than acting, and the effect is to weaken the prose and to distance the reader from the action.

The passive voice does have an important place in fiction, precisely because it expresses a sense that the character is being acted upon. If a prison guard is kicking the hero, then *I was slammed into the wall; I was struck blindingly from behind and forced to the floor* appropriately carries the sense of his helplessness.

In general, however, you should seek to use the active voice in all prose and to use the passive only when the actor is unknown or insignificant or when you want to achieve special stylistic effects like the one above.

But there is one other common grammatical construction that is *in effect* passive and can distance the reader from a sense of immediate experience. The verbs that we learn in school to call *linking verbs* are effectively passive because verbs with auxiliaries suggest an indefinite time and are never as sharply focused as active verbs. (Further editing his example cited earlier, Gardner contrasts the phrase "two snakes were fighting" with the improved "two snakes fought," which pinpoints a specific moment; he further suggests substitution of active verbs, as in "two snakes whipped and lashed, striking at each other.")

Linking verbs also invite complements that tend to be generalized or judgmental: *Her hair* looked *beautiful. He was very happy. The room* seemed *expensively furnished. They* became *morose.* Let her hair bounce, tumble, cascade, or swing; we'll see better. Let him laugh, leap, cry, or hug a tree; we'll experience his joy.

The following is a passage with very little action, nevertheless made vital by the use of active verbs:

> At Mixt she neither drinks nor eats. Each of the sisters furtively stares at her as she tranquilly sits in post-Communion meditation with her hands immersed in her habit. *Lectio* has been halted for the morning, so there is only the Great Silence and the tinks of cutlery, but handsigns are being traded as the sisters lard their hunks of bread or fold and ring their dinner napkins. When the prioress stands, all rise up with her for the blessing, and then Sister Aimee gives Mariette the handsigns. *You, infirmary.*
>
> Ron Hansen, *Mariette in Ecstasy*

Here, though the convent meal is silent and action is minimal, a number of the verbs suggest suppressed power: *stares, sits, lard, fold, ring, stands, rise, gives.*

Compare the first passage about Debbie on page 24 with the second of the rewrites on page 25. In the generalized original we have *was stubborn, was doing things, was executive, was able, was indifferent.* Apart from the compound verb *was doing*, all these are linking verbs. In the rewrite the characters *brought, called, threw, knelt, retrieved, replaced, said, reminded, justified, toured, spent,* and *curled up.* What energetic people! The rewrite contains two linking verbs: Mr. Strum *was stockholder* and *was proud*; these properly represent static states, a position and an attitude.

One beneficial side effect of active verbs is that they tend to call forth significant details. If you say "she was shocked," you are telling us; but if you are to show us that she was shocked through an action, you are likely to have to search for an image as well. "She clenched the arm of the chair so hard that her knuckles whitened." *Clenched* and *whitened* actively suggest shock, and at the same time we see her knuckles on the arm of the chair.

On Active Verbs

A general verb creates a general impression, but a precise, active verb conveys the exact picture in the reader's mind. For example:

General	Specific
walk	Does the waiter *scurry* or *amble*?
yell	Does the coach *demand* or *bellow*?
swim	Does the child *splash* or *glide*?
climb	Does the hiker *stumble up the hill* or *stride*?

To be is the most common of the linking verbs and also the most overused, but all the linking verbs invite generalization and distance. *To feel, to seem, to look, to appear, to experience, to express, to show, to demonstrate, to convey, to display*—all these suggest in fiction that the character is being acted upon or observed by someone rather than doing something. She felt *happy/sad/amused/mortified* does not convince us. We want to see her and infer her emotion for ourselves. *He very clearly conveyed his displeasure.* It isn't clear to us. How did he convey it? To whom?

Linking verbs, like the passive voice, can appropriately convey a sense of passivity or helplessness when that is the desired effect. Notice that in the passage by Mann quoted earlier in this chapter, where Felix Krull is momentarily stunned by the sight of the food before him, linking verbs are used: *It was a narrow room, there were rows and rows,* while all the colors and shapes buffet his senses. Only as he gradually recovers can he *stand, breathe, speak,* and eventually *grab*.

I don't mean to suggest that as an author you should analyze your grammar as you go along. Most word choice is instinctive, and instinct is often the best guide. However, I do mean to suggest that you should be aware of the vigor and variety of available verbs, and that if a passage lacks energy, it may be because your instinct has let you down. How often *are* subjects portrayed in some condition or are they acted *upon*, when they could more forcefully *do*?

A note of caution about active verbs: Make sparing use of what John Ruskin called the "pathetic fallacy"—the attributing of human emotions to natural and man-made objects. Even a description of a static scene can be invigorated if the houses *stand*, the streets *wander*, and the trees *bend*. But if the houses *frown*, the streets *stagger drunkenly*, and the trees *weep*, we will feel more strain than energy in the writing.

Prose Rhythm

Novelists and short-story writers are not under the same obligation as poets to reinforce sense with sound. In prose, on the whole, the rhythm is all right if it isn't clearly wrong. But it can be wrong if, for example, the cadence contradicts the meaning; on the other hand, rhythm can greatly enhance the meaning if it is sensitively used.

> The river moved slowly. It seemed sluggish. The surface lay flat. Birds circled lazily overhead. Jon's boat slipped forward.

In this extreme example, the short, clipped sentences and their parallel structures—subject, verb, modifier—work against the sense of slow, flowing movement. The rhythm could be effective if the character whose eyes we're using is not appreciating or sharing the calm; otherwise it needs recasting.

> The surface lay flat on the sluggish, slow-moving river, and the birds circled lazily overhead as Jon's boat slipped forward.

There is nothing very striking about the rhythm of this version, but at least it moves forward without obstructing the flow of the river.

> The first impression I had as I stopped in the doorway of the immense City Room was of extreme rush and bustle, with the reporters moving rapidly back and forth in the long aisles in order to shove their copy at each other or making frantic gestures as they shouted into their many telephones.

This long and leisurely sentence cannot possibly provide a sense of rush and bustle. The phrases need to move as fast as the reporters; the verbiage must be pared down because it slows them down.

> I stopped in the doorway. The City Room was immense, reporters rushing down the aisles, shoving copy at each other, bustling back again, flinging gestures, shouting into telephones.

The poet Rolfe Humphries remarked that "*very* is the least very word in the language." It is frequently true that adverbs expressing emphasis or suddenness—*extremely, rapidly, suddenly, phenomenally, quickly, immediately, instantly, definitely, terribly, awfully*—slow the sentence down so as to dilute the force of the intended meaning. "'It's a very nice day,'" said Humphries, "is not as nice a day as 'It's a day!'" Likewise, "They stopped very abruptly" is not as abrupt as "They stopped."

Just as action and character can find an echo in prose rhythm, so it is possible to help us experience a character's emotions and attitudes through control of the starts and stops of prose tempo. In the following passage from *Persuasion*, Jane Austen combines generalization, passive verbs, and a staccato speech pattern to produce a kind of breathless blindness in the heroine.

> ...[A] thousand feelings rushed on Anne, of which this was the most consoling, that it would soon be over. And it was soon over. In two minutes after Charles's preparation, the others appeared; they were in the drawing room. Her eye half met Captain Wentworth's, a bow, a courtesy passed; she heard his voice; he talked to Mary, said all that was right, said something to the Miss Musgroves, enough to mark an easy footing; the room seemed full, full of persons and voices, but a few minutes ended it.

The opening paragraph of the Stuart Dybek story "We Didn't" (included at the end of this chapter) consists of several sentences, all of which open with the phrase "we didn't" followed by a prepositional phrase identifying a place where the young couple did not consummate their relationship. The repetition reveals the narrator's frustrations and introduces the complexities of the relationship described.

Often an abrupt change in the prose rhythm will signal a discovery or change in mood; such a shift can also reinforce a contrast in characters, actions, and attitudes. In this passage from Frederick Busch's short story "Company," a woman whose movements are relatively confined watches her husband move, stop, and move again.

Every day did not start with Vince awake that early, dressing in the dark, moving with whispery sounds down the stairs and through the kitchen, out into the autumn morning while groundfog lay on the milkweed burst open and on the stumps of harvested corn. But enough of them did.

I went to the bedroom window to watch him hunt in a business suit.

He moved with his feet in the slowly stirring fog, moving slowly himself with the rifle held across his body and his shoulders stiff. Then he stopped in a frozen watch for woodchucks. His stillness made the fog look faster as it blew across our field behind the barn. Vince stood. He waited for something to shoot. I went back to bed and lay between our covers again. I heard the bolt click. I heard the unemphatic shot, and then the second one, and after a while his feet on the porch, and soon the rush of water, the rattle of the pots on top of the stove, and later his feet again, and the car starting up as he left for work an hour before he had to.

The long opening sentence is arranged in a series of short phrases to move Vince forward. By contrast, "But enough of them did" comes abruptly, its abruptness as well as the sense of the words suggesting the woman's alienation. When Vince starts off again more slowly, the repetition of "moved, slowly stirring, moving slowly," slows down the sentence to match his strides. "Vince stood" again stills him, but the author also needs to convey that Vince stands for a long time, waiting, so we have the repetitions "he stopped, his stillness, Vince stood, he waited." As his activity speeds up again, the tempo of the prose speeds up with another series of short phrases, of which only the last is drawn out with a dependent clause, "as he left for work an hour before he had to," so that we feel the retreat of the car in the distance. Notice that Busch chooses the phrase "the rush of water," not the flow or splash of water, and how the word "rush" also points to Vince's actions. Here, meaning reinforces a tempo that, in turn, reinforces meaning. (An added bonus is that variety in sentence lengths and rhythms helps to hold readers' attention.)

"The Things They Carried" by Tim O'Brien demonstrates a range of rhythms with a rich variation of effects. Here is one:

The things they carried were largely determined by necessity. Among the necessities or near-necessities were P-38 can openers, pocket knives, heat tabs, wristwatches, dog tags, mosquito repellent, chewing gum, candy, cigarettes, salt tablets, packets of Kool-Aid, lighters, matches, sewing kits, Military Payment Certificates, C rations, and two or three canteens of water. Together, these items weighed between 15 and 20 pounds. . . .

In this passage the piling of items one on the other has the effect of loading the men down and at the same time increasingly suggests the rhythm of their marching as they "hump" their stuff. Similar lists through the story create a rhythmic thread, while variations and stoppages underlie shifts of emotion and sudden crises.

> THE DIFFERENCE BETWEEN THE RIGHT WORD and the almost right word…is the difference between lightning and the lightning bug.
>
> MARK TWAIN

Mechanics

Significant detail, the active voice, and prose rhythm are techniques for achieving the sensuous in fiction, means of helping the reader "sink into the dream" of the story, in John Gardner's phrase. Yet no technique is of much use if the reader's eye is wrenched back to the surface by misspellings or grammatical errors, for once the reader has been startled out of the story's "vivid and continuous dream," that reader may not return.

Spelling, grammar, paragraphing, and punctuation are a kind of magic; their purpose is to be invisible. If the sleight of hand works, we will not notice a comma or a quotation mark but will translate each instantly into a pause or an awareness of voice; we will not focus on the individual letters of a word but extract its sense whole. When the mechanics are incorrectly used, the trick is revealed and the magic fails; the reader's focus is shifted from the story to its surface. The reader is irritated at the author, and of all the emotions the reader is willing to experience, irritation at the author is not one.

There is no intrinsic virtue in standardized mechanics, and you can depart from them whenever you produce a result that adequately compensates for a distracting effect. But only then. Poor mechanics signal amateurism to an editor and suggest that the story itself may be flawed. Unlike the techniques of narrative, the rules of spelling, grammar, and punctuation can be coldly learned anywhere in the English-speaking world—and they should be learned by anyone who aspires to write.

We Didn't

STUART DYBEK

We did it in front of the mirror
And in the light. We did it in darkness,
In water, and in the high grass.

Yehuda Amichai, "We Did It"

We didn't in the light; we didn't in darkness. We didn't in the fresh-cut summer grass or in the mounds of autumn leaves or on the snow where moonlight threw down our shadows. We didn't in your room on the canopy bed you slept in, the bed you'd slept in as a child, or in the backseat of my father's rusted Rambler, which smelled of the smoked chubs and kielbasa he delivered on weekends from my uncle Vincent's meat market. We didn't in your mother's Buick Eight, where a rosary twined the rearview mirror like a beaded, black snake with silver, cruciform fangs.

At the dead end of our lovers' lane—a side street of abandoned factories—where I perfected the pinch that springs open a bra; behind the lilac bushes in Marquette Park, where you first touched me through my jeans and your nipples, swollen against transparent cotton, seemed the shade of lilacs; in the balcony of the now defunct Clark Theater, where I wiped popcorn salt from my palms and slid them up your thighs and you whispered, "I feel like Doris Day is watching us," we didn't.

How adept we were at fumbling, how perfectly mistimed our timing, how utterly we confused energy with ecstasy.

Remember that night becalmed by heat, and the two of us, fused by sweat, trembling as if a wind from outer space that only we could feel was gusting across Oak Street Beach? Entwined in your faded Navajo blanket, we lay soul-kissing until you wept with wanting.

We'd been kissing all day—all summer—kisses tasting of different shades of lip gloss and too many Cokes. The lake had turned hot pink, rose rapture, pearl amethyst with dusk, then washed in night black with a ruff of silver foam. Beyond a momentary horizon, silent bolts of heat lightning throbbed, perhaps setting barns on fire somewhere in Indiana. The beach that had been so crowded was deserted as if there was a curfew. Only the bodies of lovers remained, visible in lightning flashes, scattered like the fallen on a battlefield, a few of them moaning, waiting for the gulls to pick them clean.

On my fingers your slick scent mixed with the coconut musk of the suntan lotion we'd repeatedly smeared over each other's bodies. When your bikini top fell away, my hands caught your breasts, memorizing their delicate weight, my palms cupped as if bringing water to parched lips.

Along the Gold Coast, high-rises began to glow, window added to window, against the dark. In every lighted bedroom, couples home from work were stripping off their business suits, falling to the bed, and doing it. They did it before mirrors and pressed against the glass in streaming shower stalls; they did it against walls and on the furniture in ways that required previously unimagined gymnastics, which they invented on the spot. They did it in honor of man and woman, in honor of beast, in honor of God. They did it because they'd been released, because they were home free, alive, and private, because they couldn't wait any longer, couldn't wait for the appointed hour, for the right time or temperature, couldn't wait for the future, for Messiahs, for peace on earth and justice for all. They did it because of the Bomb, because of pollution, because of the Four Horsemen of the Apocalypse, because extinction might be just a blink away. They did it because it was Friday night. It was Friday night and somewhere delirious music was playing—flutter-tongued flutes, muted trumpets meowing like cats in heat, feverish plucking and twanging, tom-toms, congas, and gongs all pounding the same pulsebeat.

I stripped your bikini bottom down the skinny rails of your legs, and you tugged my swimsuit past my tan. Swimsuits at our ankles, we kicked like swimmers to free our legs, almost expecting a tide to wash over us the way the tide rushes in on Burt Lancaster and Deborah Kerr in *From Here to Eternity*—a love scene so famous that although neither of us had seen the movie, our bodies assumed the exact position of movie stars on the sand and you whispered to me softly, "I'm afraid of getting pregnant," and I whispered back, "Don't worry, I have protection," then, still kissing you, felt for my discarded cutoffs and the wallet in which for the last several months I had carried a Trojan as if it was a talisman. Still kissing, I tore its flattened, dried-out wrapper, and it sprang through my fingers like a spring from a clock and dropped to the sand between our legs. My hands were shaking. In a panic, I groped for it, found it, tried to dust it off, tried as Burt Lancaster never had to, to slip it on without breaking the mood, felt the grains of sand inside it, a throb of lightning, and the Great Lake behind us became, for all practical purposes, the Pacific, and your skin tasted of salt and to the insistent question that my hips were asking your body answered yes, your thighs opened like wings from my waist as we surfaced panting from a kiss that left you pleading *Oh, Christ yes*, a *yes* gasped sharply as a cry of pain so that for a moment I thought that we *were* already doing it and that somehow I had missed the instant when I entered you, entered you in the bloodless way in which a young man discards his own virginity, entered you as if passing through a gateway into the rest of my life, into a life as I wanted it to be lived *yes* but Oh then I realized that we were still floundering unconnected in the slick between us and there was sand in the Trojan as we slammed together still feeling for that perfect fit, still in the *Here* groping for an *Eternity* that was only a fine adjustment away, just a millimeter to the left or a fraction of an inch farther south though with all the adjusting the sandy Trojan was slipping off and then it was gone but *yes* you kept repeating although your head was shaking *no-not-quite-almost* and our hearts were going like mad and you said, *Yes. Yes wait...Stop!*

"What?" I asked, still futilely thrusting as if I hadn't quite heard you.

"Oh. God!" You gasped, pushing yourself up. "What's coming?"

"Gin, what's the matter?" I asked, confused, and then the beam of a spotlight swept over us and I glanced into its blinding eye.

All around us lights were coming, speeding across the sand. Blinking blindness away, I rolled from your body to my knees, feeling utterly defenseless in the way that only nakedness can leave one feeling. Headlights bounded toward us, spotlights crisscrossing, blue dome lights revolving as squad cars converged. I could see other lovers, caught in the beams, fleeing bare-assed through the litter of garbage that daytime hordes had left behind and that night had deceptively concealed. You were crying, clutching the Navajo blanket to your breasts with one hand and clawing for your bikini with the other, and I was trying to calm your terror with reassuring phrases such as "Holy shit! I don't fucking believe this!"

Swerving and fishtailing in the sand, police calls pouring from their radios, the squad cars were on us, and then they were by us while we struggled to pull on our clothes.

They braked at the water's edge, and cops slammed out, brandishing huge flashlights, their beams deflecting over the dark water. Beyond the darting of those beams, the far-off throbs of lightning seemed faint by comparison.

"Over there, goddamn it!" one of them hollered, and two cops sloshed out into the shallow water without even pausing to kick off their shoes, huffing aloud for breath, their leather cartridge belts creaking against their bellies.

"Grab the sonofabitch! It ain't gonna bite!" one of them yelled, then they came sloshing back to shore with a body slung between them.

It was a woman—young, naked, her body limp and bluish beneath the play of flashlight beams. They set her on the sand just past the ring of drying, washed-up alewives. Her face was almost totally concealed by her hair. Her hair was brown and tangled in a way that even wind or sleep can't tangle hair, tangled as if it had absorbed the ripples of water—thick strands, slimy looking like dead seaweed.

"She's been in there awhile, that's for sure," a cop with a beer belly said to a younger, crew-cut cop, who had knelt beside the body and removed his hat as if he might be considering the kiss of life.

The crew-cut officer brushed the hair away from her face, and the flashlight beams settled there. Her eyes were closed. A bruise or a birthmark stained the side of one eye. Her features appeared swollen, her lower lip protruding as if she was pouting.

An ambulance siren echoed across the sand, its revolving red light rapidly approaching.

"Might as well take their sweet-ass time," the beer-bellied cop said.

We had joined the circle of police surrounding the drowned woman almost without realizing that we had. You were back in your bikini, robed in the Navajo blanket, and I had slipped on my cutoffs, my underwear dangling out of a back pocket.

Their flashlight beams explored her body, causing its whiteness to gleam. Her breasts were floppy; her nipples looked shriveled. Her belly appeared inflated by gallons of water. For a moment, a beam focused on her mound of pubic hair, which was overlapped by the swell of her belly, and then moved almost shyly away down her legs, and the cops all glanced at us—at you, especially—above their lights, and you hugged your blanket closer as if they might confiscate it as evidence or to use as a shroud.

When the ambulance pulled up, one of the black attendants immediately put a stethoscope to the drowned woman's swollen belly and announced, "Drowned the baby, too."

Without saying anything, we turned from the group, as unconsciously as we'd joined them, and walked off across the sand, stopping only long enough at the spot where we had lain together like lovers, in order to stuff the rest of our gear into a beach bag, to gather our shoes, and for me to find my wallet and kick sand over the forlorn, deflated Trojan that you pretended not to notice. I was grateful for that.

Behind us, the police were snapping photos, flashbulbs throbbing like lightning flashes, and the lightning itself, still distant but moving in closer, rumbling audibly now, driving a lake wind before it so that gusts of sand tingled against the metal sides of the ambulance.

Squinting, we walked toward the lighted windows of the Gold Coast, while the shadows of gapers attracted by the whirling emergency lights hurried past us toward the shore.

"What happened? What's going on?" they asked without waiting for an answer, and we didn't offer one, just continued walking silently in the dark.

It was only later that we talked about it, and once we began talking about the drowned woman it seemed we couldn't stop.

"She was pregnant," you said. "I mean, I don't want to sound morbid, but I can't help thinking how the whole time we were, we almost—you know—there was this poor, dead woman and her unborn child washing in and out behind us."

"It's not like we could have done anything for her even if we had known she was there."

"But what if we *had* found her? What if after we had—you know," you said, your eyes glancing away from mine and your voice tailing into a whisper, "what if after we did it, we went for a night swim and found her in the water?"

"But, Gin, we didn't," I tried to reason, though it was no more a matter of reason than anything else between us had ever been.

It began to seem as if each time we went somewhere to make out—on the back porch of your half-deaf, whiskery Italian grandmother, who sat in the front of the apartment cackling at *I Love Lucy* reruns; or in your girlfriend Tina's basement rec room when her parents were away on bowling league nights and Tina was upstairs with her current crush, Brad; or way off in the burbs, at the Giant Twin Drive-In during the weekend they called Elvis Fest—the drowned woman was with us.

We would kiss, your mouth would open, and when your tongue flicked repeatedly after mine, I would unbutton the first button of your blouse, revealing the beauty spot at the base of your throat, which matched a smaller spot I loved above a corner of your lips, and then the second button, which opened on a delicate gold cross—which I had always tried to regard as merely a fashion statement—dangling above the cleft of your breasts. The third button exposed the lacy swell of your bra, and I would slide my hand over the patterned mesh, feeling for the firmness of your nipple rising to my fingertip, but you would pull slightly away, and behind your rapid breath your kiss would grow distant, and I would kiss harder, trying to lure you back from wherever you had gone, and finally, holding you as if only consoling a friend, I'd ask, "What are you thinking?" although of course I knew.

"I don't want to think about her but I can't help it. I mean, it seems like some kind of weird omen or something, you know?"

"No, I don't know," I said. "It was just a coincidence."

"Maybe if she'd been farther away down the beach, but she was so close to us. A good wave could have washed her up right beside us."

"Great, then we could have had a ménage à trois."

"Gross! I don't believe you just said that! Just because you said it in French doesn't make it less disgusting."

"You're driving me to it. Come on, Gin, I'm sorry," I said. "I was just making a dumb joke to get a little different perspective on things."

"What's so goddamn funny about a woman who drowned herself and her baby?"

"We don't even know for sure she did."

"Yeah, right, it was just an accident. Like she just happened to be going for a walk pregnant and naked, and she fell in."

"She could have been on a sailboat or something. Accidents happen; so do murders."

"Oh, like murder makes it less horrible? Don't think that hasn't occurred to me. Maybe the bastard who knocked her up killed her, huh?"

"How should I know? You're the one who says you don't want to talk about it and then gets obsessed with all kinds of theories and scenarios. Why are we arguing about a woman we don't even know, who doesn't have the slightest thing to do with us?"

"I *do* know about her," you said. "I dream about her."

"You dream about her?" I repeated, surprised. "Dreams you remember?"

"Sometimes they wake me up. In one I'm at my *nonna*'s cottage in Michigan, swimming for a raft that keeps drifting farther away, until I'm too tired to turn back. Then I notice there's a naked person sunning on the raft and start yelling, 'Help!' and she looks up and offers me a hand, but I'm too afraid to take it even though I'm drowning because it's her."

"God! Gin, that's creepy."

"I dreamed you and I are at the beach and you bring us a couple hot dogs but forget the mustard, so you have to go all the way back to the stand for it."

"Hot dogs, no mustard—a little too Freudian, isn't it?"

"Honest to God, I dreamed it. You go back for mustard and I'm wondering why you're gone so long, then a woman screams that a kid has drowned and everyone stampedes for the water. I'm swept in by the mob and forced under, and I think, This is it, I'm going to drown, but I'm able to hold my breath longer than could ever be possible. It feels like a flying dream—flying under water—and then I see this baby down there flying, too, and realize it's the kid everyone thinks has drowned, but he's no more drowned than I am. He looks like Cupid or one of those baby angels that cluster around the face of God."

"Pretty weird. What do you think all the symbols mean?—hot dogs, water, drowning..."

"It means the baby who drowned inside her that night was a love child—a boy—and his soul was released there to wander through the water."

"You don't really believe that?"

We argued about the interpretation of dreams, about whether dreams are symbolic or psychic, prophetic or just plain nonsense, until you said, "Look, Dr. Freud, you can believe what you want about your dreams, but keep your nose out of mine, okay?"

We argued about the drowned woman, about whether her death was a suicide or a murder, about whether her appearance that night was an omen or a coincidence which, you argued, is what an omen is anyway: a coincidence that means something. By the end of summer, even if we were no longer arguing about the woman, we had acquired the habit of arguing about everything else. What was better: dogs or cats, rock or jazz, Cubs or Sox, tacos or egg rolls, right or left, night or day?—we could argue about anything.

It no longer required arguing or necking to summon the drowned woman; everywhere we went she surfaced by her own volition: at Rocky's Italian Beef, at Lindo Mexico, at the House of Dong, our favorite Chinese restaurant, a place we still frequented because when we'd first started seeing each other they had let us sit and talk until late over tiny cups of jasmine tea and broken fortune cookies. We would always kid about going there. "Are you in the mood for Dong tonight?" I'd whisper conspiratorially. It was a dopey joke, meant for you to roll your eyes at its repeated dopiness. Back then, in winter, if one of us ordered the garlic shrimp we would both be sure to eat them so that later our mouths tasted the same when we kissed.

Even when she wasn't mentioned, she was there with her drowned body—so dumpy next to yours—and her sad breasts, with their wrinkled nipples and sour milk—so saggy beside yours, which were still budding—with her swollen belly and her pubic bush colorless in the glare of electric light, with her tangled, slimy hair and her pouting, placid face—so lifeless beside yours—and her skin a pallid white, lightning-flash white, flash-bulb white, a whiteness that couldn't be duplicated in daylight—how I'd come to hate that pallor, so cold beside the flush of your skin.

There wasn't a particular night when we finally broke up, just as there wasn't a particular night when we began going together, but it was a night in fall when I guessed that it was over. We were parked in the Rambler at the dead end of the street of factories that had been our lovers' lane, listening to a drizzle of rain and dry leaves sprinkle the hood. As always, rain revitalized the smells of smoked fish and kielbasa in the upholstery. The radio was on too low to hear, the windshield wipers swished at intervals as if we were driving, and the windows were steamed as if we'd been making out. But we'd been arguing, as usual, this time about a woman poet who had committed suicide, whose work you were reading. We were sitting, no longer talking or touching, and I remember thinking that I didn't want to argue with you anymore. I didn't want to sit like this in hurt silence; I wanted to talk excitedly all night as we once had. I wanted to find some way that wasn't corny sounding to tell you how much fun I'd had in your company, how much knowing you had meant to me, and how I had suddenly realized that I'd been so intent on becoming lovers that I'd overlooked how close we'd been as friends. I wanted you to like me again.

"It's sad," I started to say, meaning that I was sorry we had reached the point of silence, but before I could continue you challenged the statement.

"What makes you so sure it's sad?"

"What do you mean, what makes me so sure?" I asked, confused by your question.

You looked at me as if what was sad was that I would never understand. "For all either one of us knows," you said, "death could have been her triumph!"

Maybe when it really ended was the night I felt we had just reached the beginning, that one time on the beach in the summer when our bodies rammed so desperately together that for a moment I thought we did it, and maybe in our hearts we did, although for me, then, doing it in one's heart didn't quite count. If it did, I supposed we'd all be Casanovas.

We rode home together on the El train that night, and I felt sick and defeated in a way I was embarrassed to mention. Our mute reflections emerged like negative exposures on the dark, greasy window of the train. Lightning branched over the city, and when the train entered the subway tunnel, the lights inside flickered as if the power was disrupted, though the train continued rocketing beneath the Loop.

When the train emerged again we were on the South Side of the city and it was pouring, a deluge as if the sky had opened to drown the innocent and guilty alike. We hurried from the El station to your house, holding the Navajo blanket over our heads until, soaked, it collapsed. In the dripping doorway of your apartment building, we said good night. You were shivering. Your bikini top showed through the thin blouse plastered to your skin. I swept the wet hair away from your face and kissed you lightly on the lips, then you turned and went inside. I stepped into the rain, and you came back out, calling after me.

"What?" I asked, feeling a surge of gladness to be summoned back into the doorway with you.

"Want an umbrella?"

I didn't. The downpour was letting up. It felt better to walk back to the station feeling the rain rinse the sand out of my hair, off my legs, until the only places where I could still feel its grit were in the crotch of my cutoffs and each squish of my shoes. A block down the street, I passed a pair of jockey shorts lying in a puddle and realized they were mine, dropped from my back pocket as we ran to your house. I left them behind, wondering if you'd see them and recognize them the next day.

By the time I had climbed the stairs back to the El platform, the rain had stopped. Your scent still hadn't washed from my fingers. The station—the entire city it seemed—dripped and steamed. The summer sound of crickets and nighthawks echoed from the drenched neighborhood. Alone, I could admit how sick I felt. For you, it was a night that would haunt your dreams. For me, it was another night when I waited, swollen and aching, for what I had secretly nicknamed the Blue Ball Express.

Literally lovesick, groaning inwardly with each lurch of the train and worried that I was damaged for good, I peered out at the passing yellow-lit stations, where lonely men stood posted before giant advertisements, pictures of glamorous models defaced by graffiti—the same old scrawled insults and pleas: fuck you, eat me. At this late hour the world seemed given over to men without women, men waiting in abject patience for something indeterminate, the way I waited for our next times. I avoided their eyes so that they wouldn't see the pity in mine, pity for them because I'd just been with you, your scent was still on my hands, and there seemed to be so much future ahead.

For me it was another night like that, and by the time I reached my stop I knew I would be feeling better, recovered enough to walk the dark street home making up poems of longing that I never wrote down. I was the D. H. Lawrence of not doing it, the voice of all the would-be lovers who ached and squirmed. From our contortions in doorways, on stairwells, and in the bucket seats of cars we could have composed a Kama Sutra of interrupted bliss. It must have been that night when I recalled all the other times of walking home after seeing you, so that it seemed as if I was falling into step behind a parade of my former selves—myself walking home on the night we first kissed, myself on the night when I unbuttoned your blouse and kissed your breasts, myself on the night when I lifted your skirt above your thighs and dropped to my knees— each succeeding self another step closer to that irrevocable moment for which our lives seemed poised.

But we didn't, not in the moonlight, or by the phosphorescent lanterns of lightning bugs in your back yard, not beneath the constellations we couldn't see, let alone decipher, or in the dark glow that replaced the real darkness of night, a darkness already stolen from us, not with the skyline rising behind us while a city gradually decayed, not in the heat of summer while a Cold War raged, despite the freedom of youth and the license of first love—because of fate, karma, luck, what does it matter?—we made not doing it a wonder, and yet we didn't, we didn't, we never did.

◈

Big Me

DAN CHAON

It all started when I was twelve years old. Before that, everything was a peaceful blur of childhood, growing up in the small town of Beck, Nebraska. A "town," we called it. Really, the population was just under two hundred, and it was one of those dots along Highway 30 that people didn't usually even slow down for, though strangers sometimes stopped at the little gas station near the grain elevator or ate at the café. My mother and father owned a bar called The Crossroads, at the edge of town. We lived in a little house behind it, and behind our house was the junkyard, and beyond that were wheat fields, which ran all the way to a line of bluffs and barren hills, full of yucca and rattlesnakes.

Back then I spent a lot of time in my mind, building a city up toward those hills. This imaginary place was also called Beck, but it was a metropolis of a million people. The wise though cowardly mayor lived in a mansion in the hills above the interstate, as did the bullish, Teddy Roosevelt-like police commissioner, Winthrop Golding. There were other members of the rich and powerful who lived in enormous old Victorian houses along the bluffs, and many of them harbored dreadful secrets or were involved in one way or another with the powerful Beck underworld.

One wealthy, respectable citizen, Mr. Karaffa, turned out to be a lycan-thrope who preyed on the lovely, virginal junior high-school girls, muti-lating them beyond recognition, until I shot him with a silver bullet. I was the city Detective, though I was often underappreciated and, because of my radical notions, in danger of being fired by the cowardly mayor. The police commissioner always defended me, even when he was exasperated by my unorthodox methods. He respected my integrity.

I don't know how many of my childhood years took place in this imagi-nary city. By the age of eight I had become the Detective, and shortly thereafter I began drawing maps of the metropolis. By the time we left Beck, I had a folder six inches thick, full of street guides and architec-ture and subway schedules. In the real town, I was known as the strange kid who wandered around talking to himself. Old people would find me in their backyard gardens and come out and yell at me. Chil-dren would see me playing on their swing sets, and when they came out to challenge me, I would run away. I trapped people's cats and bound their arms and legs, harshly forcing confessions from them. Since no one locked their doors, I went into people's houses and stole things, which I pretended were clues to the mystery I was trying to solve.

Everyone real also played a secret role in my city. My parents, for example, were the landlord and his wife, who lived downstairs from my modest one-room apartment. They were well-meaning but unimagina-tive people, and I was polite to them. There were a number of comic episodes in which the nosy landlady had to be tricked and defeated. My brother Mark was the district attorney, my nemesis. My younger sister Kathy was my secretary, Miss Kathy, whom I sometimes loved. I would have married her if I weren't such a lone wolf.

My family thought of me as a certain person, a role I knew well enough to perform from time to time. Now that they are far away, it sometimes hurts to think that we knew so little of one another. Some-times I think if no one knows you, then you are no one.

In the spring of my twelfth year, a man moved into a house at the end of my block. The house had belonged to an old woman who had died and left her home fully furnished but tenantless for years, until her heir had finally gotten around to having the estate liquidated, the old furni-ture sold, the place cleared out and put up for sale. This was the house I had taken cats to, the hideout where I had extracted their yowling confessions. Then finally the house was emptied, and the man took up residence.

I first saw the man in what must have been late May. The lilac bush in his front yard was in full bloom, thick with spade-shaped leaves and clusters of perfumed flowers. The man was mowing the lawn as I passed, and I stopped to stare.

It immediately struck me that there was something familiar about him—the wavy dark hair and gloomy eyes, the round face and dimpled chin. At first I thought he looked like someone I'd seen on TV. And then I realized: he looked like me! Or rather, he looked like an older version of me—me grown up. As he got closer with his push lawnmower, I was aware that our eyes were the same odd, pale shade of gray, that we had the same map of freckles across the bridge of our noses, the same stubby fingers. He lifted his hand solemnly as he reached the edge of his lawn, and I lifted my opposite hand, so that for a moment we were mirror images of one another. I felt terribly worked up and hurried home.

That night, considering the encounter, I wondered whether the man actually *was* me. I thought about all that I'd heard about time travel, and considered the possibility that my older self had come back for some unknown purpose—perhaps to save me from some mistake I was about to make or to warn me. Maybe he was fleeing some future disaster and hoped to change the course of things.

I suppose this tells you a lot about what I was like as a boy, but these were among the first ideas I considered. I believed wholeheartedly in the notion that time travel would soon be a reality, just as I believed in UFOs and ESP and Bigfoot. I used to worry, in all seriousness, whether humanity would last as long as the dinosaurs had lasted. What if we were just a brief, passing phase on the planet? I felt strongly that we needed to explore other solar systems and establish colonies. The survival of the human species was very important to me.

Perhaps it was because of this that I began to keep a journal. I had recently read *The Diary of Anne Frank* and had been deeply moved by the idea that a piece of you, words on a page, could live on after you were dead. I imagined that, after a nuclear holocaust, an extraterrestrial boy might find my journal, floating among some bits of meteorite and pieces of buildings and furniture that had once been Earth. The extraterrestrial boy would translate my diary, and it would become a bestseller on his planet. Eventually, the aliens would be so stirred by my story that they would call off the intergalactic war they were waging and make a truce.

In these journals I would frequently write messages to myself, a person whom I addressed as "Big Me," or "The Future Me." Rereading these entries as the addressee, I try not to be insulted, since my former self admonishes me frequently. "I hope you are not a failure," he says. "I hope you are happy," he says. It gives me pause.

I'm trying to remember what was going on in the world when I was twelve. My brother Mark says it was the worst year of his life. He remembers it as a year of terrible fights between my parents. "They were drunk every night, up till three and four in the morning, screaming at each other. Do you remember the night Mom drove the car into the tree?"

I don't. In my mind, they seemed happy together, in the bantering, ironic manner of sitcom couples, and their arguments seemed full of comedy, as if a laugh track might ring out after their best put-down lines. I don't recall them drunk so much as expansive, and the bar seemed a cheerful, popular place, always full, though they would go bankrupt not long after I turned thirteen.

Mark says that was the year he tried to commit suicide, and I don't recall that either, though I do remember that he was in the hospital for a few days. Mostly, I think of him reclining on the couch, looking regal and dissipated, reading books like *I'm Okay, You're Okay*, and filling out questionnaires that told him whether or not he was normal.

The truth is, I mostly recall the Detective. He had taken an interest in the mysterious stranger who had moved in down the block. The Stranger, it turned out, would be teaching seventh grade science; he would be replacing the renowned girl's basketball coach and science teacher, Mr. Karaffa, who'd had a heart attack and died right after a big game. The Stranger was named Louis Mickleson, and he'd moved to Beck from a big city: Chicago or maybe Omaha. "He seems like a lonely type of guy," my mother commented once.

"A weirdo, you mean?" said my father.

I knew how to get into Mickleson's house. It had been my hideout, and there were a number of secret entrances: loose windows, the cellar door, the back door lock that could be dislodged with the thin, laminated edge of my library card.

He was not a very orderly person, Mr. Mickleson, or perhaps he was simply uncertain. The house was full of boxes, packed and unpacked, and the furniture was placed randomly about the house, as if he'd simply left things where the moving men had set them down. In various corners of the house were projects he'd begun and then abandoned— tilting towers of stacked books next to an empty bookcase, silverware organized in rows along the kitchen counter, a pile of winter coats left on the floor near a closet. The boxes seemed to be carefully classified. Near his bed, for example, were socks, underwear, white T-shirts— each in a separate box, neatly folded near a drawerless dresser. The drawers themselves lay on the floor and contained reams of magazines: *Popular Science* in one, *Azimov's Science Fiction* in another, and *Playboy* in yet another, though the dirty pictures had all been fastidiously scissored out.

You can imagine what a cave of wonders this was for me, piled high with riches and clues; each box almost trembled with mystery. There was a collection of costume jewelry, old coins, and keys. Here were his old lesson plans and grade books, the names of former students penciled in alongside their attendance records and grades and small comments ("messy," "lazy," "shows potential!") racked up in columns. Here were photos and letters: a gold mine!

One afternoon I was kneeling before his box of letters when I heard the front door open. Naturally, I was very still. I heard the front door close, and then Mr. Mickleson muttering to himself. I tensed as he said, "Okay, well, never mind," and read aloud from a bit of junk mail he'd gotten, using a nasal, theatrical voice: "'A special gift for you enclosed!' How lovely!" I crouched there over his cardboard box, looking at a boyhood photo of him and what must have been his sister, circa 1952, sitting in the lap of an artificially bearded Santa. I heard him chuckling as he opened the freezer and took something out. Then he turned on the TV in the living room, and other voices leapt out at me.

It never felt like danger. I was convinced of my own powers of stealth and invisibility. He would not see me because that was not part of the story I was telling myself: I was the Detective! I sensed a cool, hollow spot in my stomach, and I could glide easily behind him as he sat in his La-Z-Boy recliner, staring at the blue glow of the television, watching the news. He didn't shudder as the dark shape of me passed behind him. He couldn't see me unless I chose to be seen.

I had my first blackout that day I left Mickleson's house, not long after I'd sneaked behind him and crept out the back door. I don't know whether *blackout* is the best term, with its redolence of alcoholic excess and catatonic states, but I'm not sure what else to call it. I stepped into the backyard and remember walking cautiously along a line of weedy flowerbeds toward the gate that led to the alley. I had taken the Santa photo, and I stared at it. Yes, it could have been a photograph of me when I was five, and I shuddered at the eerie similarity. An obese calico cat hurried down the alley in front of me, disappearing into a hedge that bordered someone else's backyard.

A few seconds later, I found myself at the kitchen table, eating dinner with my family. I was in the process of bringing an ear of buttered corn to my mouth, and it felt something like waking up, only faster, as if I'd been transported in a blink from one place to another. My family had not seemed to notice that I was gone. They were all eating silently, grimly, as if everything were normal. My father was cutting his meat, his jaw firmly locked, and my mother's eyes were on her plate, as if she were watching a small round television. No one seemed surprised by my sudden appearance.

It was kind of alarming. At first, it just seemed odd—like, "Oh, how did I get here?" But then, the more I thought about it, the more my skin crawled. I looked up at the clock on the kitchen wall, grinning black cat with a clock face for a belly and a pendulum tail and eyes that shifted from left to right with each tick. I had somehow lost a considerable amount of time—at least half an hour, maybe forty-five minutes. The last thing I clearly recalled was staring at that photo—Mr. Mickleson, or myself, sitting on Santa's knee. And then, somehow, I had left my body. Where had I gone? I sat there, thinking, but there wasn't even a blur of memory. There was only a blank spot.

Once, I tried to explain it to my wife.

"A *blank* spot?" she said, and her voice grew stiff and concerned, as if I'd found a lump beneath my skin. "Do you mean a blackout? You have blackouts?"

"No, no," I said and tried to smile reassuringly. "Not exactly."

"What do you mean?" she said. "Listen, Andy," she said. "If I told you that I had periods when I...lost time...wouldn't you be concerned? Wouldn't you want me to see a doctor?"

"You're blowing this all out of proportion," I said. "It's nothing like that." And I wanted to tell her about the things that the Detective had read about in the weeks and months following the first incident—about trances and transcendental states, about astral projection and out-of-body travel. But I didn't.

"There's nothing wrong with me," I said and stretched my arms luxuriously. "I feel great," I said. "It's more like daydreaming. Only—a little different."

But she still looked concerned. "You don't have to hide anything from me," she said. "I just care about you, that's all."

"I know," I said, and I smiled as her eyes scoped my face. "It's nothing," I said, "just one of those little quirks!" And that is what I truly believe. Though my loved ones sometimes tease me about my distractedness, my forgetfulness, they do so affectionately. There haven't been any major incidents, and the only times that really worry me are when I am alone, when I am driving down one street and wake up on another. And even then, I am sure that nothing terrible has happened. I sometimes rub my hands against the steering wheel. I am always intact. It's just one of those things! There are no screams or sirens in the distance.

But back then, that first time, I was frightened. I remember asking my mother how a person would know if he had a brain tumor.

"You don't have a brain tumor," she said irritably. "It's time for bed."

A little later, perhaps feeling guilty, she came up to my room with aspirin and water.

"Do you have a headache, honey?" she said.

I shook my head as she turned off my bedside lamp. "Too much reading of comic books," she said and smiled at me exaggeratedly, as she sometimes did, pretending I was still a baby. "It would make anybody's head feel funny, Little Man!" She touched my forehead with the cold, dry pads of her fingertips, looking down into my eyes, heavily. She looked sad and for a moment lost her balance as she reached down to run a palm across my cheek. "Nothing is wrong," she whispered. "It will all seem better in the morning."

That night, I sat up writing in my diary, writing to Big Me. "I hope you are alive," I wrote. "I hope that I don't die before you are able to read this."

That particular diary entry always makes me feel philosophical. I'm not entirely sure of the person he is writing to, the future person he was imagining. I don't know whether that person is alive or not. There are so many people we could become, and we leave such a trail of bodies through our teens and twenties that it's hard to tell which one is us. How many versions do we abandon over the years? How many end up nearly forgotten, mumbling and gasping for air in some tenement room of our consciousness, like elderly relatives suffering some fatal lung disease?

Like the Detective. As I wander through my big suburban house at night, I can hear his wheezing breath in the background, still muttering about secrets that can't be named. Still hanging in there.

My wife is curled up on the sofa, sipping hot chocolate, reading, and when she looks up she smiles shyly. "What are you staring at?" she says. She is used to this sort of thing by now—finds it endearing, I think. She is a pleasant, practical woman, and I doubt that she would find much of interest in the many former selves that tap against my head, like moths.

She opens her robe. "See anything you like?" she says, and I smile back at her.

"Just peeking," I say brightly. My younger self wouldn't recognize me, I'm sure of that.

Which makes me wonder: what did I see in Mickleson, beyond the striking resemblance? I can't quite remember my train of thought, though it's clear from the diary that I latched wholeheartedly onto the idea. Some of it is obviously playacting, making drama for myself, but some of it isn't. Something about Mickleson struck a chord.

Maybe it was simply this—July 13: "If Mickleson is your future, then you took a wrong turn somewhere. Something is sinister about him! He could be a criminal on the lam! He is crazy. You have to change your life now! Don't ever think bad thoughts about Mom, Dad, or even Mark. Do a good deed every day."

I had been going to his house fairly frequently by that time. I had a notebook, into which I had pasted the Santa photo, and a sample of his handwriting, and a bit of hair from a comb. I tried to write down everything that seemed potentially significant: clues, evidence, but evidence of what, I don't know. There was the crowd of beer cans on his kitchen counter, sometimes arranged in geometric patterns. There were the boxes, unpacked then packed again. There were letters: "I am tired, un-believably tired, of going around in circles with you," a woman who signed herself "Sandi" had written. "As far as I can see, there is no point in going on. Why can't you just make a decision and stick to it?" I had copied this down in my detective's notebook.

In his living room, there was a little plaque hanging on the wall. It was a rectangular piece of dark wood; a piece of parchment paper, burned around the edges, had been lacquered to it. On the parchment paper, in careful calligraphy, was written:

I wear
the chain
I forged
in life.

This seemed like a possible secret message. I thought maybe he'd escaped from jail.

From a distance, behind a hedge, I watched Mickleson's house. He wouldn't usually appear before ten in the morning. He would pop out of his front door in his bathrobe, glancing quickly around as if he sensed someone watching, and then he would snatch up the newspaper on his doorstep. At times, he seemed aware of my eyes.

I knew I had to be cautious. Mickleson must not guess that he was being investigated, and I tried to take precautions. I stopped wearing my favorite detective hat, to avoid calling attention to myself. When I went through his garbage, I did it in the early morning, while I was fairly certain he was still asleep. Even so, one July morning I was forced to crawl under a thick hedge when Mickleson's back door unexpectedly opened at eight in the morning, and he shuffled out the alley to dump a bag into his trash can. Luckily I was wearing brown and green, so I blended in with the shrubbery. I lay there, prone against the dirt, star-ing at his bare feet and hairy ankles. He was wearing nothing but boxer shorts, so I could see that his clothes had been concealing a large quan-tity of dark, vaguely sickening body hair; there was even some on his back! I had recently read a Classics Illustrated comic book version of *Dr. Jekyll and Mr. Hyde*, and I recalled the description of Hyde as "some-thing troglodytic," which was a word I had looked up in the dictionary and now applied as Mickleson dumped his bag into the trash can. I had just begun to grow a few hairs on my own body and was chilled to think I might end up like this. I heard the clank of beer cans, then he walked away. I lay still, feeling uneasy.

At home, after dinner, I would sit in my bedroom, reading through my notes, puzzling. I would flip through my lists, trying to find clues I could link together. I'd sift through the cigar box full of things I'd taken from his home: photographs, keys, a Swiss army knife, a check stub with his signature, which I'd compared against my own. But nothing seemed to fit. All I knew was that he was mysterious. He had some secret.

Late one night that summer, I thought I heard my parents talking about me. I was reading, and their conversation had been mere background, rising and falling, until I heard my name. "Andrew...how he's turning out...not fair to anybody!" Then, loudly: "What will happen to him?"

I sat up straight, my heart beating heavily, because it seemed that something must have happened, that they must have discovered something. I felt certain I was about to be exposed: my spying, my breaking and entering, my stealing. I was quiet, frightened, and then after a while, I got up and crept downstairs. My mother and father were at the kitchen table, speaking softly, staring at the full ashtray that sat between them.

My mother looked up when I came in and clenched her teeth. "Oh, for God's sake," she said. "Andy, it's two-thirty in the morning! What are you doing up?"

I stood there in the doorway, uncertainly. I wished that I were a little kid again, that I could tell her I was scared. But I just hovered there. "I couldn't sleep," I said.

My mother frowned. "Well, try harder, God damn it," she said.

I stood there a moment longer. "Mom?" I said.

"Go to bed!" She glared.

"I thought I heard you guys saying something about that man that just moved in down the block. He didn't say anything about me, did he?"

"Listen to me, Andrew," she said. Her look darkened. "I don't want you up there listening to our conversations. This is grown-up talk, and I don't want you up there snooping."

"He's going to be the new science teacher," I said.

"I know," she said, but my father raised his eyebrows.

"Who's this?" my father said, raising his glass to his lips. "That weirdo is supposed to be a teacher? That's a laugh."

"Oh, don't start!" my mother said. "At least he's a customer! You better God damn not pick a fight with him. You've driven enough people away as it is, the way you are. It's no wonder we don't have any friends!" Then she turned on me. "I thought I told you to go to bed. Don't just stand there gaping when I tell you to do something! My God, I can't get a minute's peace!"

Back in my bedroom, I tried to forget what my parents had said—it didn't matter, I thought, as long as they didn't know anything about me. I was safe! And I sat there, relieved, slowly forgetting the fact that I was really just a strange twelve-year-old boy, a kid with no real playmates, an outsider even in his own family. I didn't like being that person, and

I sat by the window, awake, listening to my parents' slow, arguing voices downstairs, smelling the smoke that hung in a thick, rippling cloud over their heads. Outside, the lights of Beck melted into the dark field; the hills were heavy, huddled shapes against the sky. I closed my eyes, wishing hard, trying to will my imaginary city into life, envisioning roads and streetlights suddenly sprouting up through the prairie grass. And tall buildings. And freeways. And people.

It has been almost twenty years since I last saw Beck. We left the town the summer before eighth grade, after my parents had gone bankrupt, and in the succeeding years we moved through a blur of ugly states—Wyoming, Montana; Panic, Despair—while my parents' marriage dissolved.

Now we are all scattered. My sister, Kathy, suffered brain damage in a car accident when she was nineteen, out driving with her friends. She now lives in a group home in Denver, where she and the others spend their days making Native American jewelry, which is sold at truck stops. My brother, Mark, is a physical therapist who lives on a houseboat in Marina Del Ray, California. He spends his free time reading books about childhood trauma, and every time I talk to him, he has a series of complaints about our old misery: at the very least, surely I remember the night that my father was going to kill us all with his gun, how he and Kathy and I ran into the junkyard and hid in an old refrigerator box? I think he's exaggerating, but Mark is always threatening to have me hypnotized, so I'll remember.

We have all lost touch with my mother. The last anyone heard, she was living in Puerto Vallarta, married to a man who apparently has something to do with real estate development. The last time I talked to her, she didn't sound like herself: a foreign-accented lilt had crept into her voice. She laughed harshly, then began to cough, when I mentioned old times.

For a time before he died, I was closest to my father. He was working as a bartender in a small town in Idaho, and he used to call me when I was in law school. Like me, he remembered Beck fondly: the happiest time of his life, he said. "If only we could have held on a little bit longer," he told me, "it would have been a different story. A different story entirely."

Then he'd sigh. "Well, anyway," he'd say. "How are things going with Katrina?"

"Fine," I'd say. "Just the usual. She's been a little distant lately. She's very busy with her classes. I think med school takes a lot out of her."

I remember shifting silently, because the truth was, I didn't really have a girlfriend named Katrina. I didn't have a girlfriend, period. I made Katrina up one evening, on the spur of the moment, to keep my dad from worrying so much. It helped him to think that I had a woman looking after me, that I was heading into a normal life: marriage, children, a house, etcetera. Now that I have such things, I feel a bit guilty. He died not knowing the truth. He died waiting to meet her, enmeshed in my made-up drama—in the last six months of his life, Katrina and I came close to breaking up, got back together, discussed marriage, worried that we were not spending enough time together. The conversations that my father and I had about Katrina were some of the best we ever had.

I don't remember much about my father from that summer when I was twelve. We certainly weren't having conversations that I can recall, and I don't ever remember that he pursued me with a gun. He was just there; I would walk past him in the morning as he sat, sipping coffee, preparing to go to work. I'd go into the bar, and he would pour me a glass of Coke with bitters, "to put hair on my chest." I'd sit there on the barstool, stroking Suds, the bar's tomcat, in my lap, murmuring quietly to him as I imagined my detective story. My father had a bit part in my imagination, barely a speaking role.

But it was at the bar that I saw Mr. Mickleson again. I had been at his house that morning, working through a box of letters, and then I'd been out at the junkyard behind our house. In those unenlightened times, it was called The Dump. People drove out and pitched their garbage over the edge of a ravine, which had become encrusted with a layer of beer cans, broken toys, bedsprings, car parts, broken glass. It was a magical place, and I'd spent a few hours in the driver's seat of a rusted-out Studebaker, fiddling with the various dashboard knobs, pretending to drive it, to stalk suspects, to become involved in a thrilling high-speed chase. At last I had come to the bar to unwind, to drink my Coke and bitters and recreate the day in my imagination. Occasionally my father would speak to me, and I would be forced to disengage myself from the Detective, who was brooding over a glass of bourbon. He had become hardened and cynical, but he would not give up his fight for justice.

I was repeating these stirring lines in my mind when Mr. Mickleson came into the bar. I felt a little thrum when he entered. My grip tightened on Suds the cat, who struggled and sprang from my lap.

Having spent time in The Crossroads, I recognized drunkenness. I was immediately aware of Mickleson's flopping gait, the way he settled heavily against the lip of the bar. "Okay, okay," he muttered to himself, then chuckled. "No, just forget it, never mind," he said cheerfully. Then he sighed and tapped his hand against the bar. "Shot o' rum," he said. "Captain Morgan, if you have it. No ice." I watched as my father served him, then flicked my glance away when Mickleson looked warily in my direction. He leveled his gaze at me, his eyes heavy with some meaning I couldn't decipher. It was part friendly, that look, but part threatening, too, in a particularly intimate way—as if he recognized me.

"Oh, hello," Mr. Mickleson said. "If it isn't the staring boy! Hello, Staring Boy!" He grinned at me, and my father gave him a stern look. "I believe I know you," Mr. Mickleson said jauntily. "I've seen you around, haven't I?"

I just sat there, blushing. It occurred to me that perhaps, despite my precautions, Mr. Mickleson had seen me after all. "Staring Boy," he said, and I tried to think of when he might have caught me staring. How many times? I saw myself from a distance, watching his house but now also being watched, and the idea set up a panic in me that was difficult to quell. I was grateful that my father came over and called me *son*. "Son," he said, "why don't you go on outside and find something to do? You may as well enjoy some of that summer sunshine before school starts."

"All right," I said. I saw that Mickleson was still grinning at me expectantly, his eyes blank and unblinking, and I realized that he was doing an imitation of my expression—Staring Boy, meet Staring Man. I tried to step casually off the barstool, but instead I stumbled and nearly fell. "Oopsie-daisy!" Mr. Mickleson said, and my father gave him a hard look, a careful glare that checked Mr. Mickleson's grin. He shrugged.

"Ah, children, children," he said confidingly to my father, as I hurried quickly to the door. I heard my father start to speak sharply as I left, but I didn't have the nerve to stick around to hear what was said.

Instead, I crept along the outside of the bar; I staked out Mickleson's old Volkswagen and found it locked. There were no windows into the bar, so I pressed myself against the wall, trying to listen. I tried to think what I would write in my notebook: that look he'd given me, his grinning mimicry of my state. "I believe I know you," he'd said. What, exactly, did he know?

And then I had a terrible thought. Where was the notebook? I imagined, for a moment, that I had left it there, on the bar, next to my drink. I had the dreadful image of Mr. Mickleson's eyes falling on it, the theme book cover, which was decorated with stylized question marks, and on which I'd written: Andy O'Day Mystery Series #67: The Detective Meets the Dreadful Double! I saw him smiling at it, opening it, his eyes narrowing as he saw his photo pasted there on the first page.

But it wasn't in the bar. I was sure it wasn't, because I remembered not having it when I went in. I didn't have it with me, I knew, and I began to backtrack, step by step, from the Studebaker to lunchtime to my bedroom, and then I saw it, with the kind of perfect clarity my memory has always been capable of, despite everything.

I saw myself in Mickleson's living room, on my knees in front of a box of his letters. I had copied something in the notebook and put it down on the floor. It was right there, next to the box. I could see it as if through a window, and I stood there observing the image in my mind's eye, as my mother came around the corner, into the parking lot.

"Andy!" she said. "I've been calling for you! Where the hell have you been?"

She was in one of her moods. "I am so sick of this!" she said and gave me a hard shake as she grabbed my arm. "You God-damned lazy kids just think you can do as you please, all the God-damn day long! The house is a pig sty, and not a one of you will bend a finger to pick up your filthy clothes or even wash a dish." She gritted her teeth, her voice trembling, and slammed into the house, where Mark was scrubbing the floor and Kathy was standing at the sink, washing dishes. Mark glared up at me, his eyes red with crying and self-pity and hatred. I knew he was going to hit me as soon as she left. "Clean, you brats!" my mother cried. "I'm going to work, and when I get home I want this house to shine!" She was in the frilly blouse and makeup she wore when she tended bar, beautiful and flushed, her eyes hard. "I'm not going to live like this anymore. I'm not going to live this kind of life!"

"She was a toxic parent," Mark says now, in one of our rare phone conversations. "A real psycho. It haunts me, you know, the shit that we went through. It was like living in a house of terror, you know? Like, you know, a dictatorship or something. You never knew what was next, and that was the scariest part. There was a point, I think, where I really just couldn't take it anymore. I really wanted to die." I listen as he draws on his cigarette and then exhales, containing the fussy spitefulness that's creeping into his voice. "Not that you'd remember. It always fell on me, whatever it was. They thought you were so cute and spacey; you were always checked out in La-La Land while I got the brunt of everything."

I listen but don't listen. I'm on the deck behind my house, with my cell phone, reclining, watching my daughters jump through the sprinkler. Everything is green and full of sunlight, and I might as well be watching an actor portraying me in the happy ending of a movie of my life. I've never told him about my blackouts, and I don't now, though they have been bothering me again lately. I can imagine what he would come up with: fugue states, repressed memories, multiple personalities. Ridiculous stuff.

"It all seems very far away to me," I tell Mark, which is not true exactly, but it's part of the role I've been playing for many years now. "I don't really think much about it."

This much is true: I barely remember what happened that night. I wasn't even there, among the mundane details of children squabbling and cleaning and my mother's ordinary unhappiness. I was the Detective!— driving my sleek Studebaker through the streets of Beck, nervous though not panicked, edgy and white-knuckled but still planning with steely determination: The notebook! The notebook must be retrieved!

Nothing else was really happening, and when I left the house, I was in a state of focused intensity.

It must have been about eleven o'clock. Mark had been especially evil and watchful, and it wasn't until he'd settled down in front of the television with a big bowl of ice cream that I could pretend, at last, to go to bed.

Outside, out the door, down the alley: it seems to me that I should have been frightened, but mostly I recall the heave of adrenaline and determination, the necessity of the notebook, the absolute need for it. It was my story.

The lights were on at Mickleson's house, a bad sign, but I moved forward anyway, into the dense and dripping shadows of his yard, the crickets singing thickly, my hand already extended to touch the knob of his back door.

It wasn't locked. It didn't even have to be jimmied; it gave under the pressure of my hand, a little electrical jolt across my skin, the door opening smooth and uncreaking, and I passed like a shadow into the narrow back foyer that led to the kitchen. There was a silence in the house, and for a moment I felt certain that Mickleson was asleep. Still, I moved cautiously. The kitchen was brightly fluorescent and full of dirty dishes and beer cans. I slid my feet along the tile, inching along the wall. Silence, and then Mickleson's voice drifted up suddenly, a low mumble and then a firmer one, as if he were contradicting himself. My heart shrank. *Now what?* I thought as I came to the edge of the living room.

Mickleson was sitting in his chair, slumping, his foot jiggling with irritation. I heard the sail-like snap of a turning page, and I didn't even have to look to know that the notebook was in his hands. He murmured again as I stood there. I felt lightheaded. *The notebook!* I thought and leaned against the wall. I felt my head bump against something, and Mr. Mickleson's plaque tilted, then fell. I fumbled for a moment before I caught it.

But the sound made him turn. There I was, dumbly holding the slice of wood, and his eyes rested on me. His expression seemed to flicker with surprise, then terror, then annoyance, before settling on a kind of blank amusement. He cleared his throat.

"I believe I see a little person in my house," he said, and I might have fainted. I could feel the Detective leaving me, shriveling up and slumping to the floor, a suit of old clothes; the city of Beck disintegrated in the distance, streets drying up like old creek beds, skyscrapers sinking like ocean liners into the wheat fields. I was very still, his gaze pinning me. "A ghostly little person," he said, with satisfaction. He stood up for a moment, wavering, and then stumbled back against the chair for support, a look of affronted dignity freezing on his face. I didn't move.

"Well, well," he said. "Do I dare assume that I am in the presence of the author of this"—he waved my notebook vaguely—"this document?"

He paused, thumbing through it with an exaggerated, mime-like gesture. "Hmm," he murmured, almost crooning. "So—imaginative! And—there's a certain—charm—about it—I think." And then he leaned toward me. "And so at last we meet, Detective O'Day!" he said, in a deep voice. "You may call me Professor Moriarty!" He made a strange shape with his mouth and laughed softly—it wasn't sinister exactly, but musing, as if he'd just told himself a good joke, and I was somehow in on it.

"Why so quiet?" he exclaimed and waggled the notebook at me. "Haven't you come to find your future, young Detective?" I watched as he pressed his fingers to his temples, like a stage medium. "Hmm," he said and began to wave his arms and fingers in a seaweed-like floating motion, as if casting a magic spell or performing a hula dance. "Looking for his future," he said. "What lies in wait for Andy O'Day? I ask myself that question frequently. Will he grow up to be...",—and here he read aloud from my journal—"...'troglodytic' and 'sinister'? Will he ever escape the sad and lonely life of a Detective, or will he wander till the end of his days through the grim and withering streets of Beck?"

He paused then and looked up from my journal. I thought for a moment that if I leapt out, I could snatch it from him, even though the things I had written now seemed dirty and pathetic. I thought to say, "Give me back my notebook!" But I didn't really want it anymore. I just stood there, watching him finger the pages, and he leaned toward me, wavering, his eyes not exactly focused on me, but on some part of my forehead or shoulder or hair. He smiled, made another small effort to stand, then changed his mind. "What will happen to Andy O'Day?" he said again, thoughtfully. "It's such a compelling question, a very lovely question, and I can tell you the answer. Because, you see, I've come through my time machine to warn you! I have a special message for you from the future. Do you want to know what it is?"

"No," I said at last, my voice thick and uncertain.

"Oh, Andy," he said, as if very disappointed. "Andy, Andy. Look! Here I am!" He held his arms out wide, as if I'd run toward them. "Your Dreadful Double!" I watched as he straightened himself, correcting the slow tilt of his body. "I know you," Mr. Mickleson said. His head dropped, but he kept one eye on me. "You must be coming to me—for something?"

I shook my head. I didn't know. I couldn't even begin to imagine, and yet I felt—not for the last time—that I was standing in a desolate and empty prairie, the fields unraveling away from me in all directions, and the long winds running through my hair.

"Don't you want to know a secret?" he said. "Come over here, I'll whisper in your ear."

And it seemed to me, then, that he did know a secret. It seemed to me that he would tell me something terrible, something I didn't want to hear. I watched as he closed my notebook and placed it neatly on the

coffee table, next to the *TV Guide*. He balanced himself on two feet, lifting up and lurching toward me. "Hold still," he murmured. "I'll whisper."
    I turned and ran.

I once tried to explain this incident to my wife, but it didn't make much
sense to her. She nodded, as if it were merely strange, merely puzzling.
"Hmmm," she said, and I thought that perhaps it *was* odd to remember
this time so vividly, when I remembered so little else. It *was* a little
ridiculous that I should find Mr. Mickleson on my mind so frequently.
    "He was just a drunk," my wife said. "A little crazy, maybe, but…"
And she looked into my face, her lips pursing. "He didn't…*do* anything
to you, did he?" she said, awkwardly, and I shook my head.
    "No—no," I said. And I explained to her that I never saw Mr. Mickleson
again. I avoided the house after that night, of course, and when school
started he wasn't teaching Science 7. We were told, casually, that he had
had an "emergency," that he had been called away, and when, after a few
weeks, he still didn't return, he was replaced without comment by an
elderly lady substitute, who read to us from the textbook—*The World of
Living Things*—in a lilting storybook voice, and who whispered, "My
God," as she watched us, later, dissecting earthworms, pinning them to
corkboard and exposing their many hearts. We never found out where Mr.
Mickleson had gone.
    "He was probably in rehab," my wife said sensibly. "Or institutional-
ized. Your father was right. He was just a weirdo. It doesn't seem that
mysterious to me."
    Yes. I nodded a little, ready to drop the subject. I couldn't very well
explain the empty longing I had felt, the eager dread that would wash
over me, going into the classroom and thinking that he might be sitting
there behind the desk, waiting. It didn't make sense, I thought, and
I couldn't explain it, any more than I could explain why he remained in
my mind as I crisscrossed the country with my family, any more than
I could explain why he seemed to be there when I thought of them, even
now: Mark, fat and paranoid, on his houseboat; my mother in Mexico,
nodding over a cocktail; Kathy, staring at a spider in the corner of her
room in the group home, her eyes dull; my father, frightened, calling me
on the phone as his liver failed him, his body decomposing in a tiny
grave in Idaho that I'd never visited. How could I explain that Mickleson
seemed to preside over these thoughts, hovering at the edge of them
like a stage director at the back of my mind, smiling as if he'd done me
a favor?
    I didn't know why he came into my mind as I thought of them, just as
I didn't know why he seemed to appear whenever I told lies. It was just
that I could sense him. *Yes*, he whispered as I told my college friends
that my father was an archaeologist living in Peru, that my mother was

a former actress; *yes*, he murmured when I lied to my father about Katrina; *yes*, as I make excuses to my wife, when I say I am having dinner with a client when in fact I am tracing another path entirely—following a young family as they stroll through the park, or a whistling old man who might be my father, if he's gotten away, or a small, brisk-paced woman who looks like Katrina might, if Katrina weren't made up. How can I explain that I walk behind this Katrina woman for many blocks, living a different life, whistling my old man tune?

I can't. I can't explain it, no more than I can admit that I still have Mickleson's plaque, just as he probably still has my notebook; no more than I can explain why I take the plaque out of the bottom drawer of my desk and unwrap the tissue paper I've folded it in, reading the inscription over, like a secret message: "I wear the chains I forged in life." I know it's just a cheap Dickens allusion, but it still seems important. I can hear him say, "Hold still. I'll whisper."

"Hmmm," my wife would say, puzzled and perhaps a bit disturbed. She's a practical woman, and so I say nothing. It's probably best that she doesn't think any more about it, and I keep to myself the private warmth I feel when I sense a blackout coming, the darkness clasping its hands over my eyes. It's better this way—we're all happy. I'm glad that my wife will be there when I awake, and my normal life, and my beautiful daughters, looking at me, wide-eyed, staring.

"Hello?" my wife will say, and I'll smile as she nudges me. "Are you there?" she'll say. "Are you all right?" she'll whisper.

◈

The Red Fox Fur Coat

TEOLINDA GERSÃO

TRANSLATED BY MARGARET JULL COSTA

On her way home one day, a humble bank clerk happened to see a red fox fur coat in a furrier's shop window. She stopped outside and felt a shiver of pleasure and desire run through her. For this was the coat she had always wanted. There wasn't another one like it, she thought, running her eyes over the other coats hanging from the metal rack or delicately draped over a brocade sofa. It was rare, unique; she had never seen such a color, golden, with a coppery sheen, and so bright it looked as if it were on fire. The shop was closed at the time, as she discovered when, giving in to the impulse to enter, she pushed at the door. She would come back tomorrow, as early as possible, in her lunch break, or during the morning; yes, she would find a pretext to slip out during the morning. That night she slept little and awoke feeling troubled and slightly feverish. She counted the minutes until the shop would open; her eyes wandered from the clock on the wall to her wristwatch and back, while she dealt with various customers. As soon as she could, she found an excuse to pop out and run to the shop, trembling to think that the coat might have been sold. It had not, she learned, been sold; she felt her breath return, her heartbeat ease, felt the blood drain from her face and resume its measured flow.

"It could have been made for you," said the saleswoman when the bank clerk put the coat on and looked at herself in the mirror. "It fits perfectly on the shoulders and at the waist, and the length is just right," she said, "and it really suits your skin tone. Not that I'm trying to pressure you into buying it," she added hurriedly, "obviously you're free to choose anything you like, but if you don't mind my saying so, the coat really does look as if it had been made for you. Just for you," she said again, with the hint of a smile.

"How much is it?" the bank clerk asked, half turning round—thus setting the hem of the coat swinging—because she found it hard to take her eyes off her own image in the mirror.

She recoiled, stunned, when she heard the reply. It cost far more than she had thought, five times more than she could possibly afford

"But we can spread out the payment if you like," said the saleswoman kindly.

She could always sacrifice her holidays, the bank clerk thought. Or divert some of the money intended for a car loan. She could use less heating, eat smaller meals. It would do her good, really, because she was beginning to put on a bit of weight.

"All right," she said, doing rapid calculations in her head. "I'll give you a deposit and start paying next week. But it's definitely mine now, isn't it?"

"Absolutely," said the saleswoman, attaching a "Sold" label to the coat. "You can take it away with you when you've paid the third installment."

She started visiting the shop at night, when it was closed and no one would see her, in order to gaze at the coat through the window, and each time it brought her more joy, each time it was brighter, more fiery, like red flames that did not burn, but were soft on her body, like a thick, ample, enfolding skin that moved when she moved...

It would be admired, as would she, people would turn to stare after her, but it was not this that provoked a secret smile; rather, she realized, it was an inner satisfaction, an obscure certainty, a sense of being in harmony with herself, that spilled over in all kinds of small ways. It was as if the rhythm of her breathing had changed, had grown calmer and deeper. She realized too, perhaps because she no longer felt tired, that she moved more quickly, that she could walk effortlessly now, at twice her usual speed. Her legs were agile, her feet nimble. Everything about her was lighter, quicker; her back, shoulders, and limbs all moved more easily.

It must be all the keep-fit I've been doing, she thought, because for some reason she had started taking regular exercise. For a few months now she had been spending two hours a week running at the track. But what she liked most was to go running in the forest, on the outskirts of the city, feeling the sand crunch beneath her feet, learning to place her feet on the ground in a different way—in direct, perfect, intimate contact with the earth. She was intensely aware of her body; she was more alive now, more alert. All her senses were keener too, she could hear, even from some distance away, infinitesimal sounds which, before, would have gone unnoticed: a lizard scurrying through the leaves, an invisible mouse making a twig crack, an acorn falling, a bird landing on a bush; she could sense atmospheric changes long before they happened: the wind turning, a rise in humidity, an increase in air pressure that would culminate in rain. And another aspect of all the things to which she had now become sensitized was the discovery of smells, a whole world of smells; she could find paths and trails purely by smell; it was strange how she had never before noticed that everything has a smell: the earth, the bark of trees, plants, leaves, and that every animal can be distinguished by its own peculiar smell, a whole spectrum of smells that came to her on waves through the air, and which she could draw together or separate out, sniffing the wind, imperceptibly lifting her head. She suddenly became very interested in animals and found herself leafing through encyclopedias, looking at the pictures—the hedgehog's pale, soft, tender underbelly; the swift hare, of uncertain hue, leaping; she pored over the bodies of birds, fascinated, pondering the softness of the flesh behind their feathers; and a single word kept bobbing insistently about in her mind: predator.

She seemed to be hungrier too, she thought, as she put away her books and went into the kitchen, and this negative aspect to all the physical exercise displeased her greatly. She tried to find a way to avoid putting on weight and prowled, dissatisfied, past patisseries, never finding what she was looking for, because the smell of coffee was repellent to her and made her feel nauseous. No, she was hungry for other things, although she didn't quite know what, fruit perhaps; this might be an opportunity to lose a little weight. She bought a vast quantity of grapes and apples and ate them all in one day, but still she felt hungry, a hidden hunger that gnawed at her from inside and never stopped.

She was cheered by an unexpected invitation to a party, welcoming any diversion that would make her forget that absurd hunger. She reveled in getting dressed up and in painting her lips and nails scarlet.

Her nails, she noticed, were very long, and even her hands seemed more sensitive, more elongated. Anyone she touched at the party that night would remain eternally in her power, she thought, smiling at herself in the mirror—a feline smile, it seemed to her. She narrowed her eyes and widened the smile, letting it spread over her face, which took on a pleasingly triangular shape that she further emphasized with make-up.

In the middle of the party, she noticed someone slicing up some meat, cooked very rare—roast beef, she thought, although these words had suddenly ceased to have any meaning. She reached out her hand and devoured a whole slice. Ah, she thought, the taste of almost raw meat, the action of sinking her teeth into it, of making the blood spurt, the taste of blood on her tongue, in her mouth, the innocence of devouring the whole slice, and she took another slice, already sensing that using her hand was now a pointless waste of time, that she should just pick it up directly with her mouth.

She burst out laughing and began to dance, waving her bloodstained hands in the air, feeling her own blood rise, as if some tempestuous inner force had been unleashed, a malign force that she could transmit to others, a plague or a curse, but this idea was nevertheless sweet, quiet, almost joyful, she felt, as she swayed, slightly drunk, listening to the echo of her own laughter.

She would spend the night obeying all these newly released forces and, in the morning, she would go and fetch the coat, because the day had come when it would be hers; it was part of her; she would know it even with her eyes closed, by touch alone, the soft, thick pelt burning her skin, cleaving to her, until she could no longer tell skin from skin....

"It could have been made for you," the saleswoman said again, as she removed it from the coat hanger.

The coat cleaving to her, until she could no longer tell skin from skin, as she could see in the mirror, as she turned the collar up around her head, her face disfigured, suddenly thinner, made up to look longer, her eyes narrow, restless, burning....

"Goodbye, then, and thanks," she said, rushing out of the shop, afraid that time was getting short and that people would stop in alarm to stare at her, because suddenly the impulse to go down on all fours and simply run was too strong, reincarnating her body, rediscovering her animal body; and as she fled, as she left the city behind her and simply fled, it took an almost superhuman effort to get into her car and drive to the edge of the forest, keeping tight control of her body, keeping tight control of her tremulous body for just one more minute, before that slam of the door, that first genuine leap on feet free at last, shaking her back and her tail, sniffing the air, the ground, the wind, and, with a howl of pleasure and joy, plunging off into the depths of the forest.

⧉ ⧉ ⧉

Writing Exercises

1. *Story Trigger.* One way to test your skill in the use of concrete, significant detail is to create a reality that is convincing—and yet literally impossible. To begin, draft a three-to-five-page story in which a single impossible event happens in the everyday world. (For example, a dog tells fortunes, a secret message appears on a pizza, the radio announcer speaks in an ex-husband's voice—supermarket tabloids can be a good source of ideas.) First, focus on using detail to create the reality of both the normal world and the impossible event—the more believable the reality is, the more seamlessly readers will accept the magic.

2. In the movie *Wait Until Dark*, Audrey Hepburn plays a blind woman being pursued by a killer through a darkened house. Audiences usually jump out of their seats during the film's climactic final scene because they identify so thoroughly with her character. Write a scene where your character is deprived of one of his five senses. Then, set the character in a situation where missing that particular sense would have an especially significant impact. The situation might put him at an advantage or disadvantage, but in any case, he will have to compensate, wringing every bit of useful information he can out of his other senses. Make the situation dramatic, one in which he is driven by a pressing need or desire. Here are some examples:
   - a child standing blindfolded in front of a piñata really wants to be the one to break it and get first crack at the candy inside,
   - a man (who is spying) can see, but not hear, his wife as she talks to her ex-husband,
   - someone on a very strict diet is at a party and stuck in a boring conversation near the buffet table.

3. *Touch.* We sometimes neglect to use tactile descriptions in our writing, but we do touch—all the time. Shopping for clothes, shaking hands, playing with pets, shuffling cards, scrubbing pots, shooting baskets. Think of what it means to touch an odd, rare, or even holy object. Consider temperature (*tepid, frigid*), moisture content (*arid, greasy, sticky, crisp*), texture (*crinkled, gritty, silky*), and weight (*ponderous, buoyant*). All of these sensations provide us with great descriptive words. Use some of them and find others.

   Describe the way an action or event *feels*—putting on a piece of clothing, engaging in exercise, eating a tough or squishy item of food, dancing, moving across a crowded room, carrying groceries in from the car, kissing, waking up, washing the car, whatever. What impression does your description give? Does it prompt a scene? Can you make some characters talk while they're doing one of these activities?

4. *Taste.* There are four main types of taste and each has its own words— sweet (*saccharine, sugary*), sour (*acidic, tart*), bitter (*acrid, biting*), and salty (*briny, brackish*). There are also lots of objects that have familiar, but distinctive tastes and so are useful in description (*fish, lemons, onions, candy, chocolate, pickles, beer, coffee,* and so on).

   Take some characters out for dinner—Chinese or Greek, burgers or gourmet, it doesn't matter. Describe a particular course or even a whole meal. What impression does your description give? What do the characters have to say about their meal? How do they communicate with each other through their appreciation of the food?

5. Create metaphors as quickly as you can. Write down that one thing is another. Don't censor yourself—have fun. Start with a noun. (For instance, a house is a cake. A house is a flower. A house is the wind. A house is a clock. A house is a salesman.) See how many things one thing can become. Some of your metaphors are bound to be striking and useful.

6. Create similes. What is something like? Come up with a list of nouns as sentence subjects, then finish the sentences. (For example: His hair felt like _____. The dog looked like a _____. The room smelled like _____. The train sounded like _____. Etc.) Ask yourself which comparisons work. There should be some similarity in the things compared, more so than in metaphors, which change one thing into another. Read your likenesses and assess them. Keep whatever works and use it in a story.

7. Write about something familiar from the point of view of a stranger—a foreigner, a time-traveler from the past, a prisoner released after twenty years in jail, an orphan. Pick a situation that might seem commonplace to your readers and imagine how she would perceive it through all her available senses. Send the urbanite to a small town in the Midwest, introduce the time-traveler to his own future, have the ex-prisoner spend the evening in a karaoke bar, let the orphan be adopted by a previously childless couple. The goal is to make the everyday seem strange and new again. Avoid using familiar words (your character won't know them). You might even try not to *name* the situation but let your reader figure out where the character is through your use of sensory details.

3

BUILDING CHARACTER
Characterization, Part I

• *The Direct Methods of Character Presentation*

Human character is in the foreground of all fiction, however the humanity might be disguised. Attributing human characteristics to the natural world may be frowned on in science, but it is a literary necessity. Bugs Bunny isn't a rabbit; he's a plucky youth in ears. Peter Rabbit is a mischievous boy. Brer Rabbit is a sassy rebel. The romantic heroes of *Watership Down* are out of the Arthurian tradition, not out of the hutch.

Your fiction can be only as successful as the characters who move it and move within it. Whether they are drawn from life or are pure fantasy—and all fictional characters lie somewhere between the two—we must find them interesting, we must find them believable, and we must care about what happens to them.

You ARE GOING TO LOVE SOME OF YOUR CHARACTERS, because they are you or some facet of you, and you are going to hate some of your characters for the same reason. But no matter what, you are probably going to have to let bad things happen to some of the characters you love or you won't have much of a story. Bad things happen to good characters, because our actions have consequences, and we do not all behave perfectly all the time.

ANNE LAMOTT

The Direct Methods of Character Presentation

There are six basic methods of character presentation. There are four direct methods—*dialogue, appearance, action*, and *thought*. Dialogue will be discussed in this chapter because it plays such an essential role in bringing characters to life. The other direct methods, along with the indirect methods—*authorial interpretation* and *interpretation by another character*—will be discussed in Chapter 4. Employing a variety of these methods can help you create full characters.

DIALOGUE

Speech characterizes in a way that is different from appearance, because speech represents an effort, mainly voluntary, to externalize the internal and to manifest not merely taste or preference but also deliberated thought. Like fiction itself, human dialogue attempts to marry logic to emotion.

Summary, Indirect, and Direct Dialogue.   Speech can be conveyed in fiction with varying degrees of directness. It can be *summarized* as part of the narrative so that a good deal of conversation is condensed:

> At home in the first few months, he and Maizie had talked brightly about changes that would make the company more profitable and more attractive to a prospective buyer: new cuts, new packaging, new advertising, new incentives to make supermarkets carry the brand.
>
> Joan Wickersham, "Commuter Marriage"

It can be reported in the third person as *indirect speech* so that it carries, without actual quotation, the feel of the exchange:

> Had he brought the coffee? She had been waiting all day long for coffee. They had forgot it when they ordered at the store the first day.
> Gosh, no, he hadn't. Lord, now he'd have to go back. Yes, he would if it killed him. He thought, though, he had everything else. She reminded him it was only because he didn't drink coffee himself. If he did he would remember it quick enough.
>
> Katherine Anne Porter, "Rope"

But usually when the exchange contains the possibility of discovery or decision, and therefore of dramatic action, it will be presented in *direct quotation*:

> "But I thought you hardly knew her, Mr. Morning."
> He picked up a pencil and began to doodle on a notebook page. "Did I tell you that?"

"Yes, you did."

"It's true. I didn't know her well."

"What is it you're after, then? Who was this person you're investigating?"

"I would like to know that too."

Siri Hustvedt, "Mr. Morning"

These three methods of presenting speech can be used in combination to take advantage of the virtues of each:

They differed on the issue of the holiday, and couldn't seem to find a common ground. (*Summary.*) She had an idea: why not some Caribbean island over Christmas? Well, but his mother expected them for turkey. (*Indirect.*)

"Oh, lord, yes, I wouldn't want to go without a yuletide gizzard." (*Direct.*)

Summary and indirect speech are often useful to get us quickly to the core of the scene, or when, for example, one character has to inform another of events that we already know, or when the emotional point of a conversation is that it has become tedious.

Carefully, playing down the danger, Len filled her in on the events of the long night.

Samantha claimed to be devastated. It was all very well if the Seversons wanted to let their cats run loose, but she certainly wasn't responsible for Lisbeth's parakeets, now was she?

But nothing is more frustrating to a reader than to be told that significant events are taking place in talk and to be denied the drama of the dialogue.

They whispered to each other all night long, and as he told her all about his past, she began to realize that she was falling in love with him.

Such a summary—it's *telling*—is a stingy way of treating the reader, who wants the chance to fall in love, too.

Economy in Dialogue.   Because direct dialogue has a dual nature—emotion within a logical structure—its purpose in fiction is never merely to convey information. Dialogue may do that (although information often is more naturally conveyed in narration), but it needs simultaneously to characterize, provide exposition, set the scene, advance the action, foreshadow, and/or remind. William Sloane, in *The Craft of Writing*, says:

There is a tentative rule that pertains to all fiction dialogue. It must do more than one thing at a time or it is too inert for the purposes of fiction. This may sound harsh, but I consider it an essential discipline.

In considering Sloane's "tentative rule," I place the emphasis on *rule*. With dialogue as with significant detail, when you write you are constantly at pains to mean more than you say. If a significant detail must both call up a sense image and *mean*, then the character's words, which presumably mean something, should simultaneously suggest image, personality, or emotion.

Dialogue, therefore, is not simply transcribed speech, but distilled speech—the "filler" and inert small talk of real conversation is edited away, even as the weight of implication is increased. "You don't simply copy what you heard on the street," says fiction writer Alice LaPlante. "You want to make it *sound* natural, but that doesn't mean it *is* natural. It takes careful editing to create natural-sounding dialogue. Generally, that means keeping things brief, and paying attention to the rhythm of the sentences. Sentences are short. They're not particularly grammatically correct, but rather quirky and characteristic of the speaker."

As a general rule, distilling speech into dialogue means avoiding long monologues and keeping the sense of an exchange. A character who speaks several consecutive sentences might come across as either a windbag (which, of course, might be your intention) or the author's puppet. Often the first and last words, phrases, or sentences of a character's speech can be eliminated. In this way you are separating the wheat from the chaff. The characters' intentions and preoccupations can shine through because of the leaps they make in their dialogue and because of the spaces left within their dialogue. The things they can't bring themselves to say aloud are often as revealing, or more revealing, than those they do say.

Characterizing Dialogue.   Even rote exchanges, however, can call up images. A character who says, "It is indeed a pleasure to meet you" carries his back at a different angle, dresses differently, from a character who says, "Hey, man, what's up?"

The three very brief speeches that follow portray three fictional men, sharply differentiated from each other not only by the content of what they say, but also by their diction (choice and use of words) and their syntax (the ordering of words in a sentence). Like appearance, these choices convey attributes of class, period, ethnicity, and so forth, as well as political or moral attitudes. How much do you know about each? How does each look?

"I had a female cousin one time—a Rockefeller, as it happened—" said the Senator, "and she confessed to me that she spent the fifteenth, sixteenth and seventeenth years of her life saying nothing but, No, thank you. Which is all very well for a girl of that age and station. But it would have been a damned unattractive trait in a male Rockefeller."

Kurt Vonnegut, *God Bless You, Mr. Rosewater*

"You think you the only one ever felt this way?" he asked. "You think I never felt this way? You think she never felt this way? Every last one of them back there one time in they life wanted to give up. She want to give up now. You know that? You got any idea how sick she is? Soon after he go, she's going too. I won't give her another year. I want her to believe he'll be up there waiting for her. And you can help me do it. And you the only one."

Ernest Gaines, A Lesson Before Dying

The Knight looked surprised at the question. "What does it matter where my body happens to be?" he said. "My mind goes on working all the same. In fact, the more head downward I am, the more I keep inventing new things.

"Now, the cleverest thing of the sort that I ever did," he went on after a pause, "was inventing a new pudding during the meat course."

Lewis Carroll, Through the Looking Glass

There are forms of insanity that condemn people to hear voices against their will, but as writers we invite ourselves to hear voices without relinquishing our hold on reality or our right to control. The trick to writing good dialogue is hearing voice. The question is, what would he or she say? The answer is entirely in language. The choice of language reveals content, character, and conflict, as well as type.

It's logical that if you must develop voices in order to develop dialogue, you'd do well to start with monologue and develop voices one by one. Use your journal to experiment with speech patterns that will characterize. Some people speak in telegraphically short sentences missing various parts of speech. Some speak in convoluted eloquence or in rhythms tedious with qualifying phrases. Some rush headlong without a pause for breath until they're breathless; others are measured or terse or begrudge even forming a sentence. Trust your "inner ear" and use your journal to practice catching voices. Freewriting is invaluable to dialogue writing because it is the manner of composition closest to speech. There is no time to mull or edit. Any qualifications, corrections, and disavowals must be made part of the process and the text.

To increase your ability to "hear" dialogue, try carrying a small pocket notebook with you and noting vivid lines or exchanges of eavesdropped dialogue verbatim. At home, look back through your notebook for speech that interests you and freedraft a monologue passage of that speech in your writing journal. Don't look for words that seem right; just listen to the voice and let it flow. You'll begin to develop your own range of voices whether you catch a particular voice or not, and may even develop your ear by the very process of "hearing" it go wrong at times.

Other Uses of Dialogue.   You can also limber up in your journal by setting yourself deliberate exercises in making dialogue—or monologue—do more than one thing at a time. In addition to revealing character, dialogue can *set the scene.*

> "We didn't know no one was here. We thought hit a summer camp all closed up. Curtains all closed up. Nothing here. No cars or gear nor nothing. Looks closed to me, don't hit to you, J.J.?"
>
> Joy Williams, "Woods"

Dialogue can *set the mood.*

> "I have a lousy trip to Philadelphia, lousy flight back, I watch my own plane blow a tire on closed-circuit TV, I go to my office, I find Suzy in tears because Warren's camped in her one-room apartment. I come home and I find my wife hasn't gotten dressed in two days."
>
> Joan Didion, *Book of Common Prayer*

Dialogue can *reveal the theme* because, as William Sloane says, the characters talk about what the story is about.

> "You feel trapped, don't you?"
> Jane looks at her.
> "Don't you?"
> "No."
> "O.K.—You just have a headache."
> "I do."...
> Milly waits a moment and then clears her throat and says, "You know, for a while there after Wally and I were married, I thought maybe I'd made a mistake. I remember realizing that I didn't like the way he laughed. I mean, let's face it, Wally laughs like a hyena...."
>
> Richard Bausch, "The Fireman's Wife"

In all of the preceding passages, the dialogue fulfills Sloane's rule because in addition to conveying its content, the dialogue either moves the story forward or enriches our understanding.

Dialogue is also one of the simplest ways to *reveal the past* (a fundamental playwriting device is to have a character who knows tell a character who doesn't know); and it is one of the most effective, because we get both the drama of the memory and the drama of the telling. Here is a passage from Toni Morrison's *The Bluest Eye* in which the past is evoked, the speaker characterized, the scene and mood set, and the theme revealed, all at the same time and in less than a dozen lines.

"The onliest time I be happy seem like was when I was in the picture show. Every time I got, I went. I'd go early, before the show started. They'd cut off the lights, and everything be black. Then the screen would light up, and I'd move right on in them pictures. White men taking such good care of they women, and they all dressed up in big clean houses with the bathtubs right in the same room with the toilet. Them pictures gave me a lot of pleasure, but it made coming home hard, and looking at Cholly hard. I don't know."

Be careful, however, that you don't succumb to the temptation to slip exposition into dialogue by allowing the characters to discuss things they both already know just for the reader's benefit.

"I've missed you so much, Margie! It's been over a month since we ran into each other at the Farmer's Market. That was the day you told me that your grandson Eddie got into Julliard!"

"Yes, Suzie, and wasn't that right before the tornado came through town? We were so scared when that siren went off! Remember how we hid underneath the rickety table with the watermelons on it?"

This kind of dialogue is both ridiculous and tedious. If we really need to know about the Farmer's Market and Eddie and the tornado, tell us in exposition. Don't weigh your characters' dialogue down with such information.

Dialogue as Action. If the telling of a memory *changes the relationship* between the teller and the listener, then you have a scene of high drama, and the dialogue can *advance the action.*

This is an important device, because dialogue is most valuable to fiction when it is itself a means of telling the story.

In the following passage, for example, the mother of a seriously ill toddler looks anxiously to a radiologist for information:

"The surgeon will speak to you," says the Radiologist.

"Are you finding something?"

"The surgeon will speak to you," the Radiologist says again. "There seems to be something there, but the surgeon will talk to you about it."

"My uncle once had something on his kidney," says the Mother. "So they removed the kidney and it turned out the something was benign."

The Radiologist smiles a broad, ominous smile. "That's always the way it is," he says. "You don't know exactly what it is until it's in the bucket."

"In the bucket," the Mother repeats.

"That's doctor talk," the Radiologist says.

"It's very appealing," says the Mother. "It's a very appealing way to talk."

Lorrie Moore, "People Like That Are the Only People Here"

Here the radiologist's speech alters the mother's feeling toward him from hopeful to hostile in one short exchange. The level of fear for the child rises, and the dialogue itself has effected change.

A crucial (and sometimes difficult) distinction to make is between speech that is mere discussion or debate and speech that is drama or action. If in doubt, ask yourself: Can this conversation between characters really change anything? *Dialogue is action when it contains the possibility of change.* When two characters have made up their minds and know each other's positions on some political or philosophical matter, for instance, they may argue with splendid eloquence but there will be no discovery and nothing to decide, and therefore no option for change. No matter how significant their topic, we are likely to find them wooden and uninteresting. The story's question *what happened next?* will suggest only *more talk*:

> "This has been the traditional fishing spot of the river people for a thousand years, and we have a moral responsibility to aid them in preserving their way of life. If you put in these rigs, it may undermine the ecosystem and destroy the aquifer of the entire county!"
>
> "Join the real world, Sybil. Free enterprise is based on this kind of technological progress, and without it we would endanger the economic base."

Ho-hum. In order to engage us emotionally in a disagreement, the characters must have an emotional stake in the outcome; we need to feel that, even if it's unlikely they would change their minds, they might change their lives.

> "If you sink that drill tomorrow morning, I'll be gone by noon."
> "Sybil, I have no choice."

Further, if you find your characters getting stuck in a repetitive conflict ("yes-you-are, no-I'm-not"), you can jump-start the action if you remember that people generally change their tactics—become charming, threatening, seductive, guilt-inducing, and so on—when they are not succeeding in getting what they badly want. And if *each* character in the scene wants something from the other, although it probably won't be the same thing, the momentum will build. It's much harder (although not impossible) to maintain dramatic energy when one of the characters simply wants to get off stage.

Text and Subtext.   Often the most forceful dialogue can be achieved by *not* having the characters say what they mean. People in extreme emotional states—whether of fear, pain, anger, or love—are at their least articulate. There is more narrative tension in a love scene where the lovers make anxious small talk, terrified of revealing their feelings, than in one where they hop into bed.

A character who is able to say "I hate you!" hates less than one who bottles the fury and pretends to submit, unwilling to expose the truth.

Dialogue can fall flat if characters define their feelings too precisely and honestly, because often the purpose of human exchange is to conceal as well as to reveal—to impress, hurt, protect, seduce, or reject. Anton Chekhov believed that a line of dialogue should always leave the sense that more could have been said. Playwright David Mamet suggests that people may or may not say what they mean, but always say something designed to get what they want.

In this example from Alice Munro's "Before the Change," the daughter of a doctor who performed illegal abortions up until his recent death takes a phone call:

> A woman on the phone wants to speak to the doctor.
> "I'm sorry. He's dead."
> "Dr. Strachan. Have I got the right doctor?"
> "Yes but I'm sorry, he's dead."
> "Is there anyone—does he by any chance have a partner I could talk to? Is there anybody else there?"
> "No. No partner."
> "Could you give me any other number I could call? Isn't there some other doctor that can—"
> "No. I haven't any number. There isn't anybody that I know of."
> "You must know what this is about. It's very crucial. There are very special circumstances—"
> "I'm sorry."

It's clear here that neither woman is willing to mention abortion, and that the daughter will also not (and probably could not) speak about her complicated feelings toward her father and his profession. The exchange is rich with irony in that both women and also the reader know the "special circumstance" they are guardedly referring to; only the daughter and the reader are privy to the events surrounding the doctor's death and to the daughter's feelings.

Notice that this is not a very articulate exchange, but it does represent dramatic action, because for both women the stakes are high; they are both emotionally involved, but in ways that put them at cross-purposes.

In "Following the Notes" by Pia Z. Ehrhardt (included at the end of this chapter) a high school-age daughter has summoned her father to her place of work because her car battery is dead, but she slips up and reveals more to him than she means to. Her subterfuge and his understanding of it are both lurking in and between the lines of their exchange:

> "You left the headlights on?" he said.
> "The passenger light," I said, pointing at the back seat. "Door wasn't shut all the way."

"Who was in the back?" he said. "I thought you were driving to work and home, only."

My daily comings and goings were charted in the kitchen, reviewed when I got back in the evening. I had the use of a Buick Century as long as I kept it filled with gas, washed it once a week in our driveway with mild detergent, and didn't joy ride with my friends.

"Sorry for the inconvenience," I said

"Don't be a smart-ass."

The idea of "reading between the lines" of dialogue is familiar to most people, for in life we tend to react more to what is implied in dialogue than to what is actually said. The linkage of text and subtext—that is, the surface, plot-related dialogue and its emotional undercurrent—was famously described by Ernest Hemingway with the analogy of an iceberg: "There is seven-eighths of it under water for every part that shows. Anything you know you can eliminate and it only strengthens your iceberg. It is the part that doesn't show."

When an unspoken subject remains unspoken, tension continues to build in a story. Often the crisis of a story occurs when the unspoken tension comes to the surface and an explosion results. "If you're trying to build pressure, don't take the lid off the pot," Jerome Stern suggests in his book *Making Shapely Fiction*. "Once people are really candid, once the unstated becomes stated, the tension is released and the effect is cathartic.... [Y]ou want to give yourself the space for a major scene. Here you do want to describe setting and action vividly, and render what they say fully. You've taken the lid off the pot and we want to feel the dialogue boil over."

IF YOU TAKE TWO STICKS AND HOLD THEM PARALLEL, you can capture that image in a photograph because it doesn't change. But if you rub those two sticks together, harder and harder, faster and faster, they will burst into flame—that's the kind of change you can capture in a story or on film. Friction is necessary for change to occur. But without the friction of conflict, there is no change. And without change, there is no story. A body at rest remains at rest unless it enters into conflict.

STEPHEN FISCHER

"No" Dialogue.   The previous Munro passage (page 81) also illustrates an essential element of conflict in dialogue: Tension and drama are heightened when characters are constantly (in one form or another) saying no to each other. In the following exchange from Ernest Hemingway's *The Old Man and the Sea*, the old man feels only love for his young protégé, and their conversation is a pledge of affection. Nevertheless, it is the old man's steady denial that lends the scene tension.

> "Can I go out and get sardines for you tomorrow?"
>
> "No. Go and play baseball. I can still row and Rogelio will throw the net."
>
> "I would like to go. If I cannot fish with you, I would like to serve in some way."
>
> "You brought me a beer," the old man said. "You are already a man."
>
> "How old was I when you first took me in a boat?"
>
> "Five and you were nearly killed when I brought the fish in too green and he nearly tore the boat to pieces. Can you remember?"
>
> "I can remember the tail slapping and banging and the thwart breaking and the noise of the clubbing. I can remember you throwing me into the bow where the wet coiled lines were and feeling the whole boat shiver and the noise of you clubbing him like chopping a tree down and the sweet blood smell all over me."
>
> "Can you really remember that or did I just tell it to you?"
>
> "I remember everything from when we first went together."
>
> The old man looked at him with his sunburned, confident loving eyes.
>
> "If you were my boy I'd take you out and gamble," he said. "But you are your father's and mother's and you are in a lucky boat."

Neither of these characters is consciously eloquent, and the dialogue is extremely simple. But look how much more it does than "one thing at a time"! It provides exposition on the beginning of the relationship, and it conveys the mutual affection of the two and the conflict within the old man between his love for the boy and his loyalty to the parents. It conveys the boy's eagerness to persuade and carries him into the emotion he had as a small child while the fish was clubbed. The dialogue represents a constant shift of power back and forth between the boy and the old man, as the boy, whatever else he is saying, continues to say *please*, and the old man, whatever else he is saying, continues to say *no*.

Another Hemingway story, "Hills Like White Elephants," also offers clear examples of "no" dialogue. Notice, however, that the conflict does not simply get stuck in a rut, because the characters continue to find new ways to ask and answer the questions as each tries to find the other's vulnerable points.

> "What should we drink?" the girl asked. She had taken off her hat and put it on the table.
>
> "It's pretty hot," the man said.
>
> "Let's drink beer."
>
> "Dos cervezas," the man said into the curtain.
>
> "Big ones?" a woman asked from the doorway.

"Yes. Two big ones."

The woman brought two glasses of beer and two felt pads. She put the felt pads and the beer glasses on the table and looked at the man and the girl. The girl was looking off at the line of hills. They were white in the sun and the country was brown and dry.

"They look like white elephants," she said.

"I've never seen one," the man drank his beer.

"No, you wouldn't have."

"I might have," the man said. "Just because you say I wouldn't have doesn't prove anything."

The girl looked at the bead curtain. "They've painted something on it," she said. "What does it say?"

Specificity. In dialogue, as in narrative, we will tend to believe a character who speaks in concrete details and to be skeptical of one who generalizes or who delivers judgments unsupported by example. When the boy in the Hemingway passage protests, "I remember everything," we believe him because of the vivid details in his memory of the fish. If one character says, "It's perfectly clear from all his actions that he adores me and would do anything for me," and another says, "I had my hands all covered with the clay slick, and he just reached over to lift a lock of hair out of my eyes and tuck it behind my ear," which character do you believe is the more loved?

Similarly, in conflict dialogue, "details are the rocks characters throw at each other," says Stephen Fischer. Our memories for hurts and slights are sadly long, and an accusation that begins as a general blame—"You never think of my feelings"—is likely to be backed up with specific proof as the argument escalates—"You said you'd pick me up at seven New Year's Eve, but you left me waiting for an hour in the snow." "There's nothing generic in our lives," Fischer explains, "and the sparks given off in conflict may reveal all the facts we need to know about the characters."

It's interesting to observe that whereas in narrative you will demonstrate control if you state the facts and let the emotional value rise off of them, in dialogue you will convey information more naturally if the emphasis is on the speaker's feelings. "My brother is due to arrive at midafternoon and is bringing his four children with him" reads as bald exposition; whereas, "That idiot brother of mine thinks he can walk in in the middle of the afternoon and plunk his four kids in my lap!" or, "I can't wait till my brother gets here at three! You'll see—those are the four sweetest kids this side of the planet"—will sound like talk and will slip us the information sideways.

Examine your dialogue to see if it does more than one thing at a time. Do the sound and syntax characterize by region, education, attitude? Do the choice of words and their syntax reveal that the character is stiff, outgoing, stifling anger, ignorant of the facts, perceptive, bigoted, afraid? Is the conflict advanced by "no" dialogue, in which the characters say *no* to each other in different ways? Is the drama heightened by the characters' inability or unwillingness to tell the whole truth?

Once you are comfortable with the voice of your character, it is well to acknowledge that everyone has many voices and that what that character says will be, within his or her verbal range, determined by the character *to whom* it is said. All of us have one sort of speech for the vicar and another for the man who pumps the gas. Huck Finn, whose voice is idiosyncratically his own, says, "Yes, sir" to the judge and "Maybe I am, maybe I ain't" to his degenerate dad.

Pacing. Economy in dialogue—distilling it, avoiding the rehash of what the reader already knows, making sure that it does more than one job at a time—is an important part of pacing. At the same time, it's important not to hurry over the unfolding drama that takes place in an exchange of speech.

One reason why readers enjoy dialogue is that it's the most direct experience of the characters we get in fiction, the only time they express themselves without any authorial interference. Therefore, it's important, when writing dialogue, not to race through it quickly with an end in mind. You might think you know what the outcome of a conversation is going to be, but dialogue is always more fun to write, and to read, if the characters surprise you. When writing dialogue take your time and listen closely to what your characters might say, based on who they are and what they want, rather than foisting your own agenda on them.

For instance, you may begin writing a scene with a plan to get in and out quickly. You may decide that this will be the scene where he breaks up with her.

"I've stopped by to tell you that it's over. I've had enough. We're finished."

"Fine. There's the door. Goodbye."

This quick exchange wouldn't allow you to discover the depth of the characters, with the consequence that the reader is cheated of the real drama. The characters come off sounding flat and unreal, whereas if you're aware as you're writing that both characters have their own desires and conflicting emotions, if you allow them to reveal some of their feelings and hide others, they will become authentic and believable. The subtext will be revealed. In a situation like this, it's important to remember that the character being abandoned is not a passive sounding board or a mere echo.

"You still need to fix that porch light. Wow, don't you look nice."

"I've got three minutes to get downtown. Jake's waiting for me. What's up?"

This dialogue is more specific and the characters are at odds, but what exactly is going to happen isn't clear. He's trying to be nonchalant, a little bit aggressive but still kind; she seems to know why he's come and has already found someone else. Or at least wants him to think so. What if he insists on coming in for three minutes? This scene wants to be longer. Keep the talkers talking. Maybe they won't break up after all—not tonight, anyway.

There are additional ways to pace yourself when writing dialogue. Timing, as it is in stand-up comedy, is crucial. Vary your sentences and the placement of your dialogue tags. Decide where you want the reader to pause, what you want to emphasize.

In this excerpt from Tobias Wolff's "Hunters in the Snow," Wolff structures the paragraph so that the reader gets the full benefit of Frank's zinger.

> Frank had his fingers fanned out, tips against the bark of the stump where he'd laid his foot. His knuckles were hairy. He wore a heavy wedding band and on his right pinky another gold ring with a flat face and an "F" in what looked like diamonds. He turned the ring this way and that. "Tub," he said, "you haven't seen your own balls in years."

In Hemingway's "Hills Like White Elephants," the silences and interruptions say as much about the characters and their conflict as their words do.

> "I don't want you to do anything that you don't want to do—"
> "Nor that isn't good for me," she said. "I know. Could we have another beer?"
> "All right, but you've got to realize—"
> "I realize," said the girl. "Can't we maybe stop talking?"

Repetition is another way to vary pace and emphasize certain words and emotions. It becomes clear that the wife in Raymond Carver's "Cathedral" worries that her guest, Robert, the blind man, will sense her husband's hostility. The husband, who is the narrator, is listening to this exchange, which is really directed at him.

> My wife covered her mouth, and then she yawned. She stretched. She said, "I think I'll go upstairs and put on my robe. I think I'll change into something else. Robert, you make yourself comfortable," she said.
> "I'm comfortable," the blind man said.
> "I want you to feel comfortable in this house," she said.
> "I am comfortable," the blind man said.

With each repetition the word *comfortable* takes on a slightly different meaning.

Fiction writers generally manage the pace of a scene by blending dialogue with description, action, and the main character's thoughts. These are also direct ways to present character and will be discussed in the next chapter.

Format and Style. The *format and style of dialogue*, like punctuation, has as its goal to be invisible; and though there may be occasions when departing from the rules is justified by some special effect, it's best to consider such occasions rare. Here are some basic guidelines:

What a character says aloud should be in quotation marks; thoughts should not. This helps clearly differentiate between the spoken and the internal, especially by acknowledging that speech is more deliberately formulated. If you feel that thoughts need to be set apart from narrative, use italics instead of quotation marks.

Begin the dialogue of each new speaker as a new paragraph. This helps orient the reader and keep clear who is speaking. If an action is described between the dialogue lines of two speakers, put that action in the paragraph of the speaker it describes:

> "I wish I'd taken that picture." Larry traced the horizon with his index finger.
>
> Janice snatched the portfolio away. "You've got chicken grease on your hands," she said, "and this is the only copy!"

Notice that the punctuation goes inside the quotation marks.

A dialogue tag tells us who has spoken—*John said, Mary said, Tim announced.* When a tag is used, it is connected to the dialogue line with a comma, even though the dialogue line may sound like a full sentence: *"I'm paying tonight,"* *Mary said.* (Misusing a period in place of the comma with a tag is one of the most common mistakes in dialogue format.)

Avoid over-using the name of the person being spoken to in dialogue—it doesn't sound conversational.

> "For God sake, Benji, my job's more important than our marathon Monopoly game."
>
> "Ah, Mom, you're always taking things the wrong way."
>
> "Benji, you know that's not true."
>
> "Yup, true, Mom, every time."

Like a luggage tag or a nametag, a dialogue tag is for the purpose of identification, and *said* is usually adequate to the task. People also *ask* and *reply* and occasionally *add, recall, remember,* or *remind.* But sometimes an unsure writer will strain for emphatic synonyms: *She gasped, he whined, they chorused, John snarled, Mary spat.* This is unnecessary and obtrusive, because although unintentional repetition usually makes for awkward style, the word *said* is as invisible as punctuation. When reading we're scarcely aware of it, whereas we are forced to be aware of *she wailed.* If it's clear who is speaking without any dialogue tag at all, don't use one. Usually an identification at the beginning of a dialogue passage and an occasional reminder are sufficient. If the speaker is inherently identified in the speech pattern, so much the better.

Similarly, tonal dialogue tags should be used sparingly: *he said with relish; she added limply*. Such phrases are blatant "telling," and the chances are that good dialogue will convey its own tone. *"Get off my case!" she said angrily*. We do not need to be told that she said this angrily. If she said it sweetly, then we would probably need to be told. If the dialogue does not give us a clue to the manner in which it is said, an action will often do so better than an adverb. *"I'll have a word with Mr. Ritter about it," he said with finality* is weaker than *"I'll have a word with Mr. Ritter about it," he said, and picked up his hat*.

It helps to make the dialogue tag unobtrusive if it comes within the spoken line: *"Don't give it a second thought," he said. "I was just going anyway."* (A midline tag has the added benefit of helping readers hear a slight pause or change in the speaker's inflection.) A tag that comes at the beginning of the line may look too much like a play script: *He said, "Don't give it a second thought…"* whereas a tag that comes after too much speech becomes confusing or superfluous: *"Don't give it a second thought. I was going anyway, and I'll just take these and drop them at the copy shop on the way," he said*. If we didn't know who was speaking long before this tag appears, it's too late to be of use and simply calls attention to itself.

Vernacular.   *Vernacular* is a tempting, and can be an excellent, means of characterizing, but it is difficult to do well and easy to overdo. Dialect, regionality, and childhood should be achieved by word choice and syntax. Misspellings should be kept to a minimum because they distract and slow the reader, and worse, they tend to make the character seem stupid. There is no point in spelling phonetically any word as it is ordinarily pronounced: Almost all of us say things like "fur" for *for*, "uv" for *of*, "wuz" for *was*, "an" for *and*, and "sez" for *says*. It's common to drop the *g* in words ending in *ing*. When you misspell these words in dialogue, you indicate that the speaker is ignorant enough to spell them that way when writing. Even if you want to indicate ignorance, you may alienate the reader by the means you choose to do so. John Updike puts this point well when he complains of a Tom Wolfe character:

> [His] pronunciations are steadfastly spelled out—'sump'm' for 'something,' 'far fat' for 'fire fight'—in a way that a Faulkner character would be spared. For Faulkner, Southern life was life; for Wolfe it is a provincial curiosity….

It is largely to avoid the charge of creating "provincial curiosities" that most fiction writers now avoid misspellings.

It can be even trickier catching the voice of a foreigner with imperfect English, because everyone has a native language, and when someone whose native language is French or Ibu starts to learn English, the grammatical mistakes they make will be based on the grammatical structure of the native language. Unless you know French or Ibu, you will make mistakes, and your dialogue is likely to sound as if it came from second-rate sitcoms.

In vernacular or standard English, the bottom-line rule is that dialogue must be speakable. If it isn't speakable, it isn't dialogue.

"Certainly I had had a fright I wouldn't soon forget," Reese would say later, "and as I slipped into bed fully dressed except for my shoes, which I flung God-knows-where, I wondered why I had subjected myself to a danger only a fool would fail to foresee for the dubious pleasure of spending one evening in the company of a somewhat less than brilliant coed."

Nobody would say this because it can't be said. It is not only convoluted beyond reason but it also stumbles over its alliteration, "only a fool would fail to foresee for," and takes more breath than the human lungs can hold.

Read your dialogue aloud and make sure it is comfortable to the mouth, the breath, and the ear. False, flabby, do-nothing dialogue will reveal itself, as will places that drag or seem rushed. This is the best way possible to tell if it's all coming together.

DIALOGUE TIPS

1. Have your characters speak no more than three sentences at a time—unless you have a good reason to do otherwise.
2. Dialogue is more interesting when characters are saying no to each other.
3. Keep exposition out of dialogue
4. Let your characters sometimes conceal or avoid instead of saying exactly what they mean.
5. Use "said" as a dialogue tag whenever possible.
6. Use an action rather than a modifier to show how a character is feeling.
7. Cut to the chase. Don't use dialogue that doesn't move the story forward and reveal character.
8. Don't let your characters be too articulate. Fragments are fine. Don't force conversations to follow a logical order (question followed by answer). No need to stay on the same subject or include clear transitions from one subject to another.
9. Vernacular is best conveyed by word choice and syntax as opposed to misspellings.

◈

Fiesta, 1980

JUNOT DIAZ

Mami's youngest sister—my tía Yrma—finally made it to the United States that year. She and tío Miguel got themselves an apartment in the Bronx, off the Grand Concourse and everybody decided that we should have a party. Actually, my pops decided, but everybody—meaning Mami, tía Yrma, tío Miguel and their neighbors—thought it a dope idea. On the afternoon of the party Papi came back from work around six. Right on time. We were all dressed by then, which was a smart move on our part. If Papi had walked in and caught us lounging around in our underwear, he would have kicked our asses something serious.

He didn't say nothing to nobody, not even my moms. He just pushed past her, held up his hand when she tried to talk to him and headed right into the shower. Rafa gave me the look and I gave it back to him; we both knew Papi had been with that Puerto Rican woman he was seeing and wanted to wash off the evidence quick.

Mami looked really nice that day. The United States had finally put some meat on her; she was no longer the same flaca who had arrived here three years before. She had cut her hair short and was wearing tons of cheapass jewelry which on her didn't look too lousy. She smelled like herself, like the wind through a tree. She always waited until the last possible minute to put on her perfume because she said it was a waste to spray it on early and then have to spray it on again once you got to the party.

We—meaning me, my brother, my little sister and Mami—waited for Papi to finish his shower. Mami seemed anxious, in her usual dispassionate way. Her hands adjusted the buckle of her belt over and over again. That morning, when she had gotten us up for school, Mami told us that she wanted to have a good time at the party. I want to dance, she said, but now, with the sun sliding out of the sky like spit off a wall, she seemed ready just to get this over with.

Rafa didn't much want to go to no party either, and me, I never wanted to go anywhere with my family. There was a baseball game in the parking lot outside and we could hear our friends, yelling, Hey, and, Cabrón, to one another. We heard the pop of a ball as it sailed over the cars, the clatter of an aluminium bat dropping to the concrete. Not that me or Rafa loved baseball; we just liked playing with the local kids, thrashing them at anything they were doing. By the sounds of the shouting, we both knew the game was close, either of us could have made a difference. Rafa frowned and when I frowned back, he put up his fist. Don't you mirror me, he said.

Don't you mirror me, I said.

He punched me—I would have hit him back but Papi marched into the living room with his towel around his waist, looking a lot smaller than he did when he was dressed. He had a few strands of hair around his nipples and a surly closed-mouth expression, like maybe he'd scalded his tongue or something.

Have they eaten? he asked Mami.

She nodded. I made you something.

You didn't let him eat, did you?

Ay, Dios mío, she said, letting her arms fall to her side.

Ay, Dios mío is right, Papi said.

I was never supposed to eat before our car trips, but earlier, when she had put out our dinner of rice, beans and sweet platanos, guess who had been the first one to clean his plate? You couldn't blame Mami really, she had been busy—cooking, getting ready, dressing my sister Madai. I should have reminded her not to feed me but I wasn't that sort of son.

Papi turned to me. Coño, muchacho, why did you eat?

Rafa had already started inching away from me. I'd once told him I considered him a low-down chickenshit for moving out of the way every time Papi was going to smack me.

Collateral damage, Rafa had said. Ever heard of it?

No.

Look it up.

Chickenshit or not, I didn't dare glance at him. Papi was old fashioned; he expected your undivided attention when you were getting your ass whupped. You couldn't look him in the eye either—that wasn't allowed. Better to stare at his belly button, which was perfectly round and immaculate. Papi pulled me to my feet by my ear.

If you throw up—

I won't, I cried, tears in my eyes, more out of reflex than pain.

Ya, Ramón, ya. It's not his fault, Mami said.

They've known about this party forever. How did they think we were going to get there? Fly?

He finally let go of my ear and I sat back down. Madai was too scared to open her eyes. Being around Papi all her life had turned her into a major-league wuss. Anytime Papi raised his voice her lip would start trembling, like some specialized tuning fork. Rafa pretended that he had knuckles to crack and when I shoved him, he gave me a *Don't start* look. But even that little bit of recognition made me feel better.

I was the one who was always in trouble with my dad. It was like my God-given duty to piss him off, to do everything the way he hated. Our fights didn't bother me too much. I still wanted him to love me, something that never seemed strange or contradictory until years later, when he was out of our lives.

By the time my ear stopped stinging Papi was dressed and Mami was crossing each one of us, solemnly, like we were heading off to war. We said, in turn, Bendición, Mami, and she poked us in our five cardinal spots while saying, Que Dios te bendiga.

This was how all our trips began, the words that followed me every time I left the house.

None of us spoke until we were inside Papi's Volkswagen van. Brand-new, lime-green and bought to impress. Oh, we were impressed, but me, every time I was in that VW and Papi went above twenty miles an hour, I vomited. I'd never had trouble with cars before—that van was like my curse. Mami suspected it was the upholstery. In her mind, American things—appliances, mouthwash, funny-looking upholstery—all seemed to have an intrinsic badness about them. Papi was careful about taking me anywhere in the VW, but when he had to, I rode up front in Mami's usual seat so I could throw up out a window.

¿Cómo te sientes? Mami asked over my shoulder when Papi pulled onto the turnpike. She had her hand on the base of my neck. One thing about Mami, her palms never sweated.

I'm OK, I said, keeping my eyes straight ahead. I definitely didn't want to trade glances with Papi. He had this one look, furious and sharp, that always left me feeling bruised.

Toma. Mami handed me four mentas. She had thrown three out her window at the beginning of our trip, an offering to Eshú; the rest were for me.

I took one and sucked it slowly, my tongue knocking it up against my teeth. We passed Newark Airport without any incident. If Madai had been awake she would have cried because the planes flew so close to the cars.

How's he feeling? Papi asked.

Fine, I said. I glanced back at Rafa and he pretended like he didn't see me. That was the way he was, at school and at home. When I was in trouble, he didn't know me. Madai was solidly asleep, but even with her face all wrinkled up and drooling she looked cute, her hair all separated into twists.

I turned around and concentrated on the candy. Papi even started to joke that we might not have to scrub the van out tonight. He was beginning to loosen up, not checking his watch too much. Maybe he was thinking about that Puerto Rican woman or maybe he was just happy that we were all together. I could never tell. At the toll, he was feeling positive enough to actually get out of the van and search around under the basket for dropped coins. It was something he had once done to amuse Madai, but now it was habit. Cars behind us honked their horns and I slid down in my seat. Rafa didn't care; he grinned back at the other cars and waved. His actual job was to make sure no cops were coming. Mami shook Madai awake and as soon as she saw Papi stooping for a couple of quarters she let out this screech of delight that almost took off the top of my head.

That was the end of the good times. Just outside the Washington Bridge, I started feeling woozy. The smell of the upholstery got all up inside my head and I found myself with a mouthful of saliva. Mami's hand tensed on my shoulder and when I caught Papi's eye, he was like, No way. Don't do it.

The first time I got sick in the van Papi was taking me to the library. Rafa was with us and he couldn't believe I threw up. I was famous for my steel-lined stomach. A third-world childhood could give you that. Papi was worried enough that just as quick as Rafa could drop off the books we were on our way home. Mami fixed me one of her honey-and-onion concoctions and that made my stomach feel better. A week later we tried the library again and on this go-around I couldn't get the window open in time. When Papi got me home, he went and cleaned out the van himself, an expression of askho on his face. This was a big deal, since Papi almost never cleaned anything himself. He came back inside and found me sitting on the couch feeling like hell.

It's the car, he said to Mami. It's making him sick.

This time the damage was pretty minimal, nothing Papi couldn't wash off the door with a blast of the hose. He was pissed, though; he jammed his finger into my cheek, a nice solid thrust. That was the way he was with his punishments: imaginative. Earlier that year I'd written an essay in school called "My Father the Torturer," but the teacher made me write a new one. She thought I was kidding.

We drove the rest of the way to the Bronx in silence. We only stopped once, so I could brush my teeth. Mami had brought along my toothbrush and a tube of toothpaste and while every car known to man sped by us she stood outside with me so I wouldn't feel alone.

Tío Miguel was about seven feet tall and had his hair combed up and out, into a demi-fro. He gave me and Rafa big spleen-crushing hugs and then kissed Mami and finally ended up with Madai on his shoulder. The last time I'd seen Tío was at the airport, his first day in the United States. I remembered how he hadn't seemed all that troubled to be in another country.

He looked down at me. Carajo, Yunior, you look horrible!

He threw up, my brother explained.

I pushed Rafa. Thanks a lot, ass-face.

Hey, he said. Tío asked.

Tío clapped a bricklayer's hand on my shoulder. Everybody gets sick sometimes, he said. You should have seen me on the plane over here. Dios mio! He rolled his Asian-looking eyes for emphasis. I thought we were all going to die.

Everybody could tell he was lying. I smiled like he was making me feel better.

Do you want me to get you a drink? Tío asked. We got beer and rum.

Miguel, Mami said. He's young.

Young? Back in Santo Domingo, he'd be getting laid by now.

Mami thinned her lips, which took some doing.

Well, it's true, Tío said.

So, Mami, I said. When do I get to go visit the D.R.?

That's enough, Yunior.

It's the only pussy you'll ever get, Rafa said to me in English.

Not counting your girlfriend, of course.

Rafa smiled. He had to give me that one.

Papi came in from parking the van. He and Miguel gave each other the sort of handshakes that would have turned my fingers into Wonder bread.

Coño, compa'i, ¿cómo va todo? they said to each other.

Tía came out then, with an apron on and maybe the longest Lee Press-On Nails I've ever seen in my life. There was this one guru motherfucker in the *Guinness Book of World Records* who had longer nails, but I tell you, it was close. She gave everybody kisses, told me and Rafa how guapo we were—Rafa, of course, believed her—told Madai how bella she was, but when she got to Papi, she froze a little, like maybe she'd seen a wasp on the tip of his nose, but then kissed him all the same.

Mami told us to join the other kids in the living room. Tío said, Wait a minute, I want to show you the apartment. I was glad Tía said, Hold on, because from what I'd seen so far, the place had been furnished in Contemporary Dominican Tacky. The less I saw, the better. I mean, I liked plastic sofa covers but damn, Tío and Tía had taken it to another level. They had a disco ball hanging in the living room and the type of stucco ceilings that looked like stalactite heaven. The sofas all had golden tassels dangling from their edges. Tía came out of the kitchen with some people I didn't know and by the time she got done introducing everybody, only Papi and Mami were given the guided tour of the four-room third-floor apartment. Me and Rafa joined the kids in the living room. They'd already started eating. We were hungry, one of the girls explained, a pastelito in hand. The boy was about three years younger than me but the girl who'd spoken, Leti, was my age. She and another girl were on the sofa together and they were cute as hell.

Leti introduced them: the boy was her brother Wilquins and the other girl was her neighbor Mari. Leti had some serious tetas and I could tell that my brother was going to gun for her. His taste in girls was predictable. He sat down right between Leti and Mari and by the way they were smiling at him I knew he'd do fine. Neither of the girls gave me more than a cursory one-two, which didn't bother me. Sure, I liked girls but I was always too terrified to speak to them unless we were arguing or I was calling them stupidos, which was one of my favorite words that year. I turned to Wilquins and asked him what there was to do around here. Mari, who had the lowest voice I'd ever heard, said, He can't speak.

What does that mean?

He's mute.

I looked at Wilquins incredulously. He smiled and nodded, as if he'd won a prize or something.

Does he understand? I asked.

Of course he understands, Rafa said. He's not dumb.

I could tell Rafa had said that just to score points with the girls. Both of them nodded. Low-voice Mari said, He's the best student in his grade.

I thought, Not bad for a mute. I sat next to Wilquins. After about two seconds of TV Wilquins whipped out a bag of dominos and motioned to me. Did I want to play? Sure. Me and him played Rafa and Leti and we whupped their collective asses twice, which put Rafa in a real bad mood. He looked at me like maybe he wanted to take a swing, just one to make him feel better. Leti kept whispering into Rafa's ear, telling him it was OK.

In the kitchen I could hear my parents slipping into their usual modes. Papi's voice was loud and argumentative; you didn't have to be anywhere near him to catch his drift. And Mami, you had to put cups to your ears to hear hers. I went into the kitchen a few times—once so the tíos could show off how much bullshit I'd been able to cram in my head the last few years; another time for a bucket-sized cup of soda. Mami and Tía were frying tostones and the last of the pastelitos. She appeared happier now and the way her hands worked on our dinner you would think she had a life somewhere else making rare and precious things. She nudged Tia every now and then, shit they must have been doing all their lives. As soon as Mami saw me though, she gave me the eye. Don't stay long, that eye said. Don't piss your old man off.

Papi was too busy arguing about Elvis to notice me. Then somebody mentioned María Montez and Papi barked, María Montez? Let me tell *you* about María Montez, compa'i.

Maybe I was used to him. His voice—louder than most adults'—didn't bother me none, though the other kids shifted uneasily in their seats. Wilquins was about to raise the volume on the TV, but Rafa said, I wouldn't do that. Muteboy had balls, though. He did it anyway and then sat down. Wilquins's pop came into the living room a second later, a bottle of Presidente in hand. That dude must have had Spider-senses or something. Did you raise that? he asked Wilquins and Wilquins nodded.

Is this your house? his pops asked. He looked ready to beat Wilquins silly but he lowered the volume instead.

See, Rafa said. You nearly got your ass *kicked*.

I met the Puerto Rican woman right after Papi had gotten the van. He was taking me on short trips, trying to cure me of my vomiting. It wasn't really working but I looked forward to our trips, even though at the end of each one I'd be sick. These were the only times me and Papi did anything together. When we were alone he treated me much better, like maybe I was his son or something.

Before each drive Mami would cross me.

Bendición, Mami, I'd say.

She'd kiss my forehead. Que Dios te bendiga. And then she would give me a handful of mentas because she wanted me to be OK. Mami didn't think these excursions would cure anything, but the one time she had brought it up to Papi he had told her to shut up, what did she know about anything anyway?

Me and Papi didn't talk much. We just drove around our neighborhood. Occasionally he'd ask, How is it?

And I'd nod, no matter how I felt.

One day I was sick outside of Perth Amboy. Instead of taking me home he went the other way on Industrial Avenue, stopping a few minutes later in front of a light blue house I didn't recognize. It reminded me of the Easter eggs we colored at school, the ones we threw out the bus windows at other cars.

The Puerto Rican woman was there and she helped me clean up. She had dry papery hands and when she rubbed the towel on my chest, she did it hard, like I was a bumper she was waxing. She was very thin and had a cloud of brown hair rising above her narrow face and the sharpest blackest eyes you've ever seen.

He's cute, she said to Papi.

Not when he's throwing up, Papi said.

What's your name? she asked me. Are you Rafa?

I shook my head.

Then it's Yunior, right?

I nodded.

You're the smart one, she said, suddenly happy with herself. Maybe you want to see my books?

They weren't hers. I recognized them as ones my father must have left in her house. Papi was a voracious reader, couldn't even go cheating without a paperback in his pocket.

Why don't you go watch TV? Papi suggested. He was looking at her like she was the last piece of chicken on earth.

We got plenty of channels, she said. Use the remote if you want.

The two of them went upstairs and I was too scared of what was happening to poke around. I just sat there, ashamed, expecting something big and fiery to crash down on our heads. I watched a whole hour of the news before Papi came downstairs and said, Let's go.

About two hours later the women laid out the food and like always nobody but the kids thanked them. It must be some Dominican tradition or something. There was everything I liked—chicharrones, fried chicken, tostones, sancocho, rice, fried cheese, yuca, avocado, potato salad, a meteor-sized hunk of pernil, even a tossed salad which I could do without—but when I joined the other kids around the serving table, Papi said, Oh no you don't, and took the paper plate out of my hand. His fingers weren't gentle.

What's wrong now? Tia asked, handing me another plate.

He ain't eating, Papi said. Mami pretended to help Rafa with the pernil.

Why can't he eat?

Because I said so.

The adults who didn't know us made like they hadn't heard a thing and Tio just smiled sheepishly and told everybody to go ahead and eat. All the kids—about ten of them now—trooped back into the living room with their plates a-heaping and all the adults ducked into the kitchen and the dining room, where the radio was playing loud-ass bachatas. I was the only one without a plate. Papi stopped me before I could get away from him. He kept his voice nice and low so nobody else could hear him.

If you eat anything, I'm going to beat you. ¿Entiendes?

I nodded.

And if your brother gives you any food, I'll beat him too. Right here in front of everybody. ¿Entiendes?

I nodded again. I wanted to kill him and he must have sensed it because he gave my head a little shove.

All the kids watched me come in and sit down in front of the TV.

What's wrong with your dad? Leti asked.

He's a dick, I said.

Rafa shook his head. Don't say that shit in front of people.

Easy for you to be nice when you're eating, I said.

Hey, if I was a pukey little baby, I wouldn't get no food either.

I almost said something back but I concentrated on the TV. I wasn't going to start it. No fucking way. So I watched Bruce Lee beat Chuck Norris into the floor of the Colosseum and tried to pretend that there was no food anywhere in the house. It was Tia who finally saved me. She came into the living room and said, since you ain't eating, Yunior, you can at least help me get some ice.

I didn't want to, but she mistook my reluctance for something else.

I already asked your father.

She held my hand while we walked; Tia didn't have any kids but I could tell she wanted them. She was the sort of relative who always remembered your birthday but who you only went to visit because you had to. We didn't get past the first-floor landing before she opened her pocketbook and handed me the first of three pastelitos she had smuggled out of the apartment.

Go ahead, she said. And as soon as you get inside make sure you brush your teeth.

Thanks a lot, Tía, I said.

Those pastelitos didn't stand a chance.

She sat next to me on the stairs and smoked her cigarette. All the way down on the first floor and we could still hear the music and the adults and the television. Tía looked a ton like Mami; the two of them were both short and light-skinned. Tía smiled a lot and that was what set them apart the most.

How is it at home, Yunior?

What do you mean?

How's it going in the apartment? Are you kids OK?

I knew an interrogation when I heard one, no matter how sugar-coated it was. I didn't say anything. Don't get me wrong, I loved my tía, but something told me to keep my mouth shut. Maybe it was family loyalty, maybe I just wanted to protect Mami or I was afraid that Papi would find out—it could have been anything really.

Is your mom all right?

I shrugged.

Have there been lots of fights?

None, I said. Too many shrugs would have been just as bad as an answer. Papi's at work too much.

Work, Tía said, like it was somebody's name she didn't like.

Me and Rafa, we didn't talk much about the Puerto Rican woman. When we ate dinner at her house, the few times Papi had taken us over there, we still acted like nothing was out of the ordinary. Pass the ketchup, man. No sweat, bro. The affair was like a hole in our living room floor, one we'd gotten so used to circumnavigating that we sometimes forgot it was there.

By midnight all the adults were crazy dancing. I was sitting outside Tía's bedroom—where Madai was sleeping—trying not to attract attention. Rafa had me guarding the door; he and Leti were in there too, with some of the other kids, getting busy no doubt. Wilquins had gone across the hall to bed so I had me and the roaches to mess around with.

Whenever I peered into the main room I saw about twenty moms and dads dancing and drinking beers. Every now and then somebody yelled, ¡Quisqueya! And then everybody else would yell and stomp their feet. From what I could see my parents seemed to be enjoying themselves.

Mami and Tía spent a lot of time side by side, whispering, and I kept expecting something to come of this, a brawl maybe. I'd never once been out with my family when it hadn't turned to shit. We weren't even theatrical or straight crazy like other families. We fought like sixth-graders,

without any real dignity. I guess the whole night I'd been waiting for a blowup, something between Papi and Mami. This was how I always figured Papi would be exposed, out in public, where everybody would know.
You're a cheater!

But everything was calmer than usual. And Mami didn't look like she was about to say anything to Papi. The two of them danced every now and then but they never lasted more than a song before Mami joined Tía again in whatever conversation they were having.

I tried to imagine Mami before Papi. Maybe I was tired, or just sad, thinking about the way my family was. Maybe I already knew how it would all end up in a few years, Mami without Papi, and that was why I did it. Picturing her alone wasn't easy. It seemed like Papi had always been with her, even when we were waiting in Santo Domingo for him to send for us.

The only photograph our family had of Mami as a young woman, before she married Papi, was the one that somebody took of her at an election party that I found one day while rummaging for money to go to the arcade. Mami had it tucked into her immigration papers. In the photo, she's surrounded by laughing cousins I will never meet, who are all shiny from dancing, whose clothes are rumpled and loose. You can tell it's night and hot and that the mosquitos have been biting. She sits straight and even in a crowd she stands out, smiling quietly like maybe she's the one everybody's celebrating. You can't see her hands but I imagined they're knotting a straw or a bit of thread. This was the woman my father met a year later on the Malecón, the woman Mami thought she'd always be.

Mami must have caught me studying her because she stopped what she was doing and gave me a smile, maybe her first one of the night. Suddenly I wanted to go over and hug her, for no other reason than I loved her, but there were about eleven fat jiggling bodies between us. So I sat down on the tiled floor and waited.

I must have fallen asleep because the next thing I knew Rafa was kicking me and saying, Let's go. He looked like he'd been hitting those girls off; he was all smiles. I got to my feet in time to kiss Tía and Tío good-bye. Mami was holding the serving dish she had brought with her.

Where's Papi? I asked.

He's downstairs, bringing the van around. Mami leaned down to kiss me.

You were good today, she said.

And then Papi burst in and told us to get the hell downstairs before some pendejo cop gave him a ticket. More kisses, more handshakes and then we were gone.

I don't remember being out of sorts after I met the Puerto Rican woman, but I must have been because Mami only asked me questions when she thought something was wrong in my life. It took her about ten passes but finally she cornered me one afternoon when we were alone in the apartment. Our upstairs neighbors were beating the crap out of their kids, and me and her had been listening to it all afternoon. She put her hand on mine and said, Is everything OK, Yunior? Have you been fighting with your brother?

Me and Rafa had already talked. We'd been in the basement, where our parents couldn't hear us. He told me that yeah, he knew about her.

Papi's taken me there twice now, he said.

Why didn't you tell me? I asked.

What the hell was I going to say? *Hey, Yunior, guess what happened yesterday? I met Papi's sucia!*

I didn't say anything to Mami either. She watched me, very very closely. Later I would think, maybe if I had told her, she would have confronted him, would have done something, but who can know these things? I said I'd been having trouble in school and like that everything was back to normal between us. She put her hand on my shoulder and squeezed and that was that.

We were on the turnpike, just past Exit 11, when I started feeling it again. I sat up from leaning against Rafa. His fingers smelled and he'd gone to sleep almost as soon as he got into the van. Madai was out too but at least she wasn't snoring.

In the darkness, I saw that Papi had a hand on Mami's knee and that the two of them were quiet and still. They weren't slumped back or anything; they were both wide awake, bolted into their seats. I couldn't see either of their faces and no matter how hard I tried I couldn't imagine their expressions. Neither of them moved. Every now and then the van was filled with the bright rush of somebody else's headlights. Finally I said, Mami, and they both looked back, already knowing what was happening.

Every Tongue Shall Confess

ZZ PACKER

As Pastor Everett made the announcements that began the service, Clareese Mitchell stood with her choir members, knowing that once again she had to Persevere, put on the Strong Armor of God, the Breastplate of Righteousness, but she was having her monthly womanly troubles and all she wanted to do was curse the Brothers' Church Council of Greater Christ Emmanuel Pentecostal Church of the Fire Baptized, who'd decided that the Sisters had to wear *white* every Missionary Sunday, which was, of course, the day of the month when her womanly troubles were always at their absolute worst! And to think that the Brothers' Church Council of Greater Christ Emmanuel Pentecostal Church of the Fire Baptized had been the first place she'd looked for guidance and companionship nearly ten years ago when her aunt Alma had fallen ill. And why not? They were God-fearing, churchgoing men; men like Deacon Julian Jeffers, now sitting in the first row of pews, closest to the altar, right under the leafy top of the corn plant she'd brought in to make the sanctuary more homey. Two months ago she'd been reading the book of Micah and posed the idea of a Book of Micah discussion group to the Deacon Jeffers and he'd said, "Oh, Sister Clareese! We should make *you* a deacon!" Which of course they didn't. Deacons, like pastors, were men—not that she was complaining. But it still rankled that Jeffers had said he'd get back to her about the Micah discussion group and he never had.

Clareese's cross-eyes roved to the back of the church where Sister Drusclla and Sister Maxwell sat, resplendent in their identical wide-brimmed, purple-flowered hats, their unsaved guests sitting next to them. The guests wore frightened smiles, and Clareese tried to shoot them reassuring looks. The gold-lettered banner behind them read: "We Are More Than Conquerors in Christ Our Lord," and she tried to use this as a focal point. But her cross-eyes couldn't help it; they settled, at last, on Deacon McCreedy, making his way down the aisle for the second time. Oh, how she hated him!

She would never forget—never, never, never—the day he came to the hospital where she worked; she was still wearing her white nurse's uniform and he'd said he was concerned about her spiritual well-being—*Liar!*—then drove her to where she lived with her aunt Alma, whose room resounded with perpetual snores and hacking and wheezing—as if Clareese didn't have enough of this at the hospital—and while Alma slept, Clareese poured Deacon McCreedy some fruit punch, which he drank between forkfuls of chicken, plus half their pork roast. No sooner than he'd wiped his hands on the napkin—didn't bother using a fork—he stood and walked behind her, covering her cross-eyes as though she were a child, as though he were about to give her a gift—a Bible with her very own name engraved on it, perhaps—but he didn't give her anything, he'd just covered her wandering eyes and said, "Sing 'On Christ the Solid Rock I Stand.' Make sure to do the Waterfall." And she was happy to do it, happy to please Deacon McCreedy, so she began singing in her best, cleanest voice until she felt his hand slide up the scratchy white pantyhose of her nurse's uniform and up toward the control-top of her pantyhose. Before she could stop him, one finger was wriggling around inside, and by then it was too late to tell him she was having her monthly womanly troubles. He drew back in disgust—no, *hatred*—then rinsed his hand in the kitchen sink and left without saying a word, not a thanks for the chicken or the pork roast or her singing. Not a single word of apology for anything. But she could have forgiven him—if Sisters could even forgive Deacons—for she could have understood that an unmarried man might have *needs*, but what really bothered her was how he ignored her. How a few weeks later she and Aunt Alma had been waiting for the bus after Wednesday-night prayer meeting and he *drove past*. That's right. No offer of a ride, no slowing down, no nothing. Aunt Alma was nearly blind and couldn't even see it was him, but Clareese recognized his car at once.

Yes, she wanted to curse the Brothers' Church Council of Greater Christ Emmanuel Pentecostal Church of the Fire Baptized, but Sisters and Brothers could not curse, could not even swear or take an oath, for *neither shalt thou swear by thy head, because thou canst not make one hair white or black*. So no oath, no swearing, and of course no betting—an extension of swearing—which was why she'd told the other nurses at University Hospital that she would not join their betting pool to predict who would get married first, Patty or Edwina. She told them about the black and white hairs and all Nurse Holloway did was clomp her pumps—as if she was too good for the standard orthopedically correct shoes—down the green tiles of the hall and shout behind her back, "Somebody sure needs to get laid." Oh, how the other RNs tittered in their gossipy way.

Now everyone applauded when Pastor Everett announced that Sister Nina would be getting married to Harold, one of the Brothers from Broadway Tongues of Spirit Church. Then Pastor Everett said, "Sister Nina will be holding a Council so we can get husbands for the rest of the hardworking Sisters." Like Sister Clareese, is what he meant. The congregation laughed at the joke. Ha ha. And perhaps the joke *was* on her. If she'd been married, Deacon McCreedy wouldn't have dared do what he did; if she'd been married perhaps she'd also be working fewer shifts at the hospital, perhaps she would have never met that patient—that man—who'd almost gotten her fired! And at exactly that moment, it hit her, right below the gut, a sharp pain, and she imagined her uterus, that Texas-shaped organ, the Rio Grande of her monthly womanly troubles flushing out to the Gulf.

Pastor Everett had finished the announcements. Now it was time for testimony service. She tried to distract herself by thinking of suitable testimonies. Usually she testified about work. Last week, she'd testified about the poor man with a platelet count of seven, meaning he was a goner, and how Nurse Holloway had told him, "We're bringing you more platelets," and how he'd said, "That's all right. God sent me more." No one at the nurses' station—to say nothing of those atheist doctors—believed him. But when Nurse Holloway checked, sure enough, Glory be to God, he had a count of sixteen. Clareese told the congregation how she knelt on the cold tiled floor of University Hospital's corridor, right then and there, arms outstretched to Glory. And what could the other nurses say to that? Nothing, that's what.

She remembered her testimony from a month ago, how she'd been working the hotline, and a mother had called to say that her son had eaten ants, and Sister Clareese had assured the woman that ants were God's creatures, and though disturbing, they wouldn't harm the boy. But the Lord told Clareese to stay on the line with the mother, not to rush the way other nurses often did, so Clareese stayed on the line. And Glory be to God that she did! Once the mother had calmed down she'd said, "Thank goodness. The insecticide I gave Kevin must have worked." Sister Clareese had stayed after her shift to make sure the woman brought her boy into Emergency. Afterward she told the woman to hold hands with Kevin and give God the Praise he deserved.

But she had told these stories already. As she fidgeted in her choir-mistress's chair, she tried to think of new ones. The congregation wouldn't care about how she had to stay on top of codes, or how she had to triple-check patients' charts. The only patients who stuck in her mind were Mrs. Geneva Bosma, whose toe was rotting off, and Mr. Toomey, who had prostate cancer. And, of course, Mr. Cleophus Sanders, the cause of all her current problems. Cleophus was an amputee who liked to turn the volume of his television up so high that his channel-surfing sounded as if someone were being electrocuted, repeatedly. At the nurses' station she'd overheard that Cleophus Sanders was once a musician who in his heyday went by the nickname "Delta Sweetmeat." But he'd gone in and out of the music business, sometimes taking construction jobs. A crane had fallen on his leg and he'd been amputated from the below the knee. No, none of these cases was Edifying in God's sight. Her run-in with Cleophus had been downright un-Edifying.

When Mr. Sanders had been moved into Mr. Toomey's room last Monday, she'd told them both, "I hope everyone has a blessed day!" She'd made sure to say this only after she was safely inside with the door closed behind her. She had to make sure she didn't mention God until the door was closed *behind* her, because Nurse Holloway was always clomping about, trying to say that this was a *university* hospital, as well as a *research* hospital, one at the very *forefront* of medicine, and didn't Registered Nurse Clareese Mitchell recognize and *respect* that not everyone shared her beliefs? That the hospital catered not only to Christians, but to people of the Jewish faith? To Muslims, Hindus, and agnostics? Atheists, even?

This Clareese knew only too well, which was why it was all the more important for her to Spread the Gospel. So she shut the door, and said to Mr. Toomey, louder this time, "I HOPE EVERYONE HAS A BLESSED DAY!"

Mr. Toomey grunted. Heavy and completely white, he reminded Sister Clareese of a walrus: everything about him drooped, his eyes like twin frowns, his nose, perhaps even his mouth, though it was hard to make out because of his frowning blond mustache. Well, Glory be to God, she expected something like a grunt from him, she couldn't say she was surprised: junkies who detox scream and writhe before turning clean; the man with a hangover does not like to wake to the sun. So it was with sinners exposed to the harsh, curing Light of the Lord.

"Hey, sanctified lady!" Cleophus Sanders called from across the room. "He got cancer! Let the man alone."

"I *know* what he *has*," Sister Clareese said. "I'm his *nurse*." This wasn't how she wanted the patient-RN relationship to begin, but Cleophus had gotten the better of her. Yes, that was the problem, wasn't it? *He'd* gotten the better of *her*. This was how Satan worked, throwing you off a little at a time. She would have to Persevere, put on the Strong Armor of God. She tried again.

"My name is Sister Clareese Mitchell, your assigned registered nurse. I can't exactly say that I'm pleased to meet you, because that would be a lie and 'lying lips are an abomination to the Lord.' I will say that I am pleased to do my duty and help you recover."

"*Me oh my!*" Cleophus Sanders said, and he laughed big and long, the kind of laughter that could go on and on, rising and rising, restarting itself if need be, like yeast. He slapped the knee of his amputated leg, the knee that would probably come off if his infection didn't stop eating away at it. But Cleophus Sanders didn't care. He just slapped that infected knee, hooting all the while in an ornery, backwoods kind of way that made Clareese want to hit him. But of course she would never, never do that.

She busied herself by changing Mr. Toomey's catheter, then remaking his bed, rolling the walrus of him this way and that, with little help on his part. As soon as she was done with Mr. Toomey, he turned on the Knicks game. The whole time she'd changed Mr. Toomey's catheter, however, Cleophus had watched her, laughing under his breath, then outright, a waxing and waning of hilarity as if her every gesture were laughably prim and proper.

"Look, Mr. *Cleophus Sanders*," she said, glad for the chance to bite on the ridiculous name, "I am a professional. You may laugh at what I do, but in doing so you laugh at the Almighty who has given me the breath to do it!"

She'd steeled herself for a vulgar reply. But no. Mr. Toomey did the talking.

"I tell *you* what!" Mr. Toomey said, pointing his remote at Sister Clareese, "I'm going to sue this hospital for lack of peace and quiet. All your 'Almighty this' and 'Oh Glory that' is keeping me from watching the game!"

So Sister Clareese murmured her apologies to Mr. Toomey, the whole while Cleophus Sanders put on an act of restraining his amusement, body and bed quaking in seizure-like fits.

Now sunlight filtered through the yellow-tinted windows of Greater Christ Emmanuel Pentecostal Church of the Fire Baptized, lighting Brother Hopkins, the organist, with a halo-like glow. The rest of the congregation had given their testimonies, and it was now time for the choir members to testify, starting with Clareese. Was there any way she could possibly turn her incident with Cleophus Sanders into an edifying testimony experience? Just then, another hit, and she felt a cramping so hard she thought she might double over. It was her turn. Cleophus's laughter and her cramping womb seemed one and the same; he'd inhabited her body like a demon, preventing her from thinking up a proper testimony. As she rose, unsteadily, to her feet, all she managed to say was, "Pray for me."

It was almost time for Pastor Everett to preach his sermon. To introduce it, Sister Clareese had the choir sing "Every Knee Shall Bow, Every Tongue Shall Confess." It was an old fashioned hymn, unlike the hopped-up gospel songs churches were given to nowadays. And she liked the slow unfolding of its message: how without people uttering a word, all their hearts would be made plain to the Lord; that He would know you not by what you said or did, but by what you'd hoped and intended. The teens, however, mumbled over the verses, and older choir members sang without vigor. The hymn ended up sounding like the national anthem at a school assembly: a stouthearted song rendered in monotone.

"Thank you, thank you, thank you, Sister Clareese," Pastor Everett said, looking back at her, "for that wonderful tune."

Tune? She knew that Pastor Everett thought she was not the kind of person a choirmistress should be; she was quiet, nervous, skinny in all the wrong places, and completely cross-eyed. She knew he thought of her as something worse than a spinster, because she wasn't yet old.

Pastor Everett hunched close to the microphone, as though about to begin a forlorn love song. From the corners of her vision she saw him smile—only for a second but with every single tooth in his mouth. He was yam-colored, and given to wearing epaulets on the shoulders of his robes and gold braiding all down the front. Sister Clareese felt no attraction to him, but she seemed to be the only one who didn't; even the Sisters going on eighty were charmed by Pastor Everett, who, though not entirely handsome, had handsome moments.

"Sister Clareese," he said, turning to where she stood with the choir. "Sister Clareese, I know y'all just sang for us, but I need some *more* help. Satan got these Brothers and Sisters putting m'Lord on hold!"

Sister Clareese knew that everyone expected her and her choir to begin singing again, but she had been alerted to what he was up to; he had called her yesterday. He had thought nothing of asking her to un-plug her telephone—her *only* telephone, her *private* line—to bring it to church so that he could use it in some sermon about call-waiting. Hadn't even asked her how she was doing, hadn't bothered to pray over her aunt Alma's sickness. Nevertheless, she'd said, "Why certainly, Pastor Everett. Anything I can do to help."

Now Sister Clareese produced her Princess telephone from under her seat and handed it to the Pastor. Pastor Everett held the telephone aloft, shaking it as if to rid it of demons. "How many of y'all—Brothers and Sisters—got telephones?" the Pastor asked.

One by one, members of the congregation timidly raised their hands.

"All right," Pastor Everett said, as though this grieved him, "almost all of y'all." He flipped through his huge pulpit Bible. "How many of y'all—Brothers and Sisters—got call-waiting?" He turned pages quickly, then stopped, as though he didn't need to search the scripture after all. "Let me tell ya," the Pastor said, nearly kissing the microphone, "there is *Someone!* Who won't *accept* your call-waiting! There is *Someone!* Who won't *wait*, when you put Him on hold!" Sister Nancy Popwell and Sister Drusella Davies now had their eyes closed in concentration, their hands waving slowly in the air in front of them as though they were trying to make their way through a dark room.

The last phone call Sister Clareese had made was on Wednesday, to Mr. Toomey. She knew both he and Cleophus were likely to reject the Lord, but she had a policy of sorts, which was to call patients who'd been in her care for at least a week. She considered it her Christian duty to call—even on her day off—to let them know that Jesus cared, and that she cared. The other RNs resorted to callous catchphrases that they bandied about the nurses' station: "Just because I care *for* them doesn't mean I have to care *about* them," or, "I'm a nurse, not a nursery." Not Clareese. Perhaps she'd been curt with Cleophus Sanders, but she had been so in defense of God. Perhaps Mr. Toomey had been curt with her, but he was going into O.R. soon, and grouchiness was to be expected.

Nurse Patty had been switchboard operator that night and Clareese had had to endure her sighs before the girl finally connected her to Mr. Toomey.

"Praise the Lord, Mr. Toomey!"

"Who's this?"

"This is your nurse, Sister Clareese, and I'm calling to say that Jesus will be with you through your surgery."

"Who?"

"Jesus," she said.

She thought she heard the phone disconnect, then, a voice. Of course. Cleophus Sanders.

"Why ain't you called *me*?" Cleophus said.

Sister Clareese tried to explain her policy, the thing about the week.

"So you care more about some white dude than you care about good ol' Cleophus?"

"It's not that, Mr. Sanders, God cares for white and black alike. Acts 10:34 says, 'God is no respecter of persons.' Black or white. Red, purple, or green—he doesn't care, as long as you accept his salvation and live right." When he was silent on the other end she said, "It's that I've only known you for two days. I'll see you tomorrow."

She tried to hang up, but he said, "Let me play something for you. Something interesting, since all you probably listen to is monks chanting and such."

Before she could respond, there was a noise on the other end that sounded like juke music. Then he came back on the phone and said, "Like that, don't you?"

"I had the phone away from my ear."

"I thought you said 'lying is the abominable.' Do you like or do you don't?" When she said nothing he said, "Truth, now."

She answered yes.

She didn't want to answer yes. But she also didn't want to lie. And what was one to do in that circumstance? If God looked into your heart right then, what would He think? Or would He have to approve because He made your heart that way? Or were you obliged to train it against its wishes? She didn't know what to think, but on the other end Cleophus said, "What you just heard there was the blues. What you just heard there was me."

"...Let me tell ya!" Pastor Everett shouted, his voice hitting its highest octave, "*Jeeeee-zus*— did not *tell* his *Daddy*—'I'm sorry, Pops, but my girlfriend is on the other line'; *Jeeeee-zus*—never *told* the Omnipotent One, 'Can you wait a sec, I think I got a call from the electric company!' *Jeeeeeee-zus*—never told Matthew, Mark, Luke, or John, 'I'm *sorry*, but I got to put you on hold; I'm sorry, Brother Luke, but I got some mac and cheese in the oven; I'm *sorry*, but I got to eat this fried chicken'"—and at this, Pastor Everett paused, grinning in anticipation of his own punch line—"'cause it's finger-licking good!'"

Drops of sweat plunked onto his microphone.

Sister Clareese watched as the congregation cheered, the women flagging their Bibles in the air as though the Bibles were as light and yielding as handkerchiefs; their bosoms jouncing as though they were harboring sacks of potatoes in their blouses. They shook tambourines, scores of them all going at once, the sound of something sizzling and frying.

That was it? That was The Message? Of course, she'd only heard part of it, but still. Of course she believed that one's daily life shouldn't outstrip one's spiritual one, but there seemed no place for true belief at Greater Christ Emmanuel Pentecostal Church of the Fire Baptized. Everyone wanted flash and props, no one wanted the Word itself, naked in its fiery glory.

Most of the Brothers and Sisters were up on their feet. "Tell it!" yelled some, while others called out, "Go 'head on!" The organist pounded out the chords to what could have been the theme song of a TV game show.

She looked to see what Sister Drusella's and Sister Maxwell's unsaved guests were doing. Drusella's unsaved guest was her son, which made him easy to bring into the fold: he was living in her shed and had no car. He was busy turning over one of the cardboard fans donated by Hamblin and Sons Funeral Parlor, reading the words intently, then flipping it over again to stare at the picture of a gleaming casket and grieving family. Sister Donna Maxwell's guest was an ex-con she'd written to and tried to save while he was in prison. The ex-con seemed to watch the scene with approval, though one could never really know what was going on in the criminal mind. For all Sister Clareese knew, he could be counting all the pockets he planned to pick.

And they called themselves missionaries. Family members and ex-cons were easy to convince of God's will. As soon as Drusella's son took note of the pretty young Sisters his age, he'd be back. And everyone knew you could convert an ex-con with a few well-timed pecan pies.

Wednesday was her only day off besides Sunday, and though a phone call or two was her policy on days off, she very seldom visited the hospital. And yet, last Wednesday, she'd had to. The more she'd considered Cleophus's situation—his loss of limb, his devil's music, his unsettling laughter—the more she grew convinced that he was her Missionary Challenge. That he was especially in need of Saving.

Minutes after she'd talked with him on the phone, she took the number 42 bus and transferred to the crosstown H, then walked the rest of the way to the hospital.

Edwina had taken over for Patty as nurses' station attendant, and she'd said, "We have an ETOH in—where's your uniform?"

"It's not my shift," she called behind her as she rushed past Edwina and into Room 204.

She opened the door to find Cleophus sitting on the bed, still plucking chords on his unplugged electric guitar that she'd heard him playing over the phone half an hour earlier. Mr. Toomey's bed was empty; one of the nurses must have already taken him to O.R., so Cleophus had the room to himself. The right leg of Cleophus's hospital pants hung down limp and empty, and it was the first time she'd seen his guitar, curvy and shiny as a sportscar. He did not acknowledge her when she entered. He was still picking away at his guitar, singing a song about a man whose woman had left him so high and dry, she'd taken the car, the dog, the furniture. Even the wallpaper. Only when he'd strummed the final chords did Cleophus look up, as if noticing her for the first time.

"Sister *Clare-reeeese!*" He said it as if he were introducing a showgirl.

"It's your soul," Clareese said. "God wants me to help save your soul." The urgency of God's message struck her so hard, she felt the wind knocked out of her. She sat on the bed next to him.

"Really?" he said, cocking his head a little.

"Really and truly," Clareese said, "I know I said I liked your music, but I said it because God gave you that gift for you to use. For Him."

"Uhnn-huh," Cleophus said. "How about this, little lady. How about if God lets me keep this knee, I'll come to church with you. We can go out and get some dinner afterwards. Like a proper couple."

She tried not to be flattered. "The Lord does *not make* deals, Mr. Sanders. But I'm sure the Lord would love to see you in church regardless of what happens to your knee."

"Well, since you seem to be His receptionist, how about you ask the Lord if he can give you the day off. I can take you out on the town. See, if I go to church, I *know* the Lord won't show. But I'm positive you will."

"Believe you me, Mr. Sanders, the Lord is at every service. *Where two or three are gathered together in my name, there am I in the midst of them.*" She sighed, trying to remember what she came to say. *"He is the Way, the Truth and the Life. No man—"*

"*...cometh to the father,*"Cleophus said, *"but by me."*

She looked at him. "You know your Bible."

"Naw. You were speaking and I just heard it." He absently strummed his guitar. "You were talking, saying that verse, and the rest of it came to me. Not even a voice," he said, "more like...kind of like music."

She stared. Her hands clapped his, preventing him from playing further. For a moment, she was breathless. He looked at her, suddenly seeming to comprehend what he'd just said, that the Lord had actually spoken to him. For a minute, they sat there, both overjoyed at what the Lord had done, but then he had to go ruin it. He burst out laughing his biggest, most sinful laugh yet.

"Awww!" he cried, doubled over, and then flopped backward onto his hospital bed. Then he closed his eyes, laughing without sound.

She stood up, chest heaving, wondering why she even bothered with him.

"Clareese," he said, trying to clear his voice of any leftover laughter, "don't go." He looked at her with pleading eyes, then patted the space beside him on the bed.

She looked around the room for some cue. Whenever she needed an answer, she relied on some sign from the Lord; a fresh beam of sunlight through the window, the hands of a clock folded in prayer, or the flush of a commode. These were signs that whatever she was thinking of doing was right. If there was a storm cloud, or something in her path, then that was a bad sign. But nothing in the room gave her any indication whether she should stay and witness to Mr. Sanders, or go.

"What, Mr. Sanders, do you want from me? It's my day off. I decided to come by and offer you an invitation to my church because God has given you a gift. A musical gift." She dug into her purse, then pulled out a pocket-sized Bible. "But I'll leave you with this. If you need to find us— our church—the name and number is printed inside."

He took the Bible with a little smile, turning it over, then flipping through it, as if some money might be tucked away inside. "Seriously, though," he'd said, "let me ask you a question that's gonna seem dumb. Childish. Now, I want you to think long and hard about it. Why the hell's there so much suffering in the world if God's doing his job? I mean, look at me. Take old Toomey, too. We done anything *that* bad to deserve all this put on us?"

She sighed. "Because of people, that's why. Not God. It's *people* who allow suffering, people who create it. Perpetrate it."

"Maybe that explains Hitler and all them others, but I'm talking about—" He gestured at the room, the hospital in general.

Clareese tried to see what he saw when he looked at the room. At one time, the white and pale green walls of the hospital rooms had given her solace; the way everything was clean, clean, clean; the many patients that had been in each room, some nice, some dying, some willing to accept the Lord. But most, like Mr. Toomey, cast the Lord aside like wilted lettuce, and now the clean hospital room was just a reminder of the emptiness, the barrenness, of her patients' souls. Cleophus Sanders was just another patient who disrespected the Lord.

"Why does He allow natural disasters to kill people?" Clareese said, knowing that her voice was raised louder than what she meant it to be. "Why are little children born to get some rare blood disease and die? Why," she yelled, waving her arms, "does a crane fall on your leg and smash it? I don't know, Mr. Sanders. And I don't like it. But I'll say this! No one has a *right* to live! The only right we have is to die. That's it! If you get plucked out of the universe and given a chance to become a life, that's more than not having become anything at all, and for that, Mr. Sanders, you should be grateful!"

She had not known where this last bit had come from, and, she could tell, neither had he, but she could hear the other nurses coming down the hall to see who was yelling, and though Cleophus Sanders looked to have more pity on his face than true belief, he had come after her when she turned to leave. She'd heard the clatter of him gathering his crutches, and even when she heard the meaty weight of him slam onto the floor, she did not turn back. Then there it was. Pastor Everett's silly motion of cupping his hand to his ear, like he was eavesdropping on the choir, his signal that he was waiting for Sister Clareese to sing her solo, waiting to hear the voice that would send the congregation shouting, "Thank you, Jesus, Blessed Savior!"

How could she do it. She thought of Cleophus on the floor and felt ashamed. She hadn't seen him since; her yelling had been brought to the attention of the administrators, and although the hospital was understaffed, the administration had suggested that she not return until next week. They handed her the card of the staff psychiatrist. She had not told anyone at church what had happened. Not even her aunt Alma.

She didn't want to sing. Didn't feel like it, but, she thought, *I will freely sacrifice myself unto Thee: I will praise Thy name, O Lord, for it is good.* Usually thinking of a scripture would give her strength, but this time it just made her realize how much strength she was always needing.

She didn't want to, but she'd do it. She'd sing a stupid solo part—the Waterfall, they called it—not even something she'd *invented* or *planned* to do who knows how many years ago when she'd had to sneeze her brains out, but oh no, she'd tried holding it in, and when she had to sing her solo, those years ago, her near-sneeze had made the words come out tumbling in a series of staccato notes that were almost fluid, and ever since then, she'd had to sing *all* solos that way, it was expected of her, everyone loved it, it was her trademark, she sang: "All-hall other-her her groooouund—is sink-king sand!"

The congregation applauded.

"Saints," the Pastor said, winding down, "you know this world will soon be *over!* Jesus will come back to this tired, sorry Earth in *a moment and a twinkling of an eye!* So you can't use call-waiting on the Lord! *Jeeee-zus,* my friends, does not accept conference calls! You are Children of God! You need to PRAY! Put down your phone! Say goodbye to AT&T! You cannot go in God's *direction,* without a little—*genuflection!*"

The congregation went wild, clapping and banging tambourines, whirling in the aisles. But the choir remained standing in case Pastor Everett wanted another song. For the first time, Clareese found that her monthly troubles had settled down. And now that she had the wherewithal to concentrate, she couldn't. Her cross-eyes wouldn't keep steady, they roamed like the wheels of a defective shopping cart, and from one roving eye she saw her aunt Alma, waving her arms as though listening to leftover strains of Clareese's solo.

What would she do? She didn't know if she'd still have her job when she went back on Monday, didn't know what the staff psychiatrist would try to pry out of her. More important, she didn't know what her aunt Alma would do without the special medical referrals Clareese could get her. What was a Sister to do?

Clareese's gaze must have found him just a moment after everyone else's had. A stranger at the far end of the aisle, standing directly opposite Pastor Everett as though about to engage him in a duel. There was

Cleophus Sanders with his crutches, the right leg of his pinstriped pants hollow, wagging after him. Over his shoulder was a strap, attached to which was his guitar. Even Deacon McCreedy was looking.

What in heaven's name was Cleophus doing here? To bring his soul to salvation? To ridicule her? For another argument? Perhaps the doctors had told him he did not need the operation after all, and Cleophus was keeping his end of the deal with God. But he didn't seem like the type to keep promises. She saw his eyes search the congregation, and when he saw her, they locked eyes as if he had come to claim her. He did not come to get Saved, didn't care about his soul in that way, all he cared about was—

Now she knew why he'd come. He'd come for her. He'd come *despite* what she'd told him, despite his disbelief. Anyhow, she disapproved. It was God he needed, not her. Nevertheless, she remained standing for a few moments, even after the rest of the choir had already seated themselves, waving their cardboard fans to cool their sweaty faces.

◆

Following the Notes

PIA Z. EHRHARDT

In high school I had a job as the hostess at The Trawler, a seafood restaurant at Esplanade Mall. My battery went dead and my father had to come to the mall parking lot to give me a jump. He dug for the cables in his trunk, pissed that he'd been called away from the new piece of music he was writing at home. It was Father's Day and what he'd asked for was for a quiet house and lemon pie for dessert.

"You left the headlights on?" he said.

"The passenger light," I said, pointing at the back seat. "Door wasn't shut all the way."

"Who was in the back?" he said. "I thought you were driving to work and home, only."

My daily comings and goings were charted in the kitchen, reviewed when I got back in the evening. I had the use of a Buick Century as long as I kept it filled with gas, washed it once a week in our driveway with mild detergent, and didn't joy ride with my friends.

"Sorry for the inconvenience," I said

"Don't be a smart-ass." He clipped the cables on the battery. "Get in and rev the engine when I tell you."

The parking lot was dark. Some of my co-workers stood outside under the street lamp, smoking. Bugs were flying in from everywhere to swarm in the light.

My father raised his arm for me to step on the gas.

Sherman's sweatshirt lay on the back seat, where he'd stripped it off. We'd had sex there before my shift, at the far edge of the parking lot, then switched shirts for the day. He wanted my Sacred Heart tee so he could show off the muscles he was sculpting for me. That's what he'd said. I wore his faded Ninja Turtles tee, had it stuffed into my jeans. Washed a thousand times, so smooth against my skin. I zipped my jacket to my neck so my father wouldn't see.

"This isn't working," he said. "There's no juice."

I drove home with him in his old green Mercedes. Sometimes he let me drive this car. Last week I'd taken Sherman for an evening drive out in Richburg Hills to look at the twinkling lights of the power plant. Oz. The front seat was a bench and Sherman scooted next to me, his hand restless on my leg.

My father whistled what he'd been working on when I called for help. We caught every red light. I smelled like cigarette smoke and sex with a busy top layer of peppermint Tic Tac. Half a box in my mouth.

"You didn't leave the house in that shirt," he said.

"Grease stain," I mumbled. "I borrowed someone's."

Bugs out of nowhere dove into the windshield. "Is Mom feeling better?" I said. She'd been in bed when I'd left that morning, said she had a cold, but I knew it was a hangover. I'd rinsed out her mug and it smelled like scotch.

"She's okay," he said. He pressed the washer button but nothing came out.

"I showed you how to fill this." The wipers squeaked across the dry windshield, smudging the spots into a mess. "Goddammit, Liddie," he said. "I can't see."

I knew what to do to make him forget my screw-ups. I simply placed him right there in the palm of my hand. "What were you working on before I interrupted?"

He told me too much, like he'd been waiting all day for someone to ask. "A choral piece—SATB—with woodwinds. I'm setting a John Ashbery poem. *The Grapevine.*" He falsettoed the soprano part because it carried the melody.

"Lyrical," I said.

My father's readiness made me sad. The guys I liked used just a few words to explain what they meant, left the rest mysterious, but my father answered anything I asked like he had one chance left on earth.

He leaned forward, squinting through the streaks, and asked me to be another set of eyes and help get us home safely.

"Why don't we pull into a gas station, Dad? I'll get out and clean."

I called Sherman when I got home to tell him about my dead battery, but he didn't have time to talk. I heard a giggle in the background and he said it was his sister, but I knew.

For dinner we had my father's favorite meal—chicken cacciatore with a warm loaf of Italian bread for dunking. My mother was quiet and excused herself during dessert to go upstairs to watch TV. My father looked sad, dumped, and I pushed the rest of my lemon pie at him. "I'm full," I said, and wanted back the one who would always be true, so I asked if he'd play for me what he'd written that day. We sat on the piano bench. I followed the notes and turned the page when he nodded.

◨ ◨ ◨

Writing Exercises

1. Go to a mall, park, restaurant, or some other public place and eavesdrop. In your notebook, write down some lines of dialogue you overhear—anything that captures your attention. Bring your notebook to class, pick your favorite line or two, and write them on the board. Once everyone in class has done this, you can each pick a line from the board and use it to begin a scene. Somewhere along the line, incorporate at least three more lines of dialogue from the board into the scene. Write quickly, and have fun!

2. Thomas Fox Averill has found that a good way to get a scene going is by starting it with what he calls the "Non-apology." Write an exchange that begins "I'm sorry, but ..." Have the other character answer and then in the ensuing back-and-forth reveal the circumstances that got them into this situation.

3. Often we fight about the small things because the big things are too big and scary, too likely to get out of hand. Write a scene between two characters almost having a big fight, but not quite. Have the real tension be about something bigger than the trivial issue at hand (e.g., it's not really about the remote control but rather about control and being remote and power and who has it in the relationship).

4. Write an exchange in which one person is trying to teach the other how to do something. Perhaps the student is not a very good one—clumsy, distracted, or resistant. Perhaps the teacher isn't so good at the task at hand. Perhaps the teacher is really teaching a lesson that goes beyond the technicalities of the task (e.g., not just how to play pool, but how to look cool).

5. Put two characters together who have just found themselves to be at two different crossroads. I just got fired. You just landed a new job. Now what?

6. Have a character say something that reveals him or her in a new light. Maybe the revelation was meant to shock: "You're having an affair with your dentist?!" Maybe the revelation was unwitting and inadvertent: "Whoa, wait a minute, you did *what?*"

7. Flirtation. Two people are feeling each other out, not sure how far to go in revealing their feelings, not sure if the other person is just being friendly or is really interested, not sure whether to play hard to get, not sure...not sure.

8. Have one character *imagine* a conversation with another. The conversation he or she is anticipating (and, in some sense, rehearsing for) should be unavoidable. It could, however, be one of two types: a conversation your character is dreading (a shameful admission, breaking some bad news, etc.) or one your character is looking forward to (revealing a new promotion or raise, a declaration of love, etc.).

4

THE FLESH MADE WORD
Characterization, Part II

The Direct Methods of Character Presentation

APPEARANCE

Of the four methods of direct presentation—dialogue (discussed in the last chapter), appearance, action, and thought—appearance is especially important because our eyes are our most highly developed means of perception, and we therefore receive more nonsensuous information by sight than by any other sense. Beauty is only skin deep, but people are embodied, and whatever beauty—or ugliness—there is in them must somehow surface in order for us to perceive it. Such surfacing involves speech and action as well as appearance, but it is appearance that prompts our first reaction to people, and everything they wear and own presents some aspect of their inner selves.

Concerned to see beyond mere appearances, writers are sometimes inclined to neglect this power of the visible. In fact, much of the tension and conflict in character does proceed from the truth that appearance is not reality. But in order to know this, we must see the appearance first. Features, shape, style, clothing, and objects can make statements of internal values that are political, religious, social, intellectual, and essential. The man in the Ultrasuede jacket is making a different statement from the one in the holey sweatshirt. The woman with the cigarette holder is telling us something different from the one with the palmed joint. Even a person who has forsaken our materialistic society altogether, sworn off supermarkets, and gone to the country to grow organic potatoes has a special relationship with his or her hoe. However indifferent we may be to our looks, that indifference is the result of experiences with our bodies. A twenty-two-year-old Apollo who has been handsome since he was six is a very different person from the man who spent his childhood cocooned in fat and burst the chrysalis at age sixteen.

Following are two very brief portraits of women. Each is mainly characterized by such trivialities as fabric, furnishings, and cosmetics. It would nevertheless be impossible to mistake the essential nature of the one for that of the other.

How beautiful Helen is, how elegant, how timeless: how she charms Esther Songford and how she flirts with Edwin, laying a scarlet fingernail on his dusty lapel, mesmerizing.

She comes in a chauffeured car. She is all cream and roses. Her stockings are purest silk; her underskirt, just briefly showing, is lined with lace.

Fay Weldon, *Female Friends*

As soon as I entered the room, a pungent odor of phosphorus told me she'd taken rat poison. She lay groaning between the quilts. The tatami by the bed was splashed with blood, her waved hair was matted like rope waste, and a bandage tied round her throat showed up unnaturally white....The painted mouth in her waxen face created a ghastly effect, as though her lips were a gash open to the ears.

Masuji Ibuse, "Tajinko Village"

Vividness and richness of character are created in these two passages, which use nothing more than appearance to characterize.

Note that sense impressions other than sight are still a part of the way a character "appears." A limp handshake or a soft cheek; an odor of Chanel, oregano, or decay—these sense impressions can characterize much the way looks do if the narrative allows the reader to touch, smell, or taste a character.

The sound and associations of a character's name, too, can give a clue to personality: The affluent Mr. Chiddister in Chapter 2 is automatically a more elegant sort than the affluent Mr. Strum; Huck Finn must have a different life from that of the Marquis of Lumbria. Although names with a blatant meaning—Joseph Surface, Billy Pilgrim, Martha Quest—tend to stylize a character and should be used sparingly, if at all, ordinary names can hint at traits you mean to heighten, and it is worth combing any list of names, including the telephone book, to find suggestive sounds. My own telephone book yields, at a glance this morning, Linda Holladay, Marvin Entzminger, and Melba Peebles, any one of which might set me to speculating on a character.

Sound also characterizes as a part of "appearance" insofar as sound represents timbre, tenor, or quality of noise and speech, the characterizing reediness or gruffness of a voice, the lift of laughter or stiffness of delivery.

The way a character physically moves is yet another form of "appearance." It is important to understand the difference between *movement* and *action,* however, for these terms are not synonymous. Physical movement—the way he crosses his legs, the way she charges down the hall—characterizes without necessarily moving the plot forward. Often movement is part of the setup of the scene, a way of establishing the situation before change-producing action begins.

ACTION

The significant characters of a fiction must be both capable of causing an action and capable of being changed by it.

> WHAT'S VITAL FOR THE FICTION WRITER to remember is that the wicked, the violent, and the stupid do also love, in their way. Just as humble and loving and thoughtful people also hate. Hate humbly, hate lovingly, hate thoughtfully, and so on.
>
> DOUG BAUER

If we accept that a story records a process of change, how is this change brought about? Basically, human beings face chance and choice, or discovery and decision—the first of each pair involuntary and the second voluntary. Translated into action, this means that a character driven by desire takes an action with an expected result, but something intervenes. Some force outside the character presents itself, in the form of information or accident or the behavior of others or the elements. The unknown becomes known, and then the discoverer must either take action or deliberately not take action, involving readers in the tension of the narrative query: And then what happens?

Here is a passage from Toni Morrison's "Recitatif" that demonstrates first movement, then discovery, then decision:

> It was August and a bus crowd was just unloading. They would stand around a long while: going to the john, and looking at gifts and junk-for-sale machines, reluctant to sit down so soon. Even to eat. I was trying to fill the coffeepots and get them all situated on the electric burners when I saw her. She was sitting in a booth smoking a cigarette with two guys smothered in head and facial hair. Her own hair was so big and wild I could hardly see her face. But the eyes. I would know them anywhere. She had on a powder-blue halter and shorts outfit and earrings the size of bracelets. Talk about lipstick and eyebrow pencil. She made the big girls look like nuns. I couldn't get off the counter until seven o'clock, but I kept watching the booth in case they got up to leave before that. My replacement was on time for a change, so I counted and stacked my receipts as fast as I could and signed off. I walked over to the booth....

Here, unloading, milling around, and filling coffeepots is *movement* that represents scene-setting and characterization. The significant *action* begins with the discovery, "I saw her." Notice that "she" is characterized directly by appearance whereas the narrator is mainly characterized by her movements (expressed in active verbs)—*watching, counting, stacking, signing off*—until the moment when she acts on her decision. At the points of both the discovery and the decision we anticipate the possibility of change: What happens next?

In the next passage from John Cheever's "The Cure," the initial movement is seemingly innocuous before abruptly shifting toward suspense:

> I turned on a light in the living room and looked at Rachel's books. I chose one by an author named Lin Yutang and sat down on a sofa under a lamp. Our living room is comfortable. The book seemed interesting. I was in a neighborhood where most of the front doors were unlocked, and on a street that is very quiet on a summer night. All the animals are domesticated, and the only night birds that I've ever heard are some owls way down by the railroad track. So it was very quiet. I heard the Barstows' dog bark, briefly, as if he had been waked by a nightmare, and then the barking

stopped. Everything was quiet again. Then I heard, very close to me, a footstep and a cough.

I felt my flesh get hard—you know that feeling—but I didn't look up from my book, although I felt that I was being watched.

This scene is set with movement and one choice—that book—that offers no particular opportunity for change and no particular dramatic force. With the moment "Then I heard," however, a discovery or realization of a different sort occurs, and there is suddenly the possibility of real change and so, suddenly, real dramatic tension. Notice that in the second paragraph the narrator discovers a familiar and entirely involuntary reaction—"I felt my flesh get hard"—followed by the decision *not* to take what would be the instinctive action. In fiction as in life, restraint, the decision to do nothing, is fraught with possible tension.

In most cases, writers do not want their technique to be too conspicuous so they usually conceal the decision and discovery structure. In the next example, from Raymond Carver's "Neighbors," the pattern of change—Bill Miller's gradual intrusion into his neighbor's house—is based on a series of decisions that Carver does not explicitly state. The passage ends with a turning point, a moment of discovery.

> When he returned to the kitchen the cat was scratching in her box. She looked at him steadily for a minute before she turned back to the litter. He opened all the cupboards and examined the canned goods, the cereals, the packaged foods, the cocktail and wine glasses, the china, the pots and pans. He opened the refrigerator. He sniffed some celery, took two bites of cheddar cheese, and chewed on an apple as he walked into the bedroom. The bed seemed enormous, with a fluffy white bedspread draped to the floor. He pulled out a nightstand drawer, found a half-empty package of cigarettes and stuffed them into his pocket. Then he stepped to the closet and was opening it when the knock sounded at the front door.

There is hardly grand larceny being committed here, but the actions build toward tension through two distinct techniques. The first is that they do actually "build": At first Bill only "examines." The celery he only sniffs, whereas he takes two bites of the cheese, then a whole apple, then half a pack of cigarettes. He moves from the kitchen to the bedroom, which is a clearer invasion of privacy, and from cupboard to refrigerator to nightstand to closet, each a more intimate intrusion than the last.

The second technique is that the narrative subtly hints at Bill's own sense of stealth. It would be easy to imagine a vandal who performed the same actions with complete indifference. But Bill thinks the cat looks "steadily" at him, which is hardly of any importance except that he feels it to be. His awareness of the enormous white bed hints at sexual guilt. When the knock at the front door sounds, we start, as he must, in a clear sense of getting caught.

Thus it turns out that the internal or mental moment of change is where the action lies. Much movement in a story is mere event, and this is why descriptions of actions, like stage directions in a dull play, sometimes add little or nothing. When the wife picks up a cup of coffee, that is mere event. If she finds that the lipstick on the cup is not her shade, that is a dramatic event, a discovery; it makes a difference. She makes a decision to fling it at the woman with the Cherry Ice mouth. Flinging it is an action, but the dramatic change occurs with the second character's realization (discovery) that she has been hit—and so on.

Every story is a pattern of change (events connected, as the author E. M. Forster observed, primarily by cause and effect) in which small and large changes are made through decision and discovery.

THOUGHT

Fiction has a flexibility denied to film and drama, where everything the spectator knows must be shown. In fiction you have the privilege of entering a character's mind, sharing at its source internal conflict, reflection, and the crucial processes of decision and discovery. Like speech, a character's thought can be offered in summary (*He hated the way she ate*), or as indirect thought (*Why did she hold her fork straight up like that?*), or directly, as if we are overhearing the character's own mind (*My God, she's going to drop the yolk!*). As with speech, the three methods can be alternated in the same paragraph to achieve at once immediacy and pace.

Methods of presenting a character's thought will be more fully discussed in Chapter 8 on point of view. What's most important to characterization is that thought, like speech, reveals more than information. It can also set mood, reveal or betray desires, develop theme, and so forth.

The territory of a character's mind is above all likely to be the center of the action. Aristotle says that a man "is his desire," that is, his character is defined by his ultimate purpose, good or bad. *Thought*, says Aristotle, is the process by which a person works backward in his mind from his goal to determine what action he can take toward that goal at a given moment.

It is not, for example, your ultimate desire to read this book. Very likely you don't even "want" to read it; you'd rather be sleeping or jogging or making love. But your ultimate goal is, say, to be a rich, respected, and famous writer. In order to attain this goal, you reason, you must know as much about the craft as you can learn. To do this, you would like to take a graduate degree at the Writer's Workshop in Iowa. To do that, you must take an undergraduate degree in _____, where you now find yourself, and must get an A in Ms. or Mr. _____'s creative writing course. To do that, you must produce a character sketch from one of the assignments at the end of this chapter by a week from Tuesday. To do so, you must sit here reading this chapter now instead of sleeping, jogging, or making love. Your ultimate motive has led you logically backward to a deliberate "moral" decision on the action you can take at this minor crossroad. In fact, it turns out that you want to be reading after all.

The relationship that Aristotle perceives among desire, thought, and action seems to me a very useful one for an author, both in structuring plot and in creating character. What does this protagonist want to happen in the last paragraph of this story? What is the particular thought process by which this person works backward to determine what she or he will do now, in the situation that presents itself on page one?

> I was on my way to what I hoped would be *the* romantic vacation of my life, off to Door County for a whole week of sweet sane rest. More rest. I needed more rest.
>
> David Haynes, *All American Girls*

The action, of course, may be the wrong one. Thought thwarts us, because it leads to a wrong choice, or because thought is full of conflicting desires and consistent inconsistencies, or because there is enormous human tension between suppressed thought and expressed thought:

> When he shuts off the shower, the phone is ringing. A sense that it has been ringing for a long time—can a mechanical noise have a quality of desperation?—propels him naked and dripping into the living room. He picks up the phone and his caller, as he has suspected, is Mieko. . . . He is already annoyed after the first hello. Mieko's voice is sharp, high, very Japanese, although she speaks superb English. He says, "Hello, Mieko," and he sounds annoyed.
>
> Jane Smiley, "Long Distance"

A person, a character, can't do much about what he or she wants; it just is (which is another way of saying that character is desire). What we can deliberately choose is our behavior, the action we take in a given situation. Achievement of our desire would be easy if the thought process between desire and act were not so faulty and so wayward, or if there were not such an abyss between the thoughts we think and those that we are willing and able to express.

The four methods of direct characterization are forms of "showing" that bring character vividly alive. But there may also be times that you wish to shape our knowledge of and reaction to your characters by "telling" us about them, judging and interpreting for the reader.

The Indirect Methods of Character Presentation

There are two methods of indirect characterization—indirect in the sense that, rather than being presented directly to our sight and hearing, the character is described in summarized, abstract, or judgmental terms by either the author or another speaker. Both of these methods are forms of "telling," and both may shape our overall view.

AUTHORIAL INTERPRETATION

The first indirect method of presenting a character is authorial interpretation—
"telling" us the character's background, motives, values, virtues, and the like.
The advantages of this indirect method are enormous, for its use leaves you
free to move in time and space; to know anything you choose to know
whether the character knows it or not; and, godlike, to tell us what we are to
feel. The indirect method allows you to convey a great deal of information in a
short time.

> The most excellent Marquis of Lumbria lived with his two daughters,
> Caroline, the elder, and Luisa; and his second wife, Doña Vicente a woman
> with a dull brain, who, when she was not sleeping, was complaining of
> everything, especially the noise....
>
> The Marquis of Lumbria had no male children, and this was the most
> painful thorn in his existence. Shortly after having become a widower,
> he had married Doña Vicente, his present wife, in order to have a son,
> but she proved sterile.
>
> The Marquis' life was as monotonous and as quotidian, as unchanging
> and regular, as the murmur of the river below the cliff or as the liturgic
> services in the cathedral.
>
> Miguel De Unamuno, *The Marquis of Lumbria*

The disadvantage of this indirect method is that it distances the reader as
all generalizations and abstractions tend to do. Indeed, in the passage above, it
may well be part of Unamuno's purpose to convey the "monotonous" and
"quotidian" quality of the Marquis' life by this summarized and distanced
rehearsal of facts, motives, and judgments. Nearly every author will use the
indirect method occasionally, and you may find it useful when you want to
cover the exposition quickly. However, direct presentation of the characters—
showing them in action and allowing readers to draw their own conclusions—
will more actively engage the reader.

INTERPRETATION BY ANOTHER CHARACTER

A character may also be presented through the opinions of other characters,
which may be considered a second indirect method. When this method is employed, however, the second character must give his or her opinions in speech,
action, or thought. In the process, the observing character is inevitably also
characterized. Whether we accept the opinion depends on what we think of
that character as he or she is thus directly characterized. In this scene from
Jane Austen's *Mansfield Park*, for example, the busybody Mrs. Norris gives her
opinion of the heroine.

> "... [T]here is something about Fanny, I have often observed it before,—
> she likes to go her own way to work; she does not like to be dictated to;

she takes her own independent walk whenever she can; she certainly has a little spirit of secrecy, and independence, and nonsense, about her, which I would advise her to get the better of."

As a general reflection on Fanny, Sir Thomas thought nothing could be more unjust, though he had been so lately expressing the same sentiments himself, and he tried to turn the conversation, tried repeatedly before he could succeed.

Here Mrs. Norris's opinion is directly presented in her speech and Sir Thomas's in his thoughts, each of them being characterized in the process. It is left to the reader to decide (without much difficulty) whose view of Fanny is the more reliable.

Similarly, in Clyde Edgerton's contemporary novel *Raney*, the opposing outlooks of a newlywed "odd couple" are dramatized through their contradictory characterizations of a lonely and preoccupied neighbor.

"Charles," I said, "you'd rather sit down back there in the bedroom and read a book than talk to a live human being like Mrs. Moss."

"I'm not so sure I agree with your assessment of Mrs. Moss," he says.

"What do you mean by that?"

"It means I have had one conversation with Mrs. Moss and one conversation with Mrs. Moss is enough. I am not interested in her falling off the commode and having a hairline rib fracture. I am not interested in her cataract operation. Mrs. Moss is unable to comprehend anything beyond her own problems and you know it."

"...Mrs. Moss does talk about herself right much. She'll come over in her apron to borrow a cup of something. One Sunday she borrowed a cup of flour after I saw a bag of Red Band in her shopping cart—on top—at the Piggly Wiggly on Saturday. But the way I figure it is this: Mrs. Moss has had a lifetime of things happening to her and all along she's had these other people—her husband and children—to watch these things happen. So she didn't ever have to *tell* anybody. Then her husband died and her children left and there was nobody around to watch these things happen anymore, so she don't have any way to share *except* to tell. So the thing to do is listen. It's easy to cut her off when she just goes on and on. You just start talking about something else. She follows right along."

Set halfway through the novel, this argument confirms the reader's view of Charles as an urban liberal who is broad-minded in abstract principles yet impatient with actual people, while Raney, the small-town narrator, tends to be narrow-minded in the abstract but compassionate with individuals, at least those long-familiar to her. What is crystallized about this couple through their argument is even more important than what is learned about the incidental character of the neighbor.

Conflict Between Methods of Presentation

The conflict that is the essence of character can be effectively (and, if it doesn't come automatically, quite consciously) achieved in fiction by producing a conflict between methods of presentation. A character can be directly revealed to us through *appearance, dialogue, action*, and *thought*. If you set one of these methods (most frequently *thought*) at odds with the others, then dramatic tension will be produced. Imagine, for example, a character who is impeccably and expensively dressed, who speaks eloquently, who acts decisively, and whose mind is revealed to us as full of order and determination. He is inevitably a flat character. But suppose that he is impeccable, eloquent, decisive, and that his mind is a mess of wounds and panic. He is at once interesting.

Here is the opening passage of Saul Bellow's *Seize the Day*, in which appearance and action are blatantly at odds with thought. Notice that it is the tension between suppressed thought and what is expressed through appearance and action that produces the rich character conflict.

> When it came to concealing his troubles, Tommy Wilhelm was not less capable than the next fellow. So at least he thought, and there was a certain amount of evidence to back him up. He had once been an actor— no, not quite, an extra—and he knew what acting should be. Also, he was smoking a cigar, and when a man is smoking a cigar, wearing a hat, he has an advantage: it is harder to find out how he feels. He came from the twenty-third floor down to the lobby on the mezzanine to collect his mail before breakfast, and he believed—he hoped— he looked passably well: doing all right.

Tommy Wilhelm is externally composed but mentally anxious, mainly anxious about looking externally composed. By contrast, in the next passage, from Samuel Beckett's *Murphy*, the landlady, Miss Carridge, who has just discovered a suicide in one of her rooms, is anxious in speech and action but is mentally composed.

> She came speeding down the stairs one step at a time, her feet going so fast that she seemed on little caterpillar wheels, her forefinger sawing horribly at her craw for Celia's benefit. She slithered to a stop on the steps of the house and screeched for the police. She capered in the street like a consternated ostrich, with strangled distracted rushes towards the York and Caledonian Roads in turn, embarrassingly equidistant from the tragedy, tossing up her arms, undoing the good work of the samples, screeching for police aid. Her mind was so collected that she saw clearly the impropriety of letting it appear so.

In this third example, from Zora Neale Hurston's "The Gilded Six-Bits," it is the very intensity of the internal that both prevents and dictates action:

> Missie May was sobbing. Wails of weeping without words. Joe stood, and after a while he found out that he had something in his hand. And then he stood and felt without thinking and without seeing with his natural eyes. Missie May kept on crying and Joe kept on feeling so much, and not knowing what to do with all his feelings, he put Slemmon's watch charm in his pants pocket and took a good laugh and went to bed.

I have said that thought is most frequently at odds with one or more of the other three methods of direct presentation—reflecting the difficulty we have expressing ourselves openly or accurately—but this is by no means always the case. A character may be successfully, calmly, even eloquently expressing fine opinions while betraying himself by pulling at his ear, or herself by crushing her skirt. Captain Queeg of Herman Wouk's *The Caine Mutiny* is a memorable example of this, maniacally clicking the steel balls in his hand as he defends his disciplinary code.

Often we are not privy to the thoughts of a character at all, so that the conflicts must be expressed in a contradiction between the external methods of direct presentation, appearance, speech, and action. Character A may be speaking floods of friendly welcome, betraying his real feeling by backing steadily away. Character B, dressed in taffeta ruffles and ostrich plumes, may wail pityingly over the miseries of the poor. Notice that the notion of "betraying oneself" is important here: We're more likely to believe the evidence unintentionally given than deliberate expression.

A classic example of such self-betrayal is found in Leo Tolstoy's *The Death of Ivan Ilyich,* where the widow confronts her husband's colleague at the funeral.

> ...[N]oticing that the table was endangered by his cigarette ash, she immediately passed him an ashtray, saying as she did so: "I consider it an affectation to say that my grief prevents my attending to practical affairs. On the contrary, if anything can—I won't say console me, but—distract me, it is seeing to everything concerning him." She again took out her handkerchief as if preparing to cry, but suddenly, as if mastering her feeling, she shook herself and began to speak calmly. "But there is something I want to talk to you about."

It is no surprise either to the colleague or to us that Praskovya Federovna wants to talk about getting money.

Finally, character conflict can be expressed by creating a tension between the direct and the indirect methods of presentation, and this is a source of much irony. The author presents us with a judgment of the character and then lets him or her speak, appear, act, and/or think in contradiction to this judgment.

Sixty years had not dulled his response; his physical reactions, like his moral ones were guided by his will and strong character, and these could be seen plainly in his features. He had a long tube-like face with a long rounded open jaw and a large depressed nose.

Flannery O'Connor, "The Artificial Nigger"

What we see here in the details of Mr. Head's features are not will and strong character but grimly unlikable qualities. "Tube-like" is an ugly image; an "open jaw" suggests stupidity; and "depressed" connotes more than shape, while dogged repetition of "long" stretches the face grotesquely.

THE OLDER WE GET, THE MORE… you realize there's a whole range of things that you will never do, of things and people you will never be. As life becomes more and more limiting, there is something wonderful about being able to get inside the skin of people unlike yourself.

LEE SMITH

The Universal Paradox

Though critics often praise literature for exhibiting characteristics of the *individual,* the *typical,* and the *universal* all at the same time, I don't think this is of much use to the practicing writer. For though you may labor to create an individual character, and you may make that character a credible example of type, I don't think you can *set out to be* "universal."

It is true, I believe, that if literature has any social justification or use it is that readers can identify the common humanity in, and can therefore identify with, characters vastly different from themselves in century, geography, gender, culture, and beliefs; and that this enhances the scope of the reader's sympathy. Yet, paradoxically, if you aim for the universal, you're likely to achieve the pompous, whereas if you aim for the individual, you're more apt to create a character in whom a reader can see aspects of himself or herself.

Imagine this scene: The child chases a ball into the street. The tires screech, the bumper thuds, the blood geysers into the air, the pulp of the small body lies inert on the asphalt. How would a bystander react? (Is it universal?) How would a passing doctor react? (Is it typical?) How would Dr. Henry Lowes, just coming from the maternity ward of his own hospital, where his wife has had her fourth miscarriage, react? (Is it individual?) Each question narrows the range of convincing reaction, and as a writer you want to convince in each range. If you succeed in the third, you are likely to have succeeded in the other two.

My advice then is to labor in the range of the particular. If you aim for a universal character you may end up with a vague or dull or windy one. On the other hand, if you set out to write a typical character you're likely to produce a caricature, because people are typical only in the generalized qualities that lump them together. *Typical* is the most provincial adjective in a writer's vocabulary, signaling that you're writing only for those who share your assumptions. A "typical" schoolgirl in Dar es Salaam is a very different type from one in San Francisco. Furthermore, every person is typical of many things successively or simultaneously. She may be in turn a "typical" schoolgirl, bride, divorcée, and feminist. He may be at one and the same time a "typical" New Yorker, math professor, doting father, and adulterer. It is in the confrontation and convolution of types that much of our individuality is produced.

Writing in generalities and typicalities is akin to bigotry—we see only what's alike about people, not what's unique. When effective, a description of type blames the character for the failure to individualize, and if an author sets out deliberately to produce types rather than individuals, then that author invariably wants to condemn or ridicule those types. Mark Helprin, in "The Schreuderspitze," takes the ridicule of type to comic extreme:

> In Munich are many men who look like weasels. Whether by genetic accident, meticulous crossbreeding, an early and puzzling migration, coincidence, or a reason that we do not know, they exist in great numbers. Remarkably, they accentuate this unfortunate tendency by wearing mustaches, Alpine hats, and tweed. A man who resembles a rodent should never wear tweed.

This is not to say that all characters must be fully drawn or *"round."* Flat characters—who exist only to exhibit a function or a single characteristic— are useful and necessary. Eric Bentley suggests in *The Life of the Drama* that if a messenger's function in a play is to deliver his message, it would be very tedious to stop and learn about his psychology. Nevertheless, onstage even a flat character has a face and a costume, and in fiction detail can give even a flat character a few angles and contours. The servant classes in the novels of Henry James are notoriously absent as individuals because they exist only in their functions (*that excellent creature had already assembled the baggage*, etc.), whereas Charles Dickens, who peoples his novels with dozens of flat characters, brings even these alive in detail.

> And Mrs. Miff, the wheezy little pew opener—a mighty dry old lady, sparely dressed, with not an inch of fullness anywhere about her—is also here.
>
> *Dombey and Son*

To borrow a notion from George Orwell's *Animal Farm*, all good characters are created round, but some are created rounder than others.

Credibility

Though you aim at individuality and not typicality in characters, your characters will exhibit typicality in the sense of "appropriateness." A Baptist Texan behaves differently from an Italian nun; a rural schoolboy behaves differently from a professor emeritus at Harvard. If you are to succeed in creating an individual character, particular and alive, you will also inevitably know what is appropriate to that sort of person and will let us know as much as we need to know to feel the appropriateness of the behavior.

For instance, we need to know soon, preferably in the first paragraph, the character's gender, age, and race or nationality. We need to know something of his or her class, period, and region. A profession (or the clear lack of it) and a marital status help, too. *Almost any reader can identify with almost any character; what no reader can identify with is confusion.* When some or several of the fundamentals of type are withheld from us—when we don't know whether we're dealing with a man or a woman, an adult or a child—the process of identifying cannot begin, and the story is slow to move us.

None of the information need come as information; it can be implied by appearance, tone, action, or detail. In the next example Barbara Kingsolver plunges the character of Leah Price and her family into a new life for which they are clearly ill-prepared, practically and politically. Although they are focused on their destination, by the end of the first two paragraphs, we know a lot about the family and the culture they carry with them.

> We came from Bethlehem, Georgia, bearing Betty Crocker cake mixes into the jungle. My sisters and I were all counting on having one birthday apiece during our twelve-month mission. "And heaven knows," our mother predicted, "they won't have Betty Crocker in the Congo."
>
> "Where we are headed, there will *be* no buyers and sellers at all," my father corrected. His tone implied that Mother failed to grasp our mission, and that her concern with Betty Crocker confederated her with the coin-jingling sinners who vexed Jesus till he pitched a fit and threw them out of the church. "Where we are headed," he said, to make things perfectly clear, "not so much as a Piggly Wiggly." Evidently Father saw this as a point in the Congo's favor. I got the most spectacular chills, just from trying to imagine.
>
> *The Poisonwood Bible*

We know that the family is Southern, not only because their town of origin is named, but also from expressions such as "vexed" and "pitched a fit," as well as from mention of the Piggly Wiggly grocery chain. Not only do we know that they are missionaries, but further, we hear the father's sermonizing voice through his repetition of the phrase "where we are headed," preaching that is echoed in the implication that the mother is "confederated" with "the coin-jingling sinners." We also hear hints of the harsh pleasure the father will take in the family's hardship. The Betty Crocker mixes tell us that the women are trying to hang on to a little bit of home comfort, yet at the same time they are taking all-American '50s culture to a place where it is irrelevant and ultimately destructive—indeed, the cake mixes are quickly ruined by jungle humidity. And although we don't know the exact age of the narrator, she seems to be a teenager old enough to hear the subtext of her father's reprovals and to relish the false sophistication of phrases like "the most spectacular chills" and "imagine." In a very short space, Kingsolver has sketched the family, their dangerous ignorance, and the father's divisive, single-minded determination.

The following passage is an even more striking example of implied information.

> Every time the same story. Your Barbie is roommates with my Barbie, and my Barbie's boyfriend comes over and your Barbie steals him, okay? Kiss kiss kiss. Then the two Barbies fight. You dumbbell! He's mine. Oh no he's not, you stinky! Only Ken's invisible, right? Because we don't have money for a stupid-looking boy doll when we'd both rather ask for a new Barbie outfit next Christmas. We have to make do with your mean-eyed Barbie and my bubblehead Barbie and our one outfit apiece not including the sock dress.
>
> Sandra Cisneros, "Barbie-Q"

Here there is no description whatever of the characters, and no direct reference to them except for the designations *you* and *I*. What do we nevertheless know about their gender, their age, their financial status, the period in which they live, their personalities, their attitudes, their relationship, the narrator's emotions?

Students of writing are sometimes daunted by the need to give so much information immediately. The thing to remember is that credibility consists in the combination of appropriateness and specificity. The trick is to find telling details that will convey the information while our attention remains on the desire or emotion of the character. Nobody wants to read a story that begins:

> She was a twenty-eight-year-old suburban American woman, relatively affluent, who was extremely distressed when her husband, Peter, left her.

But most of that, and much more besides, could be contained in a few details.

> After Peter left with the VCR, the microwave, and the key to the garage, she went down to the kitchen and ate three jars of peanut butter without tasting a single spoonful.

I don't mean to imply that it is necessarily easy to signal the essentials of type immediately. It would be truer to say that it is necessary and hard. The opening paragraph of a story is its second strongest statement (the final paragraph is the strongest) and sets the tone for all that follows. If the right words don't come to you as a gift, you may have to sit sifting and discarding the inadequate ones for a long time before you achieve both clarity and interest.

Purpose

Your character's purpose—that is, the desire that impels her or him to action—will determine our degree of identification and sympathy on the one hand, or judgment on the other.

Aristotle, in *The Poetics*, says that "there will be an element of character if what a person says or does reveals a certain moral purpose; and a good element of character, if the purpose so revealed is good." It might seem that the antiheroes, brutes, hoods, whores, perverts, and bums who people modern literature do very little in the way of revealing good moral purpose. The history of Western literature shows a movement downward and inward: downward through society from royalty to gentry to the middle classes to the lower classes to the dropouts; inward from heroic action to social drama to individual consciousness to the subconscious to the unconscious. What has remained consistent is that, for the time spent in an author's world, we understand and identify with the protagonist or protagonists, we "see their point of view"; and the fiction succeeds largely because we are willing to grant them a goodness that we would not grant them in life. While you read, you expand your mental scope by identifying with, temporarily "becoming," a character, borrowing a different mind. Fiction, as critic Laurence Gonzales says of rock music, "lets you wander around in someone else's hell for a while and see how similar it is to your own."

Complexity

If the characters of your story are credible through being appropriate and individual, and if they invite identification or judgment through a sense of their purpose, they also need to be complex. They need to exhibit enough conflict and contradiction that we can recognize them as belonging to the contradictory human race; and they should exhibit a range of possibility so that a shift of power in the plot can also produce a shift of purpose or morality. That is, they need to be capable of change.

Conflict is at the core of character as it is of plot. If plot begins with trouble, then character begins with a person in trouble; and trouble most dramatically occurs because we all have traits, tendencies, and desires that are at war, not simply with the world and other people, but with other traits, tendencies, and desires of our own. All of us probably know a woman of the strong, striding, independent sort, attractive only to men who like a strong and striding woman. And when she falls in love? She becomes a clinging sentimentalist. All of us know a father who is generous, patient, and dependable. And when the children cross the line? He smashes crockery and wields a strap. All of us are gentle, violent; logical, schmaltzy; tough, squeamish; lusty, prudish; sloppy, meticulous; energetic, apathetic; manic, depressive. Perhaps you don't fit that particular list of contradictions, but you are sufficiently in conflict with yourself that as an author you have characters enough in your own psyche to people the work of a lifetime if you will identify, heighten, and dramatize these conflicts within character, which Aristotle called "consistent inconsistencies."

UNLIKE EVEN THOSE CLOSEST TO US IN REAL LIFE—our spouses, our lovers, our kin, whom we can never know completely—fictional people retain only as much privacy and secrecy as those who create them decide to let them keep.

DOUG BAUER

If you think of the great characters of literature, you can see how inner contradiction—consistent inconsistency—brings each to a crucial dilemma. Hamlet is a strong and decisive man who procrastinates. Dorothea Brooke of *Middlemarch* is an idealistic and intellectual young woman, a total fool in matters of the heart. Ernest Hemingway's Francis Macomber wants to test his manhood against a lion and cannot face the test. Here, in a moment of crisis from *Mom Kills Self and Kids*, Alan Saperstein reveals with great economy the consistent inconsistency of his protagonist, a man who hadn't much time for his family until their absence makes clear how dependent he has been on them.

When I arrived home from work I found my wife had killed our two sons and taken her own life.
    I uncovered a blast of foul, black steam from the pot on the stove and said, "Hi, hon, what's for dinner?" But she did not laugh. She did not bounce to her feet and pirouette into the kitchen to greet me. My little one didn't race into my legs and ask what I brought him. The seven-year-old didn't automatically beg me to play a game knowing my answer would be a tired, "Maybe later."

In "The Self as Source," Cheryl Moskowitz proposes a fiction technique that relies specifically on identifying conflicting parts of the writer's personality. She points to Robert Louis Stevenson's *The Strange Case of Dr. Jekyll and Mr. Hyde* as a fairly blatant model for such fiction, and quotes from Dr. Jekyll:

> ...I thus drew steadily nearer to that truth...that man is not truly one, but two. I say two, because the state of my own knowledge does not pass beyond that point....I hazard the guess that man will ultimately be known for a mere polity of multifarious, incongruous and independent denizens.

It is, of course, impossible to know to what degree Shakespeare, Eliot, Hemingway, or Saperstein self-consciously used their own inner contradictions to build and dramatize their characters. An author works not only from his or her own personality but also from observation and imagination, and I fully believe that you are working at full stretch only when all three are involved. The question of autobiography is a complicated one, and as writer you frequently won't know yourself how much you have experienced, how much you have observed, and how much you have invented. Actress Mildred Dunnock once observed that drama is possible "because people can feel what they haven't experienced," an observation that surely extends to the writing and reading of fiction. If you push yourself to write at the outer edge of your emotional experience—what you can imagine yourself doing, even if you might not risk such actions in life—then all your writing is autobiographical in the sense that it must have passed through your mind.

Change

In a story, as opposed to a sketch or anecdote, says poet and novelist Al Young, "stuff happens, people *change*, situations *change*, there is no standing still." Certainly the easiest way to check the plot of your story is to ask, "Does my character change from opening to end? Do I give the sense that his or her life will never be quite the same again?"

Often the notion of change is mistaken by new writers to mean change that is abrupt and contrived, from Scrooge to St. Nick—yet this rarely happens in life or in realistic fiction. Rather, change can be as subtle as a step in a new direction, a slight shift in belief, or a willingness to question a rigid view or recognize unseen value in a person or situation. Our society's belief in the power of change is reaffirmed each New Year's Day, and one of the vicarious pleasures fiction offers is the chance to experience the workings of change within a character's consciousness.

John L'Heureux offers a psychological framework for viewing change: "A story is about a single moment in a character's life when a definitive choice is made, after which nothing is the same."

The "integrity" of fiction is a concept John L'Heureux emphasizes, for in good fiction incidents lead to a single moment when the main character makes a decision that regards—and determines—his or her essential integrity, after which nothing will ever be the same. He uses integrity in its primal sense of "wholeness," since at the moment of choice the character elects to live either more in harmony or more at odds with his or her best self. The decision made in that moment affects the character's relationship with the self forever.

"What we do determines what we become," fiction writer Nancy Huddleston Packer affirms. "Because character and event are interlocked, stories don't end in accident; rather, the consequences of the story come from the character who determines events. Our decisions make us who we are forever afterward."

Reinventing Character

Here are a few other ways you can try to make a character fresh and forceful in your mind before you start writing.

If the character is based on you or on someone you know, drastically alter the model in some external way: Change blond hair to dark or thin to thick; imagine the character as the opposite gender or radically alter the setting in which the character must act. Part of the trouble with writing directly from experience is that you know too much about it—what "they" did, how you felt. Under such circumstances it's hard to know whether everything in your mind is getting onto the page. An external alteration forces you to re-see, and so to see more clearly, and so to convey more clearly what you see.

On the other hand, if the character is created primarily out of your observation or invention and is unlike yourself, try to find an internal area that you have in common with the character. If you are a blond, slender young woman and the character is a fat, balding man, do you nevertheless have in common a love of French *haute cuisine*? Are you haunted by the same sort of dream? Do you share a fear of public performance or a susceptibility to fine weather?

I can illustrate these techniques only from my own writing, because I am the only author whose self I can identify with any certainty in fictional characters. In one novel, I wanted to open with a scene in which the heroine buries a dog in her backyard. I had recently buried a dog in my backyard. I wanted to capture the look and feel of red Georgia earth at sunrise, the tangle of roots, and the smell of decay. But I knew that I was likely to make the experience too much my own, too little my character's. I set about to make her not-me. I have long dark hair and an ordinary figure, and I tend to live in Levi's. I made Shaara Soole

> ... big boned, lanky, melon-breasted, her best feature was a head of rusty barbed-wire hair that she tried to control with a wardrobe of scarves and headband things. Like most costume designers, she dressed with more originality than taste, usually on the Oriental or Polynesian side, sometimes

with voluminous loops of thong and matte metal over an ordinary shirt. This was somewhat eccentric in Hubbard, Georgia, but Shaara may have been oblivious to her eccentricity, being so concerned to keep her essential foolishness in check.

Having thus separated Shaara from myself, I was able to bury the dog with her arms and through her eyes rather than my own. On the other hand, a few pages later I was faced with the problem of introducing her ex-husband, Boyd Soole. I had voluminous notes on this character, and I knew that he was almost totally unlike me. A man, to begin with, and a huge man, a theater director with a natural air of power and authority and very little interest in domestic affairs. I sat at my desk for several days, unable to make him move convincingly. My desk oppressed me, and I felt trapped and uncomfortable, my work thwarted, it seemed, by the very chair and typewriter. Then it occurred to me that Boyd was *also* sitting at a desk trying to work.

The dresser at the Travelodge was some four inches too narrow and three inches too low. If he set his feet on the floor his knees would sit free of the drawer but would be awkwardly constricted left and right. If he crossed his legs, he could hook his right foot comfortably outside the left of the knee-hole but would bruise his thigh at the drawer. If he shifted back he was placed at an awkward distance from his script. And in this position he could not work.

This passage did not instantly allow me to live inside Boyd Soole's skin, nor did it solve all my problems with his characterization. But it did let me get on with the story, and it gave me a flash of sympathy for him that later grew much more profound than I had foreseen.

Often, identifying what you have in common with the feelings of your character will also clarify what is important about her or him to the story—why, in fact, you chose to write about such a person at all. Even if the character is presented as a villain, you have something in common, and I don't mean something forgivable. If he or she is intolerably vain, watch your own private gestures in front of the mirror and borrow them. If he or she is cruel, remember how you enjoyed hooking the worm.

There is no absolute requirement that a writer need behave honestly in life; there is absolutely no such requirement. Great writers have been public hams, domestic dictators, emotional con artists, and Nazis. What is required for fine writing is honesty on the page—not how the characters *should* react at the funeral, the surprise party, in bed, but how they *would*. In order to develop such honesty of observation on the page, you must begin with a willing honesty of observation (though mercifully not of behavior) in yourself.

Creating a Group or Crowd

Sometimes it is necessary to introduce several or many people in the same scene, and this needn't present a problem, because the principle is pretty much the same in every case, and is the same as in film: pan, then close-up. In other words, give us a sense of the larger scene first, then a few details to characterize individuals. If you begin by concentrating too long on one character only, we will tend to see that person as being alone.

> Herm peered through the windshield and eased his foot up off the gas. Damn, he thought, it's not going to let up. The yellow lights made slick pools along the shoulder. He fiddled with the dial, but all he could get was blabber-radio and somebody selling vinyl siding. His back ached. His eyes itched. A hundred and forty miles to go.

At this point, if you introduce a wife, two children, and a dog to the scene, we will have to make rapid and uncomfortable adjustments in our mental picture. Better to begin with the whole carful and then narrow it down to Herm:

> Herm peered through the windshield and glanced over at Inga, who was snoring lightly against the window. The kids hadn't made a sound for about half an hour either, and only Cheza was wheezing dogbreath now and then on the back of his neck. He eased his foot up off the gas. Damn, he thought...

If the action involves several characters who therefore need to be seen right away, introduce them as a group and then give us a few characterizing details:

> All the same there were four guns on him before he'd focused enough to count. "Peace," he said again. There were three old ones, one of them barely bigger than a midget, and the young one was fat. One of the old ones had on a uniform jacket much too big for him, hanging open on his slack chest. The young one spun a string of their language at him.

If the need is to create a crowd, it is still important, having established that there *is* a crowd, to give us a few details. We will believe more thoroughly in large numbers of people if you offer example images for us. Here, for example, is a passage from *Underworld* in which Don LeLillo introduces two parts of a crowd, the boys who are waiting to sneak into the ballpark and the last legitimate arrivals:

> ...they have found one another by means of slidy looks that detect the fellow foolhard and here they stand, black kids and white kids up from the subways or off the local Harlem streets, bandidos, fifteen in all, and according to topical legends maybe four will get through for every one that's caught.

They are waiting nervously for the ticket holders to clear the turnstiles, the last loose cluster of fans, the stragglers and loiterers. They watch the late-arriving taxis from downtown and the brilliantined men stepping dapper to the windows, policy bankers and supper club swells and Broadway hotshots, high aura'd, picking lint off their sleeves.

THE CHARACTER JOURNAL

Whether indirect, direct, or, most commonly, both direct and indirect methods are used, a full and rich fictional character will need to be both credible and complex, will show purpose (and that purpose will reveal something about his or her morality), and in the course of the story will undergo some, perhaps small but nonetheless significant, change. In order to explore these elements of character, your journal can be an invaluable help.

As a writer you may have the lucky, facile sort of imagination to which characters spring full-blown, complete with gestures, histories, and passions. Or it may be that you need to explore in order to exploit, to draw your characters out gradually and coax them into being. That can be lucky, too.

For either kind of writer, but especially the latter, the journal lets you coax and explore without committing yourself to anything or anyone. It allows you to know everything about your character whether you use it or not. Before you put a character in a story, know how well that character sleeps, what he eats for lunch, what she buys and how the bills get paid. Know how your character would prefer to spend evenings and weekends and why such plans get thwarted, what memories the character has of pets and parents, cities, snow, or school. You may end up using none of this information, but knowing it may teach you how your bookperson taps a pencil or twists a lock of hair, and when and why. When you know these things, you will have taken a step past invention toward the moment of imagination in which you become your character, live in his or her skin, and produce an action that, for the reader, rings universally true.

Use the journal to note your observations of people. Try writing down your impressions of the library assistant who annoys you or the loner at the bar who intrigues you. Try to capture a gesture or the messages that physical features and clothing send. Invent a reason for that harshness or that loneliness; invent a past. Then try taking the character out of context and setting her or him in another. Get your character in trouble, and you may be on your way to a short story.

Character: A Summary

It may be helpful to summarize the practical advice on character that this chapter and the previous chapter contain.

1. Be aware of the four methods of direct character presentation— appearance, speech, action, and thought—and of the indirect methods, authorial interpretation and the presentation by another character.

2. Reveal the character's conflicts by presenting attributes in at least one of these methods that contrast with attributes you present in the others.

3. Focus sharply on how the character looks, on what she or he wears and owns, and on how she or he moves. Let us focus on it, too.

4. Examine the character's speech to make sure it does more than convey information. Does it characterize, accomplish exposition, and reveal emotion, intent, or change? Does it advance the conflict through "no" dialogue? Speak it aloud: Does it "say"?

5. Build action by making your characters discover and decide. Make sure that what happens is action and not mere event or movement, that is, that it contains the possibility for human change.

6. Use your journal to explore and build ideas for characters.

7. Know the details of your character's life: what he or she does during every part of the day, thinks about, remembers, wants, likes and dislikes, eats, says, means.

8. Know all the influences that go into the making of your character's type: age, gender, race, nationality, marital status, region, education, religion, profession.

9. Know what your character wants, both generally out of life, and specifically in the context of the story. Keeping that desire in mind, "think backward" with the character to decide what he or she would do in any situation presented.

10. Identify, heighten, and dramatize consistent inconsistencies. What does your character want that is at odds with whatever else she wants? What patterns of thought and behavior work against his primary goal?

11. If the character is based on a real model, including yourself, make a dramatic external alteration.

12. If the character is imaginary or alien to you, identify a mental or emotional point of contact.

◈

Mule Killers

LYDIA PEELLE

My father was eighteen when the mule killers finally made it to his father's farm. He tells me that all across the state that year, big trucks loaded with mules rumbled steadily to the slaughterhouses. They drove over the roads that mules themselves had cut, the gravel and macadam that mules themselves had laid. Once or twice a day, he says, you would hear a high-pitched bray come from one of the trucks, a rattling as it went by, then silence, and you would look up from your work for a moment to listen to that silence. The mules when they were trucked away were sleek and fat on oats, work-shod and in their prime. *The best color is fat,* my grandfather used to say, when asked. But that year, my father tells me, that one heartbreaking year, the best color was dead. Pride and Jake and Willy Boy, Champ and Pete were dead, Kate and Sue and Orphan Lad, Orphan Lad was dead.

In the spring of that year, in the afternoon of a rain-brightened day, my father's father goes to Nashville and buys two International Harvester tractors for eighteen hundred dollars, cash. "We've got no choice nowadays," he tells the IHC man, counting out the bills and shaking his head. He has made every excuse not to buy a mule killer, but finally the farm's financial situation has made the decision for him. Big trucks deliver the tractors and unload them in the muddy yard in front of the barn, where for a day they hunch and sulk like children. My grandfather's tobacco fields stretch out behind them, shimmering in the spring heat. Beyond the slope of green, the Cumberland River is just visible through a fringe of trees, swollen and dark with rain.

The next morning, after chores, my grandfather calls in the hands to explain the basics of the new machines, just the way the man in Nashville has done for him. He stands next to one of the tractors for a long time, talking about the mechanics of it, one hand resting on its flank. Then with all the confidence he can muster he climbs up to start it. He tries three times before the tractor shivers violently, bucks forward, and busts the top rail of a fence. "This one ain't entirely broke yet," my grandfather jokes, struggling to back it up.

"Reckon you'll break it before it breaks you?" someone calls out, and only half of the men laugh. Most of them are used to sleeping all down the length of a tobacco row until the mules stop, waking just long enough to swing the team and start on back up the next. They all know when it's lunchtime because the mules bray, in unison, every day at five to twelve.

My father stands with the men who are laughing, laughing with them and scuffing up dust with his boot, though he is nervous about the tractors. His light eyes are squinted in the sun, and he slouches—he has his father's height, and he carries it apologetically. He is trying hard to keep certain things stuffed deep inside his chest: things like fear, sadness, and uncertainty. He expects to outgrow all of these things very soon, and in the meantime, he works hard to keep them hidden. Lately, he has become secretive about the things he loves. His love is fierce and full, but edged in guilt. He loves Orphan Lad: Orphan's sharp shoulders and soft ears, the mealy tuck of his lower lip. Music. Books and the smell of books, sun-warmed stones, and Eula Parker, who has hair thick and dark as soil. He has loved her since he was ten and once sat next to her at church; during the sermon she pinched him so hard his arm was red until Tuesday, and he had secretly kissed that red butterfly bruise. But Orphan will soon be gone, and none of the hands read books, and he laughs at the tractors just as he would laugh if one of these men made a rude comment about Eula Parker, because the most important thing, he believes, is not to let on that he loves anything at all.

Late that night, some of the hands sit on the porch to dip snuff and drink bitter cups of coffee. My father sits with them, silent on the steps. When he is with people he often finds pockets in the noise that he can crawl into and fill with his own thoughts, soft, familiar thoughts with worn, rounded corners. At this particular moment he is turning an old thought of Eula Parker over and over in his mind: he is going to marry her. If he goes so far as to conjure dark-haired children for them, I don't know, but he does build a house where they sit together on a porch, a vast and fertile farm on the other side of the river, and on this night, a shed full of bright chrome tractors, twice as big as the ones that rest still warm and ticking in his father's mule barn. He plants a flower garden for her at the foot of the porch; he buys a big Victrola for the dining room and a smaller, portable one for picnics. Guiltily he touches just the edges of one of these picnics: Eula's hair loose and wild, a warm blanket by a creek, cold chicken and hard-boiled eggs, drowsiness, possibility.

In a moment his pocket of quiet is turned inside out; the hands roar with laughter at the punch line of a joke and the screen door clatters as my grandfather comes out to the porch. "You all ever gonna sleep?" he asks them, and smiles. He is an old man, nearing seventy, and the thin length of his body has rounded to a stoop, like a sapling loaded with snow. But his eyes are still the eyes of a young man, even after years in the sun, and they are bright as he smiles and jokes. My father stands up and leans against a post, crossing his arms. His father winks at him, then waves his hand at the men and steps back into the house, shaking his head and chuckling.

My grandfather understood mule power. He celebrated it. He reveled in it. He always said that what makes a mule a better worker than the horse or the donkey is that he inherited the best from both of them: strong hindquarters from his dam and strong shoulders from his sire. He said, *The gospel according to mule is push and pull.* When his wife died young of a fever, it was not a horse but Orphan Lad who pulled her coffin slowly to the burying grounds, a thing the prouder men of the county later felt moved to comment on in the back room of the feed store. My grandfather was a man who never wore a hat, even to town. *Uncover thy head before the Lord, he said,* and the Lord he believed to be everywhere: in the trees, in the water of the creek, under Calumet cans rusting in the dirt.

Eula Parker is a slippery and mysterious girl, and my father's poor heart is constantly bewildered by her fickle ways. Like the day he walked her home from church and she allowed him to hold her cool hand, but would not let him see her all the way to the front door. Or the times when she catches him looking at her, and drops her eyes and laughs—at what, he cannot guess. With a kit he burns her name into a scrap of oak board and works up the courage to leave it at the door of her parents' house in town; when he walks by the next day and it is still there, he steals it back and takes it home to hide it shamefully beneath his bed. At church she always sits with the same girl, fifth pew back on the left, and he positions himself where he can see her: her hair swept up off her neck, thick purple-black and shining, the other girl's hanging limply down, onion-paper pale. Afterward, when people gather in the yard, the other girl always smiles at him, but he never notices; he is watching to see if Eula smiles, because sometimes she does and sometimes she doesn't. His love fattens on this until it is round and full, bursting from every seam.

At night, when he is sure his father is sleeping, he sticks the phonograph needle in a rubber eraser and holds the eraser in his front teeth. Carefully, with his nose inches from the record, he sets the needle down. With a hiss and crackle, the music reverberates through the hollows of his mouth and throat without making a sound in the room. Ignoring the cramp in his neck, this is how he listens to his favorite records night after night. Wild with thoughts of Eula with her hair like oil. Her snake-charming eyes. Her long, fine hands. How she teases him. He dreams he finds pieces of his heart in the boot scraper at her door.

On a warm and steamy afternoon my father makes a trip to town. He walks along the side of the road and passing cars do not give him any room. Several times he has to jump into the tick-heavy weeds that grow at the road's edge. At the river, a truck loaded with mules from a farm to the north passes him and bottoms out on the bridge. He keeps his head to the side until it is out of sight. Soon the truck will come for the last of his father's herd. *Oh, Orphan.* On the coldest mornings of his boyhood, his father had let him ride Orphan to school, bareback with two leads clipped to the halter. When they got to the schoolhouse he'd jump down and slap the mule's wide, wonderful haunch, and the big animal would turn without hesitation and walk directly home to be harnessed and hitched for the day's work.

Town is still and hot. The street is empty, buildings quiet, second-story shutters closed like eyes. He buys a tin of phonograph needles at the furniture store and lingers to look at the portable record players, nestled neat and tidy in their black cases. When he finally steps out of the store, head bowed in thought, he nearly runs into Eula and another girl, who stand bent close in serious conversation.

When they look up and see that it is him, they both politely say hello. Eula looks up at the store awning behind him. The other girl, the girl with the onion-pale hair, she looks down at the toe of her boot. He hears himself ask, "Want to go for a soda?" His voice is like a round stone that drops right there on the sidewalk. Eula's face closes like a door. But the other girl. The other girl, she guesses so.

He takes her to the only drugstore in town and they sit at the counter and order two sodas. She doesn't speak. They watch the clerk stocking packages on the high shelves along the wall, sliding his wooden ladder along the track in the ceiling with a satisfying, heavy sound. She seals her straw with her finger and swizzles it around the glass. She crosses her right ankle over her left, then her left ankle over her right, then hooks her heels onto the bottom of the stool. My father compliments her on her dress. The clerk drops a bag of flour and curses, then apologizes to the girl. There are hollow fly carcasses wedged into the dusty seam of the counter and the warped wood floor. Even with two ceiling fans running, the air is hot and close.

This must have been the middle of August; though my father doesn't tell me this, it is easy enough to count backwards and figure for myself. The walls of the store are painted a deep green and the paint has bubbled in some places. My father's mind fails him as he searches for something to say. He watches her twist a strand of hair around her finger, but she feels his eyes on her and abruptly stops, folding her hands in her lap.

"So, you and Eula, y'all sit together at church," he says, forgetting to make it a question.

Puzzled, the girl nods her head. She has not yet said a word. Perhaps she is having trouble believing that she is sitting here at this counter, having a soda with a boy. Or she is worrying that her hair is too pale and limp, or her wrists too big, or her dress too common. She has never believed she would find herself in this situation, and so has never rehearsed.

"I've always thought this time of year is the saddest," she finally says, looking up at my father. He lays his hand on the counter and spreads out his fingers. His chin tilts forward as if he is about to speak. Then the sleigh bells on the door jingle, shiver when it slams shut. It is Eula. She doesn't look at them. She brushes her sweat-damp hair back with two fingers and asks the clerk for something—what?—my father's ears are suddenly filled—she is asking the clerk for a tin of aspirin, peering up at the shelves behind him and blinking those eyes. The clerk stares too long before turning to his ladder. My father considers socking him one in that plug-ugly face. Eula raps her fingers along the edge of the counter and hums tunelessly, and still she won't look their way.

At this moment, my father feels his heart dissolve into a sticky bright liquid. Jealousy has seized her, she has followed them here—he is certain. Finally, a staggering proclamation of her love. His heart has begun to trickle down into the soles of his feet when the girl somehow catches Eula's eye and ripples her fingers at her.

Hello.

Then Eula unfolds her long body towards them, and smiles. An enormous, beautiful, open-faced smile: a smile with no jealousy hidden behind it at all. She takes her change and paper sack from the clerk and turns, one hand stretched out towards the door. She is simply going to leave. She is going to walk out the door and leave them here to their sodas and silence. At this point my father, frantic, takes hold of the girl on the stool next to him, leans her in Eula's direction, and kisses her recklessly, right on the mouth.

My father tells me this story in the garden, bent over and searching through the knee-high weeds for long, thick stalks of asparagus, clipping them with his pocket knife and handing them to me. Here he stops and straightens and squints east, and I know his back is starting to bother him. Why he never told me the story when I was a boy, I don't know; I am twice as old now as he was, the year of the mule killers. But still he skips the part of the story where I come in.

It doesn't matter; I can imagine it. Before the door has even closed after Eula, something has changed in my father, and as he slides from his stool he firmly takes the girl's hand. He leads her out of the drugstore, glancing back once more at the pock-faced clerk, who is carefully smoothing Eula's dollar bill into the cash register drawer. Slowly they make their way somewhere: back to the farm, most likely, where his father is sitting with the hands at supper. He takes her to the hayloft, a back field, the mule barn, the spring house: anyplace that was dark and quiet for long enough that my father could desperately try to summon Eula's face, or else hope to forever blot it from his mind. Long enough that I, like a flashbulb, could snap into existence.

"Mercy, mercy, mercy," my grandfather said, that day they finally took Orphan. "He'll be all right." He pinched the bridge of his nose and looked away when they tried to load Orphan onto the truck. The mule's big ears swung forward, his narrow withers locked, and he would not budge when he got to the loading ramp. It took four men to finally get him up, and they saw his white eye swiveling madly when they looked in through the slats. "Not stubborn, just smart," my grandfather said to the ground, then again pinched his nose and leaned against the truck as two more mules were loaded up. His herd was so big that this was the last of three trips. He had intended to send Orphan with the first load, but had put it off and put it off.

"Ain't it some kind of thanks," my grandfather said as he latched up the back of the truck, the mules inside jostling to get their footing, and Orphan's long ear had swiveled back at the sound of his voice. The best of them brought three or four cents a pound as dog meat; some of them would merely be heaved six deep into a trench that would be filled in with dirt by men on tractors. The hollow report of hooves on the truck bed echoed even after the truck had pulled onto the road and turned out of sight. The exact same sound could be heard all through the county, all across the hills of Tennessee and up through Kentucky, across Missouri and Kansas, and all the way out West, even, you could hear it. The mules' job, it was finished.

When the back of the truck is finally shut, my father is high above, hiding in the hayloft. At church the pale-haired girl had pulled him into the center aisle just before the service and told him her news, the news of me. All through the sermon his mind had flipped like a fish, and he had stared hard at the back of Eula's neck, trying to still that fish. In the hayloft he thinks of this moment as he listens to the shouts of the truck driver and the engine backfiring once before the mules are pulled away, but he doesn't come to the edge, he doesn't look down for one last glimpse of Orphan Lad.

Late that night my father creeps to the Victrola in the living room and carefully opens the top of the cabinet. He slides a record onto the turntable and turns the crank, then sets his eraser and needle between his teeth and presses it to the first groove. A fiddle plays, is joined by a guitar, and then a high lonesome voice starts in about heartbreak. Every time he listens to his records like this, the first notes take him by surprise. When the music starts to fill his head, he can't believe it is coming from the record on the turntable and not from a place within himself. He closes his eyes and imagines Eula Parker is in the room, dancing behind him in a dark red dress. He moves his face across the record, following the groove with the needle, and spit collects in the pockets of his cheeks. *Eula, Eula, Eula.* He lets her name roll around in his head until it is unclear, too, whether this sound is coming from the record on the turntable, or from the deepest hollows of his heart.

Three weeks after the last load of mules goes, a tractor overturns on a hill down by the river and nearly kills one of the hands. It is not an unexpected tragedy. My grandfather is the only one with the man, and he pulls him out from underneath the seat and searches through the grass for three scattered fingers while the engine continues to choke and whir. He drives the man to the hospital in Nashville and doesn't return until late that night. His trip home is held up by an accident at the bridge that takes nearly an hour to be cleared away. When he finally arrives back, his son is waiting on the porch to tell him about the pale-haired girl.

My father has rehearsed what he will say dozens of times to the fence posts and icebox, but when he sees his father's brown, blood-caked forearms and hands, he is startled enough to forget what it was. Weary and white in the face, my grandfather sits down next to him on the top step and touches his shoulder.

"Son," he says, "you're gonna see a future I can't even stretch my mind around. Not any of it. I can't even begin to imagine."

If my father had understood what his father was trying to tell him, maybe he would have waited until the morning to say what he now says. Maybe he would never had said anything, packed up a small bag, and left town for good. Abandoned love and any expectation of it. Instead he confesses to my grandfather, all in a rush, the same way he might have admitted that he had broken the new mower, or left the front gate open all night.

My grandfather stares hard at my father's knee and is quiet a long time.

"You done her wrong," he says. Repeats it. "You got no choice but to take care of it. You done her wrong."

In those days this was my grandfather's interpretation of the world: A thing was either right or it was wrong. Or so it seemed to my father, and he was getting tired of it.

"No, sir," he says, lips tight. "That's not what I intend. I'm in love with someone else." He takes a breath. "I'm gonna marry Eula Parker." Even as he speaks her name he is startled by this statement, like it is a giant carp he has yanked from the depths of the river. It lies on the stop before both of them, gasping.

My grandfather looks at him with sadness rimming his eyes and says quietly, "You should've thought of that before."

"But you see," my father says, as if explaining to a child, "I love her."

My grandfather grips his knees with his big hands and sighs. He reaches out for his son's arm, but my father brushes him away, stands up, and walks heavily across the porch. When he goes into the house, he lets the screen door slam behind him, and it bangs twice in the casement before clicking shut.

Late that night, after washing the dishes of a silent dinner, my father sits on the porch sharpening his pocket knife. He taps his bare feet against the hollow stairs and even whistles through his teeth. His father's words have still not completely closed in around him. Though an uneasiness is slowly creeping up, he is still certain that the future is bright chrome and glorious, full of possibility. Behind him, a string of the banjo gently twangs as it goes flat in the cooling air. It is the first night of the year that smells of autumn and my father takes a few deep breaths as he leans against the porch railing and looks out into the yard. This is when he sees something out under the old elm, a long, twisted shape leaning unsteadily against the thick trunk of the tree.

He steps off the porch onto the cool grass of the yard, thinking first he sees a ghost. As he gets closer to the shape, he believes it next to be a fallen limb, or one of the hands, drunk on moonshine—then, nothing but a forgotten ladder, then—with rising heart—Eula come to call for him in her darkest dress. But when he is just a few yards away from the tree, he sees it is his father, his back to the house, arms at his sides. He is speaking quietly, and my father knows by the quality of his voice that he is praying. He has found him like this before, in the hayfield at dusk or by the creek in the morning, eyes closed, mumbling simple private incantations. My father is about to step quietly back to the porch when his father reaches a trembling hand to the tree to steady himself, then lets his shoulders collapse. He blows his nose in his hand and my father hears him swallow back thick, jumbled sobs. When he hears this, when he realizes his father is crying, he turns and rushes blindly back to the house, waves of heat rising from beneath his ribs like startled birds from a tree.

Once behind the closed door of his room, my father makes himself small as possible on the edge of his unmade bed. Staring hard at the baseboard, he tries to slow his tumbling heart. He has never seen his father cry, not even when his mother died. Now, having witnessed it, he feels like he has pulled the rug of manhood out from under the old man's feet. He convinces himself that it must be the lost mules his father was praying for, or for the mangled man who lies unconscious in the hospital bed in Nashville, and that this is what drove him to tears. It is only much later, picking asparagus in the ghost of a garden, that he will admit who his father had really been crying for: for his son, and for *his* son.

These days, my father remembers little from the time before the tractors. The growl of their engines in his mind has long since drowned out the quieter noises: the constant stamping and shifting of mule weight in the barn, the smooth sound of oats being poured into a steel bucket. He remembers the steam that rose from the animals after work. Pooled heaps of soft leather harness waiting to be mended on the breakfast table. At the threshold of the barn door, a velvet-eared dog that was always snapping its teeth at flies. Orphan standing dark and noble in the snow, a sled hooked to his harness. Eula Parker in a dark blue hat laughing and saying his name, hurrying after him and calling out "Wait, wait," one warm Sunday as he left church for home.

He remembers too his mother's cooking spices lined up in the cupboard where they had been since her death, faded inside their tins, without scent or taste. When he knew he was alone in the house, it gave him some sad comfort to take them out one by one and open them, the contents of each as dusty and gray as the next. He has just one memory of her, just an image: the curve of her spine and the fall of her hair when she had once leaned over to sniff the sheets on his bed, the morning after he'd wet it. This is all he has of her: one moment, just one, tangled in those little threads of shame.

In the same way I only have one memory of my grandfather, one watery picture from when I was very young. When my mother and father would rock me on the porch at night, my grandfather sat with them in a straight-backed chair, playing the banjo. He would tie a little tissue paper doll to his right wrist, and it danced and jumped like a tiny white ghost. I remember sitting on my mother's lap one night, and in the darkness the only things I could see were the tissue doll, the white moon of the banjo face, my mother's pale hair. I remember watching that doll bobbing along with my grandfather's strumming and, from time to time, the white flash of his teeth when he smiled. And I can hear him sing just a piece of one of the old songs: *I know'd it, indeed I know'd it, yes, I know'd it, my bones are gonna rise again.*

This is the story that my father tells me as he bends like a wire wicket in the garden, or, I should say, what once was my mother's garden. He parts the tangle of weeds to find the asparagus, then snaps off the tough spears with his knife, straightening slowly from time to time to stretch his stiff and rounded back. The garden is like a straight-edged wilderness in the middle of the closely mowed lawn, a blasted plot of weeds and thorns and thistle. Nothing has grown here since my mother died and no one wanted to tend it. Nothing except the asparagus, which comes up year after year.

Bullet in the Brain

TOBIAS WOLFF

Anders couldn't get to the bank until just before it closed, so of course the line was endless and he got stuck behind two women whose loud, stupid conversation put him in a murderous temper. He was never in the best of tempers anyway, Anders—a book critic known for the weary, elegant savagery with which he dispatched almost everything he reviewed.

With the line still doubled around the rope, one of the tellers stuck a "POSITION CLOSED" sign in her window and walked to the back of the bank, where she leaned against a desk and began to pass the time with a man shuffling papers. The women in front of Anders broke off their conversation and watched the teller with hatred. "Oh, that's nice," one of them said. She turned to Anders and added, confident of his accord, "One of those little human touches that keep us coming back for more."

Anders had conceived his own towering hatred of the teller, but he immediately turned it on the presumptuous crybaby in front of him. "Damned unfair," he said, "Tragic, really. If they're not chopping off the wrong leg, or bombing your ancestral village, they're closing their positions."

She stood her ground. "I didn't say it was tragic," she said, "I just think it's a pretty lousy way to treat your customers."

"Unforgivable," Anders said. "Heaven will take note."

She sucked in her cheeks but stared past him and said nothing. Anders saw that the other woman, her friend, was looking in the same direction. And then the tellers stopped what they were doing, and the customers slowly turned, and silence came over the bank. Two men wearing black ski masks and blue business suits were standing to the side of the door. One of them had a pistol pressed against the guard's neck. The guard's eyes were closed, and his lips were moving. The other man had a sawed-off shotgun. "Keep your big mouth shut!" the man with the pistol said, though no one had spoken a word. "One of you tellers hits the alarm, you're all dead meat. Got it?"

The tellers nodded.

"Oh, bravo," Anders said. "*Dead meat.*" He turned to the woman in front of him. "Great script, eh? The stern, brass-knuckled poetry of the dangerous classes."

She looked at him with drowning eyes.

The man with the shotgun pushed the guard to his knees. He handed the shotgun to his partner and yanked the guard's wrists up behind his back and locked them together with a pair of handcuffs. He toppled him onto the floor with a kick between the shoulder blades. Then he took his shotgun back and went over to the security gate at the end of the counter. He was short and heavy and moved with peculiar slowness, even torpor. "Buzz him in," his partner said. The man with the shotgun opened the gate and sauntered along the line of tellers, handing each of them a Hefty bag. When he came to the empty position he looked over at the man with the pistol, who said, "Whose slot is that?"

Anders watched the teller. She put her hand to her throat and turned to the man she'd been talking to. He nodded. "Mine," she said.

"Then get your ugly ass in gear and fill that bag."

"There you go," Anders said to the woman in front of him. "Justice is done."

"Hey! Bright boy! Did I tell you to talk?"

"No," Anders said.

"Then shut your trap."

"Did you hear that?" Anders said. "'Bright boy.' Right out of 'The Killers.'"

"Please be quiet," the woman said.

"Hey, you deaf or what?" The man with the pistol walked over to Anders. He poked the weapon into Anders' gut. "You think I'm playing games?"

"No," Anders said, but the barrel tickled like a stiff finger and he had to fight back the titters. He did this by making himself stare into the man's eyes, which were clearly visible behind the holes in the mask: pale blue and rawly red-rimmed. The man's left eyelid kept twitching. He breathed out a piercing, ammoniac smell that shocked Anders more than anything that had happened, and he was beginning to develop a sense of unease when the man prodded him again with the pistol.

"You like me, bright boy!" he said. "You want to suck my dick!"

"No," Anders said.

"Then stop looking at me."

Anders fixed his gaze on the man's shiny wing-tip shoes.

"Not down there. Up there." He stuck the pistol under Anders' chin and pushed it upward until Anders was looking at the ceiling.

Anders had never paid much attention to that part of the bank, a pompous old building with marble floors and counters and pillars, and gilt scrollwork over the tellers' cages. The domed ceiling had been decorated with mythological figures whose fleshy, toga-draped ugliness Anders had taken in at a glance many years earlier and afterward declined to notice. Now he had no choice but to scrutinize the painter's work. It was even worse than he remembered, and all of it executed with the utmost gravity. The artist had a few tricks up his sleeve and used them again and again—a certain rosy blush on the underside of the clouds, a coy backward glance on the faces of the cupids and fauns. The ceiling was crowded with various dramas, but the one that caught Anders' eye was Zeus and Europa—portrayed, in this rendition, as a bull ogling a cow from behind a haystack. To make the cow sexy, the painter had canted her hips suggestively and given her long, droopy eyelashes through which she gazed back at the bull with sultry welcome. The bull wore a smirk and his eyebrows were arched. If there'd been a bubble coming out of his mouth, it would have said, "Hubba hubba."

"What's so funny, bright boy?"

"Nothing."

"You think I'm comical? You think I'm some kind of clown?"

"No."

"You think you can fuck with me?"

"No."

"Fuck with me again, you're history. *Capiche?*"

Anders burst out laughing. He covered his mouth with both hands and said, "I'm sorry, I'm sorry," then snorted helplessly through his fingers and said, "*Capiche*—oh, God, *capiche*," and at that the man with the pistol raised the pistol and shot Anders right in the head.

The bullet smashed Anders' skull and ploughed through his brain and exited behind his right ear, scattering shards of bone into the cerebral cortex, the corpus callosum, back toward the basal ganglia, and down into the thalamus. But before all this occurred, the first appearance of the bullet in the cerebrum set off a crackling chain of iron transports and neuro-transmissions. Because of their peculiar origin these traced a peculiar pattern, flukishly calling to life a summer afternoon some forty years past, and long since lost to memory. After striking the cranium the bullet was moving at 900 feet per second, a pathetically sluggish, glacial pace compared to the synaptic lightning that flashed around it. Once in the brain, that is, the bullet came under the mediation of brain time, which gave Anders plenty of leisure to contemplate the scene that, in a phrase he would have abhorred, "passed before his eyes."

It is worth noting what Anders did not remember, given what he did remember. He did not remember his first lover, Sherry, or what he had most madly loved about her, before it came to irritate him—her unembarrassed carnality, and especially the cordial way she had with his unit, which she called Mr. Mole, as in, "Uh-oh, looks like Mr. Mole wants to play," and, "let's hide Mr. Mole!" Anders did not remember his wife, whom he had also loved before she exhausted him with her predictability, or his daughter, now a sullen professor of economics at Dartmouth. He did not remember standing just outside his daughter's door as she lectured her bear about his naughtiness and described the truly appalling punishments Paws would receive unless he changed his ways. He did not remember a single line of the hundreds of poems he had committed to memory in his youth so that he could give himself the shivers at will—not "Silent, upon a peak in Darien," or "My God, I heard this day," or "All my pretty ones? Did you say all? O hell-kite! All?" None of these did he remember; not one. Anders did not remember his dying mother saying of his father, "I should have stabbed him in his sleep."

He did not remember Professor Josephs telling his class how Athenian prisoners in Sicily had been released if they could recite Aeschylus, and then reciting Aeschylus himself, right there, in the Greek. Anders did not remember how his eyes had burned at those sounds. He did not remember the surprise of seeing a college classmate's name on the jacket of a novel not long after they graduated, or the respect he had felt after reading the book. He did not remember the pleasure of giving respect.

Nor did Anders remember seeing a woman leap to her death from the building opposite his own just days after his daughter was born. He did not remember shouting, "Lord have mercy!" He did not remember deliberately crashing his father's car into a tree, or having his ribs kicked in by three policemen at an anti-war rally, or waking himself up with laughter. He did not remember when he began to regard the heap of books on his desk with boredom and dread, or when he grew angry at writers for writing them. He did not remember when everything began to remind him of something else.

This is what he remembered. Heat. A baseball field. Yellow grass, the whirr of insects, himself leaning against a tree as the boys of the neighborhood gather for a pickup game. He looks on as the others argue the relative genius of Mantle and Mays. They have been worrying this subject all summer, and it has become tedious to Anders; an oppression, like the heat.

Then the last two boys arrive, Coyle and a cousin of his from Mississippi. Anders has never met Coyle's cousin before and will never see him again. He says hi with the rest but takes no further notice of him until they've chosen sides and someone asks the cousin what position he wants to play. "Shortstop," the boy says. "Short's the best position they is." Anders turns and looks at him. He wants to hear Coyle's cousin repeat what he's just said, but he knows better than to ask. The others will think he's being a jerk, ragging the kid for his grammar. But that isn't it, not at all—it's that Anders is strangely roused, elated, by those final two words, their pure unexpectedness and their music. He takes the field in a trance, repeating them to himself.

The bullet is already in the brain; it won't be outrun forever, or charmed to a halt. In the end it will do its work and leave the troubled skull behind, dragging its comet's tail of memory and hope and talent and love into the marble hall of commerce. That can't be helped. But for now Anders can still make time. Time for the shadows to lengthen on the grass, time for the tethered dog to bark at the flying ball, time for the boy in right field to smack his sweat-blackened mitt and softly chant, *They is, they is, they is.*

◆

Tandolfo the Great

RICHARD BAUSCH

"Tandolfo," he says to his own image in the mirror over the bathroom sink. "She loves you not, you goddam fool."

He's put the makeup on, packed the bag of tricks—including the rabbit, whom he calls Chi-Chi; and the bird, attention-getter, which he calls Witch. He's to do a birthday party on the other side of the river. Some five-year-old, and so this is going to be one of those tough ones, a crowd of babies, and all the adults waiting around for him to screw up.

He has fortified himself with something, and he feels ready. He isn't particularly worried about it. But there's a little something else he has to do, first. Something on the order of the embarrassingly ridiculous: he has to make a small delivery.

This morning, at the local bakery, he picked up a big pink wedding cake, with its six tiers and its scalloped edges and its little bride and groom on top. He'd ordered it on his own: he'd taken the initiative, planning to offer it to a young woman of his acquaintance. He managed somehow to set the thing on the backseat of the car and when he got home he found a note from her announcing, all excited and happy, that she's engaged. The man she'd had such trouble with has had a change of heart; he wants to get married after all. She's going to Houston to live. She loves her dear old Tandolfo with a big kiss and a hug always, and she knows he'll have every happiness. She's so thankful for his friendship. Her magic man. He's her sweet clown. She has actually driven over here and, finding him gone, left the note for him, folded under the door knocker—her pink notepaper, with the little tangle of flowers at the top. She wants him to call her, come by as soon as he can to help celebrate. *Please,* she says. *I want to give you a big hug.* He read this and then walked out to stand on the sidewalk and look at the cake in its place on the backseat of the car.

"Good God," he said. He'd thought he would put the clown outfit on, deliver the cake in person in the evening; an elaborate proposal to a girl he's never even kissed. He's a little unbalanced, and he knows it. Over the months of their working together for the county government, he's built up tremendous feelings of loyalty and yearning toward her. He thought she felt something, too. He interpreted gestures—her hand lingering on his shoulder when he made her laugh; her endearments to him, tinged as they seemed to be with a kind of sadness, as if she were afraid for what the world might do to someone so romantic.

"You sweet clown," she said. And she said it a lot. And she talked to him about her ongoing trouble, the guy she'd been in love with who kept waffling about getting married. He wanted no commitments. Tandolfo, aka Rodney Wilbury, told her that he hated men who weren't willing to run the risks of love. Why, he personally was the type who'd always believed in marriage and children, lifelong commitments. He had caused difficulties for himself and life was a disappointment so far, but he believed in falling in love and starting a family. She didn't hear him. It all went right through her like white noise on the radio. For weeks he had come around to visit her, had invited her to watch him perform. She confided in him, and he thought of movies where the friend sticks around and is a good listener, and eventually gets the girl. They fall in love. He put his hope in that. He was optimistic; he'd ordered and bought the cake. Apparently the whole time, all through the listening and being noble with her, she thought of it as nothing more than friendship, accepting it from him because she was accustomed to being offered friendship.

Now he leans close to the mirror to look at his own eyes through the makeup. They look clear enough. "Loves you absolutely not. You must be crazy. You must be the great Tandolfo."

Yes.

Twenty-six-year-old, out-of-luck Tandolfo. In love. With a great over-sized cake in the backseat of his car. It's Sunday, a cool April day. He's a little inebriated. That's the word he prefers. It's polite; it suggests something faintly silly. Nothing could be sillier than to be dressed like this in the broad daylight, and to go driving across the bridge into Virginia to put on a magic show. Nothing, could be sillier than to have spent all that money on a completely useless purchase—a cake six tiers high. Maybe fifteen pounds of sugar.

When he has made his last check of the clown face in the mirror, and the bag of tricks and props, he goes to his front door and stands at the screen looking out at the architectural shadow of it in the backseat. The inside of the car will smell like icing for days. He'll have to keep the windows open even if it rains; he'll go to work smelling like confectionery delights. The whole thing makes him laugh. A wedding cake. He steps out of the house and makes his way in the late-afternoon sun down the sidewalk to the car. As if they have been waiting for him, three boys come skating down from the top of the hill. He has the feeling that if he tried to sneak out like this at two in the morning, someone would come by and see him anyway. "Hey, Rodney," one boy says. "I mean Tandolfo."

Tandolfo recognizes him. A neighborhood boy, a tough. Just the kind to make trouble, just the kind with no sensitivity to the suffering of others. "Leave me alone or I'll turn you into spaghetti," he says.

"Hey, guys—it's Tandolfo the Great." The boy's hair is a bright blond color, and you can see through it to his scalp.

"Scram," Tandolfo says. "Really."

"Aw, what's your hurry, man?"

"I've just set off a nuclear device," Tandolfo says with grave seriousness. "It's on a timer. Poof."

"Do a trick for us," the blond one says. "Where's that scurvy rabbit of yours?"

"I gave it the week off." Someone, last winter, poisoned the first Chi-Chi. He keeps the cage indoors now. "I'm in a hurry. No rabbit to help with the driving."

But they're interested in the cake now. "Hey, what's that in your car? Is that what I think it is?"

"Just stay back."

"Is that a cake, man? Is that real?"

Tandolfo gets his cases into the trunk, and hurries to the driver's side door. The three boys are peering into the backseat.

"Hey, man. A cake. Can we have a piece of cake?"

"Back off," Tandolfo says.

The white-haired one says, "Come on, Tandolfo."

"Hey, Tandolfo, I saw some guys looking for you, man. They said you owed them money."

He gets in, ignoring them. He starts the car.

"You sucker," one of them says.

"Hey, man. Who's the cake for?"

He drives away, thinks of himself leaving them in a cloud of exhaust. Riding through the green shade, he glances in the rear-view mirror and sees the clown face, the painted smile. It makes him want to laugh. He tells himself he's his own cliché—a clown with a broken heart. Looming behind him is the cake, like a passenger in the backseat.

He drives slow. He has always believed viscerally that gestures mean everything. When he moves his hands and brings about the effects that amaze little children, he feels larger than life, unforgettable. He learned the magic while in high school, as a way of making friends, and though it didn't really make him any friends, he's been practicing it ever since. It's an extra source of income, and lately income has had a way of disappearing too quickly. He's been in some trouble—betting the horses; betting the sports events. He's hungover all the time. There have been several polite warnings at work. He's managed so far to tease everyone out of the serious looks, the cool evaluative study of his face. The fact is, people like him in an abstract way, the way they like distant clownish figures: the comedian whose name they can't remember. He can see it in their eyes. Even the rough characters after his loose change have a certain sense of humor about it. He's a phenomenon, a subject of conversation.

There's traffic on Key Bridge, and he's stuck for a while. It becomes clear that he'll have to go straight to the birthday party. Sitting behind the wheel of the car with his cake on the backseat, he becomes aware of people in other cars noticing him. In the car to his left, a girl stares, chewing gum. She waves, rolls her window down. Two others are with her, one in the backseat. "Hey," she says. He nods. Smiles inside what he knows is the painted smile. His teeth will look dark against the makeup.

"Where's the party?" she says.

But the traffic moves again. He concentrates. The snarl is on the other side of the bridge—construction of some kind. He can see the cars lined up, waiting to go up the hill into Roslyn and beyond. Time is beginning to be a consideration. In his glove box, he has a flask of bourbon. He reaches over and takes it out, looks around himself. No police anywhere. Just the idling cars and people tuning their radios or arguing or simply staring out as if at some distressing event. The smell of the cake is making him woozy. He takes a swallow of the bourbon, then puts it back. The car with the girls in it goes by him in the left lane, and they are not even looking at him. He watches them go on ahead. He's in the wrong lane again; he can't remember a time when his lane was the only one moving. He told her once that he considered himself in the race of people who gravitate to the nonmoving lanes of highways, and who cause traffic lights to turn yellow by approaching them. She took the idea and carried it out a little—saying she was of the race of people who emitted enzymes which instilled a sense of impending doom in marriageable young men, and made them wary of long-term relationships.

"No," Tandolfo/Rodney said. "I'm living proof that isn't so. I have no such fear, and I'm with you."

"But you're of the race of people who make mine relax all the enzymes."

"You're not emitting the enzymes now, I see."

"No," she said. "It's only with marriageable young men."

"I emit enzymes that prevent people like you from seeing that I'm a marriageable young man."

"I'm too relaxed to tell," she said, and touched his shoulder. A plain affectionate moment that gave him tossing nights and fever.

Because of the traffic, he arrives late at the birthday party. He gets out of the car and two men come down from the house to greet him. He keeps his face turned away, remembering too late the breath mints in his pocket.

"Jesus," one of the men says. "Look at this. Hey—who comes out of the cake? This is a kid's birthday party."

"The cake stays."

"What does he mean, it stays? Is that a trick?"

They're both looking at him. The one spoken to must be the birthday boy's father—he's wearing a party cap that says DAD. He has long dirty-looking strands of blond hair jutting out from the cap, and there are streaks of sweaty grit on the sides of his face. "So you're the Great Tandolfo," he says, extending a meaty red hand. "Isn't it hot in that makeup?"

"No, sir."

"We've been playing volleyball."

"You've exerted yourselves."

They look at him. "What do you do with the cake?" the one in the DAD cap asks.

"Cake's not part of the show, actually."

"You just carrying it around with you?"

The other man laughs. He's wearing a T-shirt with a smile face on the chest. "This ought to be some show," he says.

They all make their way across the street and the lawn, to the porch of the house. It's a big party—bunting everywhere and children gathering quickly to see the clown.

"Ladies and gentlemen," says the man in the DAD cap. "I give you Tandolfo the Great."

Tandolfo isn't ready yet. He's got his cases open, but he needs a table to put everything on. The first trick is where he releases the bird. He'll finish with the best trick, in which the rabbit appears as if from a pan of flames: it always draws a gasp, even from the adults; the fire blooms in the pan, down goes the "lid"—it's the rabbit's tight container—the latch is tripped, and the skin of the "lid" lifts off. *Voilà!* Rabbit. The fire is put out by the fireproof cage bottom. He's gotten pretty good at making the switch, and if the crowd isn't too attentive—as children often are not—he can perform certain hand tricks with some style. But he needs a table, and he needs time to set up.

The whole crowd of children is seated in front of the door into the house. He's standing here on the porch, his back to the stairs, and he's been introduced.

"Hello, boys and girls," he says, and bows. "Tandolfo needs a table."

"A table," one of the women says. All the adults are ranged against the porch wall, behind the children. He sees light sweaters, shapely hips, and wild tresses; he sees beer cans in tight fists and heavy jowls, bright ice-blue eyes. A little row of faces, and one elderly face. He feels more inebriated than he likes now, and he tries to concentrate.

"Mommy, I want to touch him," one child says.

"Look at the cake," says another, who's sitting on the railing to Tandolfo's right, with a new pair of shiny binoculars trained on the car. "Do we get some cake?"

"There's cake," says the man in the DAD cap. "But not that cake. Get down, Ethan."

"I want that cake."

"Get down. This is Teddy's birthday."

"Mommy, I want to touch him."

"I need a table, folks. I told somebody that over the telephone."

"He did say he needed a table. I'm sorry," says a woman who is probably the birthday boy's mother. She's quite pretty, leaning in the doorframe with a sweater tied to her waist.

"A table," says another woman. Tandolfo sees the birthmark on her mouth, which looks like a stain. He thinks of this woman as a child in school, with this difference from other children, and his heart goes out to her.

"I need a table," he says to her, his voice as gentle as he can make it.

"What's he going to do, perform an operation?" says DAD.

It amazes Tandolfo how easily people fall into talking about him as though he were an inanimate object, or something on a television screen. "The Great Tandolfo can do nothing until he gets a table," he says, with as much mysteriousness and drama as he can muster under the circumstances.

"I want that cake out there," says Ethan, still perched atop the porch railing. The other children start talking about cake and ice cream, and the big cake Ethan has spotted; there's a lot of confusion, and restlessness. One of the smaller children, a girl in a blue dress, comes forward and stands gazing at Tandolfo. "What's your name?" she says, swaying slightly, her hands behind her back.

"Go sit down," he says to her. "We have to sit down or Tandolfo can't do his magic."

In the doorway, two of the men are struggling with a folding card table. It's one of those rickety ones with the skinny legs, and it won't do.

"That's kind of rickety, isn't it?" says the woman with the birthmark.

"I said Tandolfo needs a sturdy table, boys and girls."

There's more confusion. The little girl has come forward and taken hold of his pant leg. she's just standing there holding it, looking at him. "We have to go sit down," he says, bending to her, speaking sweetly, clownlike. "We have to do what Tandolfo wants."

Her small mouth opens wide, as if she's trying to yawn, and with pale blue eyes quite calm and staring she emits a screech, an ear-piercing, nonhuman shriek that brings everything to a stop. Tandolfo/Rodney steps back, with his amazement and his inebriate heart, and now everyone's gathering around the girl, who continues to scream, less piercing now, her hands fisted at her sides, those blue eyes closed tight.

"What happened?" the man in the DAD cap wants to know. "Where the hell's the magic tricks?"

"I told you all I needed a *table*."

"Whud you say to her to make her cry?" He indicates the little girl, who is not merely crying but is giving forth a series of broken, grief-stricken howls.

"I want magic tricks," the birthday boy says, loud. "Where's the magic tricks?"

"Perhaps if we moved the whole thing inside," the woman with the birthmark says, fingering her left ear and making a face.

The card table has somehow made its way to Tandolfo, through the confusion and grief. The man in the DAD cap sets it down and opens it.

"There," he says, as if his point is made.

In the next moment, Tandolfo realizes that someone's removed the little girl. Everything's relatively quiet again, though her cries are coming through the walls of one of the rooms inside the house. There are perhaps fifteen children, mostly seated before him; five or six men and women behind them, or kneeling with them. "Okay, now," DAD says. "Tandolfo the Great."

"Hello, little boys and girls," Tandolfo/Rodney says. "I'm happy to be here. Are you glad to see me?" A general uproar goes up. "Well, good," he says. "Because just look what I have in my magic bag." And with a flourish, he brings out the hat from which he will release Witch. The bird is encased inside a fold of shiny cloth, pulsing there. He can feel it. He rambles on, talking fast, or trying to, and when the time comes to reveal the bird, he almost flubs it. But Witch flaps his wings and makes enough of a commotion to distract even the adults, who applaud now, and get the children to applaud. "Isn't that wonderful," Tandolfo hears. "Where did that bird come from?"

"He had it hidden away," says the birthday boy.

"Now," Tandolfo says, "for my next spell, I need a little friend from the audience." He looks right at the birthday boy—round face, short nose, freckles. Bright red hair. Little green eyes. The whole countenance speaks of glutted appetites and sloth. This kid could be on Roman coins, an emperor. He's not used to being compelled to do anything, but he seems eager for a chance to get into the act. "How about you?" Tandolfo says to him.

The others, led by their parents, cheer.

The birthday boy gets to his feet and makes his way over the bodies of the other children to stand with Tandolfo. In order for the trick to work, Tandolfo must get everyone watching the birthday boy, and there's a funny hat he keeps in the bag for this purpose. "Now," he says to the boy, "since you're part of the show, you have to wear a costume." He produces the hat as if from behind the boy's ear. Another cheer goes up. He puts the hat on his head and adjusts it, crouching down. The green eyes stare impassively at him; there's no hint of awe or fascination in them. "There we are," he says. "What a handsome fellow."

But the birthday boy takes the hat off.

"No, no. We have to wear the hat to be onstage."

"Ain't a stage," the boy says.

"Well, but hey," Tandolfo says for the benefit of the adults. "Didn't you know that all the world's a stage?" He tries to put the hat on again, but the boy moves from under his reach and slaps his hand away. "We have to wear the hat," Tandolfo says, trying to control his anger. "We can't do the magic without our magic hats." He tries once more, and the boy waits until the hat is on, then simply removes it and holds it behind him, shying away when Tandolfo tries to retrieve it. The noise of the others now sounds like the crowd at a prizefight; there's a contest going on, and they're enjoying it. "Give Tandolfo the hat now. We want magic, don't we?"

"Do the magic," the boy demands.

"I'll do the magic if you give me the hat."

"I won't."

Nothing. No support from the adults. Perhaps if he weren't a little tipsy, perhaps if he didn't feel ridiculous and sick at heart and forlorn, with his wedding cake and his odd mistaken romance, his loneliness, which he has always borne gracefully and in humor, and his general dismay; perhaps if he were to find it in himself to deny the sudden, overwhelming sense of the unearned affection given this little slovenly version of stupid complacent spoiled satiation standing before him—he might've simply gone on to the next trick.

Instead, he leans down and in the noise of the moment, says to the boy, "Give me the hat, you little prick."

The green eyes widen slightly.

It grows quiet. Even the small children can tell that something's happened to change everything.

"Tandolfo has another trick," Rodney says, "where he makes the birthday boy pop like a balloon. Especially if he's a fat birthday boy."

A stirring among the adults.

"Especially if he's an ugly little slab of flesh like this one here."

"Now just a minute," says DAD.

"Pop," Rodney says to the birthday boy, who drops the hat and then, seeming to remember that defiance is expected, makes a face. Sticks out his tongue. Rodney/Tandolfo is quick with his hands by training, and he grabs the tongue.

"Awk," the boy says. "Aw-aw-aw."

"Abracadabra." Rodney lets go, and the boy falls backward into the lap of one of the older children. "Whoops, time to sit down," says Rodney.

Very quickly, he's being forcibly removed. They're rougher than gangsters. They lift him, punch him, tear at his costume—even the women. Someone hits him with a spoon. The whole scene boils out onto the lawn, where someone has released the case that Chi-Chi was in. Chi-Chi moves about wide eyed, hopping between running children, evading them, as Tandolfo the Great cannot evade the adults. He's being pummeled, because he keeps trying to return for his rabbit. And the adults won't let him off the curb.

"Okay," he says finally, collecting himself. He wants to let them know he's not like this all the time; wants to say it's circumstances, grief, personal pain hidden inside seeming brightness and cleverness; he's a man in love, humiliated, wrong about everything. He wants to tell them, but he can't speak for a moment, can't even quite catch his breath. He stands in the middle of the street, his funny clothes torn, his face bleeding, all his magic strewn everywhere. "I would at least like to collect my rabbit," he says, and is appalled at the absurd sound of it—its huge difference from what he intended to say. He straightens, pushes the hair out of his eyes, adjusts the clown nose, and looks at them. "I would say that even though I wasn't as patient as I could've been, the adults have not comported themselves well here," he says.

"Drunk," one of the women says.

Almost everyone's chasing Chi-Chi now. One of the older boys approaches him, carrying Witch's case. Witch looks out the air hole, impervious, quiet as an idea. And now one of the men, someone Tandolfo hasn't noticed before, an older man clearly wearing a hairpiece, brings Chi-Chi to him. "Bless you," Rodney says, staring into the man's sleepy, deploring gaze.

"I don't think we'll pay you," the man says. The others are all filing back into the house, herding the children before them.

Rodney speaks to the man. "The rabbit appears out of fire."

The man nods. "Go home and sleep it off, kid."

"Right, thank you."

He puts Chi-Chi in his compartment, stuffs everything in its place in the trunk. Then he gets in and drives away. Around the corner he stops, wipes off what he can of the makeup; it's as if he's trying to remove the grime of bad opinion and disapproval. Nothing feels any different. He drives to the little suburban street where she lives with her parents, and by the time he gets there it's almost dark. The houses are set back in the trees; he sees lighted windows, hears music, the sound of children playing in the yards. He parks the car and gets out. A breezy April dusk.

"I am Tandolfo the soft-hearted," he says. "Hearken to me." Then he sobs. He can't believe it. "Jeez," he says. "Goddam."

He opens the back door of the car, leans in to get the cake. He'd forgotten how heavy it is. Staggering with it, making his way along the sidewalk, intending to leave it on her doorstep, he has an inspiration. Hesitating only for the moment it takes to make sure there are no cars coming, he goes out and sets it down in the middle of the street.

Part of the top sags slightly, from having bumped his shoulder as he pulled it off the backseat of the car. The bride and groom are almost supine, one on top of the other. He straightens them, steps back, and looks at it. In the dusky light, it looks blue. It sags just right, with just the right angle, expressing disappointment and sorrow.

Yes, he thinks. This is the place for it. The aptness of it, sitting out like this, where anyone might come by and splatter it all over creation, actually makes him feel some faint sense of release, as if he were at the end of a story. Everything will be all right if he can think of it that way. He's wiping his eyes, thinking of moving to another town. There are money troubles and troubles at work, and failures beginning to catch up to him, and he's still aching in love. He thinks how he has suffered the pangs of failure and misadventure, but in this painful instance there's symmetry, and he will make the one eloquent gesture—leaving a wedding cake in the middle of the road, like a sugar-icinged pylon. Yes.

He walks back to the car, gets in, pulls it around, and backs into the driveway of the house across the street. Leaving the engine idling, he rolls the window down and rests his arm on the sill, gazing at the incongruous shape of it there in the falling dark. He feels almost glad, almost—in some strange inexpressible way—vindicated, and he imagines what she might do if she saw him here. In a moment he's fantasizing that she comes running from her house, calling his name, looking at the cake and admiring it. This fantasy gives way to something else: images of destruction, flying sugar and candy debris. He's quite surprised to find that he wants her to stay where she is, doing whatever she's doing. He realizes with a feeling akin to elation that what he really wants—and for the moment all he really wants—is what he now has: a perfect vantage point from which to watch oncoming cars.

Turning the engine off, he waits, concentrating on the one thing, full of anticipation—dried blood and grime on his face, his hair all on end, his eyes glazed with rage and humiliation—a man imbued with interest, and happily awaiting the results of his labor.

Writing Exercises

1. Cheryl Moskowitz suggests "character imaging," making lists of the qualities, images, and actions that describe incongruities in the writer's personality. Here is a sample list from a student exercise:

Elegant	Vulgar
silk scarf to the knees	sequins on a fringed cowhide vest
still	laughing
frowns at library noise	hands out candy
startled gazelle	slobbering puppy
Waterford crystal	souvenir plate made in Mexico
a single white rosebud	two dozen overblown red roses
walks alone into the woods	throws a costume party

At this point the contradictory lists could be transformed into two separate characters. Give Ms. "Elegant" and Mr. "Vulgar" names and have them meet. Where do they meet? In what situation might they find themselves? How would a confrontation between these two play out?

2. Sometimes, our characters are too closely based on real-life people or parts of ourselves. We identify so closely with them that we are unwilling to let them get into any serious trouble, and trouble is what a story is all about. Write a scene in which your character gets into trouble. How might you have her mess up? Perhaps she makes a fool of herself by saying or doing the wrong thing, or is stubborn even though she is dead wrong about something. Maybe someone else is at fault, maybe she's chosen to do something downright bad. An indiscretion? An "experiment"? An immoral act?

3. Write two versions of an opening paragraph of a story that introduces a character indirectly—one in which you (as the author) describe her and a second in which another character in the story does the describing.

   In your first version tell the reader some of the basics (gender, age, race/nationality, class, region, period, etc.), but go further as well, revealing some details about the character's personality and desires, values and emotions. In your second version, let another character introduce that character. What is this second character's attitude toward the first? What does he or she know, guess, conclude?

4. Every family has one—a black sheep, an eccentric, an embarrassment. For a page or two describe that person in your own family. It may well be someone others talk about and disapprove of, but whom you find intriguing. Is there the germ of a story in the rumors, the envy, and the half-told tales? Or, perhaps the story grows out of the actual encounters you or others have had with this person.

5. Have a character write a letter to someone with whom she's had a misunderstanding or disagreement, but have her do this *without addressing the problem directly*. Perhaps she's being polite, perhaps she's trying to protect herself, but in any case, she dances around the main issue in the letter, which is nevertheless clearly revealed. In the course of this letter, she will be telling us something about the second character, the one with whom she has the problem, but inadvertently, she will be telling us even more about herself—about her own prejudices, biases, insecurities, jealousies, and fears.

6. Divide up into small groups of at least three people each. Each member of the group should brainstorm a list of character names: first and last names, even nicknames if you want. One or two of the names may be blatantly symbolic, but most should be evocative: compelling but plausible, ordinary but suggestive. Everyone should come up with six to eight names.

   Now, switch lists. Pick a name from this new list and let it help you imagine a character. Write out some basic information about the character (age, race, religion, education, class, marital status, profession), and add a few interesting details about the character (hobbies, bad habits, fears, personality quirks, desires, aspirations, past experiences). Do this for three or four of the character names and see if you can use these characters to begin a story.

7. Pair up. Decide on a conflict that would arise between two characters. The more at stake the better. Each write a monologue in the point of view of one or the other of the characters. Let the character speak freely in the monologue, passionately setting forth his or her point of view. Read the monologues to each other.

Set the monologues aside, and each write a scene containing both characters in a situation that brings out the conflict between them.

8. Pair up. With your partner, decide on a situation where one character is rambling on about something and a second character is forced to listen. Now, each of you should freewrite a monologue for this character, letting her or him go on and on.

Exchange monologues, read them silently, and then, individually, rewrite the scene from the point of view of the *listener*, using the three methods of conveying speech. Use the monologue your partner gave you, but *summarize* some of it, present some of it as *indirect speech*, and finally, for use as *direct quotation*, select a few of the choicest, juiciest, most revealing lines.

5

◈

FAR, FAR AWAY
Fictional Place

♦ Place and Atmosphere

♦ Harmony and Conflict Between Character and Place

♦ Place and Character

♦ Place and Emotion

♦ Symbolic and Suggestive Place

♦ Alien and Familiar Place

♦ An Exercise in Place

"It's the job of the writer to create a world that entices you in and shows you what's at stake there," says fiction writer Nancy Huddleston Packer. For some writers, that world itself may inspire the story, while others will tend to focus on setting and atmosphere during the revision process. Still, even from the first, raw draft, it is important to remember Elizabeth Bowen's maxim that "nothing happens nowhere" and Jerome Stern's further admonition that a scene that seems to happen nowhere often seems not to happen at all. The failure to create an atmosphere, to establish a sense of where or when the story takes place, will leave readers bored or confused. And just as the rhythm of your prose must work with and not against your intention, so the use of place must work with and not against your ultimate meaning. Setting helps define a story's dimensions. Setting grounds a story in place.

Like dialogue, setting must do more than one thing at once, from illuminating the story's symbolic underpinnings to such practical kinds of "showing" as reflecting emotion or revealing subtle aspects of a character's life. Yet just as character and plot are interlinked, so character itself is a product of place and culture. We need not only know a character's gender, race, and age, but also in what atmosphere she or he operates to understand the significance of the action. For instance, could you imagine Scarlett O'Hara, from *Gone with the Wind*, without her plantation? Scarlett O'Hara acts as she does because she's a product of the Old South. The setting in which she's always lived defines and helps to explain her.

Sister Clareese in ZZ Packer's story "Every Tongue Shall Confess" doesn't challenge the hypocritical and sexist deacons of the Greater Christ Emmanuel Church of the Fire Baptized, because her church, with its familiar roles and expectations, is comforting and the most important thing in her life. The two bickering old women in Eudora Welty's story "A Visit of Charity" behave the way they do because they've been forgotten by the outside world, forced to live out their last days together in the cold, dark nursing home. The main character in Dan Chaon's story "Big Me" reacts against the unpleasant reality of his small town life by imagining an alternative small town in which good and evil are well defined and he's the one in control. His overinvolvement in this imaginary world is what causes him to take the risks that are essential to the story. And finally, setting itself may give rise to an external conflict—one as big as the Vietnam War in "The Things They Carried" or as small as the disrupted birthday party in "Tandolfo the Great." The setting need not seem scary or even problematic to us as readers—a child's birthday party seems harmless enough—but if the character—in this case a drunk, enraged, humiliated clown—finds the setting to be hostile, then a conflict is born.

WHEN I WAS WRITING *Searches and Seizure,* I was living in London, and I needed to describe a hotel room. I've been in lots of hotel rooms, of course, but I didn't want to depend upon my memory. And so I went to the Royal Garden Hotel in Kensington and rented a room, simply to study the furniture there, to feel the glossy top of the wood that is almost not wood, to get the smell of the shower, the textures in the bath, to look at the rhetoric on the cards on top of the television set. This is stuff that I could not invent, and it was important to me to have it down very, very accurately. So I took notes. Somebody watching me would have thought I was a madman.

STANLEY ELKIN

But realistic settings constructed from memory or research are only part of the challenge, for an intensely created fantasy world makes new boundaries for the mind. *Once upon a time, long ago and far away, a dream, hell, heaven, a garbage shaft, Middle Earth, Hogwarts boarding school,* and *the subconscious* all have been the settings of excellent fiction. Even Utopian fiction, set *Nowhere* with a capital *N* (or *nowhere* spelled backward, as Samuel Butler had it in *Erehwon*), happens in a nowhere with distinct physical characteristics. Outer space is an exciting setting precisely because its physical boundary is the outer edge of our familiar world. Obviously this does not absolve the writer from the necessity of giving outer space its own characteristics, atmosphere, and logic. If anything, these must be more intensely realized within the fiction, since we have less to borrow from in our own experience.

> The westering sun shining in on his face woke Shevek as the dirigible, clearing the last high pass of the Ne Theras, turned south....He pressed his face to the dusty window, and sure enough, down there between two low rusty ridges was a great walled field, the Port. He gazed eagerly, trying to see if there was a spaceship on the pad. Despicable as Urras was, still it was another world; he wanted to see a ship from another world, a voyager across the dry and terrible abyss, a thing made by alien hands. But there was no ship in the Port.
>
> Ursula K. Le Guin, *The Dispossessed*

We may be in outer space, but we are on a planet that shares certain aspects with our own—a westering sun, a mountain pass, and a walled field with two low rusty ridges—disappointingly empty. We've gone some place specific and real, and it is that reality and specificity that allow us to get lost in the story.

But what ingredients, when mixed together, make a setting? Is setting simply a description of the current weather conditions and the sights and smells and sounds immediately in the foreground of your story? Not necessarily. Fiction writer Michael Martone says that a truly effective evocation of fictional setting might resemble those old painted murals in post offices from the 1930s and early '40s. Any one of the figures in the mural has his or her own story, while at the same time those stories are embedded in the larger story of the whole painting. As we stand there observing the figures, we may see the social interactions between them but at the same time, we also observe the layers of history and social forces around these characters as evidenced in their buildings, their inventions, their appliances, their transportation, their agriculture, their efforts to tame and control nature.

"These murals attempt," says Martone, "by the design of hundreds of details, to convey the simultaneous presence of history and social life of the greater community along with the personal specific struggle of a protagonist. Purely as a practical matter, placing stories in such a fertile media will make it easy for things to happen [in a story], for characters to do things."

To illustrate this, Martone refers to a story by Rick DeMarinis titled "Under the Wheat," about a construction worker who is building nuclear silos in a nearly deserted North Dakota town. As Martone points out, the character in this story is always looking up or down through various membranes of time and space. He is dwarfed by the constructed and the natural features of the place. Here he is fishing on the still surface of the lake created by a nearby dam:

> Something takes my hook and strips off ten yards of line and then stops dead. Snag. I reel it in. The pole is bent double and the line is singing. Then something lets go but it isn't the line because I'm still snagged. It breaks the surface, a lady's shoe. It's brown and white with a short heel. I toss it into the bottom of the boat. The water is shallow here, and clear. There's something dark and wide under me like a shadow on the water. An old farmhouse, submerged when the dam filled. There's a deep current around the structure. I can see fence, tires, an old truck, feed pens. There is a fat farmer in the yard looking up at me, checking the weather, and I jump away from him, almost tipping the boat. My heart feels tangled in my ribs. But it is only a stump with arms. The current takes my boat in easy circles. A swimmer would be in serious trouble. I crank up the engine and head back. No fish today. So be it. Sometimes you come home empty-handed. The shoe is new, stylish and was made in Spain.

Setting can be rich and layered with many relics from the past—the barn, the fence, the truck. And it can be ominous—where did that lady's shoe come from?

Place and Atmosphere

Your fiction must have an *atmosphere* because without it your characters will be unable to breathe.

Part of the atmosphere of a scene or story is its setting, including the locale, period, weather, and time of day. Part of the atmosphere is its *tone*, an attitude taken by the narrative voice that can be described in terms of a quality—sinister, facetious, formal, solemn, wry. The two facets of atmosphere, setting and tone, are often inextricably mixed in the ultimate effect. A sinister atmosphere might be achieved partly by syntax, rhythm, and word choice; partly by darkness, dampness, and a desolate landscape, as is shown in the first line of Edgar Allan Poe's "The Fall of the House of Usher":

> During the whole of a dull, dark, and soundless day in the autumn of the year, when the clouds hung oppressively low in the heavens, I had been passing alone, on horseback, through a singularly dreary tract of country; and at length found myself, as the shades of the evening drew on, within view of the melancholy House of Usher.

In Annie Proulx's story "What Kind of Furniture Would Jesus Pick?" we can feel the extent of a beleaguered housewife's oppression when we read this description of the wind attacking her Wyoming ranch:

> The house lay directly in line with a gap in the encircling hills to the northwest, and through this notch the prevailing winds poured, falling on the house with ferocity. The house shuddered as the wind punched it and slid along its sides like a released torrent from a broken dam. Week after week in winter it sank and rose, attacked and feinted. When she put her head down and went out to the truck it yanked at her clothing, shot up her sleeves, whisked her hair into a raveled fright wig.

The words *encircling hills, prevailing winds, falling, ferocity, shuddered, punched, released torrent, broken dam, week after week, sank and rose, attacked and feinted, put her head down, yanked, shot, whisked,* and *raveled fright wig* leave no doubt as to how she's feeling, not only about the wind, but about her life in general.

You can orient your reader in a place with straight information (*On the southern bank of the Bayou Teche . . .*), but as with the revelation of character, you may more effectively reveal place through concrete detail (*The bugs hung over the black water in clusters of a steady hum*). Stuart Dybek offers another set of evocative details in his story "Breasts": *Joe's bedroom window was open too, and a breeze that tingled the blinds they hadn't bothered to draw seemed tinted with the glow of the new arc lights the city had erected.* In both of these examples the information is indirect. We aren't sure yet what to make of the clusters of bugs or the open blinds, but they reveal an attitude toward the setting, and we seem to experience it firsthand.

Harmony and Conflict Between Character and Place

If character is the foreground of fiction, setting is the background, and as in a painting's composition, the foreground may be in harmony or in conflict with the background. If we think of the Impressionist paintings of the late nineteenth century, we think of the harmony of, say, women with light-scattering parasols strolling against summer landscapes of light-scattering trees. By contrast, the Spanish painter José Cortijo has a portrait of a girl on her Communion day; she sits curled and ruffled, in a lace mantilla, on an ornately carved Mediterranean throne against a backdrop of stark, harshly lit, poverty-stricken shacks.

Likewise, the setting and characters of a story may be in harmony:

> The Bus to St. James's—a Protestant Episcopal school for boys and girls— started its round at eight o'clock in the morning, from a corner of Park Avenue in the Sixties. The earliness of the hour meant that some of the parents who took their children there were sleepy and still without coffee,

but with a clear sky the light struck the city at an extreme angle, the air was fresh, and it was an exceptionally cheerful time of day. It was the hour when cooks and door men walk dogs, and when porters scrub the lobby floor mats with soap and water.

John Cheever, "The Bus to St. James's"

Contentment, regularity, and peace are suggested by this passage. For the parents and the students of St. James, all is right with the world.

Or there can be an inherent conflict between the background and foreground:

...He opened the door himself and started down the walk to get her going. The sky was a dying violet and the houses stood out darkly against it, bulbous liver-colored monstrosities of a uniform ugliness though no two were alike. Since this had been a fashionable neighborhood forty years ago, his mother persisted in thinking they did well to have an apartment in it. Each house had a narrow collar of dirt around it in which sat, usually, a grubby child. Julian walked with his hands in his pockets, his head down and thrust forward and his eyes glazed with the determination to make himself completely numb during the time he would be sacrificed to her pleasure.

Flannery O'Connor, "Everything That Rises Must Converge"

Notice how images of the time of day work with concrete details of place to create very different atmospheres—on the one hand *morning, Park Avenue, earliness, clear sky, light, extreme angle, air, fresh, cheerful, dogs, scrub, soap, water*; and on the other *dying violet, darkly, bulbous liver-colored monstrosities, uniform ugliness, narrow, dirt, grubby child*. Notice also that where conflict occurs, there is already "narrative content," or the makings of a story. We might reasonably expect that in the Cheever story, where the characters are in apparent harmony with their background, there is or will be conflict in the foreground between or among those children, parents, and perhaps the servitors who keep their lives so well scrubbed. It won't surprise us when the peace and quiet of this world shatters, and the weather gets downright dangerous by the end of the story.

Place and Character

One of the most economical means of sketching a character is simply to show readers a personal space that the character has created, be it a bedroom, locker, kitchen, hideout, office cubicle, or the interior of a car. This technique is illustrated in Elizabeth Tallent's story "Prowler," as Dennis, a divorced father, surveys his thirteen-year-old son's bedroom.

Dennis believes it tells everything about Kenny: photo-realist motorcycles, chrome and highly evolved threat, grace the walls, along with a frail Kafka razor-bladed from a library book, a sin so small and so unprecedented that Dennis uncharacteristically forgot to mention it to him. If Kenny's motor-cycle paintings are depressing, surely jug-eared Kafka promises complexity, contradiction, hope?

Through the description of Kenny's room, we see that the boy is making a transition to the rocky years of adolescence, showing both a typical interest in fast, powerful, rebellious vehicles and also signs of more private teenage angst (and what is he doing with razor blades anyway?). Not every parent would interpret a Kafka portrait, much less a stolen one, as a sign of hope—in this case, the reflection may reveal as much about the observing father as about the indirectly observed son, adding a further layer of complexity.

Doug Coupland uses an even more self-conscious version of the same technique to create a quick portrait of the household of fanatical young Microsoft employees featured in his novel *Microserfs*:

> More details about our group house—Our House of Wayward Mobility.
> Because the house receives almost no sun, moss and algae tend to colo-nize what surfaces they can. There is a cherry tree, crippled by a fungus. The rear verandah, built of untreated 2×4's, has quietly rotted away, and the sliding door in the kitchen has been braced shut with a hockey stick to prevent the unwary from straying into the suburban abyss. . . .
> Inside, each of us has a bedroom. Because of the McDonald's-like turnover in the house, the public rooms—the living room, kitchen, dining room, and basement—are bleak to say the least. The dormlike atmosphere precludes heavy-duty interior design ideas. In the living room are two vel-veteen sofas that were too big and too ugly for some long-gone tenants to take with them. Littered about the Tiki Green shag carpet are:
>
> - Two Microsoft Works PC inflatable beach cushions
> - One Mitsubishi 27-inch color TV
> - Various vitamin bottles
> - Several weight-gaining system cartons (mine)
> - 86 copies of MacWEEK arranged in chronological order by Bug Barbecue, who will go berserk if you so much as move one issue out of date
> - Bone-shaped chew toys for when Mishka visits
> - Two PowerBooks
> - Three IKEA mugs encrusted with last month's blender drink sensation
> - Two 12.5 pound dumbbells (Susan's)

- A Windows NT box

- Three baseball caps (two Mariners, one A's)

- Abe's Battlestar Galactica trading card album

- Todd's pile of books on how to change your life to win! (*Getting Past OK, 7 Habits of Highly Effective People . . .*)

The kitchen is stocked with ramshackle 1970s avocado green appliances. You can almost hear the ghost of Emily Hartley yelling "Hi, Bob!" every time you open the fridge door (a sea of magnets and 4x6-inch photos of last year's house parties). Our mail is in little piles by the front door: bills, Star Trek junk mail, and the heap-o-catalogues next to the phone.

I think we'd order our lives via 1-800 numbers if we could.

Like their mold-ravaged house, the Microserfs also receive almost no sun as they pursue their project shipping deadlines round the clock; the litter of objects listed gives clues to whatever thin slices of personality remain.

What generalizations might you make about the Microserfs after reading this passage? Are they self-absorbed? Driven? Wealthy? Immature? Focused? Sloppy? All these descriptions may apply, but they seem bland and inadequate when juxtaposed with the list of specific details that bring them to life in a way that mere adjectives never could.

Here is Michael Martone again: "The reader is to be pulled in by the preponderance of the evidence that he or she has been sifting through. As you read, the details fall like snow that suddenly is ash. The character is clearly visible once he is coated, like a statue in the town square after such a storm, with a film of detail."

SUPPOSE WE THINK OF A SCENE IN YOUR NOVEL as a scene in a play. Any scene in any play takes place on some sort of set. I feel that the sets in your play are quite wonderful, but you never let us see them. A spotlight follows every move the characters make and throws an almost blinding radiance on them, but it is a little like the spotlight a burglar uses when he is cracking a safe; it illuminates a small circle and the rest of the stage is in darkness most of the time. . . . It would be better, I think, if you occasionally used a spotlight large enough to illuminate the corners of the room, for those corners have gone on existing all through the most dramatic moments.

CAROLINE GORDON TO FLANNERY O'CONNOR

Place and Emotion

Our relation to place, time, and weather, like our relation to clothes and other objects, is charged with emotion more or less subtle, more or less profound. It is filled with judgment mellow or harsh. And it alters according to what happens to us. In some rooms you are always trapped; you enter them with grim purpose and escape them as soon as you can. Others invite you to settle in, to nestle or carouse. Some landscapes lift your spirits; others depress you. Cold weather gives you energy and bounce, or else it clogs your head and makes you huddle, struggling. You describe yourself as a night person or a morning person. The house you loved as a child now makes you, precisely because you were once happy there, think of loss and death. It is central to fiction that all such emotion be used or heightened (or invented) to dramatic effect.

Imagine experiencing a thunderstorm when in the throes of a new love: The rain might seem to glitter, the lightning to sizzle, the thunder to rumble with anticipation. The downpour would refresh and exhilarate, nourishing the newly budding violets. Then imagine how the very same storm would feel in the midst of a lousy romantic breakup: The raindrops would be thick and cold, almost greasy; the lightning would slash at the clouds; the thunder would growl. Torrents of rain would beat the delicate tulips to the ground.

Because we have all had the experience of seeing our inner emotional states reflected by the outer world, we instinctively understand that setting can serve as a mirror of emotion. Seen through the eyes of a character, setting is never neutral.

In Frederick Busch's story "Ralph the Duck," the narrator thinks back on a troubling incident that had taken place during his rounds at the local college that evening. He sits with a "king-sized drink composed of sour mash whiskey and ice" and

> In our back room, which is on the northern end of the house, and cold for sitting in that close to dawn, I sat and watched the texture of the sky change. It was going to snow, and I wanted to see the storm come up the valley.

He seems to sense that there is worse trouble to come, and in fact it later arrives in the middle of an ice storm. Yet by the story's end, when he is feeling some relief and hope (to which the laconic narrator himself would never admit), we see these feelings mirrored in a very different view of the same landscape.

> I was at the northern windows, looking through the mullions down
> the valley to the faint red line along the mounds and little peaks of
> the ridge beyond the valley. The sun was going to come up, and I was
> looking for it.

Setting can help to portray a swirl of emotion, as in this moment from Joyce Carol Oates's story "Where Are You Going, Where Have You Been?" in which Arnold Friend's attempts to disorient and terrorize Connie are succeeding, and she is losing her grasp on all that is familiar, even as she feels nostalgic for the home she is leaving:

> The kitchen looked like a place she had never seen before, some room she had run inside but which wasn't good enough, wasn't going to help her. The kitchen window had never had a curtain, after three years, and there were dishes in the sink for her to do—probably—and if you ran your hand across the table you'd probably feel something sticky there.

Emotion is conveyed in these and similar passages, even as the story is being anchored in place. When a reader senses that setting is being used to reveal something important, there is no danger of its being what one student calls "the stuff you skip."

What do we skip? Self-indulgent description of setting that seems to exist only as an excuse for flowery, inflated language: "The majestic mountains rose like great behemoths above the grassy plains, and the plains themselves rolled away like a great and endless ocean." Description of setting that feels forced—an overly fastidious catalog of details, often awkwardly placed: "The dead man's pantry was stocked with canisters of oatmeal, Cream of Wheat, corn meal, flour (white and whole wheat), rice (brown and white), couscous, instant grits, and Wheatena, and bottles of various cooking oils—corn, olive, canola, sunflower and vegetable." Description that is generic and perfunctory, lacking in emotional significance or authorial judgment: "Robert's farm consisted of 1,276 acres of land, most of which was tillable, but seventy-seven acres of which was made up of woodlots and inaccessible bottomland along three different creeks."

Michael Martone, in a lecture on setting, noted: "In many stories I read, [household] appliances are often deployed neutrally, used mainly...as a way to fill up space, background things merely to run or handle, props, business for the character to perform when the real action is happening between people."

When we read any nonessential description, our eyes and minds will glaze over and we'll either skip ahead to "the good parts" or stop reading altogether.

"SWALLOWS, FLITTING OVER THE SURFACE OF THE WATER, twittered gaily"—eliminate such commonplaces. You have to choose small details in describing nature, grouping them in such a way that if you close your eyes after reading it you can picture the whole thing. For example, you'll get a picture of a moonlit night if you write that on the dam of the mill a piece of broken bottle flashed like a bright star and the black shadow of a dog or a wolf rolled by like a ball, etc.

ANTON CHEKHOV TO HIS BROTHER ALEXANDER

Symbolic and Suggestive Place

Ever since the rosy-fingered dawn came over the battlefield of Homer's *Iliad* (and no doubt well before that), poets and writers have used the context of history, night, storm, stars, sea, city, and plain to give their stories a sense of reaching out toward the universe. Sometimes the universe resonates with an answer, and in his plays Shakespeare consistently drew parallels between the conflicts of the heavenly bodies and the conflicts of nations and characters.

In "The Life You Save May Be Your Own," Flannery O'Connor uses the elements in a conscious Shakespearian way, letting the setting reflect and affect the theme.

> The old woman and her daughter were sitting on their own porch when Mr. Shiflet came up their road for the first time. The old woman slid to the edge of her chair and leaned forward, shading her eyes from the piercing sunset with her hand. The daughter could not see far in front of her and continued to play with her fingers. Although the old woman lived in this desolate spot with only her daughter, and she had never seen Mr. Shiflet before, she could tell, even from a distance, that he was a tramp and no one to be afraid of. His left coat sleeve was folded up to show there was only half an arm in it and his gaunt figure listed lightly to the side as if the breeze were pushing him. He had on a black town suit and a brown felt hat that was turned up in the front and down in the back and he carried a tin tool box by a handle. He came on at an amble, up her road, his face turned toward the sun which appeared to be balancing itself on the peak of a small mountain.

The focus in this opening paragraph of the story is on the characters and their actions, and the setting is economically, almost incidentally, established: *porch, road, sunset, breeze, peak, small mountain.* What the passage gives us is a type of landscape, rural and harsh; the only adjectives in the description of the setting are *piercing, desolate,* and *small.* But this general background works together with details of action, thought, and appearance to establish a great deal more that is both informational and emotional. The old woman's peering suggests that people on the road are not only unusual but suspicious. On the other hand, that she is reassured to see a tramp suggests both a period and a set of assumptions about country life. That Mr. Shiflet wears a town suit establishes him as a stranger to this set of assumptions. That the sun appears to be balancing itself (we are not sure whether it is the old woman's observation or the author's) leaves us, at the end of the paragraph, with a sense of anticipation and tension.

Now, what happens in the story is this: Mr. Shiflet repairs the old woman's car and (in order to get the car) marries her retarded daughter. He abandons the daughter on their honeymoon and picks up a hitchhiker who insults both Mr. Shiflet and the memory of his mother. The hitchhiker jumps out. Mr. Shiflet curses and drives on.

Throughout the story, as in the first paragraph, the focus remains on the characters and their actions. Yet the landscape and the weather make their presence felt, subtly commenting on attitudes and actions. As Mr. Shiflet's fortunes wax promising and he expresses satisfaction with his own morality, "A fat yellow moon appeared in the branches of the fig tree as if it were going to roost there with the chickens." When, hatching his plot, he sits on the steps with the mother and daughter, "The old woman's three mountains were black against the sky." Once he has abandoned the girl, the weather grows "hot and sultry, and the country had flattened out. Deep in the sky a storm was preparing very slowly and without thunder." Once more there is a sunset, but this time the sun "was a reddening ball that through his windshield was slightly flat on the bottom and top," and this deflated sun reminds us of the "balanced" one about to be punctured by the peak in its inevitable decline. When the hitchhiker has left him, a cloud covers the sun, and Mr. Shiflet in his fury prays for the Lord to "break forth and wash the slime from this earth!" His prayer is apparently answered.

> After a few minutes there was a guffawing peal of thunder from behind and fantastic raindrops, like tin-can tops, crashed over the rear of Mr. Shiflet's car. Very quickly he stepped on the gas and with his stump sticking out the window he raced the galloping shower to Mobile.

The setting in this story, as this bald summary emphasizes, is deliberately used as a comment on the actions. The behavior of the weather, in ironic juxtaposition to the title, "The Life You Save May Be Your Own," makes clear that the "slime" Mr. Shiflet has damned may be himself. Yet the reader is never aware of this as a symbolic intrusion. The setting remains natural and realistically convincing, an incidental backdrop, until the heavens are ready to make their guffawing comment.

Robert Coover's settings rarely present a symbolic or sentient universe, but they produce in us an emotionally charged expectation of what is likely to happen here. The following passages are the opening paragraphs of three short stories from a single collection, *Pricksongs and Descants*. Notice how the three different settings are achieved not only by imagery and content, but also by the very different rhythms of the sentence structure.

> A pine forest in the midafternoon. Two children follow an old man, dropping breadcrumbs, singing nursery tunes. Dense earthy greens seep into the darkening distance, flecked and streaked with filtered sunlight. Spots of red, violet, pale blue, gold, burnt orange. The girl carries a basket for gathering flowers. The boy is occupied with the crumbs. Their song tells of God's care for little ones.

> "The Gingerbread House"

Situation: television panel game, live audience. Stage strobelit and cameras insecting about. Moderator, bag shape corseted and black suited behind desk/rostrum, blinking mockmodesty at lens and lamps, practised pucker on his soft mouth and brows arched in mild goodguy astonishment. Opposite him, the panel: Aged Clown, Lovely Lady and Mr. America, fat as the continent and bald as an eagle. There is an empty chair between Lady and Mr. A, which is now filled, to the delighted squeals of all, by a spectator dragged protesting from the Audience, nondescript introduced as Unwilling Participant, or more simply, Bad Sport. Audience: same as ever, docile, responsive, good-natured, terrifying. And the Bad Sport, you ask, who is he? fool! thou art!

"Panel Game"

She arrives at 7:40, ten minutes late, but the children, Jimmy and Bitsy, are still eating supper, and their parents are not ready to go yet. From the other rooms come the sounds of a baby screaming, water running, a television musical (no words: probably a dance number—patterns of gliding figures come to mind). Mrs. Tucker sweeps into the kitchen, fussing with her hair, and snatches a baby bottle full of milk out of a pan of warm water, rushes out again. Harry! she calls. The babysitter's here already!

"The Babysitter"

Here are three quite familiar places: a fairy-tale forest, a television studio, and a suburban house. In at least the first two selections, the locale is more consciously and insistently set than in the O'Connor opening, yet all three remain suggestive backdrops rather than active participants—no guffawing or galloping here. Coover directs our attitude toward these places through imagery and tone.

In "The Gingerbread House," the forest is a neverland, and the time is once upon a time, though there are grimmer-than-Grimm hints of violence about it. Simple sentence structure helps establish the childlike quality appropriate to a fairy tale. But a more complex sentence intervenes, with surprising intensity of imagery: *dense, earthy, seep, darkening, flecked, streaked, filtered.* Because of this, the innocence of the tone is set askew, so that by the time we hear of God's care for little ones, we fully and accurately expect a brutal disillusionment.

Setting can often, and in a variety of ways, arouse reader expectation and foreshadow events to come. In "The Gingerbread House," there is an implied conflict between character and setting, between the sentimentality of the children's flowers and nursery tunes and the threatening forest, so that we are immediately aware of the central conflict of the story: innocence versus violence. As in the Cheever story "The Bus to St. James's," anticipation can also be aroused by an insistent single attitude toward setting, and in this case the reader, being a contrary sort of person, is likely to anticipate a change or paradox.

Where conflict between character and setting is immediately intro-duced, as it is in both "The Gingerbread House" and "Panel Game," it is usually because the character is unfamiliar with, or uncomfortable in, the setting. In "Panel Game" it's both. The television studio is a place of hys-teria, chaos, and hypocrisy (as evidenced by the moderator's mockmodesty and practiced pucker). The television studio, which is in fact a familiar and unthreatening place to most of us, has been made mad. This is achieved partly by violating expected grammar. The sentences are not sen-tences. They are missing vital verbs and logical connectives, so that the images are squashed against each other. The prose is cluttered, effortful, negative; as a result, as reader you know "the delighted squeals of all" do not include your own, and you're ready to sympathize with the unwilling central character (you!).

In "The Babysitter," notice that the setting is ordinary and is presented as ordinary. The sentences have standard and rather leisurely syntax; neither form nor image startles. Details are generic, not specific: the house is presented without a style; the children are named but not seen; Mrs. Tucker behaves in a way predictable and familiar to most anyone in contemporary America. What Coover has in fact done is to present us with a setting so usual, so "typical," that we begin to suspect that something unusual is afoot.

Indeed, the Tuckers, their house, their children, their car, their night out, and their babysitter remain unvaryingly typical throughout all the external actions in the course of the evening. Against this relentlessly wholesome backdrop play the individual fantasies of the characters—brilliant, brutal, sex-ual, dangerous, and violent—that provide the conflict of the story.

Alien and Familiar Place

Many poets and novelists have observed that the function of literature is to make the ordinary fresh and strange. F. Scott Fitzgerald, on the other hand, advised a young writer that reporting extreme things as if they were ordinary was the starting point of fiction. Both of these views are true, and they are particularly true of setting. Whether a place is familiar or unfamiliar, comfort-able or discomfiting in fiction has nothing to do with whether the reader actually knows the place and feels good there. It is an attitude taken, an assumption made. In his detective novels, Ross Macdonald assumes a famil-iarity toward California that is translatable into any language ("I turned left off the highway and down an old switchback blacktop to a dead end"), whereas even the natives of North Hollywood must feel alien on Tom Wolfe's version of their streets:

> ...endless scorched boulevards lined with one-story stores, shops, bowling alleys, skating rinks, taco drive-ins, all of them shaped not like rectangles but like trapezoids, from the way the roofs slant up from the back and the

plate-glass fronts slant out as if they're going to pitch forward on the sidewalk and throw up.

The Kandy-Kolored Tangerine-Flake Streamline Baby

The prose of Tom Wolfe, whether about rural North Carolina, Fifth Avenue,
or Cape Kennedy, lives in a tone of constant breathless astonishment. By contrast, Ray Bradbury's outer space is pure down-home.

It was quiet in the deep morning of Mars, as quiet as a cool black well,
with stars shining in the canal waters, and, breathing in every room, the
children curled with their spiders in closed hands.

The Martian Chronicles

One great advantage of being a writer is that you may create the world.
Places and the elements have the significance and the emotional effect you
give them in language. As a person you may be depressed by rain, but as an author you are free to make rain mean freshness, growth, bounty, and God. You
may choose; the only thing you are not free to do is not to choose.

As with character, the first requisite of effective setting is to know it fully,
to experience it mentally, and the second is to create it through significant
detail. What sort of place is this, and what are its peculiarities? What is the
weather like, the light, the season, the time of day? What are the contours of
the land and architecture? What are the social assumptions of the inhabitants,
and how familiar and comfortable are the characters with this place and its
lifestyle? These things are not less important in fiction than in life, but more
so, since their selection inevitably takes on significance.

And as in the stories at the end of this chapter, "The Sea Fairies," "Love
and Hydrogen," and "Visit of Charity" setting may become a character itself.
In Maura Stanton's "The Sea Fairies," the main character is a teenage girl from
a family of modest means who has just arrived at an elegant house where she
will be babysitting. It is Christmas, the mother of her young charges is dying in
the hospital, and the babysitter is entering a house that will ask more of her
than she yet knows:

The high-ceilinged room smelled of wax and pine. I stopped to look up at
the shadowy Christmas tree, a Norway pine with long slender needles. It
was covered with curious ornaments of different shapes. I reached out to
stroke the cold wood of the grand piano, then opened the French doors to
the dining room. There were silver candelabra on the glossy mahogany
table. The glass and china in the highboys against the wall tinkled slightly,
jarred by my footfall. I remembered how I had turned on the chandelier
the last time I was here, delighted by its crystal teardrops. But for some reason I did not feel like turning on a light yet. I wanted to see the girls first.

An Exercise in Place

Here is a series of passages about war, set in different periods and places. The first is in Russia during the campaign of Napoleon, the second on the island of Pianosa during World War II, and the third in a post-Holocaust future.

> Several tens of thousands of the slain lay in diverse postures and various uniforms. Over the whole field, previously so gaily beautiful with the glitter of bayonets and cloudlets of smoke in the morning sun, there now spread a mist of damp and smoke and a strange acid smell of saltpeter and blood. Clouds gathered and drops of rain began to fall on the dead and wounded, on the frightened, exhausted, and hesitating men, as if to say: Enough, men! Enough! Cease! Bethink yourselves! What are you doing?
>
> Leo Tolstoy, *War and Peace*

> Their only hope was that it would never stop raining, and they had no hope because they all knew it would. When it did stop raining in Pianosa, it rained in Bologna. When it stopped raining in Bologna, it began again in Pianosa. If there was no rain at all, there were freakish, inexplicable phenomena like the epidemic of diarrhea or the bomb line that moved. Four times during the first six days they were assembled and briefed and then sent back. Once, they took off and were flying in formation when the control tower summoned them down. The more it rained, the worse they suffered. The worse they suffered, the more they prayed that it would continue raining.
>
> Joseph Heller, *Catch-22*

> She liked the wild, quatrosyllabic lilt of the word, Barbarian. Then, looking beyond the wooden fence, she saw a trace of movement in the fields beyond. It was not the wind among the young corn; or, if it was wind among the young corn, it carried her the whinny of a raucous horse. It was too early for poppies but she saw a flare of scarlet. She ceased to watch the Soldiers; instead she watched the movement flow to the fences and crash through them and across the tender wheat. Bursting from the undergrowth came horseman after horseman. They flashed with curious curved plates of metal dredged up from the ruins. Their horses were bizarrely caparisoned with rags, small knives, bells and chains dangling from manes and tails, and man and horse together, unholy centaurs crudely daubed with paint, looked twice as large as life. They fired long guns. Confronted with the terrors of the night in the freshest hours of the morning, the gentle crowd scattered, wailing.
>
> Angela Carter, *Heroes and Villains*

Compare the settings. How do climate, period, imagery, and language contribute to each? To what degree is place a sentient force? Is there conflict between character and setting? How does setting affect and/or reveal the attitude taken toward the war? What mood, what emotions are implied?

◈

The Sea Fairies

MAURA STANTON

I remember how it rained that December. The temperature hovered around forty, never dropping low enough at night to freeze the drops into flakes. The yards were sodden; the yellow grass was dead, but the thick and luxuriant blades had not yet been crushed by a snowfall. There were Christmas trees in many of the windows I passed on the bus home from school, but they did not seem cheerful. I longed for snow.

That day, when I reached my own front porch, and was folding my umbrella, I saw that my mother was looking out at me through the little window in the door.

She opened the door. "Just leave your umbrella out there for now," she said. "There's an emergency at the Lundbergs' and they need you to baby-sit."

"Oh, no," I said. My feet were wet and I longed for a cup of tea. All I wanted to do was sit down in the living room and look at the lights on the Christmas tree.

"They've called everyone. They need someone to spend the night. I said you'd do it."

"What's wrong?" I shook the water off my jacket onto the little braided rug just inside the door, and wiped my shoes. My glasses steamed over. I couldn't see anything.

"Mrs. Lundberg was hurt in a car accident. She's been taken to the hospital, and Mr. Lundberg's out of town. Her sister called—she got your name from one of the neighbors. She can't keep the girls herself because her own kids have chicken pox."

"Will Mrs. Lundberg be all right?"

I took off my glasses. My mother was toying with the top button on her blouse.

"Her sister didn't seem to know much. She's pretty upset. The hospital called her, and she picked up the girls at school. As soon as you get there, she's going to the hospital."

"Those poor little girls," I said. "Let me change my clothes. I'm soaked."

I threw my books down on the end of the couch and hurried to the bedroom. I had baby-sat for the Lundberg girls only once, when their regular babysitter was sick. The Lundbergs lived five blocks away in one of the big houses across from the lake. My mother had never met Mrs. Lundberg. I had felt strange babysitting for them, awkward and shy as I was introduced to their little girls and shown through their large rooms. Mrs. Lundberg had worn a grey suit and tiny gold earrings. I remembered Mr. Lundberg's high forehead and receding, dark blond hair. He was a musician and traveled. I had liked the three girls—I could only remember two of their names, Christine and Lucia. What was the little one called?

I pulled on my jeans and laced my tennis shoes. I could hear the rain falling harder again, so I stuck an extra pair of socks into my pocket. I put my nightgown and robe into a canvas bag, then went into the bathroom for my toothbrush. One of my sisters had come home from grade school and had put a Christmas record on the record player. I listened to "Deck the Halls" as I combed my hair. I could hear the sound of pots and pans and running water from the kitchen as my mother started supper.

I went into the living room. My jacket was damp all the way through to the lining. I grabbed my books. I knew it was going to be a long night, and on Fridays there was nothing I liked on television. My sister had turned on the tree lights and was lying on the floor, rearranging the chipped plaster figures in the manger. I stopped to admire the tree and took a deep breath. I couldn't smell pine this year, but the tree looked pretty. We'd bought the right amount of tinsel and had hung it strand by strand, instead of throwing it in clumps. The old, familiar glass ornaments glittered. I looked up at my favorite silver ball, on a bough just beneath the angel at the top. Then, shivering, I went out into the rain.

The drops pouring off my umbrella seemed murky rather than clear, but I guessed it was the effect of the dusk. I passed many brightly lighted windows. I saw a white Christmas tree with blue balls and a tall Christmas tree with tiny, blinking lights. When I reached Edgewater, the houses were set so far back from the sidewalk and surrounded by so much shrubbery, that I couldn't see in the windows very well. I looked out at the sodden park and the black lake beyond it. I fancied that if I tried to walk to the lake, I would sink down through the marshy grass before I reached it. The lake seemed to have overflowed or to have risen up from underneath the ground, for the park lawn was spotted with pools of standing water.

The Lundbergs lived in a tall brick house. The front windows were blocked by two high spruce trees. I opened the wrought-iron front gate and walked up the long, curving sidewalk. The spruce boughs caught the rain like plates, then poured it off all at once when it grew too heavy, so I had to be careful not to be get soaked as I stood on the front step.

I had to bang the knocker twice. Then the door was opened abruptly by a woman with damp, blond hair who looked like Mrs. Lundberg.

"You're the baby-sitter? Thank God!"

She stood back while I shook out my umbrella and stepped inside the door. "Just leave that in the hall."

I leaned my half-shut umbrella against the inside wall. I was afraid to open it, for there was an oriental rug on the oak floor, and once again I was intimidated by the huge, open stairway.

"I'm Ellen Darrell," the blond woman said. She was clumsily pulling on her wet coat, which had been hanging on a brass coat rack. "I'm Mrs. Lundberg's sister."

"How is she?" I asked.

"Oh, God. I don't know. They wouldn't tell me much on the phone, but she's in serious condition. She was in the operating room. I've got to get there." I could hear a sob in her voice, which she was struggling to keep under control. Her hair was coming undone from her French roll.

"Do the girls know?" I asked.

She lowered her voice at once. "They're in the kitchen. I just told them she was in the hospital. I didn't tell them about the operating room. But they know I'm upset. Christine's been crying."

"Is Mr. Lundberg coming?"

"He's stuck in Vermont. He can't get a plane out until the morning." She finally got her top button through the hole. I'll try to call you later. And I'll be back in the morning—or I'll send my husband. He's trying to find someone to stay with my kids. I've got two sick ones." She looked at my jacket. "Why don't you hang that on the radiator in the kitchen. Won't this rain ever stop? No wonder Karen had an accident."

I took off my dripping jacket while Mrs. Darrell pulled a man's black umbrella out of the umbrella stand. She opened it wide to test it, then snapped it shut. "I'm going. The girls know you're here—you've been here before, haven't you?" She continued when I nodded. "I'm sure there's plenty to eat. I told the girls to make themselves sandwiches, but I saw some eggs...try to cheer them up. That's the most important thing."

"All right," I said.

She squeezed her eyes shut for a movement. "I've got to get a grip on myself." She opened her eyes, which were blue and wet. I thought she looked younger but less pretty than Mrs. Lundberg. Her face was plumper.

"I'll cheer them up." I said.

She nodded. She went outside, raising her umbrella immediately. I pulled the door shut, then wiped off my glasses. The tall grandfather clock under the stairway ticked loudly in the silence.

I went into the living room. The heavy curtains were still open. The tall side windows must have faced the direction of the wind, for the rain was beating against them. I could see nothing in the dusk outside beyond the grey waves of water on the glass.

The high-ceilinged room smelled of wax and pine. I stopped to look up at the shadowy Christmas tree, a Norway pine with long, slender needles. It was covered with curious ornaments of different shapes. I reached out to stroke the cold wood of the grand piano, then opened the French doors to the dining room. There were silver candelabra on the glossy mahogany table. The glass and china in the highboys against the wall tinkled slightly, jarred by my footfall. I remembered how I had turned on the chandelier the last time I was here, delighted by its crystal teardrops. But for some reason I did not feel like turning on a light just yet. I wanted to see the girls first.

I blinked at the glare when I pushed open the kitchen door. All the heat and light in the house seemed to be gathered in that comfortable room with its bronze-colored appliances and shiny floor. The three girls were sitting around the maple table. The smallest one was spreading peanut butter onto a piece of bread. Christine, the oldest, was leaning over the table, her head in her arms. Lucia was drinking a glass of milk. She smiled at me. There was a white ring around her mouth.

"Hello," I said, feeling awkward. "You remember me?"

Lucia nodded. Christine lifted her head. Her eyes were red and swollen. She visibly swallowed her tears. "Mother's in the hospital," she said.

"I know," I said, "I'm sure she'll be all right." I spotted the radiator Mrs. Darrell had mentioned. "I think I'll lay my jacket over there to dry out. And change my socks. It's really raining, isn't it?"

The smallest girl was looking at me suspiciously. She was holding her slice of bread and peanut butter in one hand, and flinched away as I passed her to get to the radiator. I wished I could remember her name.

"Is this enough to eat? Can I fix you something for supper?" I asked as I pulled on my socks. I hoped my tennis shoes would dry by morning. I pressed my hands against the radiator to warm them up.

"I'm not hungry," Christine said.

"I am," said Lucia. " I want some pizza."

"Is there any?"

"In the freezer," said Lucia. She scooted her chair out, and ran across the kitchen. "I'll get it. You just have to put it in the oven. We're not supposed to turn the oven on by ourselves."

I took the pizza out of the box, read the directions, and looked at the complicated stove for a long time. I finally found the right dial.

"Can we watch television after supper?" Lucia asked.

"Sure," I said.

"You've got to practice, Lucia," Christine said in a tight voice. "Just because Mother's not here —"

Lucia looked down at the floor. She sighed heavily.

"Do your play the piano?" I asked her.

"She plays the flute," Christine said.

I looked at Christine. She sat erect in her chair. She wasn't crying now, but she was pale, and the skin beneath her eyes was faintly discolored. Her thin blond hair was pushed back behind her ears. She had large, dark blue eyes. I remembered that last year she had said she was eleven.

"Do you play something?" I asked.

"The violin," she said. "Like my father. Adele is learning the piano. I play the piano, too." She stood up, smoothing her plaid wool kilt. "I'm going to practice."

"You should eat something first."

The smell of pizza was growing strong in the kitchen. She wrinkled her nose. "I'm just not hungry," she said. "I'll get a sandwich later if I am."

She left the kitchen. I glanced at Adele, who had finished her peanut butter slice and was staring at me. She had curly light brown hair with red highlights in it. I thought she must be six or seven.

"Do you want some pizza, Adele?" I asked.

"Where's Mommy? I want Mommy."

"Mommy's in the hospital, Adele," Lucia said. "She'll be home in the morning."

Adele's face puckered for a moment. I thought she was going to cry, but just then a large orange cat came out from under the table. "Kitty," she called.

"You have a cat," I said. "I didn't know you had a cat."

"His name is Whiskers," Lucia said. "Here's the pizza cutter."

I took the pizza out of the oven. I could hear Christine tuning her violin through the closed door. She began to play as I cut the pizza into even wedges.

"That's beautiful," I said, stopping to listen.

"That's her Bach partita," Lucia said. "She's been working on that for a long time."

Lucia got out three plates. I put a piece of pizza in front of Adele, but she pushed it away. "I want to play Sea Fairies," she said.

"What's Sea Fairies?" I asked.

"A game we play," Lucia said. "It comes from a book, but Christine tells us stories that aren't in the book."

"I'll show you." Adele jumped down from her chair. She ran out of the kitchen with the cat jogging behind her. During the few moments that the door was open, I could hear Christine's music clearly. It made me shiver.

"That's so lovely." I whispered.

Lucia cocked her head. She had blond hair the color of Christine's, but it was cut short and curled around her ears. "It is lovely," she said. "She's playing it perfectly tonight. She hasn't begun over once."

"Would she mind if I went in there to listen?"

"Don't," said Lucia. "It would make her nervous."

I finished my pizza. Adele came running back with a book in her hand, and again, while the door was open, the violin filled the kitchen. The beautiful notes were muffled as soon as the door was shut.

Adele put the book in front of me. It was a heavy, old book with a tattered, rose-colored cover. I opened it to the ornate title page: *The Sea Fairies* by L. Frank Baum.

"He wrote *The Wizard of Oz*," I said.

"I know." Lucia stroked the worn cover of the book.

"What's it about," I asked. "How do you play Sea Fairies?"

"First of all,' said Lucia, "the Sea Fairies are mermaids who live in a palace under the sea, the most beautiful palace in the world. It's made of pearl and coral and pink seashells."

"And glass," added Adele. "And diamonds."

"Yes," agreed Lucia. "Now in the book, Trot and Captain Bill go down to visit the Sea Fairies. Trot is just an ordinary girl, and Captain Bill has a wooden leg."

"How can they breathe under water?" I asked.

Lucia smiled. "The Sea Fairies turn them into mermaids, too. Only Captain Bill is a merman, I guess. Trot is a little scared, but she likes it. Oh, it's so wonderful down there." Lucia closed her eyes. "And the Sea Fairies are so beautiful."

"Is that all?" I asked.

Lucia opened her eyes. She looked a little scornful. "Of course not. There's danger, too. Zog is a hideous monster. He keeps trying to destroy the Sea Fairies. The squid work for him. They color the sea black to hide him when he travels."

"But how do you play the game?"

"We need Christine. We've used up all the stories in the book, so she has to tell us new ones. Then we pretend. We take turns being the Queen of the Sea Fairies, or her sister, the Princess. Then one of us is always Trot."

"What about Captain Bill?"

Lucia shrugged. "We don't need him. We pretend he's still up in the rowboat."

"I want to be a Sea Fairy this time," said Adele. "I don't want to be Trot."

Christine had finished her piece. I thought she might play something else, but in a moment she came back into the kitchen. Her mouth was trembling. "I need a drink of water," she said in a jerky voice.

She turned on the tap, and filled a glass.

"Adele wants to play Sea Fairies," Lucia said.

"All right." Christine took only a sip from her glass. "Let's go into the other room." She looked at me. "Will you play?"

"Sure," I said.

"I told her how we play," said Lucia. "Is she a Sea Fairy?"

Christine frowned. "No. She's Trot."

"Then I'm a Sea Fairy!" Adele laughed happily.

I put the pizza dishes in the sink, and we followed Christine into the living room. It was much colder in the rest of the house. I felt as if I had dived underneath the sea, leaving the sun on the surface as I swam down into the gloomy depths. Christine had turned on two end table lamps in the living room, and the light on her music stand was still burning, but the corners of the large room were still shadowy. I was going to suggest that we turn on the tree lights, when I noticed that this tree had only ornaments. There were no strings of colored lights and no tinsel. The ornaments were handmade, mostly wooden. I noticed a little carved rocking house, painted shiny red, a goldfish with blue scales, and a tiny, unpainted wooden angel.

"You sit there," Christine said, pointing to a high-backed chair beside the fireplace. I obeyed her. I could feel the coldness of the heavy brocade cushion through my jeans. "Did Lucia tell you what Zog can do? Once he made the water boiling hot, and the Sea Fairies almost died. Once he turned the water into ice."

"How did they escape?"

Christine stood erect on the tiles before the fireplace. Adele and Lucia sat side by side on the couch, watching her.

"The Sea Fairies have an invisible magic ring around them. They made one for Trot, too. If you close you eyes, you can feel it on your skin."

I saw that Adele and Lucia had closed their eyes. I closed my eyes, too. I grew conscious of my skin in the cold room. I reached up to smooth my hair and felt a tiny snap of electricity.

"Tonight," Christine said in a hushed, trembling voice, "something terrible has happened."

I opened my eyes. Adele and Lucia, holding hands now, continued to keep their eyes tightly shut. Christine's eyes were shut. I felt uneasy. I couldn't look away from Christine. She swayed slightly as she stood talking in front of the brass andirons, her face as closed as a sleeper's.

"Zog has captured the Queen of the Sea Fairies. She's prisoner in the dungeon of his terrible castle. The rest of the Sea Fairies are at home in the Palace. They don't know what to do. Zog has sent his squid to color the water black, black as ink. The Sea Fairies can hardly see each other in the black water."

"Oh," Lucia murmured. She did not open her eyes.

"Zog has learned how the Sea Fairies make their magic circle. He has a gold cup full of poison and if the Queen of the Sea Fairies drinks the poison, her magic circle will dissolve. Then he'll have her forever. The Sea Fairies have got to rescue her, but they don't know what to do."

"The Princess has a magic wand," said Lucia. There was a pleading note in her voice which started me.

"She can't find her magic wand in the black water. No, this time Trot is going to have to save the Queen of the Sea Fairies."

Christine opened her eyes and looked directly at me. "We're the Sea Fairies. Lucia is the Princess, Adele and I are hand-maidens. What should we do, Trot?"

"This is where the game starts," whispered Lucia, shaking herself and releasing Adele's hand.

"Tell us your plan, then lead us on a rescue mission," said Christine in a tight voice.

Adele stood up on the couch, bouncing on the cushions, waving her arms toward the windows. "Look at the black water," she cried.

We all looked at the windows. No one had closed the curtains. The rain was changing to sleet, and was pinging against the glass. It was completely night now, and the lights in the room were reflected dimly in the glass, as if they were really burning somewhere else, through miles of murkiness.

"Let's see," I began lamely. "I guess we've got to sneak into Zog's castle when he isn't looking."

"How will we find it?" asked Lucia. "The water's black."

"Well," I said. "The squid work for Zog, but the eels work for us. The electric eels, the ones that light up. They'll lead us there."

"Good," said Christine. She was watching me closely.

"Now let's swim there!" cried Adele. Again she began waving her arms. She jumped off the couch as if she were diving.

"Not yet," Lucia said. "Trot has to work out the plan. The castle gate is locked."

"But there's a secret passage," I said. "It's hidden by seaweed. The goldfish know where it is."

"The goldfish are good fish," Lucia said. "They've helped us before."

"But they won't this time," said Christine gloomily. "Zog made a trap for them. He caught them all in a big net, and they're down in his dungeon."

"Oh," sighed Adele.

"But one escaped," I said. I pointed at the Christmas tree, remembering the ornament I had seen earlier. "That one escaped, and it swam here to tell us."

The phone rang at that moment. Even though it was in the kitchen, and the door was shut, the shrill bell went through all of us like a knife.

"I'll get it," cried Christine. "It's Aunt Ellen."

The two younger girls ran after her. By the time I reached the kitchen, Christine was talking on the white wall phone. The others were watching her eagerly.

"But when will she be home?" I heard her say. Then she sighed. She listened for a while.

"How is she?" whispered Lucia fiercely, pulling at Christine's arm.

Christine lowered the receiver. She looked pale, and was holding herself rigidly. "She's sleeping, Aunt Ellen says. She wants to talk to you." Christine handed me the receiver.

Mrs. Darrell began speaking. Her voice was far away and so full of grief that it must surely have contradicted any reassurance she had tried to give Christine. "Are the girls still there? Are they all right?"

"Yes," I said. "They're fine."

"I just told Christine that her mother was sleeping. That's all I want the girls to know right now." Mrs. Darrell paused. "But my husband and I are coming back, and I wanted you to know, because I'd asked you to stay the night. You see, my sister passed away about an hour ago."

"Oh!" I cried involuntarily.

"Please don't say anything. I know the girls are right there. We'll tell them when we get there. Just keep them distracted until then. We'll take over. And you'll be able to go home."

"All right," I said. I wanted to say how sorry I was, but the three girls were listening intently to my every word. Christine had fastened her eyes to my face, and I was afraid that she would be able to read the least twitch of my muscles.

"We'll see you in about fifteen minutes. Or maybe longer. Someone said the roads are getting slick. But please, please don't say anything to the girls—don't tell them we're coming. This is going to be very, very hard. The doctors have given us some sedatives for them, in case..." She trailed off.

"Don't worry about anything," I said as firmly as I could. "I'll take care of them. Please don't worry."

"Goodbye, then," she whispered, and hung up.

"What did she tell you?" Christine asked quickly.

"She wants me to cheer you up, that's all," I said. I took a deep breath to steady myself. "She just doesn't want you to feel—" The word "sad" was on the tip of my tongue. "She doesn't want you to feel bored," I said.

Christine looked at me searchingly. "She talked to you for a long time."

"We have to finish our game," I said.

"Good," said Adele.

Christine turned away. "I'm tired," she said. "I don't feel well."

"Oh, Christine!" Adele pulled at her kilt.

Lucia looked at me, then at her sister's back. "Let's play, Christine. There's nothing else to do."

"I just don't—" Christine's voice was choked. She couldn't finish.

Lucia swallowed nervously. "Christine?" she called.

"We've got to talk to that goldfish," I said hastily. "Let's go back in the living room. Come on, Christine." I grabbed Adele's hand. "Come on, Lucia."

Lucia followed me, and Christine came after her reluctantly. I stopped in front of the Christmas tree and pointed up at the goldfish ornament.

"He's out of breath," I said. "It look him a long time to swim here, but now he'll show us where the secret passage is."

"He's too tired to swim back," Christine said in a hopeless voice. "He'll never make it."

"But look how small he is." I unhooked the ornament, and put it into the pocket of Adele's smock. "He can ride with Princess Adele."

Adele smiled in delight. "We're going to save the Queen! Let's swim, let's swim!"

"But here come the swordfish," said Christine. She came around beside me, and pointed toward the hallway. Her lower lip was trembling. "Zog has sent the swordfish. They'll cut us to pieces."

"But Princess Lucia has a magic whistle. When she blows it, all the whales floating up on the top of the water will come diving down. They'll frighten the swordfish away."

Lucia pursed her lips and whistled.

"You see," I said. "Here come the whales. The Queen of the Sea Fairies once pulled a harpoon out of the side of a whale, and now all the whales love her."

"But the whales are afraid of Zog," Christine said. "He blows darts into their sides and puts them to sleep. They can't go near his castle."

"We'll go alone. The goldfish will show us the secret passage in the seaweed."

"Oh," said Christine. She looked down at the rug. "We're trapped in the seaweed. We're trapped."

Lucia and Adele dropped to the floor. "We're trapped," cried Adele. "You're trapped, Trot. The seaweed is wrapped all around you."

I fell to the floor. Christine knelt down beside me.

"Zog has brought the cup of poison to the Queen." Christine covered her face with her hands. "She doesn't know it's poison. She's going to drink it. And there's nothing we can do. Nothing!"

"The clams will cut the seaweed," I said, speaking directly to Christine. "Their shells have sharp edges." Then I added in a triumphant voice, "And the Queen knows there's poison in the cup!"

Christine looked at me through her fingers. "Does she know?"

"Of course she knows. She's the Queen. She's smarter than everyone. Zog thinks she drank the poison, but a little starfish floated by just then, and he looked away." I pointed up at the star on the top of the Christmas tree. All three girls looked up at it. "There. The Queen just poured the poison into a vase."

"Now what will she do?" asked Lucia.

"Zog is coming toward her," whispered Christine. "He's going to wrap her in his cloak and take her away forever."

"But she still has her magic circle," I insisted. "Zog doesn't know that. He won't be able to touch her."

Christine stretched out one hand, as if to ward off something invisible.

"She's tricked Zog," I said. "Now the Sea Fairies are inside the castle. Trot is swimming ahead, and the Sea Fairies are behind her. They're going to find the Queen." I got to my feet. "She's just behind that iron door."

Christine, still on her knees, stared blankly in the direction I was pointing. "Who will open the door?"

"You open it, Christine."

Christine looked up at my face. I met her eyes and held them as long as I could. She sighed, then got slowly to her feet, and squeezed her lids shut. "I've opened the door. Now we're swimming into the dungeon. We're not afraid but Zog is afraid. He's afraid of mortals. If a mortal ever touches him, he'll turn to ink. When he sees Trot, he shrieks. He shoots up through the water. And now the Queen is waiting for the Sea Fairies. She's smiling. Her tail is covered with pearls, and all the goldfish in the dungeon have made a golden cloak for her, the most beautiful cloak in the world."

I felt my heart pounding. The color had come back into Christine's face. But then I heard the ominous sound of someone at the front door.

"What is it?" Christine touched my sleeve lightly. I couldn't look at her.

"It's Aunt Ellen!" cried Adele, running into the hall.

"Aunt Ellen?" Lucia said in a puzzled voice, following Adele.

Christine gasped. She took a step away from me. "She's dead!" she wailed. She ran into the hall.

I backed away. I backed away into the dining room. I heard Mrs. Darrell's voice, then a man's voice. I backed into the kitchen, letting the door fall shut behind me.

I put on my wet tennis shoes. It took me a long time to tie the laces, because my fingers were shaking. I was buttoning my jacket when Mrs. Darrell came into the kitchen.

"I want to thank you for coming over," she said in a quavering voice as she reached into her purse. She held out some bills.

"No, no, I don't want any money," I said. I clutched my books and hurried out the back door.

It was much colder, and a wind was blowing, sweeping away the clouds, and opening a space in the sky for a huge, white moon. I was startled by the brightness. Ordinary fir trees had been transformed into glass. The bare oaks and dying elms of the neighborhood were all sparkling. Their weighted limbs made a crackling and popping sound. I had trouble keeping my balance as I walked down the alley. Car windshields were sheeted with shiny ice. Garbage cans glittered in the moonlight. It was as if Zog had worked one of his spells under cover of the black water. He had frozen the kingdom of the Sea Fairies, and only Trot, the ordinary girl, was allowed to swim to the surface to resume her life as if nothing had happened.

◈

Love and Hydrogen

JIM SHEPARD

Imagine five or six city blocks could lift, with a bump, and float away. The impression the 804-foot-long *Hindenburg* gives on the ground is that of an airship built by giants and excessive even to their purposes. The fabric hull and mainframe curve upward sixteen stories high.

Meinert and Gnüss are out on the gangway ladder down to the starboard #1 engine car. They're helping out the machinists, in a pinch. Gnüss is afraid of heights, which amuses everyone. It's an open aluminum ladder with a single handrail extending eighteen feet down into the car's hatchway. They're at 2,000 feet. The clouds below strand by and dissipate. It's early in a mild May in 1937.

Their leather caps are buckled around their chins, but they have no goggles. The air buffets by at eighty-five miles per hour. Meinert shows him how to hook his arm around the leading edge of the ladder to keep from being blown off as he leaves the hull. Even through the sheepskin gloves the metal is shockingly cold from the slipstream. The outer suede of the grip doesn't provide quite the purchase they would wish when hanging their keisters out over the open Atlantic. Every raised foot is wrenched from the rung and flung into space.

Servicing the engines inside the cupola, they're out of the blast, but not the cold. Raising a head out of the shielded area is like being cuffed by a bear. It's a pusher arrangement, thank God. The back ends of the cupolas are open to facilitate maintenance on the blocks and engine mounts. The engines are 1,100-horsepower diesels four feet high. The propellers are twenty-two feet long. When they're down on their hands and knees adjusting the vibration dampers, those props are a foot and a half away. The sound is like God losing his temper, kettledrums in the sinuses, fists in the face.

Meinert and Gnüss are both Regensburgers. Meinert was in his twenties and Gnüss a child during the absolute worst years of the inflation. They lived on mustard sandwiches, boiled kale, and turnip mash. Gnüss's most cherished toy for a year and a half was a clothespin on which his father had painted a face. They're ecstatic to have found positions like this. Their work fills them with elation, and the kind of spuriously proprietary pride that mortal tour guides might feel on Olympus. Meals that seem giddily baronial—plates crowded with sausages, tureens of soups, platters of venison or trout or buttered potatoes—appear daily, once the passengers have been served, courtesy of Luftschiffbau Zeppelin. Their sleeping berths, aboard and ashore, are more luxurious than any other place they've previously laid their heads.

Meinert and Gnüss are in love. This complicates just about everything. They steal moments when they can—on the last Frankfurt to Rio run, they exchanged an intense and acrobatic series of caresses 135 feet up inside the superstructure, when Meinert was supposed to have been checking a seam on one of the gasbags for wear, their glue pots clacking and clocking together—but mostly their ardor is channeled so smoothly into underground streams that even their siblings, watching them work, would be satisfied with their rectitude.

Meinert loves Gnüss's fussiness with detail, his loving solicitude with all schedules and plans, the way he seems to husband good feeling and pass it around among his shipmates. He loves the celebratory delight Gnüss takes in all meals, and watches him with the anticipatory excitement that an enthusiast might bring to a sublime stretch of *Aïda*. Gnüss has a shy and diffident sense of humor that's particularly effective in groups. At the base of his neck, so it's hidden by a collar, he has a tattoo of a figure eight of rope: an infinity sign. He's exceedingly well proportioned.

Gnüss loves Meinert's shoulders, his way of making every physical act worthy of a Johnny Weissmuller, and the way he can play the irresponsible daredevil and still erode others' disapproval or righteous indignation. He's openmouthed at the way Meinert flaunts the sort of insidious and disreputable charm that all mothers warn against. In his bunk at night, Gnüss sometimes thinks, *I refuse to list all his other qualities*, for fear of agitating himself too completely. He calls Meinert *Old Shatterhand*. They joke about the age difference.

It goes without saying that the penalty for exposed homosexuality in this case would begin at the loss of one's position. Captain Pruss, a fair man and an excellent captain, a month ago remarked in Gnüss's presence that he'd throw any fairy he came across bodily out of the control car.

Meinert bunks with Egk; Gnüss with Thoolen. It couldn't be helped. Gnüss had wanted to petition for their reassignment as bunkmates—what was so untoward about friends wanting to spend more time together?—but Meinert the daredevil had refused to risk it. Each night Meinert lies in his bunk wishing they'd risked it. As a consolation, he passed along to Gnüss his grandfather's antique silver pocket watch. It had already been engraved *To My Dearest Boy*.

Egk is a fat little man with boils. Meinert considers him to have been well named. He whistles the same thirteen-note motif each night before lights out.

How much happiness is someone entitled to? This is the question that Gnüss turns this way and that in his aluminum bunk in the darkness. The ship betrays no tremor or sense of movement as it slips through the sky like a fish.

He is proud of his feelings for Meinert. He can count on one hand the number of people he's known he believes to be capable of feelings as exalted as his.

Meinert, meanwhile, has developed a flirtation with one of the passengers: perhaps the only relationship possible that would be more forbidden than his relationship with Gnüss. The flirtation alternately irritates and frightens Gnüss.

The passenger is one of those languid teenagers who own the world. She has a boy's haircut. She has a boy's chest. She paints her lips but otherwise wears no makeup. Her parents are briskly polite with the crew and clearly excited by their first adventure on an airship; she is not. She has an Eastern name: Tereska.

Gnüss had to endure their exchange of looks when the girl's family first came aboard. Passengers had formed a docile line at the base of the main gangway. Gnüss and Meinert had been shanghaied to help the chief steward inspect luggage and personal valises for matches, lighters, camera flashbulbs, flashlights, even a child's sparking toy pistol: anything that might mix apocalyptically with their ship's seven million cubic feet of hydrogen. Two hundred stevedores in the ground crew were arrayed every ten feet or so around their perimeter, dragging slightly back and forth on their ropes with each shift in the wind. Meinert made a joke about drones pulling a queen. The late afternoon was blue with rain and fog. A small, soaked Hitler Youth contingent with two bedraggled Party pennants stood at attention to see them off.

Moinert was handed Tereska's valise, and Tereska wrestled it back, rummaging through it shoulder to shoulder with him. They'd given one another playful bumps.

The two friends finished their inspections and waited at attention until all the passengers were up the gangway. "Isn't she the charming little rogue," Gnüss remarked.

"Don't scold, Auntie," Meinert answered.

The first signal bell sounded. Loved ones who came to see the travelers off waved and shouted. A passenger unbuckled his wrist-watch and tossed it from one of the observation windows as a farewell present. Meinert and Gnüss were the last ones aboard and secured the gangway. Two thousand pounds of water ballast was dropped. The splash routed the ranks of the Hitler Youth contingent. At 150 feet the signal bells of the engine telegraphs jangled, and the engines one by one roared to life. At 300 feet the bells rang again, calling for higher revolutions.

On the way to their subsequent duties, the two friends took a moment at a free spot at an observation window, watching the ground recede. The passengers were oohing and aahing the mountains of Switzerland and Austria as they fell away to the south, inverted in the mirrorlike expanse of the lake. The ship lifted with the smoothness of planetary motion.

Aloft, their lives had really become a pair of stupefying narratives. Frankfurt to Rio in three and a half days. Frankfurt to New York in two. The twenty-five passenger cabins on A deck slept two in state-room comfort and featured featherlight and whisper-quiet sliding doors. On B deck passengers could lather up in the world's first airborne shower. The smoking room, off the bar and double-sealed all the way round, stayed open until the last guests said good night. The fabric-covered walls in the lounge and public areas were decorated with hand-painted artwork. Each room had its own theme: the main salon, a map of the world crosshatched by the routes of famous explorers; the reading room, scenes of the history of postal delivery. An aluminum bust of General von Hindenberg sat in a halo of light on an ebony base in a niche at the top of the main gangway. A place setting for two for dinner involved fifty-eight pieces of Dresden china and silver. The butter knives' handles were themselves minizeppelins. Complimentary sleeping caps were bordered with the legend *An Bord Des Luftschiffes Hindenburg*. Luggage tags were stamped *Im Zeppelin Über Den Ozean* and featured an image of the *Hindenburg* bearing down, midocean, on what looked like the Santa Maria.

When he can put Tereska out of his head, Gnüss is giddy with the danger and improbability of it all. The axial catwalk is 10 inches wide at its base and 782 feet long and 110 feet above the passenger and crew compartments below. Crew members require the nimbleness of structural steelworkers. The top of the gas cells can only be inspected from the vertical ringed ladders running along the inflation pipes: sixteen stories up into the radial and spiraling bracing wires and mainframe. Up that high, the airship's interior seems to have its own weather. Mists form. The vast cell walls holding the seven million cubic feet of hydrogen billow and flex.

At the very top of Ladder #4 on the second morning out, Meinert hangs from one hand. He spins slowly above Gnüss, down below with the glue pots, like a high-wire act seen at such a distance that all the spectacle is gone. He sings one of his songs from the war, when as a seventeen-year-old he served on the LZ-98 and bombed London when the winds let them reach it. His voice is a floating echo from above:

> *In Paris people shake all over*
> *In terror as they wait.*
> *The Count prefers to come at night,*
> *Expect us at half past eight!*

Gnüss nestles in and listens. On either side of the catwalk, great tanks carry 143,000 pounds of diesel oil and water. Alongside the tanks, bays hold food supplies, freight, and mail. This is one of his favorite places to steal time. They sometimes linger here for the privacy and the ready excuses—inspection or errands—that all this storage space affords.

Good news: Meinert signals that he's located a worn patch, necessitating help. Gnüss climbs to him with another glue pot and a pot of the gelatin latex used to render the heavy-duty sailmaker's cotton gas-tight. His erection grows as he climbs.

Their repairs complete, they're both strapped in on the ladder near the top, mostly hidden in the gloom and curtaining folds of the gas cell. Gnüss, in a reverie after their lovemaking, asks Meinert if he can locate the most ecstatic feeling he's ever experienced. Meinert can. It was when he'd served as an observer on a night attack on Calais.

Gnüss still has Meinert's warm sex in his hand. This had been the LZ-98, captained by Lehmann, Meinert reminds him. They'd gotten nowhere on a hunt for fogbound targets in England, but conditions over Calais had been ideal for the observation basket: thick cloud at 4,000 feet, but the air beneath crystalline. The big airships were much safer when operating above cloud. But then: how to see their targets?

The solution was exhilarating: on their approach they throttled the motors as far back as they could while retaining the power to maneuver. The zeppelin was leveled out at 500 feet above the cloud layer, and then, with a winch and a cable, Meinert, as Air Observer, was lowered 2,000 feet in the observation basket, a hollow metal capsule scalloped open at the top. He had a clear view downward, and his gondola, so relatively tiny, was invisible from the ground.

Dropping into space in that little bucket had been the most frightening and electric thing he'd ever done. He'd been swept along alone under the cloud ceiling and over the lights of the city, like the messenger of the gods.

The garrison of the fort had heard the sound of their motors, and the light artillery had begun firing in that direction. But only once had a salvo come close enough to have startled him with its crash.

His cable extended above his head into the darkness and murk. It bowed forward. The capsule canted from the pull. The wind streamed past him. The lights rolled by below. From his wicker seat he directed the immense invisible ship above by telephone, and set and reset their courses by eye and by compass. He crisscrossed them over the fort for forty-five minutes, signaling when to drop their small bombs and phosphorus incendiaries. The experience was that of a sorcerer's, hurling thunderbolts on his own. That night he'd been a regular Regensburg Zeus. The bombs and incendiaries detonated on the railroad station, the warehouses, and the munitions dumps. When they fell they spiraled silently out of the darkness above and plummeted past his capsule, the explosions carried away behind him. Every so often luminous ovals from the fort's searchlights rippled the bottoms of the clouds like a hand lamp beneath a tablecloth.

Gnüss, still hanging in his harness, is disconcerted by the story. He tucks Meinert's sex back into the opened pants.

"That feeling comes back to me when I'm my happiest: hiking or alone," Meinert muses. "And when I'm with you, as well," he adds, after having seen Gnüss's face.

Gnüss buckles his own pants, unhooks his harness, and begins his careful descent. "I don't think I make you feel like Zeus," he says, a little sadly.

"Well, like Pan, anyway," Meinert calls out from above him.

That evening darkness falls on the ocean below while the sun is still a glare on the frames of the observation windows. Meinert and Gnüss have their evening duties, as waiters. Their stations are across the room from one another. The dining room is the very picture of a fine hotel restaurant, without the candles. After dinner, they continue to ferry drinks from the bar on B deck to thirsty guests in the lounge and reading rooms. Through the windows, the upper surfaces of the clouds in the moonlight are as brilliant as breaking surf. Tereska is nowhere to be found.

Upon retiring, passengers leave their shoes in the corridor, as on shipboard. Newspaper correspondents stay up late in the salon, typing bulletins to send by wireless ahead to America. In the darkness and quiet before they themselves turn in, Gnüss leads Meinert halfway up Ladder #4 yet again, to reward him for having had no contact whatsoever with that teenager. Their continuing recklessness feels like Love itself.

Like their airship, their new home when not flying is Friedrichshafen, beside the flatly placid Lake Constance. The Company's presence has transformed the little town. In gratitude the town fathers have erected a Zeppelin fountain in the courtyard of the Rathaus, the centerpiece of which is the Count bestride a globe, holding a log-sized airship in his arms.

Friedrichshafen is on the north side of the lake, with the Swiss mountains across the water to the south, including the snowcapped Säntis, rising some 8,000 feet. Meinert has tutored Gnüss in mountain hiking, and Gnüss has tutored Meinert in oral sex above the tree line. They've taken chances as though cultivating a death wish: in a lift in the famous Insel Hotel, in rented rooms in the wood-carving town of Überlingen and Meersburg with its old castle dating back to the seventh century. In vineyards on the southern exposures of hillsides. Even, once in a lavatory in the Maybach engine plant, near the gear manufacturing works.

When not perversely risking everything they had for no real reason, they lived like the locals, with their coffee and cake on Sunday afternoon and their raw smoked ham as the ubiquitous appetizer for every meal. They maintained their privacy as weekend hikers and developed the southerner's endless capacity for arguing the merits of various mountain trails. By their third year in Friedrichshafen their motto was "A mountain each weekend." They spent nights in mountain huts, and in winter they might go entire days skiing without seeing other adventurers. If Meinert had asked his friend which experience had been the most ecstatic of *his* young life, Gnüss would have cited the week they spent alone in a hut over one Christmas holiday.

Neither has been back to Regensburg for years. Gnüss's most vivid memory of it, for reason he can't locate, is of the scrape and desolation of his dentist's tooth-cleaning instruments one rainy March morning. Meinert usually refers to their hometown as Vitality's Graveyard. His younger brother still writes to him twice a week. Gnüss still sends a portion of his pay home to his parents and sisters.

Gnüss knows that he's being the young and foolish one but nevertheless can't resist comparing the invincible intensity of his feelings for Meinert with his pride at serving on this airship—this machine that conquers two oceans at once, the one above and the one below—this machine that brought their country supremacy in passenger, mail, and freight service to the North and South American continents only seventeen years after the Treaty of Versailles.

Even calm, cold, practical minds that worked on logarithms or carburetors felt the strange joy, the uncanny fascination, the radiance of atmospheric and gravitational freedom. They'd watched the *Graf Zeppelin*, their sister ship, take off one beautiful morning, the sun dazzling on its aluminum dope as if it were levitating on light, and it was like watching Juggernaut float free of the earth. One night they'd gone down almost to touch the waves and scared a fishing boat in the fog, and had joked afterward about what the boat's crew must have experienced: looking back to see a great dark, whirring thing rise like a monster upon them out of the murky air.

They're both party members. They were over Aachen during the national referendum on the annexation of the Rhineland, and helped the chief steward rig up a polling booth on the port promenade deck. The Yes vote had carried among the passengers and crew by a count of 103 to 1.

Meals in flight are so relaxed that some guests arrive for breakfast in their pajamas. Tereska is one such guest, and Gnüss from his station watches Meinert chatting and flirting with her. *She's only an annoyance*, he reminds himself, but his brain seizes and charges around enough to make him dizzy.

The great mass of the airship is off-limits to passengers except for those on guided tours. Soon after the breakfast service is cleared, Meinert informs him, with insufficient contrition, that Tereska's family has requested him as their guide. An hour later, when it's time for the tour to begin, there's Tereska alone, in her boyish shirt and sailor pants. She jokes with Meinert and lays a hand on his forearm. He jokes with her.

Gnüss, beside himself, contrives to approach her parents, sunning themselves by a port observation window. He asks if they'd missed the tour. It transpires that the bitch has forewarned them that it would involve a good deal of uncomfortable climbing and claustrophobic poking about.

He stumbles about below decks, only half-remembering his current task. What's happened to his autonomy? What's happened to his ability to generate contentment for himself independent of Meinert's behavior? Before all this he saw himself in the long term as First Officer, or at least Chief Sailmaker: a solitary and much admired figure of cool judgments and sober self-mastery. Instead, now he feels overheated and coursed through with kineticism, like an agitated and kenneled dog.

He delivers the status report on the ongoing inspection of the gas cells. "Why are you *weeping*?" Sauter, the Chief Engineer, asks.

Responsibility has flown out the window. He takes to carrying Meinert's grandfather's watch inside his pants. His briefs barely hold the weight. It bumps and sidles against his genitals. Does it show? Who cares?

He sees Meinert only once all afternoon, and then from a distance. He searches for him as much as he dares during free moments. During lunch the Chief Steward slaps him on the back of the head for gathering wool.

Three hours are spent in a solitary and melancholy inspection of the rearmost gas cell. In the end he can't say for sure what he's seen. If the cell had disappeared entirely, it's not clear he would have noticed.

Rhine salmon for the final dinner. Fresh trout from the Black Forest. There's an all-night party among the passengers to celebrate their arrival in America. At the bar the man who'd thrown away his wristwatch on departure amuses himself by balancing a fountain pen on its flat end.

They continue to be separated for most of the evening, which creeps along glacially. Gnüss sorts glassware for storage upon landing, and Meinert lends a hand back at the engine gondolas, helping record fuel consumption. The time seems out of joint, and Gnüss finally figures out why: a prankster has set the clock in the bar back, to extend the length of the celebration.

On third watch he takes a break. He goes below and stops by the crew's quarters. No luck. He listens in on a discussion of suitable first names for children conceived aloft in a zeppelin. The consensus favors Shelium, if a girl.

Someone asks if he's seen Meinert. Startled, he eyes the questioner. Apparently the captain's looking for him. Two machinists exchange looks.

Has Gnüss seen him or not? the questioner wants to know. He realizes he hasn't answered. The whole room has taken note of his paralysis. He says he hasn't, and excuses himself.

He finds Meinert on the catwalk heading aft. Relief and anger and frustration swarm the cockleshell of his head. His frontal lobe is in tumult. Before he can speak Meinert tells him to keep his voice down, and that the party may be over. What does *that* mean? Gnüss wants to know. His friend doesn't answer.

They go hunting for privacy without success. A crossbrace near the bottom of the tail supports a card game.

On the way back forward, they're confronted by their two room-mates, Egk and Thoolen, who block the catwalk as though they've formed an alliance. Perhaps they feel neglected. "Do you two *ever* separate?" Egk asks. "Night and day I see you together." Thoolen nods unpleasantly. One is Hamburg at its most insolent, the other Bremerhaven at its foggiest. "Shut up, you fat bellhop," Meinert says.

They roughly squeeze past, and Egk and Thoolen watch them go. *"I'm so in love!"* Egk sings out. Thoolen laughs.

Gnüss follows his friend in silence until they reach the ladder down to B deck. It's a busy hub. Crew members come and go briskly. Meinert hesitates. He seems absorbed in a recessed light fixture. It breaks Gnüss's heart to see that much sadness in the contours of his preoccupation.

"What do you mean: the party may be over?" Gnüss demands quietly.

"Pruss wants to see me. He says for disciplinary matters. After that, you know as much as I," Meinert says.

The radio officer and the ship's doctor pass through the corridor at the bottom of the stairs, glancing up as they go, without stopping their quiet conversation.

When Gnüss is unable to respond, Meinert adds, "Maybe he just wants me to police up my uniform."

At a loss, Gnüss finally puts a hand on Meinert's arm. Meinert smiles, and whispers, *"You are the most important thing in the world right now."*

The unexpectedness of it brings tears to Gnüss's eyes. Meinert murmurs that he needs to get into his dining room whites. It's nearly time to serve the third breakfast. They've served two luncheons, two dinners, and now three breakfasts.

They descend the stairs together. Gnüss is already dressed and so gives his friend another squeeze on the arm and tells him not to worry, and then goes straight to the galley. His eyes still bleary with tears, he loads linen napkins into the dumbwaiter. Anxiety is like a whirling pillar in his chest. He remembers another of Meinert's war stories, one whispered to him in the early morning after they'd first spent the night together. They'd soaked each other and the bed linens with love and then had collapsed. He woke to words in his ear, and at first thought his bedmate was talking in his sleep. The story concerned Meinert's captain after a disastrous raid one moonless night over the Channel. Meinert had been at his post in the control car. The captain had started talking to himself. He'd said that both radios were smashed, not that it mattered, both radiomen being dead. And that both outboard engines were beyond repair, not that *that* mattered, since they had no fuel.

Around four A.M., the passengers start exclaiming at the lights of Long Island. The all-night party has petered out into knots of people waiting and chatting along the promenade. Gnüss and Meinert set out the china, sick with worry. Once the place settings are all correct, they allow themselves a look out an open window. They see below that they've overtaken the liner *Staatendam*, coming into New York Harbor. She salutes them with blasts of her siren. Passengers crowd her decks waving handkerchiefs.

They're diverted north to avoid a front of thunderstorms. All morning, they drift over New England, gradually working their way back to Long Island Sound.

At lunch Captain Pruss appears in the doorway for a moment, and then is gone. They bus tables. The passengers all abandon their seats to look out on New York City. From the exclamations they make, it's apparently some sight. Steam whistles sound from boats on the Hudson and East Rivers. Someone at the window points out the *Bremen* just before it bellows a greeting. The *Hindenburg*'s passengers wave back with a kind of patriotic madness.

The tables cleared, the waiters drift back to the windows. Gnüss puts an arm around Meinert's shoulders, despair making him courageous. Through patchy cloud they can see shoal water, or tiderips, beneath them.

Pelicans flock in their wake. What looks like a whale races to keep pace with their shadow.

In New Jersey they circle over miles of stunted pines and bogs, their shadow running along the ground like a big fish on the surface.

It's time for them to take their landing stations.

Sauter passes them on their way to the catwalk and says that they should give the bracing wires near Ladder #4 another check and that he'd noticed a bit of hum.

By the time they reach the base of #4, it's more than a bit of a hum. Gnüss volunteers to go, anxious to do something concrete for his disconsolate beloved. He wipes his eyes and climbs swiftly while Meinert waits below on the catwalk.

Meinert's grandfather's pocket watch bumps and tumbles about his testicles while he climbs. Once or twice he has to stop to rearrange himself. The hum is near the top, hard to locate. At their favorite perch, he stops and hooks on his harness. His weight supported, he turns his head slightly to try and make his ears direction finders. He runs a thumb and forefinger along nearby cables to test for vibration. The cables are covered in graphite to suppress sparks. The slickness seems sexual to him. He's dismayed by his single-mindedness.

On impulse, he takes the watch, pleasingly warm, from his pants. He loops it around one of the cable bolts just so he can look at it. The short chain keeps slipping from the weight. He wraps it once around the nut on the other side of the beam. The nut feels loose to him. He removes and pockets the watch, finds the spanner on his tool belt, fits it snugly over the nut, and tightens it, and then, uncertain, tightens it again. There's a short, high-pitched sound of metal under stress or tearing.

Below him, his lover, tremendously resourceful in all sorts of chameleon-like self-renovations, and suffused with what he understands to be an unprecedented feeling for his young young boy, has been thinking to himself, *Imagine instead that you were perfectly happy.* Shivering, with his coat collar turned up as though he was sitting around a big cold aerodrome, he leans against a cradle of wires and stays and reexperiences unimaginable views, unearthly lightness, the hull starlit at altitude, electrical storms and the incandescence of clouds, and Gnüss's lips on his throat. He remembers his younger brother's iridescent fingers after having blown soap bubbles as a child.

Below the ship, frightened horses spook like flying fish discharged from seas of yellow grass. Miles away, necklaces of lightning drop and fork.

Inside the hangarlike hull, they can feel the gravitational forces as Captain Pruss brings the ship up to the docking mast in a tight turn. The sharpness of the turn overstresses the after-hull structure, and the bracing wire bolt that Gnüss overtightened snaps like a rifle shot. The recoiling wire slashes open the gas cell opposite. Seven or eight feet above Gnüss's alarmed head, the escaping hydrogen encounters the prevailing St. Elmo's fire playing atop the ship.

From the ground, in Lakehurst, New Jersey, the *Hindenburg* malingers in a last wide circle, uneasy in the uneasy air.

The fireball explodes outward and upward, annihilating Gnüss at its center. More than 100 feet below on the axial catwalk, as the blinding light envelops everything below it, Meinert knows that whatever time has come is theirs, and won't be like anything else.

Four hundred and eighty feet away, loitering on the windblown and sandy flats weedy with dune grass, Gerhard Fichte, chief American representative of Luftschiffbau Zeppelin and senior liaison to Goodyear, hears a sound like surf in a cavern and sees the hull interior blooming orange, lit from within like a Japanese lantern, and understands the catastrophe to his company even before the ship fully explodes. He thinks: *Life, motion, everything was untrammeled and without limitation, pathless, ours.*

◈

A Visit of Charity

EUDORA WELTY

It was mid-morning—a very cold, bright day. Holding a potted plant before her, a girl of fourteen jumped off the bus in front of the Old Ladies' Home, on the outskirts of town. She wore a red coat, and her straight yellow hair was hanging down loose from the pointed white cap all the little girls were wearing that year. She stopped for a moment beside one of the prickly dark shrubs with which the city had beautified the Home, and then proceeded slowly toward the building, which was of whitewashed brick and reflected the winter sunlight like a block of ice. As she walked vaguely up the steps she shifted the small pot from hand to hand; then she had to set it down and remove her mittens before she could open the heavy door.

"I'm a Campfire Girl...I have to pay a visit to some old lady," she told the nurse at the desk. This was a woman in a white uniform who looked as if she were cold; she had close-cut hair which stood up on the very top of her head exactly like a sea wave. Marian, the little girl, did not tell her that this visit would give her a minimum of only three points in her score.

"Acquainted with any of our residents?" asked the nurse. She lifted one eyebrow and spoke like a man.

"With any old ladies? No—but—that is, any of them will do," Marian stammered. With her free hand she pushed her hair behind her ears, as she did when it was time to study Science.

The nurse shrugged and rose. "You have a nice *multiflora cineraria* there," she remarked as she walked ahead down the hall of closed doors to pick out an old lady.

There was loose, bulging linoleum on the floor. Marian felt as if she were walking on the waves, but the nurse paid no attention to it. There was a smell in the hall like the interior of a clock. Everything was silent until, behind one of the doors, an old lady of some kind cleared her throat like a sheep bleating. This decided the nurse. Stopping in her tracks, she first extended her arm, bent her elbow, and leaned forward from the hips—all to examine the watch strapped to her wrist; then she gave a loud double-rap on the door.

"There are two in each room," the nurse remarked over her shoulder.

"Two what?" asked Marian without thinking. The sound like a sheep's bleating almost made her turn around and run back.

One old woman was pulling the door open in short, gradual jerks, and when she saw the nurse a strange smile forced her old face dangerously awry. Marian, suddenly propelled by the strong, impatient arm of the nurse, saw next the side-face of another old woman, even older, who was lying flat in bed with a cap on and a counterpane drawn up to her chin.

"Visitor," said the nurse, and after one more shove she was off up the hall.

Marian stood tongue-tied; both hands held the potted plant. The old woman, still with that terrible, square smile (which was a smile of welcome) stamped on her bony face, was waiting....Perhaps she said something. The old woman in bed said nothing at all, and she did not look around.

Suddenly Marian saw a hand, quick as a bird claw, reach up in the air and pluck the white cap off her head. At the same time, another claw to match drew her all the way into the room, and the next moment the door closed behind her.

"My, my, my," said the old lady at her side.

Marian stood enclosed by a bed, a washstand and a chair; the tiny room had altogether too much furniture. Everything smelled wet—even the bare floor. She held on to the back of the chair, which was wicker and felt soft and damp. Her heart beat more and more slowly, her hands got colder and colder, and she could not hear whether the old women were saying anything or not. She could not see them very clearly. How dark it was! The window shade was down, and the only door was shut. Marian looked at the ceiling....It was like being caught in a robbers' cave, just before one was murdered.

"Did you come to be our little girl for a while?" the first robber asked.

Then something was snatched from Marian's hand—the little potted plant.

"Flowers!" screamed the old woman. She stood holding the pot in an undecided way. "Pretty flowers," she added.

Then the old woman in bed cleared her throat and spoke. "They are not pretty," she said, still without looking around, but very distinctly.

Marian suddenly pitched against the chair and sat down in it.

"Pretty flowers," the first old woman insisted. "Pretty—pretty..."

Marian wished she had the little pot back for just a moment—she had forgotten to look at the plant herself before giving it away. What did it look like?

"Stinkweeds," said the other old woman sharply. She had a bunchy white forehead and red eyes like a sheep. Now she turned them toward Marian. The fogginess seemed to rise in her throat again, and she bleated, "Who—are—you?"

To her surprise, Marian could not remember her name. "I'm a Camp-fire Girl," she said finally.

"Watch out for the germs," said the old woman like a sheep, not addressing anyone.

"One came out last month to see us," said the first old woman.

A sheep or a germ? wondered Marian dreamily, holding on to the chair.

"Did not!" cried the other old woman.

"Did so! Read to us out of the Bible, and we enjoyed it!" screamed the first.

"Who enjoyed it!" said the woman in bed. Her mouth was unexpectedly small and sorrowful, like a pet's.

"We enjoyed it," insisted the other. "You enjoyed it—I enjoyed it."

"We all enjoyed it," said Marian, without realizing that she had said a word.

The first old woman had just finished putting the potted plant high, high on the top of the wardrobe, where it could hardly be seen from below. Marian wondered how she had ever succeeded in placing it there, how she could ever have reached so high.

"You mustn't pay any attention to old Addie," she now said to the little girl. "She's ailing today."

"Will you shut your mouth?" said the woman in bed. "I am not."

"You're a story."

"I can't stay but a minute—really, I can't," said Marian suddenly. She looked down at the wet floor and thought that if she were sick in here they would have to let her go.

With much to-do the first old woman sat down in a rocking chair— still another piece of furniture!—and began to rock. With the fingers of one hand she touched a very dirty cameo pin on her chest. "What do you do at school?" she asked.

"I don't know..." said Marian. She tried to think but she could not.

"Oh, but the flowers are beautiful," the old woman whispered. She seemed to rock faster and faster; Marian did not see how anyone could rock so fast.

"Ugly," said the woman in bed.

"If we bring flowers—" Marian began, and then fell silent. She had almost said that if Campfire Girls brought flowers to the Old Ladies' Home, the visit would count one extra point, and if they took a Bible with them on the bus and read it to the old ladies, it counted double. But the old woman had not listened, anyway; she was rocking and watching the other one, who watched back from the bed.

"Poor Addie is ailing. She has to take medicine—see?" she said, pointing a horny finger at a row of bottles on the table, and rocking so high that her black comfort shoes lifted off the floor like a little child's.

"I am no more sick than you are," said the woman in bed.

"Oh, yes you are!"

"I just got more sense than you have, that's all," said the other old woman, nodding her head.

"That's only the contrary way she talks when *you all* come," said the first old lady with sudden intimacy. She stopped the rocker with a neat pat of her feet and leaned toward Marian. Her hand reached over—it felt like a petunia leaf, clinging and just a little sticky.

"Will you hush! Will you hush!" cried the other one.

Marian leaned back rigidly in her chair.

"When I was a little girl like you, I went to school and all," said the old woman in the same intimate, menacing voice. "Not here—another town..."

"Hush!" said the sick woman. "You never went to school. You never came and you never went. You never were anything—only here. You never were born! You don't know anything. Your head is empty, your heart and hands and your old black purse are all empty, even that little old box that you brought with you you brought empty—you showed it to me. And yet you talk, talk, talk, talk, talk all the time until I think I'm losing my mind! Who are you? You're a stranger—a perfect stranger! Don't you know you're a stranger? Is it possible that they have actually done a thing like this to anyone—sent them in a stranger to talk, and rock, and tell away her whole long rigmarole? Do they seriously suppose that I'll be able to keep it up, day in, day out, night in, night out, living in the same room with a terrible old woman—forever?"

Marian saw the old woman's eyes grow bright and turn toward her. This old woman was looking at her with despair and calculation in her face. Her small lips suddenly dropped apart, and exposed a half circle of false teeth with tan gums.

"Come here, I want to tell you something," she whispered. "Come here!"

Marian was trembling, and her heart nearly stopped beating altogether for a moment.

"Now, now, Addie," said the first old woman. "That's not polite. Do you know what's really the matter with old Addie today?" She, too, looked at Marian; one of her eyelids dropped low.

"The matter?" the child repeated stupidly. "What's the matter with her?"

"Why, she's mad because it's her birthday!" said the first old woman, beginning to rock again and giving a little crow as though she had answered her own riddle.

"It is not, it is not!" screamed the old woman in bed. "It is not my birthday, no one knows when that is but myself, and will you please be quiet and say nothing more, or I'll go straight out of my mind!" She turned her eyes toward Marian again, and presently she said in the soft, foggy voice, "When the worst comes to the worst, I ring this bell, and the nurse comes." One of her hands was drawn out from under the patched counterpane—a thin little hand with enormous black freckles. With a finger which would not hold still she pointed to a little bell on the table among the bottles.

"How old are you?" Marian breathed. Now she could see the old woman in bed very closely and plainly, and very abruptly, from all sides, as in dreams. She wondered about her—she wondered for a moment as though there was nothing else in the world to wonder about. It was the first time such a thing had happened to Marian.

"I won't tell!"

The old face on the pillow, where Marian was bending over it, slowly gathered and collapsed. Soft whimpers came out of the small open mouth. It was a sheep that she sounded like—a little lamb. Marian's face drew very close, the yellow hair hung forward.

"She's crying!" She turned a bright, burning face up to the first old woman.

"That's Addie for you," the old woman said spitefully.

Marian jumped up and moved toward the door. For the second time, the claw almost touched her hair, but it was not quick enough. The little girl put her cap on.

"Well, it was a real visit," said the old woman, following Marian through the doorway and all the way out into the hall. Then from behind she suddenly clutched the child with her sharp little fingers. In an affected, high-pitched whine she cried, "Oh, little girl, have you a penny to spare for a poor old woman that's not got anything of her own? We don't have a thing in the world—not a penny for candy—not a thing! Little girl, just a nickel—a penny—".

Marian pulled violently against the old hands for a moment before she was free. Then she ran down the hall, without looking behind her and without looking at the nurse, who was reading *Field & Stream* at her desk. The nurse, after another triple motion to consult her wrist watch, asked automatically the question put to visitors in all institutions: "Won't you stay and have dinner with *us*?"

Marian never replied. She pushed the heavy door open into the cold air and ran down the steps.

Under the prickly shrub she stooped and quickly, without being seen, retrieved a red apple she had hidden there.

Her yellow hair under the white cap, her scarlet coat, her bare knees all flashed in the sunlight as she ran to meet the big bus rocketing through the street.

"Wait for me!" she shouted. As though at an imperial command, the bus ground to a stop.

She jumped on and took a big bite out of the apple.

◩ ◩ ◩

Writing Exercises

1. This exercise involves two steps. First, describe a public place from your own childhood that continues to evoke powerful, emotional memories. It could be a movie theater, shopping mall, ballpark, the parking lot at your high school, or even the town dump. Now set a scene in this location. Use dialogue, description, action, and the thoughts of at least one of your characters. The scene should involve at least two characters, both of whom are uncomfortable in this setting.

2. Have your character accept a ride from someone she doesn't know well. Describe the ride and the car, particularly its interior. Instead of naming or generalizing about your character's feelings, focus on the details and let them reveal her emotional state and comfort level. Let the details tell us whether the car is luxurious, pristine, a family runabout, a mess. You're the author and so may know the future. Will the character's impressions of the owner, based on the car's condition, prove accurate?

3. Put a character in conflict with a setting. Imagine a character who misunderstands the nature of the place, or overlooks something important, or is oblivious of the danger suggested by certain details. Or imagine a character whose reaction to a place is the opposite of what we would expect: She is carefree in a dark urban alley; he is tranquil and reflective at the shooting range; he is contented in the funeral home.

4. Describe a place where a character feels trapped. It could be obvious—a jail cell, dentist's chair, elevator, or orphanage—but it might be less obvious—an RV, an amusement park, a wedding rehearsal, or a library. Use sensory details to suggest your character's discomfort, claustrophobia, and dread.

5. Photographers and filmmakers use a technique called depth of field. So do fiction writers. Write a scene in which you move back and forth between two "fields of action." Have two things going at once—one involving your characters in the foreground and a second having to do with the background. For instance, you might give us some dialogue among the characters on a picnic, then a paragraph about that storm brewing on the horizon, then back to the picnic, and so on. Don't worry too much about making explicit connections or creating transitions between paragraphs. In time, the two strands will figure out their own way of interweaving.

6. As a class, create a "virtual" dorm room on the blackboard. Going around the room, have everyone name an object in the room. Be as specific as possible: Is the stereo top of the line and brand new, or is it an obscure brand, fifteen years old, with a broken tape deck? List some CDs, books, and magazines. Describe the condition of things, how they are organized (or disorganized). Use brand names. What's in the closet? The drawers?

     Important: before starting this exercise, no one should suggest anything about the person who lives in the room; instead, let the character emerge as the room comes into focus, as individuals build on the suggestions of those who spoke before them. You may not even want to specify gender; let the room tell you!

     When everyone has added something, discuss the room you have created and the person who lives there. Are there any especially surprising elements? Are there details that seem contradictory? Which objects are the most revealing and intriguing? What story or stories might emerge from the details? What is going to happen to this character?

6

LONG AGO
Fictional Time

+ *Summary and Scene*

+ *Revising Summary and Scene*

+ *Flashback*

+ *Slow Motion*

Literature is, by virtue of its nature and subject matter, tied to time in a way the other arts are not. A painting represents a frozen instant that viewers experience at a time of their own choosing. Music bridges a span of time, which also dictates tempo and rhythm, but the time scheme is self-enclosed and makes no reference to time in the world outside itself. In fiction, the concern is *content time*, the period covered in the story. It is quite possible to write a story that takes about twenty minutes to read and covers about twenty minutes of action (Jean-Paul Sartre performed experiments in this *durational realism*), but no one has suggested such a correspondence as a fictional requirement. Sometimes the time period covered is telescoped, sometimes stretched. John Gould's "Feelers," which appears at the end of this chapter, is only a few pages long but includes a scene in the present time as well as several flashbacks and flashforwards. The history of the world up until now can be covered in a sentence; four seconds of crisis may take a chapter. It's even possible to do both at once: William Golding's entire novel *Pincher Martin* takes place between the time the drowning protagonist begins to take off his boots and the moment he dies with his boots still on. But when asked by a student, "How long does it really take?" Golding replied, "Eternity."

Summary and Scene

Summary and *scene* are methods of treating time in fiction. A summary covers a relatively long period of time in relatively short compass; a scene deals at length with a relatively short period of time.

Summary narration is a useful and often necessary device: It may give information, fill in a character's background, let us understand a motive, alter pace, create a transition, leap moments or years. For example, early in *The Poisonwood Bible*, summary is used both to fast-forward through time to the story's present moment and to set the political context:

> In the year of our Lord 1960 a monkey barreled through space in an American rocket; a Kennedy boy took the chair out from under a fatherly general named Ike; and the whole world turned on an axis called the Congo. The monkey sailed right overhead, and on a more earthly plane men in locked rooms bargained for the Congo's treasure. But I was there. Right on the head of that pin.

In the following example from Ian McEwan's *Enduring Love*, the narrator is preparing to pick up his wife at the airport. The summary leading up to their reunion doesn't tell us every single thing he did that morning (information we don't really need) but gives us enough description of his preparations to let us know how eagerly he's looking forward to his wife's return:

> On the way out to Heathrow I had made a detour into Covent Garden and found a semilegal place to park, near Carluccio's. I went in and put together a picnic whose centerpiece was a great ball of mozzarella, which the assistant fished out of an earthenware vat with a wooden claw. I also bought black olives, mixed salad, and focaccia. Then I hurried up Long Acre to Rota's to take delivery of Clarissa's birthday present. Apart from the flat and our car, it was the most expensive single item I had ever bought. The rarity of this little book seemed to give off a heat I could feel through the thick brown wrapping paper as I walked back up the street. Forty minutes later I was scanning the screens for arrival information.

Short bits of summary often come in the middle of a scene, as in this excerpt from Alice Munro's story "Hateship, Friendship, Courtship, Loveship, Marriage." The main character, Johanna, is trying on potential wedding dresses in a clothing store, and the summary explores her reasons for having blurted out her secret to the saleswoman:

> "It's likely what I'll get married in," said Johanna.
>
>   She was surprised at that coming out of her mouth. It wasn't a major error—the woman didn't know who she was and would probably not be

talking to anybody who did know. Still, she had meant to keep absolutely quiet. She must have felt she owed this person something—that they'd been through the disaster of the green suit and the discovery of the brown dress together and that was a bond. Which was nonsense. The woman was in the business of selling clothes, and she'd succeeded in doing just that.

"Oh!" the woman cried out. "How wonderful!"

Even the history of a relationship can be given in summary, as seen in this paragraph from Munro's "What Is Remembered":

Pierre and Jonas had grown up together in West Vancouver—they could remember it before the Lion's Gate Bridge was built, when it seemed like a small town. Their parents were friends. When they were eleven or twelve years old they had built a rowboat and launched it at Dundarave Pier. At the university they had parted company for awhile—Jonas was studying to be an engineer, while Pierre was enrolled in the Classics, and the Arts and Engineering students traditionally despised each other. But in the years since then the friendship had to some extent been revived. Jonas, who was not married, came to visit Pierre and Meriel, and sometimes stayed with them for a week at a time.

All four of these summaries use concrete details to engage the reader—the monkey barreling through space, a giant ball of mozzarella, the disaster of the green suit, launching a rowboat. Vivid and specific summary is enlightening and enjoyable to read. On the other hand, a general, perfunctory summary—"They met a few years ago and fell in love. He thought she was beautiful, she thought he was cute. They had many lively dates together before they got engaged"—is likely to be one of those passages that readers skip.

Summary can be called the mortar of the story, but scenes are the building blocks. Scene is the crucial means of allowing your reader to experience the story with the characters. Basically defined, a scene is dialogue and action that take place between two or more characters over a set period of "real" time. Like a story, on its own small scale, a scene has a turning point or mini-crisis that propels the story forward toward its conclusion. Scene is *always* necessary to fiction, for it allows readers to see, hear, and sense the story's drama moment to moment. Jerome Stern, in *Making Shapely Fiction*, astutely observes that like a child in a tantrum, when you want everyone's full attention you "make a scene," using the writer's full complement of "dialogue, physical reactions, gestures, smells, sounds, and thoughts." A confrontation, a turning point, or a crisis occurs at given moments that take on significance as moments and cannot be summarized. The form of a story requires confrontations, turning points, and crises, and therefore requires scenes.

It is quite possible to write a short story in a single scene, with hardly any summary at all, as demonstrated by "A Visit of Charity" (included at the end of Chapter 5) and "Hominids" by Jill McCorkle (included at the end of this chapter). It is nearly impossible, however, to write a successful story entirely in summary. One of the most common errors beginning fiction writers make is to summarize events rather than to realize them as moments.

Here is a moment in the story "Tandolfo the Great," which I've summarized to show the limitations of summary. The clown, Rodney, has just called the birthday boy a name: "Then Rodney decides to insult the boy further, and when the boy sticks out his tongue, Rodney grabs it and lets go, causing the boy to sit down hard. The boy's parents and their friends roughly remove Rodney, take him outside and prevent him from rescuing his rabbit. He tries to stick up for himself, but nobody takes him seriously."

This summary keeps us at a distance from the action and characters, just when we expect, and need, to be up close. This particular moment is a turning point, and in the scene, as Richard Bausch actually wrote it, we are right there, experiencing everything along with Rodney, delighting in his attack on the birthday boy, suffering his humiliation when he's manhandled, feeling his need to rescue Chi-Chi the rabbit, squirming in discomfort when he reveals his drunken state:

It grows quiet. Even the small children can tell that something's happened to change everything.

"Tandolfo has another trick," Rodney says, "where he makes the birthday boy pop like a balloon. Especially if he's a fat birthday boy."

A stirring among the adults.

"Especially if he's an ugly little slab of flesh like this one here."

"Now just a minute," says DAD.

"Pop," Rodney says to the birthday boy, who drops the hat and then, seeming to remember that defiance is expected, makes a face. Sticks out his tongue. Rodney/Tandolfo is quick with his hands by training, and he grabs the tongue.

"Awk," the boy says. "Aw-aw-aw."

"Abracadabra." Rodney lets go, and the boy falls backward into the lap of one of the older children. "Whoops, time to sit down," says Rodney.

Very quickly, he's being forcibly removed. They're rougher than gangsters. They lift him, punch him, tear at his costume—even the women. Someone hits him with a spoon. The whole scene boils out onto the lawn, where someone has released the cage that Chi-Chi was in. Chi-Chi moves about wide-eyed, hopping between running children, evading them, as Tandolfo the Great cannot evade the adults. He's being pummeled, because he keeps trying to return for his rabbit. And the adults won't let him off the curb....

He straightens, pushes the hair out of his eyes, adjusts the clown nose, and looks at them. "I would say that even though I wasn't as patient as I could've been, the adults have not comported themselves well here," he says.

"Drunk," one of the women says.

Transitions between summary and scene must also be carefully crafted. In the following paragraph from Margaret Atwood's *Lady Oracle*, the narrator has been walking home from her Brownie troop with older girls who tease and terrify her with threats of a bad man. The first paragraph of this quotation summarizes the way things were over a period of a few months and then makes a transition to one of the afternoons:

> The snow finally changed to slush and then to water, which trickled down the hill of the bridge in two rivulets, one on either side of the path; the path itself turned to mud. The bridge was damp, it smelled rotten, the willow branches turned yellow, the skipping ropes came out. It was light again in the afternoons, and on one of them, when for a change Elizabeth hadn't run off but was merely discussing the possibilities with the others, a real man actually appeared.

The second paragraph, the beginning of a scene, specifies a particular moment:

> He was standing at the far side of the bridge, a little off the path, holding a bunch of daffodils in front of him. He was a nice-looking man, neither old nor young, wearing a good tweed coat, not at all shabby or disreputable. He didn't have a hat on, his taffy-colored hair was receding and the sunlight gleamed on his high forehead.

Notice that the scene is introduced when an element of conflict and confrontation occurs. That the threatened bad man does appear and that he is surprisingly innocuous promises a turn of events and a change in the relationship among the girls. We need to see the moment when this change occurs.

Throughout *Lady Oracle*, a typical pattern recurs: a summary leading up to, and followed by, a scene that represents a turning point. Here is another example—one with a different setting and characters—from later in the novel:

> My own job was fairly simple. I stood at the back of the archery range, wearing a red leather change apron, and rented out the arrows. When the barrels of arrows were almost used up, I'd go down to the straw targets. The difficulty was that we couldn't make sure all the arrows had actually been shot before we went down to clear the targets. Rob would shout, Bows DOWN, please, arrows OFF the string, but occasionally someone would let an arrow go, on purpose or by accident. This was how I got shot. We'd pulled the arrows and the men were carrying the barrels back to the line; I was replacing a target face, and I'd just bent over.

To get comfortable with this pattern of storytelling, it may help to think of your own past as a movement through time: *I was born in Arizona and lived there with my parents until I was eighteen; then I spent three years in New York before going on to England.* Or you might instead remember the way things were during a period of that time: *In New York we used to go down Broadway for a midnight snack, and Judy would always dare us to do some nonsense or other before we got back.* But when you think of the events that significantly altered your life, your mind will present you with a scene: *Then one afternoon Professor Bovie stopped me in the hall after class and wagged his glasses at me. "Have you thought about studying in England?"*

The moments that altered your life you remember at length and in detail; your memory tells you your story, and it is a great natural storyteller.

A STORY ISN'T ABOUT A MOMENT IN TIME, a story is about *the* moment in time.

W. D. WETHERELL

Scene and summary are often intermixed, of course, and summary may serve precisely to heighten scene.

As we saw in a previous example from the Munro story about the women in the clothing store, summary used within a scene can suggest contrast with the past, intensify mood, or delay while creating suspense about what will happen next. This example from Rosellen Brown's *Before and After*—in which a father, disturbed by reports of a young girl's murder, is checking out his son's car in a dark garage—does all three.

> The snow was lavender where the light came down on it, like the weird illumination you see in planetariums that changes every color and makes white electric blue. Jacob and I loved to go to the science museum in Boston—not that long ago he had been at that age when the noisy saga of whirling planets and inexplicable anti-gravitational feats, narrated by a man with a deep official-facts voice, was thrilling. He was easily, unstintingly thrilled, or used to be. Not now, though.

Notice how Brown uses brief summaries both of the way things used to be and the way things have changed over time, as well as images of time, weather, and even the whirling cosmos to rouse our fear toward the "instant" in which major change occurs:

> At the last instant I thought I'd look at the trunk. I was beginning to feel relief wash over me like that moon-white air outside—a mystery still, where he might be, but nothing suspicious. The trunk snapped open and rose with the slow deliberation of a drawbridge, and then I thought I'd fall over for lack of breath. Because I knew I was looking at blood.

In this excerpt from *Saturday* by Ian McEwan, a novel that takes place on one Saturday, the main character, a neurosurgeon, has awakened in the middle of the night and is staring out the window at the street below. A bit of summary in this scene lets us know how things appear outside his window right now as opposed to how they usually look. Notice the smooth transitions between the time periods and how the sensory descriptions ground us in both:

He leans forward, pressing his weight onto his palms against the sill, exulting in the emptiness and clarity of the scene. His vision—always good—seems to have sharpened. He sees the paving stone mica glistening in the pedestrianised square, pigeon excrement hardened by distance and cold into something almost beautiful, like a scattering of snow. He likes the symmetry of black cast-iron posts and their even darker shadows, and the lattice of cobbled gutters. The overfull litter baskets suggest abundance rather than squalor; the vacant benches set around the circular gardens look benignly expectant of their daily traffic—cheerful lunchtime office crowds, the solemn, studious boys from the Indian hostel, lovers in quiet raptures or crisis, the crepuscular drug dealers, the ruined old lady with her wild haunting calls. Go away! She'll shout for hours at a time, and squawk harshly, sounding like some marsh bird or zoo creature.

Standing here, as immune to the cold as a marble statue, gazing towards Charlotte Street, towards a foreshortened jumble of facades, scaffolding and pitched roofs, Henry thinks the city is a success....

The movements between scene and summary can be quite fluid—you can easily move in and out and back and forth between them quite easily as long as the reader is not confused, and as long as both scene and summary seem relevant and engaging.

It is crucial that a fiction writer understand the difference between the two and know when and how to best use both of them.

O NE SIMPLE TRICK TO HELP YOU CONCENTRATE ON writing a scene at a specific time in a specific location is to state, right away, something like this: 10 A.M., NYC Athletic Club, Jim and John. If you know when, where, and how, you could probably jump in, and if not, add one more element: what. What are they competing for? What are they in conflict about?

JOSIP NOVAKOVICH

Revising Summary and Scene

Some writers have a tendency to oversummarize, racing through more time and more events than are necessary to tell the story. The danger there is lack of depth. Other writers undersummarize, finding it difficult to deal with quick leaps and transitions, dwelling at excessive length on every scene, including the scenes of the past. The danger of such writing is that readers may not sense which scenes are more important than others. The writer seems not to have made this decision himself or herself. Reluctant to do the writer's job, a reader may lose patience.

After you have written (and especially workshopped) a few stories, you will know which sort of writer you are, and in which direction you need to work.

Following are some comments you may hear in workshop—and suggestions for revising your story accordingly:

- If people say *you have enough material for a novel*, then you have probably not distilled your material down to the very few scenes that contain the significance you seek.

  —Pick one event of all those you have included that contains a moment of crucial change in your character. Write *that* scene in detail, moment by moment. Take time to create the place and the period. Make us see, taste, smell. Let characters speak. Is there a way to indicate, sketch, contain—or simply omit—all that earlier life you raced through in summary? If this proves too difficult, have you really found out yet what your story is about? Explore the scene, rather than the summary, for clues.

  —Try condensing an unnecessary scene to a sentence. Every scene should feel necessary to the story. Each one should build on the one before, and in each scene something surprising should happen—the conflict should escalate. Scenes in which nothing important happens can be summarized. For instance, this exchange of information between the characters does not merit a scene: "Suzie stopped by her parents' house to talk to her mother about the missing money, but her father told her that her mother had gone to visit a sick friend. She said she'd call later and went back to her apartment."

  —Try fusing two or even three such scenes into one. Ask yourself what is being accomplished in each scene, and try to determine whether or not one scene could do the work for all of them. For instance, in the previous example, you might have a scene following the one where Suzie visits her parent's house in which, back at her apartment, Suzie's boyfriend tells her that her mother has called and wants to speak to her right away. Another scene might include a telephone call between Suzie and her mother, in which her mother asks her to come to the casino and bring her credit card, and then, finally, you may have a scene where Suzie enters the casino and finds her mother standing, zombie-like, in front of the slot machines. This final scene is likely to be the only one really necessary. There might be some summary of the visit with her father and the telephone call with her mother, or Suzie might mention some or all of these things to her mother when she sees her in the casino—perhaps this is the third time in a week that her mother has called in a panic, which upsets not only Suzie but her boyfriend too. And why is her mother continuing to lie to Suzie's father? Sick friend, indeed.

This scene-combining may seem impossible at first, and it may involve sacrificing a delicious phrase or a nifty nuance, but it is simply the necessary work of plotting.

- If your critics say *you write long* or *your story really begins on page three* (or *six*, or *eleven*), have you indulged yourself in setting things up, or dwelt on the story's past at the expense of its present? Where the writer begins writing the story is not necessarily where the final version of the story will begin. Look through your story for a better place to begin.

Chekhov advised his fellow writers to tear the story in half and begin in the middle; in fact, most stories begin as close to the end as possible. Nancy Huddleston Packer says: "The first line of a story should hook readers' attention and pull them into the middle of the action. You want readers to feel like the train is leaving without them, so they'd better get on board and keep reading as fast as they can."

John Gardner described a story as being a "vivid and continuous dream" that the writer creates in the mind of the reader. John L'Heureux applies this notion to the opening of a story, saying that the first paragraph should be designed to help readers "sink into the dream of the story." Like the opening frame of a movie, the opening paragraph entices readers into the story-dream, economically setting the tone; establishing the world, level of reality, and point of view; indirectly conveying information; and "promising" that certain concerns will be dealt with over the course of the story. Often the possible ground for some change or reversal is established in the opening as well.

- If your readers are *confused by what happens at the end*, it may very well be that you have summarized the crisis instead of realizing it in a scene. The crisis moment in a story *must always be presented as a scene*. This is the moment we have been waiting for. This is the payoff when the slipper fits. We want to be there. We want to feel the moment that change happens, hear it, taste it, see it in color in close-up on the wide screen of our minds. This is also a hard job, sometimes the hardest a writer has to do—it's draining to summon up all that emotion in all its intensity. And there isn't always a glass slipper handy when you need one; it may be difficult enough to identify the moment when you need that scene.

Many writers avoid writing crisis scenes in early drafts, perhaps because in fiction, as in our lives, we often try to avoid intense conflict. In order to write a vivid close-up scene for the reader, a writer must first fully imagine that scene, must place him- or herself in it and emotionally experience it, moment by moment. Many writers find it necessary to take it a step further, as Dan Chaon did when he wrote "Big Me":

> I'll also tell you that the hardest part of the story for me—the final confrontation between Andy and Mickleson—was ultimately written as I actually acted out the scene late at night. Imagine our poor neighbor lady glancing over and seeing me prancing around my study, gesticulating and saying things like "Hold still, I'll whisper," and then writing wildly on a legal pad. My neighbor closed her curtain discreetly, as I suppose I should have as well.

It is often the case that such scenes, even in the imagination, are uncomfortable places to be. However, your job as a writer is to recognize the need for such a scene and to try to overcome your squeamishness about going there.

So when is the right time to end your story? As the following writers suggest, the best place to look for an answer to this question is the story itself.

> It will turn out that your first page has a lot to do with your last page. Just as in a poem, the first line has a lot to do with the last line, even though you didn't know what it was going to be.
>
> Doris Betts

> An ending that seems unsatisfactory might actually be fine. The trouble with the ending might be that the beginning or the middle doesn't set up the ending. A problem scene may not be a problem because of the way it is written. The revision of the ending might need to be carried out back in the beginning of the story.... You start writing the ending when you write your first word.
>
> Jerome Stern, *Making Shapely Fiction*

> The climax is that major event, usually toward the end, that brings all the tunes you have been playing so far into one major chord, after which at least one of your people is profoundly changed. If someone isn't changed, then what is the point of your story? For the climax, there must be a killing or a healing or a domination. It can be a real killing, a murder, or it can be a killing of the spirit, or of something terrible inside one's soul, or it can be a killing of a deadness within, after which the person becomes alive again. The healing may be about union, reclamation, the rescue of a fragile prize. But whatever happens, we need to feel that it was inevitable, that even though we may be amazed, it feels absolutely right, that of course things would come to this, of course they would shake down in this way.
>
> Anne Lamott, *Bird by Bird*

I don't like endings that feel like they've got a big bow or THE END sign. What I really like in an ending is to feel satisfied that there was completion within the story, and yet, in some way, the story is still open.

Jill McCorkle

Flashback

Flashback—in either scene or summary—is one of the most magical of fiction's contrivances, easier and more effective in this medium than in any other, because the reader's mind is a swifter mechanism for getting into the past than anything that has been devised for stage or even film. In fiction you can give the reader a smoothly worded transition into the past, and the force of the story will be time-warped to whenever and wherever you want it.

Nevertheless, many beginning writers use unnecessary flashbacks. While flashback can be a useful way to provide background to character or the history of events—the information that screenwriters call *backstory*—it isn't the only way. Rather, dialogue, brief summary, a reference, or detail can often tell us all we need to know.

If you are tempted to use flashback to fill in the whole past, try using your journal for exploring background. Write down everything, fast. Then take a hard look at it to decide just how *little* of it you can use, how much of it the reader can infer, how you can sharpen an image to imply a past incident or condense a grief into a line of dialogue. Trust the reader's experience of life to understand events from attitudes. And keep the present of the story moving.

For instance, when thinking about the backstory for the scene involving Suzie and her gambling-addicted mother, you might write in your journal about the escalation of Suzie's mother's problem with money—how it started when Suzie's older sister ran away from home, how her mother began buying gadgets and appliances she saw on TV, how Suzie came home one day to find her mother rearranging brand-new living room furniture, the "old" furniture she'd bought six months ago already sitting out in the yard. Then riverboat casinos came to Davenport, and when her mother's friends decided to go there on a lark, only Suzie's mother stayed all night, Suzie and her father were frantic with worry, etc., etc.

When looking at all this material, you might be tempted to use some of it in flashbacks—a scene when Suzie and her parents discover that their older daughter has run away? Or when Suzie finds her mother rearranging the furniture? Or when the mother stays out all night at the casino and Suzie and her father are calling everyone they know? But should you interrupt the present story for any of these potential flashbacks? Are they worth bringing it to a halt? I'd say no, except for possibly the first example—the aftermath of the older daughter's disappearance. That scene could have deep emotional resonance and help us to better understand the mother's problems.

The other examples could appear in the story in summary form, if they need to appear at all.

Writing out all of this background material is never a waste of time. Even if most of it is never mentioned in either scene or summary, it will inform your understanding of the characters and allow you to understand their problems and empathize with them, helping you to create a fuller, richer, more plausible story.

Flashback is effectively used in fiction to *reveal* at the *right point*. It does not so much distract us from, as contribute to, the central action of the story, deepening our understanding of character and theme. If you find that you do need to use a flashback to reveal, at some point, why the character reacts as she does, or how totally he is misunderstood by those around him, or some other point of emotional significance, then there are several ways to help the reader make that leap in time.

- Provide a smooth, clear transition between present and past. A connection between what's happening in the present and what happened in the past will often best transport the reader, just as it does the character. But avoid overly blatant transitions such as, "Henry thought back to the time" and "I drifted back in memory." Assume the reader's intelligence and ability to follow a leap back. For example:

  The kid in the Converse high-tops lifted off on the tips of his toes and slam-dunked it in.

  Joe'd done that once, in the lot off Seymour Street, when he was still four inches shorter than Ruppert and had already started getting zits. It was early fall, and…

- A graceful transition to the past allows you to summarize necessary background quickly, as in this example from James W. Hall's *Under Cover of Daylight*.

  Thorn watched as Sugarman made a quick inspection of the gallery. Thorn sat on the couch where he'd done his homework as a boy, the one that looked out across the seawall toward Carysfort light.

  That was how his nights had been once, read a little Thoreau, do some algebra, and look up, shifting his body so he could see through the louvers the fragile pulse of that marker light, and let his mind roam, first out the twelve miles to the reef and then pushing farther, out past the shipping lanes into a world he pictured as gaudy and loud, chaotic. Bright colors and horns honking, exotic vegetables and market stalls, and water, clear and deep and shadowy, an ocean of fish, larger and more powerful than those he had hauled to light. Beyond the reef.

- If you are writing in the past tense, begin the flashback in the past perfect (*she had driven; he had worked*) and use the construction "had + (verb)" two or three times more. Then switch to the simple past (*he raced; she crept*); the reader will be with you. If you are writing in the present tense, you may want to keep the whole flashback in the past tense.

- Try to avoid a flashback within a flashback. If you find yourself tempted by this awkward shape, it probably means you're trying to let flashback carry too much of the story.

- When the flashback ends, be very clear that you are catching up to the present again. Repeat an action or image that the reader will remember belonging to the basic time period of the story. For instance, if in the present time of the story the characters are eating dinner in a fancy restaurant, you could bring us back into the present by mentioning some of the sights and smells of the place— the sight of the annoying waiter coming toward them again, the delicious smell of the coffee in the cup your character is savoring. Or you could have the character set down his fork and glance at the other character across the table. However you decide to do it, you must place the reader firmly where he or she belongs. Often simply beginning the paragraph with "Now..." will accomplish the reorientation.

Slow Motion

Flashback is a term borrowed from film, and I want to borrow another—*slow motion*—to point out a correlation between narrative time and significant detail.

When people experience moments of great intensity, their senses become especially alert and they register, literally, more than usual. In extreme crisis people have the odd sensation that time is slowing down, and they see, hear, smell, and remember ordinary sensations with extraordinary clarity. This psychological fact can work artistically in reverse: You can create the intensity by using detail with special focus and precision. The phenomenon is so universal that it has become a standard film technique to register a physical blow, gunshot, sexual passion, or extreme fear in slow motion. The technique works forcefully in fiction as well.

Ian McEwan, in *A Child in Time*, demonstrates the technique:

...He was preparing to overtake when something happened—he did not quite see what—in the region of the lorry's wheels, a hiatus, a cloud of dust, and then something black and long snaked through a hundred feet towards him. It slapped the windscreen, clung there a moment and was whisked away before he had time to understand what it was. And then—or did this happen in the same moment?—the rear of the lorry made a complicated set of move-ments, a bouncing and swaying, and slewed in a wide spray of sparks, bright even in sunshine. Something curved and metallic flew off to one side. So far Stephen had had time to move his foot towards the brake, time to notice a padlock swinging on a loose flange, and 'Wash me please' scrawled in grime. There was a whinnying of scraped metal and new sparks, dense enough to form a white flame which seemed to propel the rear of the lorry into the air.

Anyone who has faced some sort of accident can identify with the experi-ence of sensuous slowdown McEwan records. But the slow-motion technique works also with experiences most of us have not had and to which we must submit in imagination:

Blood was spurting from an artery in my left leg. I could not see it, and I do not recall how I knew it...for a short time I was alone with Patrick. I told myself I was in good hands, but I did not do this with words; I surrendered myself. I focused on breathing. I slowed my breathing, and tried to remain absolutely in the present, in each moment...waiting to die or stay alive was like getting an injection as a child, when you first learned not to think, but to gather yourself into the present, to breathe slowly, to relax your muscles, even your arm as the nurse swabbed it with alcohol, to feel the cool alcohol, to smell it, to feel your feet on the floor and see the color of the wall, and nothing else as your slow breathing opened you up to the incredible length and breadth and depth of one second.

Andre Dubus, "Breathing"

And the technique will work when the intensity or trauma of the moment is not physical but emotional:

They were in the deep sleep of midnight when Pauline came quietly into her son's room and saw that there were two in his bed. She turned on the light. The room was cold and stuffy; warm in the core of it was the smell of a body she had known since she gave birth to him, unmistakable to her as the scent that leads a bitch to her puppy, and it was mingled with the scents of sexuality caressed from the female nectary. The cat was a rolled fur glove in an angle made by Sasha's bent knees. The two in the bed opened their eyes; they focussed out of sleep and saw Pauline. She was looking at them, at their naked shoulders above the covers....

Nadine Gordimer, *A Sport of Nature*

Central to this technique are the alert but matter-of-fact acceptance of the event and the observation of small, sometimes apparently random, details.

The characters do not say, "Oh my God, we're going to die!" or "What an outrage!" Instead they record a padlock swinging, the cool feel of an alcohol swab, a cat rolled into the angle of bent knees.

Beginning writers often overuse summary in their fiction because it seems to be the fastest and most direct way of getting information across. Often, however, we want the reader to linger awhile and experience certain moments along with the characters. Once you become adept at the skill of manipulating time in fiction, you will find that the necessity of setting your story at some specific time is a liberating opportunity.

IN OUR EFFORT TO KEEP THE ACTION FROM lagging, we hurry the reader over crucial moments. But anything that is very exciting can't be taken in hurriedly. If somebody is killed in an automobile accident, people who were involved in the accident or who merely witnessed it will be busy for days afterwards piecing together a picture of what happened. They simply couldn't take it all in at that time. When we are writing fiction, we have to give the reader ample time to take in what is happening, particularly if it is very important.

CAROLINE GORDON TO FLANNERY O'CONNER

Hominids

JILL MCCORKLE

"I'm thinking I will have myself a restaurant known as Peckers, and as my model I will use Hooters, where one of Bill's buddies likes to go on Friday night. I will have a woodpecker instead of an owl and waiters instead of waitresses. They will wear uniforms that are, shall I say, a bit revealing below the belt and as manager my job will be saying who looks good in the outfit and who doesn't. Sorry, that's business. It's not harassment if you say right up front that Peckers is all about peckers. The Pecker Burger, the Pecker Shake, the foot-long Peckerdog, the Pecker who serves you. There will be lots of cute puns about wood, redheaded, etc. I think it will be a huge success."

I make this speech to the group—Bill's old friends and their wives—gathered for the golf weekend Bill pulls together every year. Golf is the excuse for the get-together even though sometimes only a couple of them actually play. Most of the time is spent drinking and telling tales. Bill has just told how he and the boys could not help but pull off of I-95 and check out Cafe Risqué, which advertises all up and down the highway. I also say, "So why not South of the Border? They have lots of billboards on the highway, too, and they have liquor by the drink. They even have fireworks you can buy. Sombreros. Enchiladas. As a matter of fact, you can buy just about anything at South of the Border, except for the señoritas, *unless*," I add, feigning great suprise, "that's why you went to Cafe Risqué instead."

The signs say that Cafe Risqué is open all night and that the women are topless. The women on the signs look like supermodels—shiny healthy hair and white well-cared-for teeth. I'm certain that what's on the billboards is not what you find inside, especially at eight o'clock in the morning, or two o'clock in the afternoon. Or any time, for that matter. I'm betting you find track marks, illiteracy, scars of at least one abusive relationship. At least that would be my uneducated guess.

I'm guessing stretched-out titties, the children who stretched them cold and alone at home waiting for mama to get off work. Or maybe the women have no children and they eye every man who comes in through that darkened glass door as a potential future, a ticket to a better, cleaner existence. Men, for instance, like my spouse, Bill, who is college educated and should know better, and his sidekick, Ed, an old fraternity brother who has flown in from Atlanta and who chooses to spend part of his day this way while his wife and newborn are back at home.

I voice my sadness at this scene. I politely question Bill's participation in this event and ask how he will explain such a place, should the question ever arise, to our son and daughter, who are on the threshold of adolescence. And still the conversation in the room turns to breasts. Ethan—former college fraternity brother from Winston-Salem—just can't get over the whole scene. He is imitating, swinging his pathetic khaki-clad body side to side. He discusses ta-ta size like you might a pumpkin, while his wife stands there and giggles. I catch her eye and she stops cold. She knows better but like many of us she has learned that it's easier to look the other way, pretend that you really did not see or hear what you thought you did.

You can learn a lot on a weekend like this. I look around the room—my dining room—as they gather here for cocktails and hors d'oeuvres, and I might as well be on another planet even though it's a scene I have lived through for over a decade by now.

There is always at least one man going through the motions of separation or divorce. That one normally arrives with a woman twenty years younger or comes alone and flirts with all the wives. This year it is Dennis, from D.C., who grew up in this very town but has gone to great lengths to rid himself of any traces of his native origin. It is as if he has no memory of a mother or a childhood or an education here. He would have the world believe that he simply sprang forth in a business suit with a fat wallet boasting membership in the NRA, a Rolex on his wrist, and a BMW parked by the curb. Right now he seems to be checking out everyone's cleavage. I watch him and keep thinking that before the night is over, I will go and get my high school yearbook and pass it around so everyone can check out when he was a Future Farmer of America and a Teen Dem and a relatively decent guy. I will ask how his mother—a woman who put in forty years as a receptionist at the courthouse and who raised a child all by her-self—is faring out at Turtle Bay Nursing Home, which he visits only at Christmas if then. He keeps trying to catch my eye and wink like the two of us are somehow in on something. My glance back at him says *You suck.*

I tell everybody that I think men who are attracted to breasts in a major way are still yearning to suckle their mamas. Isn't it true there's a whole generation of formula-fed men who never had that opportunity and now they are suffering? They want to latch on; they want to make their mothers draw sharp breaths in with the tight wrench just before that glo-rious letdown. I say that knowing that they are all Enfamil men with mamas who claim they couldn't nurse when the truth is nobody taught them how. I don't think evolution would have allowed a whole generation to die out; it certainly hasn't happened that way in the animal kingdom. You don't see animals making fun of teats and udders. I doubt if it happens among humans in Third World countries either. But maybe this was the period in history when society began to look at the breast in a whole differ-ent way. Maybe this is when the breast went from a source of nourishment for the young to something for men to pinch and make jokes about.

I can tell that they are tiring of my lecture; I can feel the tension ris-ing so I choose to sink back and away. I ask them to tell us all about their games that day, no one even noticing that this is a way of defusing the situation, a way for me to sit and sip my drink and fade off into my own thoughts. Like the time I accompanied my son and his third-grade class to the science museum where we stood before the model of Lucy—our first woman—her thumb visible, her body emerging from a previous simian form. She was only three and a half feet tall, her head the size of a softball. She was only in her twenties when she died and already her backbone was deformed; she suffered a terrible form of arthritis. She was found at the edge of a lake and scientists are unsure if she drowned or if she simply died of an illness. Did anyone even consider the possibility that perhaps she grew so tired, her heart so heavy, that she simply lay facedown on the shore and waited for the water to carry her into an eter-nal sleep? Did such a desire even exist in this early human form or was it the result of years of domestication, demands that went far beyond what life out in the wild would have required? Lucy's breasts were not huge;

they were thin and stretched. The kids pointed at her nipples and butt crack. They were children and had that right. They still had every opportunity to grow up and imagine the infant kept alive by Lucy's milk—a whole world's population nourished by Lucy's milk.

* * *

The discussion of golf comes around to the old story about Johnny Carson asking Arnold Palmer what he did for good luck before a match. Palmer replied, "My wife kisses my balls," to which Carson said, "Bet that makes your putter stand up." No one in the room actually saw the interview so we're not sure how much if any of it is true. The discussion of Ethan's swing leads right back into the swing of the hips of the woman who was clearly attracted to him at Cafe Risqué. Then the swing of her breasts, which Ethan said made him think of Loni Anderson. "Not the face, of course," he said. "Jesus Christ."

"Can you give it a rest?" Ethan's wife finally says. She is on her third cosmopolitan and feeling strong if only momentarily.

"So men like breasts," Dennis says and looks around to get moral support. "Is that news? What's the big deal?"

I say that if there were a disease the cure of which required men to have their penises removed they would be a bit more sensitive to body parts. I say this knowing that Dennis's mother had a double mastectomy when he was still in high school; there she was, a divorced mother, not so common at the time, working a forty-hour week, with a disease no one ever mentioned. There were no support groups, no magazine articles in which other women told their stories.

Ethan, who is lounging back on my sofa with his shiny little loafers propped on one silk-upholstered arm and who has had one too many, tells us, apropos of nothing, that he takes Viagra. There is absolute silence. Ethan's wife, Joyce, who had gone to the bathroom (she said, though I know that really she slipped by the liquor cabinet to freshen her drink), now returns to silence.

"What's up?" she asks.

"Ethan apparently," I say, and after the roar of laughter dies down, I continue. "He was just telling us about how he takes Viagra."

"Ethan!" There is horror all over her face: I am horrified just to imagine the man tuned up like an Eveready. Horrified that poor Joyce has to live with him. And now horrified at myself for making a joke at her expense as well as his.

"Do you see blue?" one man asks. "I've heard it can affect your vision."

"Temporary," Ethan answers smugly. Mr. All Knowing. Mr. Thinks He's Big. Nothing can slow him down.

"And it works?"

"Oh, *yeah*, it works." Ethan is enjoying his five minutes in the sun as he and Joyce knock back the liquor for very different reasons.

"So this was for a medical reason?" I ask.

"You mean impotence?" Dennis yells.

"No," Ethan spits. He wants to call me something really really bad, but he thinks better with Bill there beside me. He can't call Dennis anything because Dennis is a rung or two higher than he is on the man's man ladder. "I was just curious."

"Oh," I say. "Curious."

Bill catches my eye and I can't tell if it's to apologize or to say *Give me a break, I only entertain these guys once a year, let us act like boys. Let us have some fun.* I've heard it all before. And there were the years when the women thought the way we could compete was to act just like them, to go to clubs and drink too much and watch men strip. Scream out things like *Wooo wooo wooo, shake it baby yeah,* whistle wolf calls, salivate like Pavlovian dogs. You know, you never really do get into that and you sure get tired of trying to. Personally I'd rather be watching old movies—Bette Davis, Charles Boyer. I'd rather be in my nightgown with a mug of hot chocolate and my children snuggled under a down comforter watching reruns of *Andy Griffith* or *Leave It to Beaver.* I can't imagine Andy Taylor or Ward Cleaver going to Cafe Risqué. The long and short of it (no pun intended) is that very often at the end of a day, I am tired. My breasts are tired. My legs, back, brain. I would like nothing better than to stretch out and close my eyes, disappear, if only briefly.

The men, in spite of everything that has been said, return to the Cafe Risqué topic. Apparently there was one sexy waitress who was considerably overweight. (Ethan: "See? We aren't prejudiced against fat ones. The one that really liked me was the *fat* one.") Another skinny Asian one, Dennis informs us, needs a good orthodontist. (Plus her G-string was nasty looking; her thighs had purple stretch marks.) The one pouring coffee had a tattoo of a snake wrapping around her throat. A really fat ass. I am about to comment about how they all must have left nose prints on the glass of her cage when I walk over and stand next to Bill just in time to hear Ethan deliver his punch line about how to screw a fat girl: "Roll her in flour and look for the wet spots."

"What a hoot!" I slap him on the back as hard as I can. "Aren't you *funny?*" I avoid looking at Joyce, who I have known for a very long time. She was in my wedding. Bill is the godfather of their son. She drinks a little bit more, I notice, at each gathering.

"I've got one for you," I say. "Where do men go after they go to Hooter's?"

"Where?"

"The Hootel. And why don't women date Wood*peckers*?" I emphasize the last two syllables.

"Why?"

"Always boring." The women like that one. "And why does a dog lick his balls?"

"Wait, I know this one," Ron says. "Because he can."

"And did you hear about what happened when the woman showed her size 36C breasts? No? None of you guys have heard this one?"

They all shake their heads, Bill included, as they wait for the punch.

"God, this is an old one. I hear it at least once a week. And I can follow it with the one about the 36B and the 32A and the 48DD."

"So tell us already," Dennis says. He and Ethan are standing there nudging each other like prepubescent boys.

"Well, they all had cancer. They all had to have their breasts surgically removed." The women look down at my rug, the lovely intricate pattern of color. I'm sure there's at least one bad Pap smear in this room. One lump that has caused fear and worry. "Like your mother, Dennis."

They are all quiet now. The women are moving toward the warm yellow glow of my kitchen, where I have promised them a comfortable seat and a glass of good wine while I finish preparing the meal. "Maybe this is the reason the women go to the kitchen," Ron's wife, a relatively new wife, says quietly. "I wish we had done it sooner."

Now you can hear a pin drop. Now you can hear the cars passing on the highway, a rise and fall like ocean waves, and my mind is there by the highway with those women walking around inside Cafe Risqué. And wouldn't any one of them give everything she owned to be standing in this very room, in this privileged life where people actually have hobbies and children fuss about the full plate of good food you put before them and men take for granted the women they married, the bodies they like to roll on top of in the middle of the night, the breasts they pinch and knead like dough.

"Honey," Bill says and calls me back to the doorway. "Let it drop, okay? This is a party, not some New Age awareness group."

Tears spring to my eyes and I have to look away. I look out the window into our backyard at the array of Little Tikes apparatus that no longer gets used. He looks over at all of his buddies, especially Dennis, and laughs as if to apologize for the interruption. I can tell he wants to whisper all of the choice words—*hormones, premenstrual, girl things*—but to me he says, "I'm sorry. It was all a joke." He grips my hands in his. "Truce?"

The men are talking in low cautious voices. They are talking about birdies and bogeys and woods and irons, which in many ways is the same conversation with different nouns. The women have sprung to action and have begun setting my dining table with crystal and silver and Wedgwood china, all wedding presents eighteen years ago. They are laughing now about things their children have said and done. They are talking about their perennial beds, knowing that soon enough I will have to join in.

The peonies are just on the verge of bursting into full bloom and Joyce knows that next to the first breath of autumn this is my very favorite time of the year.

When my son and I stood in front of the model of Lucy, it was as if the world stopped for just a second, just long enough for us to take note of how far we had come and how far we had to go. He waited until his classmates ran off in hysterical laughter and then—could he have sensed my great respect for this ancient little hominid?—took my hand and whispered, "I bet she was real pretty for her time." My heart leapt forward a couple of millennia. This boy, this future man, was evolution in action. I tell this story and the women all smile; they relax in a way that they haven't all night long. It begins a whole ring of conversation around topics of love and warmth, desire and longing. I am easily drawn into the circle but a part of me is still thinking about bare breasts and day-old coffee, empty bank accounts and biopsies, neglected children and scar tissue. I am thinking of Lucy as she limped her way to the water's edge seeking rest; I am thinking of her as she lay there millions of years ago staring out at this world for the very last time.

◈

Mrs. Dutta Writes a Letter

CHITRA BANERJEE DIVAKARUNI

When the alarm goes off at 5:00 A.M., buzzing like a trapped wasp, Mrs. Dutta has been lying awake for quite a while. Though it has now been two months, she still has difficulty sleeping on the Perma Rest mattress Sagar and Shyamoli, her son and daughter-in-law, have bought specially for her. It is too American-soft, unlike the reassuringly solid copra ticking she is used to at home. *Except this is home now*, she reminds herself. She reaches hurriedly to turn off the alarm, but in the dark her fingers get confused among the knobs, and the electric clock falls with a thud to the floor. Its insistent metallic call vibrates out through the walls of her room until she is sure it will wake everyone. She yanks frantically at the wire until she feels it give, and in the abrupt silence that follows she hears herself breathing, a sound harsh and uneven and full of guilt.

Mrs. Dutta knows, of course, that this turmoil is her own fault. She should just not set the alarm. There is no need for her to get up early here in Sunnyvale, in her son's house. But the habit, taught to her by her mother-in-law when she was a bride of seventeen, *a good wife wakes before the rest of the household*, is one she finds impossible to break. How hard it was then to pull her unwilling body away from her husband's sleep-warm clasp, Sagar's father whom she had just learned to love. To stumble to the kitchen that smelled of stale garam masala and light the coal unoon so she could make morning tea for them all—her parents-in-law, her husband, his two younger brothers, the widow aunt who lived with them.

After dinner, when the family sits in front of the TV, she attempts to tell her grandchildren about those days. "I was never good at starting that unoon—the smoke stung my eyes, making me cough and cough. Breakfast was never ready on time, and my mother-in-law—oh, how she scolded me until I was in tears. Every night I would pray to Goddess Durga, please let me sleep late, just one morning!"

"Mmmm," Pradeep says, bent over a model plane.

"Oooh, how awful," says Mrinalini, wrinkling her nose politely before she turns back to a show filled with jokes that Mrs. Dutta does not understand.

"That's why you should sleep in now, Mother," says Shyamoli, smiling from the recliner where she sits looking through the *Wall Street Journal*. With her legs crossed so elegantly under the shimmery blue skirt she has changed into after work, and her unusually fair skin, she could pass for an American, thinks Mrs. Dutta, whose own skin is brown as roasted cumin. The thought fills her with an uneasy pride.

From the floor where he leans against Shyamoli's knee, Sagar adds, "We want you to be comfortable, Ma. To rest. That's why we brought you to America."

In spite of his thinning hair and the gold-rimmed glasses which he has recently taken to wearing, Sagar's face seems to Mrs. Dutta still that of the boy she used to send off to primary school with his metal tiffin box. She remembers how he crawled into her bed on stormy monsoon nights, how when he was ill no one else could make him drink his barley water. Her heart balloons in sudden gladness because she is really here, with him and his children in America. "Oh, Sagar"—she smiles—"now you're talking like this! But did you give me a moment's rest while you were growing up?" And she launches into a description of childhood pranks that has him shaking his head indulgently while disembodied TV laughter echoes through the room.

But later he comes into her bedroom and says, a little shamefaced, "Mother, please, don't get up so early in the morning. All that noise in the bathroom, it wakes us up, and Molli has such a long day at work..."

And she, turning a little so he shouldn't see her foolish eyes filling with tears as though she were a teenage bride again and not a woman well over sixty, nods her head, *yes, yes*.

Waiting for the sounds of the stirring household to release her from the embrace of her Perma Rest mattress, Mrs. Dutta repeats the 108 holy names of God. *Om Keshavaya Namah, Om Narayanaya Namah, Om*

Madhavaya Namah. But underneath she is thinking of the bleached-blue aerogram from Mrs. Basu that has been waiting unanswered on her bedside table all week, filled with news from home. There was a robbery at Sandhya Jewelry Store, the bandits had guns but luckily no one was hurt. Mr. Joshi's daughter, that sweet-faced child, has run away with her singing teacher, who would've thought it. Mrs. Barucha's daughter-in-law had one more baby girl, yes, their fourth, you'd think they'd know better than to keep trying for a boy. Last Tuesday was Bangla Bandh, another labor strike, everything closed down, even the buses not running, but you can't really blame them, can you, after all factory workers have to eat, too. Mrs. Basu's tenants, whom she'd been trying to evict forever, had finally moved out, good riddance, but you should see the state of the flat.

At the very bottom Mrs. Basu wrote, *Are you happy in America?*

Mrs. Dutta knows that Mrs. Basu, who has been her closest friend since they both came to Ghoshpara Lane as young brides, cannot be fobbed off with descriptions of Fisherman's Wharf and the Golden Gate Bridge, or even anecdotes involving grandchildren. And so she has been putting off her reply while in her heart family loyalty battles with insidious feelings of—but she turns from them quickly and will not name them even to herself.

Now Sagar is knocking on the children's doors—a curious custom, this, children being allowed to close their doors against their parents—and with relief Mrs. Dutta gathers up her bathroom things. She has plenty of time. It will take a second rapping from their mother before Pradeep and Mrinalini open their doors and stumble out. Still, she is not one to waste the precious morning. She splashes cold water on her face and neck (she does not believe in pampering herself), scrapes the night's gumminess from her tongue with her metal tongue cleaner, and brushes vigorously, though the minty toothpaste does not leave her mouth feeling as clean as did the bittersweet neem stick she'd been using all her life. She combs the knots out of her hair. Even at her age, it is thicker and silkier than her daughter-in-law's permed curls. *Such vanity*, she scolds her reflection, *and you a grandmother and a widow besides*. Still, as she deftly fashions her hair into a neat coil, she remembers how her husband would always compare it to night rain.

She hears a commotion outside.

"Pat! Minnie! What d'you mean you still haven't washed up? I'm late every morning to work nowadays because of you kids."

"But, Mom, *she's* in there. She's been there forever..." says Mrinalini.

Pause. Then, "So go to the downstairs bathroom."

"But all our stuff is here," says Pradeep, and Mrinalini adds, "It's not fair. Why can't *she* go downstairs?"

A longer pause. Inside the bathroom Mrs. Dutta hopes Shyamoli will not be too harsh on the girl. But a child who refers to elders in that disrespectful way ought to be punished. How many times had she slapped Sagar for something far less, though he was her only one, the jewel of her eye, come to her after she had been married for seven years and everyone had given up hope already? Whenever she lifted her hand to him it was as though her heart was being put through a masala grinder. Such is a mother's duty.

But Shyamoli only says, in a tired voice, "That's enough! Go put on your clothes, hurry."

The grumblings recede. Footsteps clatter down the stairs. Inside the bathroom Mrs. Dutta bends over the sink, gripping the folds of her sari. Hard to think through the pounding in her head to what it is she feels most—anger at the children for their rudeness, or at Shyamoli for letting them go unrebuked. Or is it shame that clogs her throat, stinging, sulfuric, indigestible?

It is 9.00 A.M. and the house, after the flurry of departures, of frantic "I can't find my socks," and "Mom, he took my lunch money," and "I swear I'll leave you kids behind if you're not in the car in exactly one minute," has settled into its placid daytime rhythms.

Busy in the kitchen, Mrs. Dutta has recovered her spirits. It is too exhausting to hold on to grudges, and, besides, the kitchen—sunlight sliding across its countertops while the refrigerator hums reassuringly—is her favorite place.

Mrs. Dutta hums too as she fries potatoes for alu dum. Her voice is rusty and slightly off-key. In India she would never have ventured to sing, but with everyone gone, the house is too quiet, all that silence pressing down on her like the heel of a giant hand, and the TV voices, with their unreal accents, are no help at all. As the potatoes turn golden-brown, she permits herself a moment of nostalgia for her Calcutta kitchen—the new gas stove bought with the birthday money Sagar sent, the scoured brass pots stacked by the meat safe, the window with the lotus-pattern grille through which she could look down on children playing cricket after school. The mouth-watering smell of ginger and chili paste, ground fresh by Reba the maid, and, in the evening, strong black Assam cha brewing in the kettle when Mrs. Basu came by to visit. In her mind she writes to Mrs. Basu, *Oh, Roma, I miss it all so much, sometimes I feel that someone has reached in and torn out a handful of my chest.*

But only fools indulge in nostalgia, so Mrs. Dutta shakes her head clear of images and straightens up the kitchen. She pours the half-drunk glasses of milk down the sink, though Shyamoli has told her to save them in the refrigerator. But surely Shyamoli, a girl from a good Hindu family, doesn't expect her to put contaminated jutha things in with the rest of the food? She washes the breakfast dishes by hand instead of letting them wait inside the dishwater till night, breeding germs. With practiced fingers she throws an assortment of spices into the blender: coriander, cumin, cloves, black pepper, a few red chilies for vigor. No stale bottled curry powder for *her! At least the family's eating well since I arrived*, she writes in her mind, *proper Indian food, rotis that puff up the way they should, fish curry in mustard sauce, and real pulao with raisins and cashews and ghee—the way you taught me, Roma—instead of Rice-a-roni*. She would like to add, *They love it*, but thinking of Shyamoli she hesitates.

At first Shyamoli had been happy enough to have someone take over the cooking. It's wonderful to come home to a hot dinner, she'd say, or, Mother, what crispy papads, and your fish gravy is out of this world. But recently she's taken to picking at her food, and once or twice from the kitchen Mrs. Dutta has caught wisps of words, intensely whispered: *cholesterol, all putting on weight, she's spoiling you*. And though Shyamoli always refuses when the children ask if they can have burritos from the freezer instead, Mrs. Dutta suspects that she would really like to say yes.

The children. A heaviness pulls at Mrs. Dutta's entire body when she thinks of them. Like so much in this country they have turned out to be—yes, she might as well admit it—a disappointment.

For this she blames, in part, the Olan Mills portrait. Perhaps it had been impractical of her to set so much store on a photograph, especially one taken years ago. But it was such a charming scene—Mrinalini in a ruffled white dress with her arm around her brother, Pradeep chubby and dimpled in a suit and bow tie, a glorious autumn forest blazing red and yellow behind them. (Later Mrs. Dutta would learn, with a sense of having been betrayed, that the forest was merely a backdrop in a studio in California, where real trees did not turn such colors.)

The picture had arrived, silver-framed and wrapped in a plastic sheet filled with bubbles, with a note from Shyamoli explaining that it was a Mother's Day gift. (A strange concept, a day set aside to honor mothers. Did the sahebs not honor their mothers the rest of the year, then?) For a week Mrs. Dutta could not decide where it should be hung. If she put it in the drawing room, visitors would be able to admire her grandchildren, but if she put it on the bedroom wall, she would be able to see the photo, last thing, before she fell asleep. She had finally opted for the bedroom, and later, when she was too ill with pneumonia to leave her bed for a month, she'd been glad of it.

Mrs. Dutta was not unused to living on her own. She had done it for the last three years, since Sagar's father died, politely but stubbornly declining the offers of various relatives, well-meaning and otherwise, to come and stay with her. In this she had surprised herself as well as others, who thought of her as a shy, sheltered woman, one who would surely fall apart without her husband to handle things for her. But she managed quite well. She missed Sagar's father, of course, especially in the evenings, when it had been his habit to read to her the more amusing parts of the newspaper while she rolled out rotis. But once the grief receded, she found it rather pleasant to be mistress of her own life, as she confided to Mrs. Basu. She liked being able, for the first time ever, to lie in bed all evening and read a new novel of Shankar's straight through if she wanted, or to send out for hot brinjal pakoras on a rainy day without feeling guilty that she wasn't serving up a balanced meal.

When the pneumonia hit, everything changed.

Mrs. Dutta had been ill before, but those illnesses had been different. Even in bed she'd been at the center of the household, with Reba coming to find out what should be cooked, Sagar's father bringing her shirts with missing buttons, her mother-in-law, now old and tamed, complaining that the cook didn't brew her tea strong enough, and Sagar running in crying because he'd had a fight with the neighbor boy. But now there was no one to ask her, querulously, *Just how long do you plan to remain sick*, no one waiting in impatient exasperation for her to take on her duties again, no one whose life was inconvenienced the least bit by her illness.

There was, therefore, no reason for her to get well.

When this thought occurred to Mrs. Dutta, she was so frightened that her body grew numb. The walls of the room spun into blackness, the bed on which she lay, a vast four-poster she had shared with Sagar's father since her marriage, rocked like a mastless dinghy caught in a storm, and a great, muted roar reverberated in the cavities of her skull. For a moment, unable to move or see, she thought, *I'm dead.* Then her vision, desperate and blurry, caught on the portrait. *My grandchildren.* She focused, with some difficulty, on the bright, oblivious sheen of their child faces, the eyes so like Sagar's that for a moment she could feel heartsickness cramping her joints like arthritis. She drew in a shuddering breath; the roaring seemed to recede. When the afternoon post brought another letter from Sagar, *Mother, you really should come and live with us, we worry about you all alone in India, especially when you're sick like this*, she wrote back the same day, with fingers that still shook a little, *You're right, my place is with you, with my grandchildren.*

But now that she is here on the other side of the world, she is wrenched by doubt. She knows the grandchildren love her—how can it be otherwise among family? And she loves them, she reminds herself, though they have put away, somewhere in the back of a closet, the vellum-bound *Ramayana for Young Readers* that she carried all the way from India in her hand luggage. Though their bodies twitch with impatience when she tries to tell them stories of her girlhood. Though they offer the most transparent excuses when she asks them to sit with her while she chants the evening arati. *They're flesh of my flesh, blood of my blood*, she reminds herself. But sometimes when she listens, from the other room, to them speaking on the phone, their American voices rising in excitement as they discuss a glittering alien world of Power Rangers, Spice Girls, and Spirit Week at school, she almost cannot believe it.

Stepping into the backyard with a bucket of newly washed clothes, Mrs. Dutta views the sky with some anxiety. The butter-gold sunlight is gone, black-bellied clouds have taken over the horizon, and the air feels still and heavy on her face, as before a Bengal storm. What if her clothes don't dry by the time the others return home?

Washing clothes has been a problem for Mrs. Dutta ever since she arrived in California.

"We can't, Mother," Shyamoli had said with a sigh when Mrs. Dutta asked Sagar to put up a clothesline for her in the backyard. (Shyamoli sighed often nowadays. Perhaps it was an American habit? Mrs. Dutta did not remember the Indian Shyamoli, the docile bride she'd mothered for a month before putting her on a Pan Am flight to join her husband, pursing her lips in quite this way to let out a breath at once patient and vexed.) "It's just not *done*, not in a nice neighborhood like this one. And being the only Indian family on the street, we have to be extra careful. People here, sometimes—." She'd broken off with a shake of her head. "Why don't you just keep your dirty clothes in the hamper I've put in your room, and I'll wash them on Sunday along with everyone else's."

Afraid of causing another sigh, Mrs. Dutta had agreed reluctantly. But she knew she should not store unclean clothes in the same room where she kept the pictures of her gods. That brought bad luck; and the odor. Lying in bed at night she could smell it distinctly, even though Shyamoli claimed the hamper was airtight. The sour, starchy old-women smell embarrassed her.

What embarrassed her more was when, Sunday afternoons, Shyamoli brought the laundry into the family room to fold. Mrs. Dutta would bend intensely over her knitting, face tingling with shame, as her daughter-in-law nonchalantly shook out the wisps of lace, magenta and sea-green and black, that were her panties, laying them next to a stack of Sagar's briefs. And when, right in front of everyone, Shyamoli pulled out Mrs. Dutta's own crumpled, baggy bras from the clothes heap, she wished the ground would open up and swallow her, like the Sita of mythology.

Then one day Shyamoli set the clothes basket down in front of Sagar.

"Can you do them today, Sagar?" (Mrs. Dutta, who had never, through the forty-two years of her marriage, addressed Sagar's father by name, tried not to wince.) "I've got to get that sales report into the computer by tonight."

Before Sagar could respond, Mrs. Dutta was out of her chair, knitting needles dropping to the floor.

"No no no, clothes and all is no work for the man of the house. I'll do it." The thought of her son's hands searching through the basket and lifting up his wife's—and her own—underclothes filled her with horror.

"Mother!" Shyamoli said. "This is why Indian men are so useless around the house. Here in America we don't believe in men's work and women's work. Don't I work outside all day, just like Sagar? How'll I manage if he doesn't help me at home?"

"I'll help you instead," Mrs. Dutta ventured.

"You don't understand, do you, Mother?" Shyamoli said with a shaky smile. Then she went into the study.

Mrs. Dutta sat down in her chair and tried to understand. But after a while she gave up and whispered to Sagar that she wanted him to teach her how to run the washer and dryer.

"Why, Mother? Molli's quite happy to..."

"I've got to learn it...." Her voice warped with distress as she rummaged through the tangled heap for her clothes.

Her son began to object, then shrugged. "Oh very well. If that's what you really want."

But later, when she faced them alone, the machines with their cryptic symbols and rows of gleaming knobs terrified her. What if she pressed the wrong button and flooded the entire floor with soapsuds? What if she couldn't turn the machines off and they kept going, whirring maniacally, until they exploded? (This had happened to a women on a TV show just the other day, and she had jumped up and down, screaming. Everyone else found it hilarious, but Mrs. Dutta sat stiff-spined, gripping the armrest of her chair.) So she took to washing her clothes in the bathtub when she was alone. She had never done such a chore before, but she remembered how the village washerwomen of her childhood would beat their saris clean against river rocks. And a curious satisfaction filled her as her clothes hit the porcelain with the same solid wet *thunk*.

My small victory, my secret.

This is why everything must be dried and put safely away before Shyamoli returns. Ignorance, as Mrs. Dutta knows well from years of managing a household, is a great promoter of harmony. So she keeps an eye on the menacing advance of the clouds as she hangs up her blouse and underwear. As she drapes her sari along the redwood fence that separates her son's property from the neighbor's, first wiping it clean with a dish towel she has secretly taken from the bottom drawer of the kitchen. But she isn't too worried. Hasn't she managed every time, even after that freak hailstorm last month when she had to use the iron from the laundry closet to press everything dry? The memory pleases her. In her mind she writes to Mrs. Basu, *I'm fitting in so well here, you'd never guess I came only two months back. I've found new ways of doing things, of solving problems creatively. You would be most proud if you saw me.*

When Mrs. Dutta decided to give up her home of forty-five years, her relatives showed far less surprise than she had expected.

"Oh, we all knew you'd end up in America sooner or later," they said. "It was a foolishness to stay on alone so long after Sagar's father, may he find eternal peace, passed away. Good thing that boy of yours came to his senses and called you to join him. Everyone knows a wife's place is with her husband, and a widow's with her son."

Mrs. Dutta had nodded meek agreement, ashamed to let anyone know that the night before she had awakened weeping.

"Well, now that you're going, what'll happen to all your things?"

Mrs. Dutta, still troubled over those treacherous tears, had offered up her household effects in propitiation. "Here, Didi, you take this cutwork bedspread. Mashima, for a long time I meant for you to have these Corning Ware dishes, I know how much you admire them. And, Boudi, this tape recorder that Sagar sent a year back is for you. Yes yes, I'm quite sure. I can always tell Sagar to buy me another one when I get there."

Mrs. Basu, coming in just as a cousin made off triumphantly with a bone china tea set, had protested. "Prameela, have you gone crazy? That tea set used to belong to your mother-in-law."

"But what'll I do with it in America? Shyamoli has her own set—"

A look that Mrs. Dutta couldn't read flitted across Mrs. Basu's face. "But do you want to drink from it for the rest of your life?"

"What do you mean?"

Mrs. Basu hesitated. Then she said, "What if you don't like it there?"

"How can I not like it, Roma?" Mrs. Dutta's voice was strident, even to her own ears. With an effort she controlled it and continued, "I'll miss my friends, I know—and you most of all. The things we do together—evening tea, our walk around Rabindra Sarobar Lake, Thursday night Bhagavat Geeta class. But Sagar—they're my only family. And blood is blood after all."

"I wonder," Mrs. Basu said dryly, and Mrs. Dutta recalled that though both of Mrs. Basu's children lived just a day's journey away, they came to see her only on occasions when common decency demanded their presence. Perhaps they were tightfisted in money matters too. Perhaps that was why Mrs. Basu had started renting out her downstairs a few years ago, even though, as anyone in Calcutta knew, tenants were more trouble than they were worth. Such filial neglect must be hard to take, though Mrs. Basu, loyal to her children as indeed a mother should be, never complained. In a way Mrs. Dutta had been better off, with Sagar too far away for her to put his love to the test.

"At least don't give up the house," Mrs. Basu was saying. "It'll be impossible to find another place in case—"

"In case what?" Mrs. Dutta asked, her words like stone chips. She was surprised to find that she was angrier with Mrs. Basu than she'd ever been. Or was it fear? *My son isn't like yours,* she'd been on the verge of spitting out. She took a deep breath and made herself smile, made herself remember that she might never see her friend again.

"Ah, Roma," she said, putting her arm around Mrs. Basu, "you think I'm such an old witch that my Sagar and my Shyamoli will be unable to live with me?"

Mrs. Dutta hums a popular Rabindra Sangeet as she pulls her sari from the fence. It's been a good day, as good as it can be in a country where you might stare out the window for hours and not see one living soul. No vegetable vendors with wicker baskets balanced on their heads, no knife-sharpeners calling *scissors-knives-choppers, scissors-knives-choppers* to bring the children running. No dehati women with tattoos on their arms to sell you cookware in exchange for your old silk saris. Why, even the animals that frequented Ghoshpara Lane had personality. Stray dogs that knew to line up outside the kitchen door just when leftovers were likely to be thrown out, the goat who maneuvered its head through the garden grille hoping to get at her dahlias, cows who planted themselves majestically in the center of the road, ignoring honking drivers. And right across the street was Mrs. Basu's two-story house, which Mrs. Dutta knew as well as her own. How many times had she walked up the stairs to that airy room painted sea-green and filled with plants where her friend would be waiting for her.

What took you so long today, Prameela? Your tea is cold already.

Wait till you hear what happened, Roma. Then you won't scold me for being late....

Stop it, you silly woman, Mrs. Dutta tells herself severely. Every single one of your relatives would give an arm and a leg to be in your place, you know that. After lunch you're going to write a nice, long letter to Roma, telling her exactly how delighted you are to be here.

From where Mrs. Dutta stands, gathering up petticoats and blouses, she can look into the next yard. Not that there's much to see, just tidy grass and a few pale blue flowers whose name she doesn't know. There are two wooden chairs under a tree, but Mrs. Dutta has never seen anyone using them. What's the point of having such a big yard if you're not even going to sit in it? she thinks. Calcutta pushes itself into her mind again, Calcutta with its narrow, blackened flats where families of six and eight and ten squeeze themselves into two tiny rooms, and her heart fills with a sense of loss she knows to be illogical.

When she first arrived in Sagar's home, Mrs. Dutta wanted to go over and meet her next-door neighbors, maybe take them some of her special rose-water rasogollahs, as she'd often done with Mrs. Basu. But Shyamoli said she shouldn't. Such things were not the custom in California, she explained earnestly. You didn't just drop in on people without calling ahead.

Here everyone was busy, they didn't sit around chatting, drinking endless cups of sugar tea. Why, they might even say something unpleasant to her.

"For what?" Mrs. Dutta had asked disbelievingly, and Shyamoli had said, "Because Americans don't like neighbors to"—here she used an English phrase—"invade their privacy." Mrs. Dutta, who didn't fully understand the word *privacy* because there was no such term in Bengali, had gazed at her daughter-in-law in some bewilderment. But she understood enough to not ask again. In the following months, though, she often looked over the fence, hoping to make contact. People were people, whether in India or America, and everyone appreciated a friendly face. When Shyamoli was as old as Mrs. Dutta, she would know that, too.

Today, just as she is about to turn away, out of the corner of her eye Mrs. Dutta notices a movement. At one of the windows a woman is standing, her hair a sleek gold like that of the TV heroines whose exploits baffle Mrs. Dutta when sometimes she tunes in to an afternoon serial. She is smoking a cigarette, and a curl of gray rises lazily, elegantly from her fingers. Mrs. Dutta is so happy to see another human being in the middle of her solitary day that she forgets how much she disapproves of smoking, especially in women. She lifts her hand in the gesture she has seen her grandchildren use to wave an eager hello.

The woman stares back at Mrs. Dutta. Her lips are a perfect-painted red, and when she raises her cigarette to her mouth, its tip glows like an animal's eye. She does not wave back or smile. Perhaps she is not well? Mrs. Dutta feels sorry for her, alone in her illness in a silent house with only cigarettes for solace, and she wishes the etiquette of America had not prevented her from walking over with a word of cheer and a bowl of her fresh-cooked alu dum.

Mrs. Dutta rarely gets a chance to be alone with her son. In the morning he is in too much of a hurry even to drink the fragrant cardamom tea which she (remembering how as a child he would always beg for a sip from her cup) offers to make him. He doesn't return until dinnertime, and afterward he must help the children with their homework, read the paper, hear the details of Shyamoli's day, watch his favorite TV crime show in order to unwind, and take out the garbage. In between, for he is a solicitous son, he converses with Mrs. Dutta. In response to his questions she assures him that her arthritis is much better now; no, no, she's not growing bored being at home all the time; she has everything she needs—Shyamoli has been so kind—but perhaps he could pick up a few aerograms on his way back tomorrow? She recites obediently for him an edited list of her day's activities and smiles when he praises her cooking. But when he says, "Oh, well, time to turn in, another working day tomorrow," she is racked by a vague pain, like hunger, in the region of her heart.

So it is with the delighted air of a child who has been offered an unexpected gift that she leaves her half-written letter to greet Sagar at the door today, a good hour before Shyamoli is due back. The children are busy in the family room doing homework and watching cartoons (mostly the latter, Mrs. Dutta suspects). But for once she doesn't mind because they race in to give their father hurried hugs and then race back again. And she has him, her son, all to herself in a kitchen filled with the familiar, pungent odors of tamarind sauce and chopped coriander leaves.

"Khoka," she says, calling him by the childhood name she hasn't used in years, "I could fry you two-three hot-hot luchis, if you like." As she waits for his reply she can feel, in the hollow of her throat, the rapid beat of her blood. And when he says yes, that would be very nice, she shuts her eyes and takes a deep breath, and it is as though merciful time has given her back her youth, that sweet, aching urgency of being needed again.

Mrs. Dutta is telling Sagar a story.

"When you were a child, how scared you were of injections! One time, when the government doctor came to give us compulsory typhoid shots, you locked yourself in the bathroom and refused to come out. Do you remember what your father finally did? He went into the garden and caught a lizard and threw it in the bathroom window, because you were even more scared of lizards than of shots. And in exactly one second you ran out screaming—right into the waiting doctor's arms."

Sagar laughs so hard that he almost upsets his tea (made with real sugar, because Mrs. Dutta knows it is better for her son than that chemical powder Shyamoli likes to use). There are tears in his eyes, and Mrs. Dutta, who had not dared to hope he would find her story so amusing, feels gratified. When he takes off his glasses to wipe them, his face is oddly young, not like a father's at all, or even a husband's, and she has to suppress an impulse to put out her hand and rub away the indentations the glasses have left on his nose.

"I'd totally forgotten," says Sagar. "How can you keep track of those old, old things?"

Because it is the lot of mothers to remember what no one else cares to, Mrs. Dutta thinks. To tell them over and over until they are lodged, perforce, in family lore. We are the keepers of the heart's dusty corners.

But as she starts to say this, the front door creaks open, and she hears the faint click of Shyamoli's high heels. Mrs. Dutta rises, collecting the dirty dishes.

"Call me fifteen minutes before you're ready to eat so I can fry fresh luchis for everyone," she tells Sagar.

"You don't have to leave, Mother," he says.

Mrs. Dutta smiles her pleasure but doesn't stop. She knows Shyamoli likes to be alone with her husband at this time, and today in her happiness she does not grudge her this.

"You think I've nothing to do, only sit and gossip with you?" she mock-scolds. "I want you to know I have a very important letter to finish."

Somewhere behind her she hears a thud, a briefcase falling over. This surprises her. Shyamoli is always so careful with her case because it was a gift from Sagar when she was finally made a manager in her company.

"Hi!" Sagar calls, and when there's no answer, "Hey, Molli, you okay?"

Shyamoli comes into the room slowly, her hair disheveled as though she's been running her fingers through it. A hectic color blotches her cheeks.

"What's the matter, Molli?" Sagar walks over to give her a kiss. "Bad day at work?" Mrs. Dutta, embarrassed as always by this display of marital affection, turns toward the window, but not before she sees Shyamoli move her face away.

"Leave me alone." Her voice is wobbly. "Just leave me alone."

"But what is it?" Sagar says in concern.

"I don't want to talk about it right now." Shyamoli lowers herself into a kitchen chair and puts her face in her hands. Sagar stands in the middle of the room, looking helpless. He raises his hand and lets it fall, as though he wants to comfort his wife but is afraid of what she might do.

A protective anger for her son surges inside Mrs. Dutta, but she leaves the room silently. In her mind-letter she writes, *Women need to be strong, not react to every little thing like this. You and I, Roma, we had far worse to cry about, but we shed our tears invisibly. We were good wives and daughters-in-law, good mothers. Dutiful, uncomplaining. Never putting ourselves first.*

A sudden memory comes to her, one she hasn't thought of in years, a day when she scorched a special kheer dessert. Her mother-in-law had shouted at her, "Didn't your mother teach you anything, you useless girl?" As punishment she refused to let Mrs. Dutta go with Mrs. Basu to the cinema, even though *Sahib, Bibi aur Ghulam,* which all Calcutta was crazy about, was playing, and their tickets were bought already. Mrs. Dutta had wept the entire afternoon, but before Sagar's father came home she washed her face carefully with cold water and applied kajal to her eyes so he wouldn't know.

But everything is getting mixed up, and her own young, trying-not-to-cry face blurs into another—why, it's Shyamoli's—and a thought hits her so sharply in the chest she has to hold on to the bedroom wall. *And what good did it do? The more we bent, the more people pushed us, until one day we'd forgotten that we could stand up straight. Maybe Shyamoli's doing the right thing, after all....*

Mrs. Dutta lowers herself heavily on to her bed, trying to erase such an insidious idea from her mind. Oh, this new country where all the rules are upside down, it's confusing her. Her mind feels muddy, like a pond in which too many water buffaloes have been wading. Maybe things will settle down if she can focus on the letter to Roma.

Then she remembers that she has left the half-written aerogram on the kitchen table. She knows she should wait until after dinner, after her son and his wife have sorted things out. But a restlessness—or is it defiance?—has taken hold of her. She's sorry Shyamoli's upset, but why should she have to waste her evening because of that? She'll go get her letter—it's no crime, is it? She'll march right in and pick it up, and even if Shyamoli stops in midsentence with another one of those sighs, she'll refuse to feel apologetic. Besides, by now they're probably in the family room, watching TV.

Really, Roma, she writes in her head as she feels her way along the unlighted corridor, *the amount of TV they watch here is quite scandalous. The children too, sitting for hours in front of that box like they've been turned into painted Kesto Nagar dolls, and then talking back when I tell them to turn it off.* Of course, she will never put such blasphemy into a real letter. Still, it makes her feel better to say it, if only to herself.

In the family room the TV is on, but for once no one is paying it any attention. Shyamoli and Sagar sit on the sofa, conversing. From where she stands in the corridor, Mrs. Dutta cannot see them, but their shadows—enormous against the wall where the table lamp has cast them—seem to flicker and leap at her.

She is about to slip unseen into the kitchen when Shyamoli's rising voice arrests her. In its raw, shaking unhappiness it is so unlike her daughter-in-law's assured tones that Mrs. Dutta is no more able to move away from it than if she had heard the call of the nishi, the lost souls of the dead on whose tales she grew up.

"It's easy for you to say 'Calm down.' I'd like to see how calm *you'd* be if she came up to you and said, 'Kindly tell the old lady not to hang her clothes over the fence into my yard.' She said it twice, like I didn't understand English, like I was an idiot. All these years I've been so careful not to give these Americans a chance to say something like this, and now—"

"Shhh Shyamoli, I *said* I'd talk to Mother about it."

"You always say that, but you never *do* anything. You're too busy being the perfect son, tiptoeing around her feelings. But how about mine?"

"Hush, Molli, the children..."

"Let them hear. I don't care anymore. They're not stupid. They already know what a hard time I've been having with her. You're the only one who refuses to see it."

In the passage Mrs. Dutta shrinks against the wall. She wants to move away, to not hear anything else, but her feet are formed of cement, impossible to lift, and Shyamoli's words pour into her ears like smoking oil.

"I've explained over and over, and she still keeps on doing what I've asked her not to—throwing away perfectly good food, leaving dishes to drip all over the countertops. Ordering my children to stop doing things

I've given them permission for. She's taken over the entire kitchen, cooking whatever she likes. You come in the door and the smell of grease is everywhere, in all our clothes. I feel like this isn't my house anymore."

"Be patient, Molli, she's an old woman, after all."

"I know. That's why I tried so hard. I know having her here is important to you. But I can't do it any longer. I just can't. Some days I feel like taking the kids and leaving." Shyamoli's voice disappears into a sob.

A shadow stumbles across the wall to her, and then another. Behind the weatherman's nasal tones announcing a week of sunny days, Mrs. Dutta can hear a high, frightened weeping. The children, she thinks. It's probably the first time they've seen their mother cry.

"Don't talk like that, sweetheart." Sagar leans forward, his voice, too, miserable. All the shadows on the wall shiver and merge into a single dark silhouette.

Mrs. Dutta stares at that silhouette, the solidarity of it. Sagar and Shyamoli's murmurs are lost beneath a noise—is it in her veins, this dry humming, the way the taps in Calcutta used to hum when the municipality turned the water off? After a while she discovers that she has reached her room. In darkness she lowers herself on to her bed very gently, as though her body is made of the thinnest glass. Or perhaps ice, she is so cold. She sits for a long time with her eyes closed, while inside her head thoughts whirl faster and faster until they disappear in a gray dust storm.

When Pradeep finally comes to call her for dinner, Mrs. Dutta follows him to the kitchen where she fries luchis for everyone, the perfect circles of dough puffing up crisp and golden as always. Sagar and Shyamoli have reached a truce of some kind: she gives him a small smile, and he puts out a casual hand to massage the back of her neck. Mrs. Dutta demonstrates no embarrassment at this. She eats her dinner. She answers questions put to her. She smiles when someone makes a joke. If her face is still, as though she has been given a shot of Novocain, no one notices. When the table is cleared, she excuses herself, saying she has to finish her letter.

Now Mrs. Dutta sits on her bed, reading over what she wrote in the innocent afternoon.

Dear Roma,

Although I miss you, I know you will be pleased to hear how happy I am in America. There is much here that needs getting used to, but we are no strangers to adjusting, we old women. After all, haven't we been doing it all our lives?

Today I'm cooking one of Sagar's favorite dishes, alu-dum.... It gives me such pleasure to see my family gathered around the table, eating my food. The children are still a little shy of me, but I am hopeful that we'll soon be friends. And Shyamoli, so confident and successful—you should see her when she's all dressed for work. I can't believe she's the same timid bride I sent off to America just a few years ago. But, Sagar, most of all, is the joy of my old age....

With the edge of her sari Mrs. Dutta carefully wipes a tear that has fallen on the aerogram. She blows on the damp spot until it is completely dry, so the pen will not leave an incriminating smudge. Even though Roma would not tell a soul, she cannot risk it. She can already hear them, the avid relatives in India who have been waiting for something just like this to happen. *That Dutta-ginni, so set in her ways, we knew she'd never get along with her daughter-in-law.* Or worse, *Did you hear about poor Prameela, how her family treated her, yes, even her son, can you imagine?*

This much surely she owes to Sagar.

And what does she owe herself, Mrs. Dutta, falling through black night with all the certainties she trusted in collapsed upon themselves like imploded stars, and only an image inside her eyelids for company? A silhouette—man, wife, children—joined on a wall, showing her how alone she is in this land of young people. And how unnecessary.

She is not sure how long she sits under the glare of the overhead light, how long her hands clench themselves in her lap. When she opens them, nail marks line the soft flesh of her palms, red hieroglyphs—her body's language, telling her what to do.

Dear Roma, Mrs. Dutta writes,

I cannot answer your question about whether I am happy, for I am no longer sure I know what happiness is. All I know is that it isn't what I thought it to be. It isn't about being needed. It isn't about being with family either. It has something to do with love, I still think that, but in a different way than I believed earlier, a way I don't have the words to explain. Perhaps we can figure it out together, two old women drinking cha in your downstairs-flat (for I do hope you will rent it to me on my return), while around us gossip falls—but lightly, like summer rain, for that is all we will allow it to be. If I'm lucky—and perhaps, in spite of all that has happened, I am—the happiness will be in the figuring out.

Pausing to read over what she has written, Mrs. Dutta is surprised to discover this: Now that she no longer cares whether tears blotch her letter, she feels no need to weep.

◆

Feelers

JOHN GOULD

"An entomologist, did you say?" says Harlan, incredulous. He's been here at the Bougainvillea Resort and Spa about an hour and already something wild is happening to him. "From the Greek *entomon*, insect? From the neuter of *entomos*, cut up, from *temnein*, to cut?"

"Um, I guess so," says the woman standing next to him—head cocked, arms akimbo—before the rack of brochures. "Bugs."

"Because you see I'm an etymologist," says Harlan. "Entomologist, etymologist, don't you think that's kind of uncanny?"

"Etymologist?" says the woman. "Like, words?"

"Right," says Harlan. "From the Greek *etymon*, from *etymos*, true, and of course *logion*, diminutive of *logos*"—no way to stop himself when he's wound this tight—"a saying, especially a saying of Christ's. Can I buy you a drink?"

"Sure," says the woman. "My name's Miriam."

"Harlan," says Harlan.

They place their orders—gin and tonic for Harlan, virgin Caesar for Miriam ("Hal" from Harlan)—and wander out onto a little patio overlooking one of the pools. It's dusk, but birds still—mockingbirds, presumably, as promised by the resort's literature. Poring over the pamphlet at home a few weeks ago, Harlan strove to imagine the mockingbird's evening cry. He failed. Failure comes easily to Harlan. Most recently he failed at marriage. This trip, an impulsive purchase which will max out all three of his credit cards, was inspired by the arrival of his divorce papers.

Harlan and Miriam take seats at a lime table by a potted palm with a view of the setting sun—a hot-pink smear over the tennis courts—cross their legs and start chatting. During their conversation they discover all sorts of things about one another. They discover that they're both from Toronto, that they've both just arrived at the Bougainvillea Resort and Spa, that they were both on the same flight, Harlan in seat 7E (seven, coincidentally, being the most blessed of all numbers according to the faith of her fathers, to say nothing of her mothers), Miriam in seat 34D (Harlan's eyebrows going up here—the figure's just about right, judging by the trippy distortion of the stripes on her blouse). They discover that Harlan had the chicken, Miriam the pasta. They discover that neither of them ever goes on a vacation like this, or has a spouse, or a child.

Inevitably, though, the things they discover about one another are way outnumbered by the things they don't discover about one another. For example, Miriam doesn't discover that as a boy Harlan indulged in a dark practice for which he later coined the term *entomosadism*—yanking not the limbs but the antennae, the fine feelers, from various creepy-crawlies. Nor does she discover that Harlan is here recovering from his botched marriage, a knowledge which, a couple of months down the road, will fill her with remorse. Harlan, for his part, doesn't discover that as a girl Miriam consistently misheard the Torah passage, "I will make him an help meet for him" (God taking pity on his lonesome man of clay), as "I will make him an elk meat form." Worse, perhaps, he doesn't discover that Miriam is here recovering (still) from the loss of her child, a baby girl known as Toots who died at the age of three hours, before she could get herself a proper name—all of this nine years ago now, when Miriam was twenty-five years old. A couple of months down the road this knowledge will inspire in him a sense of awe for the human heart—Miriam's, for example, and his own—the depth to which it can be damaged, the weird miracle of its healing.

For the next ten days, though, the two will flourish in a state of blissful ignorance of these and umpteen other details. They'll come to adore one another's little quirks, the affected way Harlan has of twirling his walking stick—a brass-and-mahogany heirloom from somebody else's family he scooped at a swap meet years ago, and has never since gone without—or the way Miriam bares her teeth like a baboon on the cusp of each orgasm.

"Love," Harlan will sigh, "from the Old English *lufu*, akin to the Latin *lubere*, to please."

A couple of months from now, when Miriam dumps Harlan, she'll do it with a gift, a plastic terrarium which will appear, at first, to be bereft of life. Taped to the glass will be this note:

Harlan, my dear, this is a carausius morosus, a "walking stick"—thought you'd enjoy the wordplay. I've named her Toots, after the little girl I lost many years ago. I'm sorry I could never bring myself to tell you. She likes brambles, please, fresh every day. She'll have babies, even though she has no mate. Do you know the word parthenogenesis? Of course you do. I'm afraid that pill I popped every morning wasn't THE pill, as I let you assume, it was just something for my allergies. Again, I'm sorry. I wanted your height, and your intellect—a flair for the humanities to balance out my science. And anyway I liked you, I really did. I swear to God I won't come after you for child support. Please just forgive me, if you can, and then forget us. Love, Babs

Eventually Harlan will spot her, a greenish bug about the length of his pinky, a stick with six stick-legs and two antennae. "Hello, Toots," he'll say. "Parthenogenesis," he'll say, "from the Greek *parthenos*, virgin, and Latin *genesis*. Virgin birth, baby." Harlan will wonder whether he's ever had anything irreplaceable, whether he's lost it. Brambles? he'll wonder. Where the hell am I going to find brambles in this town?

◘ ◘ ◘

Writing Exercises

1. Think of a time you remember well and can write about with authority. The memory could have to do with a job, an activity, a family tradition, a physical condition, or something similar.

   Write a summary of a typical day during this period—what usually happened, what you were in the habit of doing.

   Then move to a specific moment: "One time. . . ." This moment should be significant, introducing a conflict or representing a turning point. Create the scene. Use dialogue and significant details.

2. Make a list of activities that take place over a brief period of time, a few hours at most. Choose one of these and write a short (five-page) story confined within that period of time.

3. Imagine an accident. It might be minor—a finger cut, a knocked-over vase—or it might be major—a car wreck, a fire. Now, write several versions of the accident: a one-sentence summary, a one-paragraph summary, a full scene, and finally, a slo-o-o-o-wed down version of the scene. It may help to think of filmmaking. Begin with a panoramic establishing shot and let the camera keep zooming in, closer and closer, to an extreme close-up.

4. Even if the action of your story takes place mainly in 2001, your character might at some point remember in vivid detail an important event that happened in 1968. Most stories include at least a short flashback.

   Write a flashback, a scene involving one of your characters that took place before the opening of the story. Your goal is to reveal who that character used to be. The flashback should help explain or illuminate the main story. You might want to base this flashback on something that actually happened to you, or to someone you know, in order to give the flashback an air of authority.

5. Write a story that takes place over a fairly long period of time (at least six months, perhaps several years). Make a list of possible events in the story; you may even want to draw a time line. Sketch out your story, bearing in mind that you will have to cover great stretches of time. What will you show in scenes? What can be summarized? For common or everyday experiences, can one scene or summary suggest the rest? (A single scene of newlyweds fighting can convey the nature of all their arguments. Likewise, a summary of a specific/generalized day at the office can give a sense of a character's everyday life.)

6. Write a very short (two- to three-page) story in which you use (in miniature) scene, summary, flashback, and slow motion.

7

THE TOWER AND THE NET
Story Form, Plot, and Structure

- *Conflict, Crisis, and Resolution*

- *The Arc of the Story*

- *Patterns of Power*

- *Connection and Disconnection*

- *Story Form as an Inverted Check Mark*

- *Story and Plot*

- *The Short Story and the Novel*

What makes you want to write?

It seems likely that the earliest storytellers—in the tent or the harem, around the campfire or on the Viking ship— made themselves popular by distracting their listeners from a dull or dangerous evening with heroic exploits and a skill at creating suspense: What happened next? And after that? And then what happened?

Natural storytellers are still around, and a few of them are very rich. Some are on the best-seller list; more are in television and film. But it's probable that your impulse to write has little to do with the desire or the skill to work out a plot. On the contrary, you want to write because you are a sensitive observer. You have something to say that does not answer the question *What happened next?* You share with most—and the best—contemporary fiction writers a sense of the injustice, the absurdity, and the beauty of the world; and you want to register your protest, your laughter, and your affirmation.

Yet readers still want to wonder what happened next, and unless you make them wonder, they will not turn the page. You must master plot, because no matter how profound or illuminating your vision of the world may be, you cannot convey it to those who do not read you.

When editors take the trouble to write a rejection letter to a young author (and they do so only when they think the author talented), the gist of the letter most frequently is: "This piece is sensitive (perceptive, vivid, original, brilliant, funny, moving), but it is not a *story*."

How do you know when you have written a story? And if you're not a natural-born wandering minstrel, can you go about learning to write one?

STRUCTURE IS THE ART THAT CONCEALS ITSELF—you only *see* the structure in a badly structured story, and call it formula.

STEPHEN FISCHER

It's interesting that we react with such different attitudes to the words "formula" and "form" as they apply to a story. A formula story is hackwork. To write one, you pick a sitcom plot line or a blockbuster hero, shuffle the characters and the situations around a little, and hope the trick works once more. By contrast, *form* is a term of the highest artistic approbation, even reverence, with overtones of *order, harmony, model, archetype*.

And "story" is a "form" of literature. Like a face, it has necessary features in a necessary harmony. We're aware of the infinite variety of human faces, aware of their unique individuality, which is so powerful that once you know a face you can recognize it twenty years after you last saw it, despite the changes it has undergone. We're aware that minute alterations in the features can express grief, anger, or joy. If you place side by side two photographs of, say, Anne Hathaway and Geronimo, you are instantly aware of the fundamental differences of age, race, sex, class, and century; yet these two faces are more like each other than either is like a foot or a fern, both of which have their own distinctive forms. Every face has two eyes, a nose between them, a mouth below, a forehead, two cheeks, two ears, and a jaw. If a face is missing one of these features, you may say, "I love this face in spite of its lacking a nose," but you must acknowledge the *in spite of*. You can't simply say, "This is a wonderful face."

The same is true of a story. You might say, "I love this piece even though there's no crisis action in it." You can't simply say, "This is a wonderful *story*."

Conflict, Crisis, and Resolution

One of the useful ways of describing the necessary features of story form is to speak of *conflict*, *crisis*, and *resolution*.

Conflict is a fundamental element of fiction. Playwright Elia Kazan describes it simply as "two dogs fighting over a bone"; William Faulkner reminds us that in addition to a conflict of wills, fiction also shows "the heart in conflict with itself," so that conflict seethes both within and between characters. In life, "conflict" often carries negative connotations, yet in fiction, be it comic or tragic, dramatic conflict is fundamental because in literature only trouble is interesting.

Only trouble is interesting. This is not so in life. Life offers periods of comfortable communication, peaceful pleasure, and productive work, all of which are extremely interesting to those involved. But passages about such times by themselves make for dull reading; they can be used as lulls in an otherwise tense situation, as a resolution, even as a hint that something awful is about to happen. They cannot be used as a whole plot.

> ALMOST ALL GOOD STORIES ARE SAD because it is the human struggle that engages us readers and listeners the most. To watch characters confront their hardships and uncertainties makes us feel better about our own conflicts and confusions and fears. We have a sense of community, of sympathy, a cleansing sympathy, as Aristotle said, and relief that we are safe in our room only reading the story.
>
> ROBERT MORGAN

Suppose, for example, you go on a picnic. You find a beautiful deserted meadow with a lake nearby. The weather is splendid and so is the company. The food's delicious, the water's fine, and the insects have taken the day off. Afterward, someone asks you how your picnic was. "Terrific," you reply, "really perfect." No story.

But suppose the next week you go back for a rerun. You set your picnic blanket on an anthill. You all race for the lake to get cold water on the bites, and one of your friends goes too far out on the plastic raft, which deflates. He can't swim and you have to save him. On the way in you gash your foot on a broken bottle. When you get back to the picnic, the ants have taken over the cake and a possum has demolished the chicken. Just then the sky opens up. When you gather your things to race for the car, you notice an irritated bull has broken through the fence. The others run for it, but because of your bleeding heel the best you can do is hobble. You have two choices: try to outrun him or stand perfectly still and hope he's interested only in a moving target. At this point, you don't know if your friends can be counted on for help, even the nerd whose life you saved. You don't know if it's true that a bull is attracted by the smell of blood.

A year later, assuming you're around to tell about it, you are still saying, "Let me *tell* you what happened last year." And your listeners are saying, "What a story!"

As Charles Baxter, in *Burning Down the House*, more vividly puts it:

> Say what you will about it, Hell is story-friendly. If you want a compelling story, put your protagonist among the damned. The mechanisms of hell are nicely attuned to the mechanisms of narrative. Not so the pleasures of Paradise. Paradise is not a story. It's about what happens when the stories are over.

If it takes trouble to make a picnic into a story, this is equally true of the great themes of life: birth, love, sex, work, and death. Here is a very interesting love story to live: Jan and Jon meet in college. Both are beautiful, intelligent, talented, popular, and well adjusted. They're of the same race, class, religion, and political persuasion. They are sexually compatible. Their parents become fast friends. They marry on graduating, and both get rewarding work in the same city. They have three children, all of whom are healthy, happy, beautiful, intelligent, and popular; the children love and respect their parents to a degree that is the envy of everyone. All the children succeed in work and marriage. Jan and Jon die peacefully, of natural causes, at the same moment, at the age of eighty-two, and are buried in the same grave.

No doubt this love story is very interesting to Jan and Jon, but you can't make a novel of it. Great love stories involve intense passion and a monumental impediment to that passion's fulfillment. So: They love each other passionately, but their parents are sworn enemies (*Romeo and Juliet*). Or: They love each other passionately, but he's black and she's white, and he has an enemy who wants to punish him (*Othello*). Or: They love each other passionately, but she's married (*Anna Karenina*). Or: He loves her passionately, but she falls in love with him only when she has worn out his passion ("Frankly, my dear, I don't give a damn.")

In each of these plots, there is both intense desire and great danger to the achievement of that desire; generally speaking, this shape holds good for all plots. It can be called 3-D: *Drama* equals *desire* plus *danger*. One common fault of talented young writers is to create a main character who is essentially passive. This is an understandable fault; as a writer you are an observer of human nature and activity, and so you identify easily with a character who observes, reflects, and suffers. But such a character's passivity transmits itself to the page, and the story also becomes passive. Charles Baxter regrets that

"In writing workshops, this kind of story is often the rule rather than the exception." He calls it:

> the fiction of finger-pointing.... In such fiction, people and events are often accused of turning the protagonist into the kind of person the protagonist is, usually an unhappy person. That's the whole story. When blame has been assigned, the story is over.

In such flawed stories, the central character (and by implication, the story's author) seems to take no responsibility for what that character wants to have happen. This is quite different from Aristotle's rather startling claim that a man *is* his desire.

FICTION IS THE ART FORM OF HUMAN YEARNING. That is absolutely essential to any work of fictional narrative art—a character who yearns. And that is not the same as a character who simply has problems.... The yearning is also the thing that generates what we call plot, because the elements of the plot come from thwarted or blocked or challenged attempts to fulfill that yearning.

ROBERT OLEN BUTLER

In fiction, in order to engage our attention and sympathy, the protagonist must *want*, and want intensely. The thing that the character wants need not be violent or spectacular; it is the intensity of the wanting that introduces an element of danger. A character may want, like the protagonist in David Madden's *The Suicide's Wife*, no more than to get her driver's license, but if so, she must feel that her identity and her future depend on her getting a driver's license, while a corrupt highway patrolman tries to manipulate her. A character may want, like Samuel Beckett's Murphy, only to tie himself to his rocking chair and rock, but if so, he will also want a woman who nags him to get up and get a job. A character may want, like the heroine of Margaret Atwood's *Bodily Harm*, only to get away from it all for a rest, but if so, she must need rest for her survival, while tourists and terrorists involve her in machinations that begin in discomfort and end in mortal danger.

It's important to realize that the great dangers in life and in literature are not necessarily the most spectacular. Another mistake frequently made by young writers is to think that they can best introduce drama into their stories by way of murderers, chase scenes, crashes, and vampires, the external stock dangers of pulp and TV. In fact, all of us know that the most profound impediments to our desire usually lie close to home, in our own bodies, personalities, friends, lovers, and families. Fewer people have cause to panic at the approach of a stranger with a gun than at the approach of Mama with the curling iron. More passion is destroyed at the breakfast table than in a time warp.

A frequently used critical tool divides possible conflicts into several basic categories: man against man, man against nature, man against society, man against machine, man against God, man against himself. Most stories fall into these categories, and in a literature class they can provide a useful way of discussing and comparing works. But the employment of categories can be misleading insofar as it suggests that literary conflicts take place in these abstract, cosmic dimensions. A writer needs a specific story to tell, and if you sit down to pit "man" against "nature," you will have less of a story than if you pit seventeen-year-old James Tucker of Weehawken, New Jersey, against a two-and-a-half-foot bigmouth bass in the backwoods of Toomsuba, Mississippi. (The value of specificity is a point to which we return again and again.)

Once conflict is established and developed in a story, the conflict must come to a crisis—the final turning point—and a resolution. Order is a major value that literature offers us, and order implies that the subject has been brought to closure. In life this never quite happens, but whether or not the lives of fictional characters end, the story does, and we are left with a satisfying sense of completion.

What I want to do now is to present several ways—they are all essentially metaphors—of seeing this pattern of *conflict-crisis-resolution* in order to make the shape and its variations clearer, and particularly to indicate what a crisis action is.

The Arc of the Story

Novelist John L'Heureux says that a story is about a single moment in a character's life that culminates in a defining choice after which nothing will be the same again. The editor and teacher Mel McKee states flatly that "a story is a war. It is sustained and immediate combat." He offers four imperatives for the writing of this "war" story: (1) get your fighters fighting, (2) have something—the stake—worth their fighting over, (3) have the fight dive into a series of battles with the last battle in the series the biggest and most dangerous of all, (4) have a walking away from the fight. The stake over which wars are fought is usually a territory, and it's important that this "territory" in a story be as tangible and specific as the Gaza Strip.

Just as a minor "police action" may gradually escalate into a holocaust, story form follows its most natural order of "complications" when each battle is bigger than the last. It begins with a ground skirmish, which does not decide the war. Then one side brings in spies, and the other, guerrillas; these actions do not decide the war. So one side brings in the air force, and the other answers with antiaircraft. One side takes to missiles, and the other answers with rockets. One side has poison gas, and the other has a hand on the nuclear button. Metaphorically, this is what happens in a story. As long as one antagonist can recoup enough power to counterattack, the conflict goes on. But, at some point in the story, one of the antagonists will produce a weapon from which the other cannot recover. *The crisis action is the last battle and makes the outcome inevitable;* there can no longer be any doubt who wins the particular territory—though there can be much doubt about moral victory. When this has happened the conflict ends with a significant and permanent *change*—which is the definition, in fiction, of a resolution.

Notice that although a plot involves a desire and a danger to that desire, it does not necessarily end happily if the desire is achieved, nor unhappily if it is not. The more morally complex the story, the less straightforward the idea of winning and losing becomes. In *Hamlet*, Hamlet's desire is to kill King Claudius, and he is prevented from doing so for most of the play by other characters, intrigues, and his own mental state. When he finally succeeds, it is at the cost of every significant life in the play, including his own. Although the hero "wins" his particular "territory," the play is a tragedy. In Margaret Atwood's *Bodily Harm*, on the other hand, the heroine ends up in a political prison. Yet the discovery of her own strength and commitment is such that we know she has achieved salvation. *What does my character win by losing his struggle, or lose by winning?* John L'Heureux suggests the writer ask himself or herself.

Patterns of Power

Novelist Michael Shaara described a story as a power struggle between equal forces. It is imperative, he argued, that each antagonist have sufficient power that the reader is left in doubt about the outcome. We may be wholly in sympathy with one character and even reasonably confident that she or he will triumph. But the antagonist must represent a real and potent danger, and the pattern of the story's complications will be achieved by *shifting the power back and forth from one antagonist to the other.* Finally, an action will occur that will shift the power irretrievably in one direction.

"Power" takes many forms—physical strength, charm, knowledge, moral power, wealth, ownership, rank, and so on. Most obvious is the power of brute force, as wielded by mobster Max Blue in Leslie Marmon Silko's epic novel *Almanac of the Dead*:

> ...Max thinks of himself as an executive producer of one-night-only performances, dramas played out in the warm California night breezes, in a phone booth in downtown Long Beach. All Max had done was dial a phone number and listen while the pigeon repeats, "Hello? Hello? Hello? Hello?" until .22-pistol shots snap *pop!pop!* and Max hangs up.

A character who blends several types of power—good looks, artistic talent, social privilege, and the self-assurance that stems from it—is Zavier Chalfant, son of a furniture factory owner in Donald Secreast's story "Summer Help." Zavier is seen through the eyes of Wanda, a longtime employee assigned the coveted job of painting designs on the most expensive pieces. As the plant supervisor introduces them:

> ...Zavier Chalfant was letting his gaze rest lightly on Wanda. Most boys— and that's what Zavier was, after all, a boy of about twenty-one—were very embarrassed their first day on the job. Zavier, in contrast, seemed more amused than embarrassed.... His thick blond hair covered the collar of his jacket but was clean and expertly cut so he looked more like a knight than a hippie.... [H]is face looked like a Viking's face; she'd always been partial to Vikings. Of course, Zavier was too thin to be a Viking all the way down, but he had the face of an adventurer. Of an artist.

Wanda's awe of Zavier's power is confirmed when he easily paints a design she must labor over.

> "Color is my specialty." Zavier deftly added the highlights to the woman's face and hands. "It's everything." He finished the flesh parts in a matter of minutes. He took another brush from Wanda and in six or seven strokes had filled in the woman's robe.

Yet if power is entirely one-sided, suspense will be lost, so it is important to identify a source of power for each character surrounding the story's conflict. Remember that "power" takes many forms, some of which have the external appearance of weakness. Anyone who has ever been tied to the demands of an invalid can understand this: Sickness can be great strength. Weakness, need, passivity, an ostensible desire not to be any trouble to anybody—all these can be used as manipulative tools to prevent the protagonist from achieving his or her desire. Martyrdom is immensely powerful, whether we sympathize with it or not; a dying man absorbs all our energies.

The power of weakness has generated the central conflict in many stories and in such plays as *Uncle Vanya* and *The Glass Menagerie*. Here is a passage in which it is swiftly and deftly sketched:

> This sepulchral atmosphere owed a lot to the presence of Mrs. Taylor her- self. She was a tall, stooped woman with deep-set eyes. She sat in her living room all day long and chain-smoked cigarettes and stared out the picture window with an air of unutterable sadness, as if she knew things beyond mortal bearing. Sometimes she would call Taylor over and wrap her arms around him, then close her eyes and hoarsely whisper, "Terence, Terence!" Eyes still closed, she would turn her head and resolutely push him away.

> Tobias Wolff, *This Boy's Life*

Connection and Disconnection

Some students, as well as critics, object to the description of narrative as a war or power struggle. Seeing the world in terms of conflict and crisis, of enemies and warring factions, not only constricts the possibilities of literature, they argue, but also promulgates an aggressive and antagonistic view of our own lives.

Speaking of the "gladiatorial view of fiction," Ursula Le Guin writes:

> People are cross-grained, aggressive, and full of trouble, the storytellers tell us; people fight themselves and one another, and their stories are full of their struggles. But to say that that *is* the story is to use one aspect of existence, conflict, to subsume all other aspects, many of which it does not include and does not comprehend.
>
> *Romeo and Juliet* is a story of the conflict between two families, and its plot involves the conflict of two individuals with those families. Is that all it involves? Isn't *Romeo and Juliet* about something else, and isn't it the something else that makes the otherwise trivial tale of a feud into a tragedy?

I'm indebted to dramatist Claudia Johnson for this further—and, it seems to me, crucial—insight about that "something else": Whereas the dynamic of the power struggle has long been acknowledged, narrative is also driven by a pattern of connection and disconnection between characters that is the main source of its emotional effect. Over the course of a story, and within the smaller scale of a scene, characters make and break emotional bonds of trust, love, understanding, or compassion with one another. A connection may be as obvious as a kiss or as subtle as a glimpse; a connection may be broken with an action as obvious as a slap or as subtle as an arched eyebrow.

In *Romeo and Juliet,* for example, the Montague and Capulet families are fiercely disconnected, but the young lovers manage to connect in spite of that. Throughout the play they meet and part, disconnect from their families in order to connect with each other, finally part from life in order to be with each other eternally. Their ultimate departure in death reconnects the feuding families.

Johnson puts it this way:

> ...[U]nderlying any good story, fictitious or true—is a deeper pattern of change, a pattern of connection and disconnection. The conflict and the surface events are like waves, but underneath is an emotional tide, the ebb and flow of human connection....

Patterns of conflict and connection occur in every story, and sometimes they are evident in much smaller compass, as in this scene from Leslee Becker's story "The Personals." The story takes place shortly after the Loma

Prieta earthquake, a catastrophe that has united the community, in the eyes of bookshop owner Alice, while reminding her how cut off from others she actually is. The story centers around her nervous first date with Warren, a shoe salesman and widower still grieving his wife Doris. Described by one reviewer as "factory irregulars," the lonely couple ends their date with an after-hours visit to Warren's shoe store.

> Suddenly, music began, and Warren emerged from the back room, holding liquor, glasses, shoe boxes, and stockings. "For you," he said, spreading the things at her feet. He opened a box and removed shoes with dramatic high heels. "I've got hand bags, too," he said. "For you, Doris."
>
> She knew he had not realized his mistake, and she said nothing as he sat on the floor in front of her. She felt his hand on her heel, her shoe sliding off effortlessly. She watched the back of him in the mirror and did not want to look at herself as he lifted her foot and pressed it against his chest.
>
> "I don't want to be alone anymore," he said.
>
> She felt her foot slipping out of his hand, the stocking rasping under his fingers. He got to his feet immediately and sat next to her. She looked to the mirror and saw him touch his toupee and wince.
>
> "It's all right," she said. "Warren…"
>
> "I'll take you home," he said.
>
> The moment she reached for his hand he got up and began replacing the shoes in the box. "Please," she said. "I know what you're feeling."
>
> "How can you? I don't even know. I'll take you back."
>
> He went into the back room, and the music stopped. While she slipped her shoe on, she felt small and dishonest.
>
> As soon as they returned to the car, she told him what she had done after the earthquake. "I was in a huge department store. Nobody was paying attention to me. I stole things."
>
> "Promise me," he said, "you won't tell anyone about tonight."
>
> "But nothing happened."
>
> "Yeah," he said.

In this short excerpt, Warren tries to connect with Alice through a generous display of shoes, only to blunder and break the fragile connection by calling her by his dead wife's name. When he presses further, Alice withdraws, then tries to ease his humiliation by first offering common emotional experience and then admitting a secret. But it is too late, at least for the present, and Warren refuses to reconnect, perhaps ashamed of the neediness he has revealed.

While the pattern of either conflict or connection may dominate in a given work, "stories are about *both* conflict and connection," says novelist and poet Robert Morgan.

> A story which is only about conflict will be shallow. There must be some deepening of our understanding of the characters. Stories are rarely just

about conflicts between good and bad. They are more often about conflicts of loyalty, one good versus another: does a man join up to serve his country, or stay home to help protect and raise his children? The writer strives to bring art to a level where a story is not so much a plot as about human connection, and not just about the conflict of good versus bad, but about the conflict of loyalty with loyalty.

Human wills clash; human belonging is necessary. In discussing human behavior, psychologists speak in terms of "tower" and "network" patterns, the need to climb (which implies conflict) and the need for community, the need to win out over others and the need to belong to others; and these two forces also drive fiction. Like conflict and its complications, connection and its complications can produce a pattern of change, and both inform the process of change recorded in scene and story.

Story Form as an Inverted Check Mark

The nineteenth-century German critic Gustav Freitag analyzed plot in terms of a pyramid of five actions: an exposition, followed by a complication (or *nouement*, "knotting up," of the situation), leading to a crisis, which is followed by a "falling action" or anticlimax, resulting in a resolution (or *dénouement*, "unknotting").

In the compact short-story form, the falling action is likely to be very brief or nonexistent, and often the crisis action itself implies the resolution, which is not necessarily stated but exists as an idea established in the reader's mind.

So for our purposes it is probably more useful to think of story shape not as a pyramid with sides of equal length but as an inverted check mark. If we take the familiar tale of Cinderella and diagram its power struggle using this model, we can see how the various elements reveal themselves even in this simple children's story.

At the opening of the tale we're given the basic conflict: Cinderella's mother has died, and her father has married a brutal woman with two waspish daughters. Cinderella is made to do all the dirtiest and most menial work, and she weeps among the cinders. The Stepmother has on her side the strength of ugliness and evil (two very powerful qualities in literature as in life). With her daughters she also has the strength of numbers, and she has parental authority. Cinderella has only beauty and goodness, but (in literature and life) these are also very powerful.

At the beginning of the struggle in "Cinderella," the power is very clearly on the Stepmother's side. But the first event (action, battle) of the story is that an invitation arrives from the Prince, which explicitly states that *all* the ladies of the land are invited to a ball. Notice that Cinderella's desire is not to triumph over her Stepmother (though she eventually will, much to our satisfaction); such a desire would diminish her goodness. She simply wants to be relieved of her mistreatment. She wants equality, so that the Prince's invitation, which

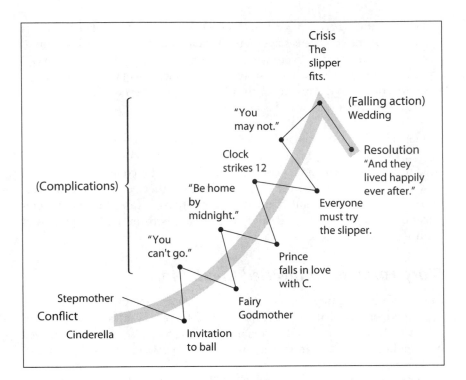

specifically gives her a right equal to the Stepmother's and Stepsisters' rights, shifts the power to her.

The Stepmother takes the power back by blunt force: You may not go; you must get us ready to go. Cinderella does so, and the three leave for the ball.

Then what happens? The Fairy Godmother appears. It is *very* powerful to have magic on your side. The Fairy Godmother offers Cinderella a gown, glass slippers, and a coach with horses and footmen, giving her more force than she has yet had.

But the magic is not all-potent. It has a qualification that portends bad luck. It will last only until midnight (unlike the Stepmother's authority), and Cinderella must leave the ball before the clock strikes twelve or risk exposure and defeat.

What happens next? She goes to the ball and the Prince falls in love with her—and love is an even more powerful weapon than magic in a literary war. In some versions of the tale, the Stepmother and Stepsisters are made to marvel at the beauty of the Princess they don't recognize, pointing to the irony of Cinderella's new power.

And then? The magic quits. The clock strikes twelve, and Cinderella runs down the steps in her rags to her rats and pumpkin, losing a slipper, bereft of her power in every way.

But after that, the Prince sends out a messenger with the glass slipper and a dictum (a dramatic repetition of the original invitation in which all ladies were invited to the ball) that every female in the land is to try on the slipper. Cinderella is given her rights again by royal decree.

What happens then? In most good retellings of the tale, the Stepmother also repeats her assumption of brute authority by hiding Cinderella away, while our expectation of triumph is tantalizingly delayed with grotesque comedy: One sister cuts off a toe, the other a heel, trying to fit into the heroine's rightful slipper.

After that, Cinderella tries on the slipper and it fits. *This is the crisis action.* Magic, love, and royalty join to recognize the heroine's true self; evil, numbers, and authority are powerless against them. At this point, the power struggle has been decided; the outcome is inevitable. When the slipper fits, no further action can occur that will deprive Cinderella of her desire. Nothing will be the same again: The change in the lives of all concerned is significant and permanent.

The tale has a brief "falling action" or "walking away from the fight": The Prince sweeps Cinderella up on his white horse and gallops away to their wedding. The story comes to closure with the classic resolution of all comedy: They lived happily ever after.

If we also look at "Cinderella" in terms of connection/disconnection, we see a pattern as clear as that represented by the power struggle. The first painful disconnection is that Cinderella's mother has died; her father has married (connected with) a woman who spurns (disconnects from) her; the Prince's invitation offers connection; the Stepmother's cruelty alienates again. The Fairy Godmother connects as a magical friend, but the disappearance of the coach and gown disconnect Cinderella temporarily from that grand and glorious fairy-tale union, marriage to the Prince. If we consult the emotions that this tale engenders—pity, anger, hope, fear, romance, anticipation, disappointment, triumph—we see that both the struggle between antagonist/protagonist and the pattern of alienation/connectedness is necessary to ensure, not only that there is an action, but also that we care about its outcome. The traditional happy ending is the grand connection, marriage; the traditional tragic outcome is the final disconnection, death.

ART IS PLEASING YOURSELF....But you can please yourself and it won't be art. Art is having the mastery to take your experience, whether it's visual or mental, and make meaningful shapes that convey a reality to others.

GAIL GODWIN

In the *Poetics*, the first extensive work of extant Western literary criticism, Aristotle referred to the crisis action of a tragedy as a *peripeteia*, or reversal of the protagonist's fortunes. Critics and editors agree that a reversal of some sort is necessary to all story structure, comic as well as tragic. Although the protagonist need not lose power, land, or life, he or she must in some significant way be changed or moved by the action. Aristotle specified that this reversal came about because of *hamartia*, which has for centuries been translated as a "tragic flaw" in the protagonist's character, usually assumed to be, or defined as, pride. But more recent critics have defined and translated *hamartia* much more narrowly as a "mistake in identity" with the reversal coming about in a "recognition."

It is true that recognition scenes have played a disproportionately large role in the crisis actions of plots both comic and tragic, and that these scenes frequently stretch credibility. In real life, you are unlikely to mistake the face of your mother, son, uncle, or even friend, and yet such mistakes have provided the turning point of many traditional plots. If, however, the notion of "recognition" is extended to more abstract and subtle realms, it becomes a powerful metaphor for moments of "realization." In other words, the "recognition scene" in literature may stand for that moment in life when we "recognize" that the man we have considered good is evil, the event we have considered insignificant is crucial, the woman we have thought out of touch with reality is a genius, the object we have thought desirable is poison. There is in this symbolic way a recognition in "Cinderella." We knew that she was essentially a princess, but until the Prince recognizes her as one, our knowledge must be frustrated.

James Joyce developed a similar idea when he spoke of, and recorded both in his notebooks and in his stories, moments of what he called *epiphany*. As Joyce saw it, epiphany is a crisis action in the mind, a moment when a person, an event, or a thing is seen in a light so new that it is as if it has never been seen before. At this recognition, the mental landscape of the viewer is permanently changed.

In many of the finest modern short stories and novels, the true territory of struggle is the main character's mind, and so the real crisis action must occur there. Yet it is important to grasp that Joyce chose the word *epiphany* to represent this moment of reversal, and that the word means "a *manifestation* of a supernatural being"; specifically, in Christian doctrine, "the manifestation of Christ to the gentiles." By extension, then, in a short story any mental reversal that takes place in the crisis of a story must be *manifested*; it must be triggered or shown by an action. The slipper must fit. It would not do if the Stepmother just happened to change her mind and give up the struggle; it would not do if the Prince just happened to notice that Cinderella looked like his love. The moment of recognition must be manifested in an action.

This point, that the crisis must be manifested or externalized in an action, is absolutely central, although sometimes difficult to grasp when the struggle of the story takes place in a character's mind. In a revenge story, it is easy to see how the conflict must come to crisis. The common revenge plot, from *Hamlet* to *Inglourious Basterds*, takes this form: Someone important to the hero (family member, lover, friend) is killed, and for some reason the authorities who ought to be in charge of justice can't as won't avenge the death. The hero (or heroes) must do so, then, and the crisis action is manifested in the dagger, the sword, the pistol, the poison, or the explosion.

But suppose the story is about a struggle between two brothers on a fishing trip, and the change that takes place is that the protagonist, believing for most of the action that he holds his older brother in contempt, discovers at the end of the story that they are deeply bound by love and family history. Clearly this change is an epiphany, a mental reversal. A writer insufficiently aware of the nature of crisis action might signal the change in a paragraph that begins "Suddenly Larry remembered their father and realized that Jeff was very much like him." Well, unless that memory and that realization are manifested in an action, the reader is unable to share them, and therefore cannot be moved with the character.

> Jeff reached for the old net and neatly bagged the trout, swinging round to offer it with a triumphant, "Got it! We got it, didn't we?" The trout flipped and struggled, giving off a smell of weed and water and fecund mud. Jeff's knuckles were lined with grime. The knuckles and the rich river smell filled him with a memory of their first fishing trip together, the sight of their father's hands on the same scarred net....

Here the epiphany, a memory leading to a realization, is triggered by an action and sensory details that the reader can share; the reader now has a good chance of also being able to share the epiphany. Less commonly, a story may offer readers an epiphany that the main character neglects to see, as in the short story "Everything That Rises Must Converge," which appears at the end of this chapter. Such characters are often on the verge of great change, yet lack the maturity or courage to take that difficult leap to recognition.

Much great fiction, and the preponderance of serious modern fiction, echoes life in its suggestion that there are no clear or permanent solutions, that the conflicts of character, relationship, and the cosmos cannot be permanently resolved. Most of the stories in this volume end, in Vladimir Nabokov's words, "with no definite full-stop, but with the natural motion of life." None could end "they lived happily ever after" or even "they lived unhappily ever after."

Yet the story form demands a resolution. Is there such a thing as a no-resolution resolution? Yes, and it has a very specific form. Go back to the metaphor that "a story is a war." After the skirmish, after the guerrillas, after the air strike, after the poison gas and the nuclear holocaust, imagine that the two surviving combatants, one on each side, emerge from their fallout shelters.

They crawl, then stumble to the fence that marks the border. Each possessively grasps the barbed wire with a bloodied fist. The "resolution" of this battle is that neither side will ever give up and that no one will ever win; *there will never be a resolution*. This is a distinct reversal (the recognition takes place in the reader's mind) of the opening scene, in which it seemed eminently worthwhile to open a ground skirmish. In the statement of the conflict was an inherent possibility that one side or the other could win. Inherent in the resolution is a statement that no one can ever win. That is a distinct reversal and a powerful change.

Story and Plot

So far, I have used the words "story" and "plot" interchangeably. The equation of the two terms is so common that they are often comfortably understood as synonyms. When an editor says, "This is not a story," the implication is not that it lacks characters, theme, setting, or even incident, but that it has no plot.

Yet there is a distinction frequently drawn between the two terms, a distinction that although simple in itself, gives rise to manifold subtleties in the craft of narrative and that also represents a vital decision that you as a writer must make: Where should your narrative begin?

The distinction is easily made. A *story* is a series of events recorded in their chronological order. A *plot* is a series of events deliberately arranged so as to reveal their dramatic, thematic, and emotional significance. A story gives us only "what happened next," whereas plot's concern is "what, how, and why," with scenes ordered to highlight the workings of cause and effect.

Here, for example, is a fairly standard story: A sober, industrious, and rather dull young man meets the woman of his dreams. She is beautiful, brilliant, passionate, and compassionate; more wonderful still, she loves him. They plan to marry, and on the eve of their wedding his friends give him a stag party in the course of which they tease him, ply him with liquor, and drag him off to a whorehouse for a last fling. There he stumbles into a cubicle...to find himself facing his bride-to-be.

Where does this story become interesting? Where does the *plot* begin?

You may start, if you like, with the young man's *Mayflower* ancestry. But if you do, it's going to be a very long story, and we're likely to close the book about the middle of the nineteenth century. You may begin with the first time he meets the extraordinary woman, but even then you must cover at least weeks, probably months, in a few pages; and that means you must summarize, skip, and generalize, and you'll have a hard time both maintaining your credibility and holding our attention. Begin at the stag party? Better. If you do so, you will somehow have to let us know all that has gone before, either through dialogue or through the young man's memory, but you have only one evening of action to cover, and we'll get to the conflict quickly. Suppose you begin instead the next morning, when the man wakes with a hangover in bed in a brothel with his bride on his wedding day. Is that, perhaps, the best of all? An immediate conflict that must lead to a quick and striking crisis?

E. M. Forster distinguishes between plot and story by describing story as:

> the chopped off length of the tape worm of time . . . a narrative of events arranged in their time sequence. A plot is also a narrative of events, the emphasis falling on causality. "The king died, and then the queen died," is a story. "The king died, and then the queen died of grief," is a plot. The time sequence is preserved, but the sense of causality overshadows it. Or again: "The queen died, no one knew why, until it was discovered that it was through grief at the death of the king." This is a plot with a mystery in it, a form capable of high development. It suspends the time sequence, it moves as far away from the story as its limitations will allow. Consider the death of the queen. If it is in a story we say, "and then?" If it is in a plot we ask, "why?"

The human desire to know *why* is as powerful as the desire to know what happened next, and it is a desire of a higher order. Once we have the facts, we inevitably look for the links between them, and only when we find such links are we satisfied that we "understand." Rote memorization in a science class bores almost everyone. Grasp and a sense of discovery begin only when we perceive *why* "a body in motion tends to remain in motion" and what an immense effect this actuality has on the phenomena of our lives.

A STORY HAS TO BE A GOOD DATE, because the reader can stop at any time. . . . Remember, readers are selfish and have no compulsion to be decent about anything.

KURT VONNEGUT

The same is true of the events of a story. Random incidents neither move nor illuminate; we want to know why one thing leads to another and to feel the inevitability of cause and effect.

Here is a series of uninteresting events chronologically arranged.

Ariadne had a bad dream.
She woke up tired and cross.
She ate breakfast.
She headed for class.
She saw Leroy.
She fell on the steps and broke her ankle.

Leroy offered to take notes for her.
She went to a hospital.

This series of events does not constitute a plot, and if you wish to fashion it into a plot, you can do so only by letting us know the meaningful relations among the events. We first assume that Ariadne woke in a temper because of her bad dream, and that Leroy offered to take notes for her because she broke her ankle. But why did she fall? Perhaps because she saw Leroy? Does that suggest that her bad dream was about him? Was she, then, thinking about his dream-rejection as she broke her egg irritably on the edge of the frying pan? What is the effect of his offer? Is it a triumph or just another polite form of rejection when, really, he could have missed class once to drive her to the x-ray lab? The emotional and dramatic significance of these ordinary events emerges in the relation of cause to effect, and where such relation can be shown, a possible plot comes into existence. Notice also that in this brief attempt to form the events into a plot, I have introduced both conflict and a pattern of connection/disconnection.

Ariadne's is a story you might very well choose to tell chronologically: It needs to cover only an hour or two, and that much can be handled in the compressed form of the short story. But such a choice of plot is not inevitable even in this short compass. Might it be more gripping to begin with the wince of pain as she stumbles? Leroy comes to help her up and the yolk yellow of his T-shirt fills her field of vision. In the shock of pain she is immediately back in her dream. . . .

When "nothing happens" in a story, it is because we fail to sense the causal relationship between what happens first and what happens next. When something does "happen," it is because the resolution of a short story or a novel describes a change in the character's life, an effect of the events that have gone before. This is why Aristotle insisted with such apparent simplicity on "a beginning, a middle, and an end." A story is capable of many meanings, and it is first of all in the choice of structure—which portion of the story forms the plot—that you offer us the gratifying sense that we "understand."

The Short Story and the Novel

Many editors and writers insist that the short story and the novel are vastly different creatures. It is my belief, however, that, like the distinction between story and plot, the distinction between the two forms is very simple, and the many and profound possibilities of difference proceed from that simple source: A short story is short, and a novel is long.

Because of this, a short story can waste no words. It usually features the perspective of one or a very few characters. It may recount only one central action and one major change in the life of the central character or characters. It can afford no digression that does not directly affect the action. A short story strives to create what Edgar Allan Poe called "the single effect"—a single emotional impact that imparts a flash of understanding, though both impact and understanding may be complex. The virtue of a short story is its density, for it raises a single "what if" question, while a novel may raise many. If it is tight, sharp, economical, well knit, and charged, then it is a good short story because it has exploited a central attribute of the form—that it is short.

Occasionally in workshops, a new writer struggling to craft the shape of conflict-crisis-resolution may wonder if a story's lack of one of these elements means the work "must be a novel." Tempting as this hope may be, it only sidesteps the inevitable challenge of plotting, for not only must a novel have a large-scale plot structure, but individual chapters or episodes frequently are shaped around a pattern of conflict-crisis-incremental change that propels the novel onward.

Further, while no literary form is superior to another, few novelists achieve publication without first having crafted any number of short stories. The greater the limitation of space, the greater the necessity for pace, sharpness, and density. Short stories ask the writer to rise to the challenges of shaping, "showing," and making significance again and again, experiences that later may save that writer countless hours and pages when the time to tackle a novel comes along.

The form of the novel is an expanded story form. It asks for a conflict, a crisis, and a resolution, and no technique described in this book is irrelevant to its effectiveness.

What You Pawn I Will Redeem

SHERMAN ALEXIE

NOON

One day you have a home and the next you don't, but I'm not going to tell you my particular reasons for being homeless, because it's my secret story, and Indians have to work hard to keep secrets from hungry white folks.

I'm a Spokane Indian boy, an Interior Salish, and my people have lived within a hundred-mile radius of Spokane, Washington, for at least ten thousand years. I grew up in Spokane, moved to Seattle twenty-three years ago for college, flunked out after two semesters, worked various blue- and bluer-collar jobs, married two or three times, fathered two or three kids, and then went crazy. Of course, crazy is not the official definition of my mental problem, but I don't think asocial disorder fits it, either, because that makes me sound like I'm a serial killer or something. I've never hurt another human being, or, at least, not physically. I've broken a few hearts in my time, but we've all done that, so I'm nothing special in that regard. I'm a boring heartbreaker, too. I never dated or married more than one woman at a time. I didn't break hearts into pieces overnight. I broke them slowly and carefully. And I didn't set any land-speed records running out the door. Piece by piece, I disappeared. I've been disappearing ever since.

I've been homeless for six years now. If there's such a thing as an effective homeless man, then I suppose I'm effective. Being homeless is probably the only thing I've ever been good at. I know where to get the best free food. I've made friends with restaurant and convenience store managers who let me use their bathrooms. And I don't mean the public bathrooms, either. I mean employee's bathrooms, the clean ones hidden behind the kitchen or the pantry or the cooler. I know it sounds strange to be proud of this, but it means a lot to me, being trustworthy enough to piss in somebody else's clean bathroom. Maybe you don't understand the value of a clean bathroom, but I do.

Probably none of this interests you. Homeless Indians are everywhere in Seattle. We're common and boring, and you walk right on by us, with maybe a look of anger or disgust or even sadness at the terrible fate of the noble savage. But we have dreams and families. I'm friends with a homeless Plains Indian man whose son is the editor of a bigtime newspaper back east. Of course, that's his story, but we Indians are great storytellers and liars and mythmakers, so maybe that Plains Indian hobo is just a plain old everyday Indian. I'm kind of suspicious of him, because he identifies himself only as Plains Indian, a generic term, and not by a specific tribe. When I asked him why he wouldn't tell me exactly what he is, he said, "Do any of us know exactly what we are?" Yeah, great, a philosophizing Indian. "Hey," I said, "you got to have a home to be that homely." He just laughed and flipped me the eagle and walked away.

I wander the streets with a regular crew—my teammates, my defenders, my posse. It's Rose of Sharon, Junior, and me. We matter to one another if we don't matter to anybody else. Rose of Sharon is a big woman, about seven feet tall if you're measuring overall effect and about five feet tall if you're only talking about the physical. She's a Yakama Indian of the Wishram variety. Junior is a Colville, but there are about 199 tribes that make up the Colville, so he could be anything. He's good-looking, though, like he just stepped out of some "Don't Litter the Earth" public service advertisement. He's got those great big cheekbones that are like planets, you know, with little moons orbiting them. He gets me jealous, jealous, and jealous. If you put Junior and me next to each other, he's the Before Columbus Arrived Indian and I'm the After Columbus Arrived Indian. I am living proof of the horrible damage that colonialism has done to us Skins. But I'm not going to let you know how scared I sometimes get of history and its way. I'm a strong man, and I know that silence is the best method of dealing with white folks.

This whole story really started at lunchtime, when Rose of Sharon, Junior, and I were panning the handle down at Pike Place Market. After about two hours of negotiating, we earned five dollars—good enough for a bottle of fortified courage from the most beautiful 7-Eleven in the world. So we headed over that way, feeling like warrior drunks, and we walked past this pawnshop I'd never noticed before. And that was strange, because we Indians have built-in pawnshop radar. But the strangest thing of all was the old powwow-dance regalia I saw hanging in the window.

"That's my grandmother's regalia," I said to Rose of Sharon and Junior.

"How you know for sure?" Junior asked.

I didn't know for sure, because I hadn't seen that regalia in person ever. I'd only seen photographs of my grandmother dancing in it. And those were taken before somebody stole it from her, fifty years ago. But it sure looked like my memory of it, and it had all the same color feathers and beads that my family sewed into our powwow regalia.

"There's only one way to know for sure," I said.

So Rose of Sharon, Junior, and I walked into the pawnshop and greeted the old white man working behind the counter.

"How can I help you?" he asked.

"That's my grandmother's powwow regalia in your window," I said. "Somebody stole in from her fifty years ago, and my family has been searching for it ever since."

The pawnbroker looked at me like I was a liar. I understood. Pawnshops are filled with liars.

"I'm not lying," I said. "Ask my friends here. They'll tell you."

"He's the most honest Indian I know," Rose of Sharon said.

"All right, honest Indian," the pawnbroker said. "I'll give you the benefit of the doubt. Can you prove it's your grandmother's regalia?"

Because they don't want to be perfect, because only God is perfect, Indian people sew flaws into their powwow regalia. My family always sewed one yellow bead somewhere on our regalia. But we always hid it so that you had to search really hard to find it.

"If it really is my grandmother's," I said, "there will be one yellow bead hidden somewhere on it."

"All right, then," the pawnbroker said. "Let's take a look."

He pulled the regalia out of the window, laid it down on the glass counter, and we searched for that yellow bead and found it hidden beneath the armpit.

"There it is," the pawnbroker said. He didn't sound surprised. "You were right. This is your grandmother's regalia."

"It's been missing for fifty years," Junior said.

"Hey, Junior," I said. "It's my family's story. Let me tell it."

"All right," he said. "I apologize. You go ahead."

"It's been missing for fifty years," I said.

"That's his family's sad story," Rose of Sharon said. "Are you going to give it back to him?"

"That would be the right thing to do," the pawnbroker said. "But I can't afford to do the right thing. I paid a thousand dollars for this. I can't just give away a thousand dollars."

"We could go to the cops and tell them it was stolen," Rose of Sharon said.

"Hey," I said to her. "Don't go threatening people."

The pawnbroker sighed. He was thinking about the possibilities.

"Well, I suppose you could go to the cops," he said. "But I don't think they'd believe a word you said."

He sounded sad about that. As if he was sorry for taking advantage of our disadvantages.

"What's your name?" the pawnbroker asked me.

"Jackson," I said.

"Is that first or last?"

"Both," I said.

"Are you serious?"

"Yes, it's true. My mother and father named me Jackson Jackson. My family nickname is Jackson Squared. My family is funny."

"All right, Jackson Jackson," the pawnbroker said. "You wouldn't happen to have a thousand dollars, would you?"

"We've got five dollars total," I said.

"That's too bad," he said, and thought hard about the possibilities. "I'd sell it to you for a thousand dollars if you had it. Heck, to make it fair, I'd sell it to you for nine hundred and ninety-nine dollars. I'd lose a dollar. That would be the moral thing to do in this case. To lose a dollar would be the right thing."

"We've got five dollars total," I said again.

"That's too bad," he said once more, and thought harder about the possibilities. "How about this? I'll give you twenty-four hours to come up with nine hundred and ninety-nine dollars. You come back here at lunchtime tomorrow with the money and I'll sell it back to you. How does that sound?"

"It sounds all right," I said.

"All right, then," he said. "We have a deal. And I'll get you started. Here's twenty bucks."

He opened up his wallet and pulled out a crisp twenty-dollar bill and gave it to me. And Rose of Sharon, Junior, and I walked out into the daylight to search for nine hundred and seventy-four more dollars.

1 P.M.

Rose of Sharon, Junior, and I carried our twenty-dollar bill and our five dollars in loose change over to the 7-Eleven and bought three bottles of imagination. We needed to figure out how to raise all that money in only one day. Thinking hard, we huddled in an alley beneath the Alaska Way Viaduct and finished off those bottles—one, two, and three.

2 P.M.

Rose of Sharon was gone when I woke up. I heard later that she had hitchhiked back to Toppenish and was living with her sister on the reservation.

Junior had passed out beside me and was covered in his own vomit, or maybe somebody else's vomit, and my head hurt from thinking, so I left him alone and walked down to the water. I love the smell of ocean water. Salt always smells like memory.

When I got to the wharf, I ran into three Aleut cousins, who sat on a wooden bench and stared out at the bay and cried. Most of the homeless Indians in Seattle come from Alaska. One by one, each of them hopped a big working boat in Anchorage or Barrow or Juneau, fished his way south to Seattle, jumped off the boat with a pocketful of cash to party hard at one of the highly sacred and traditional Indian bars, went broke and broker, and has been trying to find his way back to the boat and the frozen north ever since.

These Aleuts smelled like salmon, I thought, and they told me they were going to sit on that wooden bench until their boat came back.

"How long has your boat been gone?" I asked.

"Eleven years," the elder Aleut said.

I cried with them for a while.

"Hey," I said. "Do you guys have any money I can borrow?"

They didn't.

3 P.M.

I walked back to Junior. He was still out cold. I put my face down near his mouth to make sure he was breathing. He was alive, so I dug around in his blue jeans pockets and found half a cigarette. I smoked it all the way down and thought about my grandmother.

Her name was Agnes, and she died of breast cancer when I was fourteen. My father always thought Agnes caught her tumors from the uranium mine on the reservation. But my mother said the disease started when Agnes was walking back from a powwow one night and got run over by a motorcycle. She broke three ribs, and my mother always said those ribs never healed right, and tumors take over when you don't heal right.

Sitting beside Junior, smelling the smoke and the salt and the vomit, I wondered if my grandmother's cancer started when somebody stole her powwow regalia. Maybe the cancer started in her broken heart and then leaked out into her breasts. I know it's crazy, but I wondered whether I could bring my grandmother back to life if I bought back her regalia.

I needed money, big money, so I left Junior and walked over to the Real Change office.

4 P.M.

Real Change is a multifaceted organization that publishes a newspaper, supports cultural projects that empower the poor and the homeless, and mobilizes the public around poverty issues. Real Change's mission is to organize, educate, and build alliances to create solutions to homelessness and poverty. It exists to provide a voice for poor people in our community.

I memorized Real Change's mission statement because I sometimes sell the newspaper on the streets. But you have to stay sober to sell it, and I'm not always good at staying sober. Anybody can sell the paper. You buy each copy for thirty cents and sell it for a dollar, and you keep the profit.

"I need one thousand four hundred and thirty papers," I said to the Big Boss.

"That's a strange number," he said. "And that's a lot of papers."

"I need them."

The Big Boss pulled out his calculator and did the math.

"It will cost you four hundred and twenty-nine dollars for that many," he said.

"If I had that kind of money, I wouldn't need to sell the papers."

"What's going on, Jackson-to-the-Second-Power?" he asked. He is the only person who calls me that. He's a funny and kind man.

I told him about my grandmother's powwow regalia and how much money I needed in order to buy it back.

"We should call the police," he said.

"I don't want to do that," I said. "It's a quest now. I need to win it back by myself."

"I understand," he said. "And, to be honest, I'd give you the papers to sell if I thought it would work. But the record for the most papers sold in one day by one vender is only three hundred and two."

"That would net me about two hundred bucks," I said.

The Big Boss used his calculator. "Two hundred and eleven dollars and forty cents," he said.

"That's not enough," I said.

"And the most money anybody has made in one day is five hundred and twenty-five. And that's because somebody gave Old Blue five hundred-dollar bills for some dang reason. The average daily net is about thirty dollars."

"This isn't going to work."

"No."

"Can you lend me some money?"

"I can't do that," he said. "If I lend you money, I have to lend money to everybody."

"What can you do?"

"I'll give you fifty papers for free. But don't tell anybody I did it."

"O.K." I said.

He gathered up the newspapers and handed them to me. I held them to my chest. He hugged me. I carried the newspapers back toward the water.

5 P.M.

Back on the wharf, I stood near the Bainbridge Island Terminal and tried to sell papers to business commuters boarding the ferry.

I sold five in one hour, dumped the other forty-five in a garbage can, and walked into McDonald's, ordered four cheeseburgers for a dollar each, and slowly ate them.

After eating, I walked outside and vomited on the sidewalk. I hated to lose my food so soon after eating it. As an alcoholic Indian with a busted stomach, I always hope I can keep enough food in me to stay alive.

6 P.M.

With one dollar in my pocket, I walked back to Junior. He was still passed out, and I put my ear to his chest and listened for his heartbeat. He was alive, so I took off his shoes and socks and found one dollar in his left sock and fifty cents in his right sock.

With two dollars and fifty cents in my hand, I sat beside Junior and thought about my grandmother and her stories.

When I was thirteen, my grandmother told me a story about the Second World War. She was a nurse at a military hospital in Sydney, Australia. For two years, she healed and comforted American and Australian soldiers.

One day, she tended to a wounded Maori soldier, who had lost his legs to an artillery attack. He was very dark-skinned. His hair was black and curly and his eyes were black and warm. His face was covered with bright tattoos.

"Are you Maori?" he asked my grandmother.

"No," she said. "I'm Spokane Indian. From the United States."

"Ah, yes," he said. "I have heard of your tribes. But you are the first American Indian I have ever met."

"There's a lot of Indian soldiers fighting for the United States," she said. "I have a brother fighting in Germany, and I lost another brother on Okinawa."

"I am sorry," he said. "I was on Okinawa as well. It was terrible."

"I am sorry about your legs," my grandmother said.

"It's funny, isn't it?" he said.

"What's funny?"

"How we brown people are killing other brown people so white people will remain free."

"I hadn't thought of it that way."

"Well, sometimes I think of it that way. And other times I think of it the way they want me to think of it. I get confused."

She fed him morphine.

"Do you believe in heaven?" he asked.

"Which heaven?" she asked.

"I'm talking about the heaven where my legs are waiting for me."

They laughed.

"Of course," he said, "my legs will probably run away from me when I get to heaven. And how will I ever catch them?"

"You have to get your arms strong," my grandmother said, "So you can run on your hands."

They laughed again.

Sitting beside Junior, I laughed at the memory of my grandmother's story. I put my hand close to Junior's mouth to make sure he was still breathing. Yes, Junior was alive, so I took my two dollars and fifty cents and walked to the Korean grocery store in Pioneer Square.

7 P.M.

At the Korean grocery store, I bought a fifty-cent cigar and two scratch lottery tickets for a dollar each. The maximum cash prize was five hundred dollars a ticket. If I won both, I would have enough money to buy back the regalia.

I loved Mary, the young Korean woman who worked the register. She was the daughter of the owners, and she sang all day.

"I love you," I said when I handed her the money.

"You always say you love me," she said.

"That's because I will always love you."

"You are a sentimental fool."

"I'm a romantic old man."

"Too old for me."

"I know I'm too old for you, but I can dream."

"O.K.," she said. "I agree to be a part of your dreams, but I will only hold your hand in your dreams. No kissing and no sex. Not even in your dreams."

"O.K.," I said. "No sex. Just romance."

"Goodbye, Jackson Jackson, my love. I will see you soon."

I left the store, walked over to Occidental Park, sat on a bench, and smoked my cigar all the way down.

Ten minutes after I finished the cigar, I scratched my first lottery ticket and won nothing. I could win only five hundred dollars now, and that would be only half of what I needed.

Ten minutes after I lost, I scratched the other ticket and won a free ticket—a small consolation and one more chance to win some money.

I walked back to Mary.

"Jackson Jackson," she said. "Have you come back to claim my heart?"

"I won a free ticket," I said.

"Just like a man," she said. "You love money and power more than you love me."

"It's true," I said. "And I'm sorry it's true."

She gave me another scratch ticket, and I took it outside. I like to scratch my tickets in private. Hopeful and sad, I scratched that third ticket and won real money. I carried it back inside to Mary.

"I won a hundred dollars," I said.

She examined the ticket and laughed.

"That's a fortune," she said, and counted out five twenties. Our fingertips touched as she handed me the money. I felt electric and constant.

"Thank you," I said, and gave her one of the bills.

"I can't take that," she said. "It's your money."

"No, it's tribal. It's an Indian thing. When you win, you're supposed to share with your family."

"I'm not your family."

"Yes, you are."

She smiled. She kept the money. With eighty dollars in my pocket, I said goodbye to my dear Mary and walked out into the cold night air.

8 P.M.

I wanted to share the good news with Junior. I walked back to him, but he was gone. I heard later that he had hitchhiked down to Portland, Oregon, and died of exposure in an alley behind the Hilton Hotel.

9 P.M.

Lonesome for Indians, I carried my eighty dollars over to Big Heart's in South Downtown. Big Heart's is an all-Indian bar. Nobody knows how or why Indians migrate to one bar and turn it into an official Indian bar. But Big Heart's has been an Indian bar for twenty-three years. It used to be way up on Aurora Avenue, but a crazy Lummi Indian burned that one down, and the owners moved to the new location, a few blocks south of Safeco Field.

I walked into Big Heart's and counted fifteen Indians—eight men and seven women. I didn't know any of them, but Indians like to belong, so we all pretended to be cousins.

"How much for whiskey shots?" I asked the bartender, a fat white guy.

"You want the bad stuff or the badder stuff?"

"As bad as you got."

"One dollar a shot."

I laid my eighty dollars on the bar top.

"All right," I said. "Me and all my cousins here are going to be drinking eighty shots. How many is that apiece?"

"Counting you," a woman shouted from behind me, "that's five shots for everybody."

I turned to look at her. She was a chubby and pale Indian woman, sitting with a tall and skinny Indian man.

"All right, math genius," I said to her, and then shouted for the whole bar to hear. "Five drinks for everybody!"

All the other Indians rushed the bar, but I sat with the mathematician and her skinny friend. We took our time with our whiskey shots.

"What's your tribe?" I asked.

"I'm Duwamish," she said. "And he's Crow."

"You're a long way from Montana," I said to him.

"I'm Crow," he said. "I flew here."

"What's your name?" I asked them.

"I'm Irene Muse," she said. "And this is Honey Boy."

She shook my hand hard, but he offered his hand as if I was supposed to kiss it. So I did. He giggled and blushed, as much as a dark-skinned Crow can blush.

"You're one of them two-spirits, aren't you?" I asked him.

"I love women," he said. "And I love men."

"Sometimes both at the same time," Irene said.

We laughed.

"Man," I said to Honey Boy. "So you must have about eight or nine spirits going on inside you, enit?"

"Sweetie," he said. "I'll be whatever you want me to be."

"Oh, no," Irene said. "Honey Boy is falling in love."

"It has nothing to do with love," he said.

We laughed.

"Wow," I said. "I'm flattered, Honey Boy, but I don't play on your team."

"Never say never," he said.

"You better be careful," Irene said. "Honey Boy knows all sorts of magic."

"Honey Boy," I said, "you can try to seduce me, but my heart belongs to a woman named Mary."

"Is your Mary a virgin?" Honey Boy asked.

We laughed.

And we drank our whiskey shots until they were gone. But the other Indians bought me more whiskey shots, because I'd been so generous with my money. And Honey Boy pulled out his credit card, and I drank and sailed on that plastic boat.

After a dozen shots, I asked Irene to dance. She refused. But Honey Boy shuffled over to the jukebox, dropped in a quarter, and selected

Willie Nelson's "Help Me Make It Through the Night." As Irene and I sat at the table and laughed and drank more whiskey, Honey Boy danced a slow circle around us and sang along with Willie.

"Are you serenading me?" I asked him.

He kept singing and dancing.

"Are you serenading me?" I asked him again.

"He's going to put a spell on you," Irene said.

I leaned over the table, spilling a few drinks, and kissed Irene hard. She kissed me back.

10 P.M.

Irene pushed me into the women's bathroom, into a stall, shut the door behind us, and shoved her hand down my pants. She was short, so I had to lean over to kiss her. I grabbed and squeezed her everwhere I could reach, and she was wonderfully fat, and every part of ther body felt like a large, warm, soft breast.

MIDNIGHT

Nearly blind with alcohol, I stood alone at the bar and swore I had been standing in the bathroom with Irene only a minute ago.

"One more shot!" I yelled at the bartender.

"You've got no more money!" he yelled back.

"Somebody buy me a drink!" I shouted.

"They've got no more money!"

"Where are Irene and Honey Boy?"

"Long gone!"

2 A.M.

"Closing time!" the bartender shouted at the three or four Indians who were still drinking hard after a long, hard day of drinking. Indian alcoholics are either sprinters or marathoners.

"Where are Irene and Honey Boy?" I asked.

"They've been gone for hours," the bartender said.

"Where'd they go?"

"I told you a hundred times, I don't know."

"What am I supposed to do?"

"It's closing time. I don't care where you go, but you're not staying here."

"You are an ungrateful bastard. I've been good to you."

"You don't leave right now, I'm going to kick your ass."

"Come on, I know how to fight."

He came at me. I don't remember what happened after that.

4 A.M.

I emerged from the blackness and discovered myself walking behind a big warehouse. I didn't know where I was. My face hurt. I felt my nose and decided that it might be broken. Exhausted and cold, I pulled a plastic tarp from a truck bed, wrapped it around me like a faithful lover, and fell asleep in the dirt.

6 A.M.

Somebody kicked me in the ribs. I opened my eyes and looked up at a white cop.

"Jackson," the cop said. "Is that you?"

"Officer Williams," I said. He was a good cop with a sweet tooth. He'd given me hundreds of candy bars over the years. I wonder if he knew I was diabetic.

"What the hell are you doing here?" he asked.

"I was cold and sleepy," I said. "So I lay down."

"You dumb-ass, you passed out on the railroad tracks."

I sat up and looked around. I was lying on the railroad tracks. Dock workers stared at me. I should have been a railroad-track pizza, a double Indian pepperoni with extra cheese. Sick and scared, I leaned over and puked whiskey.

"What the hell's wrong with you?" Officer Williams asked. "You've never been this stupid."

"It's my grandmother," I said. "She died."

"I'm sorry, man. When did she die?"

"Nineteen seventy-two."

"And you're killing yourself now?"

"I've been killing myself ever since she died."

He shook his head. He was sad for me. Like I said, he was a good cop.

"And somebody beat the hell out of you," he said. "You remember who?"

"Mr. Grief and I went a few rounds."

"It looks like Mr. Grief knocked you out."

"Mr. Grief always wins."

"Come on," he said. "Let's get you out of here."

He helped me up and led me over to his squad car. He put me in the back. "You throw up in there and you're cleaning it up," he said.

"That's fair."

He walked around the car and sat in the driver's seat. "I'm taking you over to detox," he said.

"No, man, that place is awful," I said. "It's full of drunk Indians."

We laughed. He drove away from the docks.

"I don't know how you guys do it," he said.

"What guys?" I asked.

"You Indians. How the hell do you laugh so much? I just picked your ass off the railroad tracks, and you're making jokes. Why the hell do you do that?"

"The two funniest tribes I've ever been around are Indians and Jews, so I guess that says something about the inherent humor of genocide."

We laughed.

"Listen to you, Jackson. You're so smart. Why the hell are you on the street?"

"Give me a thousand dollars and I'll tell you."

"You bet I'd give you a thousand dollars if I knew you'd straighten up your life."

He meant it. He was the second-best cop I'd ever known.

"You're a good cop," I said.

"Come on, Jackson," he said. "Don't blow smoke up my ass."

"No, really, you remind me of my grandfather."

"Yeah, that's what you Indians always tell me."

"No, man, my grandfather was a tribal cop. He was a good cop. He never arrested people. He took care of them. Just like you."

"I've arrested hundreds of scumbags, Jackson. And I've shot a couple in the ass."

"It don't matter. You're not a killer."

"I didn't kill them. I killed their asses. I'm an ass-killer."

We drove through downtown. The missions and shelters had already released their overnighters. Sleepy homeless men and women stood on street corners and stared up at a gray sky. It was the morning after the night of the living dead.

"Do you ever get scared?" I asked Officer Williams.

"What do you mean?"

"I mean, being a cop, is it scary?"

He thought about that for a while. He contemplated it. I liked that about him.

"I guess I try not to think too much about being afraid," he said. "If you think about fear, then you'll be afraid. The job is boring most of the time. Just driving and looking into dark corners, you know, and seeing nothing. But then things get heavy. You're chasing somebody, or fighting them or walking around a dark house, and you just know some crazy guy is hiding around a corner, and hell, yes, it's scary."

"My grandfather was killed in the line of duty," I said.

"I'm sorry. How'd it happen?"

I knew he'd listen closely to my story.

"He worked on the reservation. Everybody knew everybody. It was safe. We aren't like those crazy Sioux or Apache or any of those other warrior tribes. There've only been three murders on my reservation in the last hundred years."

"That is safe."

"Yeah, we Spokane, we're passive, you know. We're mean with words. And we'll cuss out anybody. But we don't shoot people. Or stab them. Not much, anyway."

"So what happened to your grandfather?"

"This man and his girlfriend were fighting down by Little Falls."

"Domestic dispute. Those are the worst."

"Yeah, but this guy was my grandfather's brother. My great-uncle."

"Oh, no."

"Yeah, it was awful. My grandfather just strolled into the house. He'd been there a thousand times. And his brother and his girlfriend were drunk and beating on each other. And my grandfather stepped between them, just as he'd done a hundred times before. And the girlfriend tripped or something. She fell down and hit her head and started crying. And my grandfather kneeled down beside her to make sure she was all right. And for some reason my great-uncle reached down, pulled my grandfather's pistol out of the holster, and shot him in the head."

"That's terrible. I'm sorry."

"Yeah, my great-uncle could never figure out why he did it. He went to prison forever, you know, and he always wrote these long letters. Like fifty pages of tiny little handwriting. And he was always trying to figure out why he did it. He'd write and write and write and try to figure it out. He never did. It's a great big mystery."

"Do you remember your grandfather?"

"A little bit. I remember the funeral. My grandmother wouldn't let them bury him. My father had to drag her away from the grave."

"I don't know what to say."

"I don't, either."

We stopped in front of the detox center.

"We're here," Officer Williams said.

"I can't go in there," I said.

"You have to."

"Please, no. They'll keep me for twenty-four hours. And then it will be too late."

"Too late for what?"

I told him about my grandmother's regalia and the deadline for buying it back.

"If it was stolen, you need to file a report," he said. "I'll investigate it myself. If that thing is really your grandmother's, I'll get it back for you. Legally."

"No," I said. "That's not fair. The pawnbroker didn't know it was stolen. And, besides, I'm on a mission here. I want to be a hero, you know? I want to win it back, like a knight."

"That's romantic crap."

"That may be. But I care about it. It's been a long time since I really cared about something."

Officer Williams turned around in his seat and stared at me. He studied me.

"I'll give you some money," he said. "I don't have much. Only thirty bucks. I'm short until payday. And it's not enough to get back the regalia. But it's something."

"I'll take it," I said.

"I'm giving it to you because I believe in what you believe. I'm hoping, and I don't know why I'm hoping it, but I hope you can turn thirty bucks into a thousand somehow."

"I believe in magic."

"I believe you'll take my money and get drunk on it."

"Then why are you giving it to me?"

"There ain't no such thing as an atheist cop."

"Sure, there is."

"Yeah, well, I'm not an atheist cop."

He let me out of the car, handed me two fivers and a twenty, and shook my hand.

"Take care of yourself, Jackson," he said. "Stay off the railroad tracks."

"I'll try," I said.

He drove away. Carrying money, I headed back toward the water.

8 A.M.

On the wharf, those three Aleuts still waited on the wooden bench.

"Have you seen your ship?" I asked.

"Seen a lot of ships," the elder Aleut said. "But not our ship."

I sat on the bench with them. We sat in silence for a long time. I wondered if we would fossilize if we sat there long enough.

I thought about my grandmother. I'd never seen her dance in her regalia. And, more than anything. I wished I'd seen her dance at a powwow.

"Do you guys know any songs?" I asked the Aleuts.

"I know all of Hank Williams," the elder Aleut said.

"How about Indian songs?"

"Hank Williams is Indian."

"How about sacred songs?"

"Hank Williams is sacred."

"I'm talking about ceremonial songs. You know, religious ones. The songs you sing back home when you're wishing and hoping."

"What are you wishing and hoping for?"

"I'm wishing my grandmother was still alive."

"Every song I know is about that."

"Well, sing me as many as you can."

The Aleuts sang their strange and beautiful songs. I listened. They sang about my grandmother and about their grandmothers. They were lonesome for the cold and the snow. I was lonesome for everything.

10 A.M.

After the Aleuts finished their last song, we sat in silence for a while. Indians are good at silence.

"Was that the last song?" I asked.

"We sang all the ones we could," the elder Aleut said. "The others are just for our people."

I understood. We Indians have to keep our secrets. And these Aleuts were so secretive they didn't refer to themselves as Indians.

"Are you guys hungry?" I asked.

They looked at one another and communicated without talking.

"We could eat," the elder Aleut said.

11 A.M.

The Aleuts and I walked over to the Big Kitchen, a greasy diner in the International District. I knew they served homeless Indians who'd lucked into money.

"Four for breakfast?" the waitress asked when we stepped inside.

"Yes, we're very hungry," the elder Aleut said.

She took us to a booth near the kitchen. I could smell the food cooking. My stomach growled.

"You guys want separate checks?" the waitress asked.

"No, I'm paying," I said.

"Aren't you the generous one," she said.

"Don't do that," I said.

"Do what?" she asked.

"Don't ask me rhetorical questions. They scare me."

She looked puzzled, and then she laughed.

"O.K., professor," she said. "I'll only ask you real questions from now on."

"Thank you."

"What do you guys want to eat?"

"That's the best question anybody can ask anybody," I said. "What have you got?"

"How much money you got?" she asked.

"Another good question," I said. "I've got twenty-five dollars I can spend. Bring us all the breakfast you can, plus your tip."

She knew the math.

"All right, that's four specials and four coffees and fifteen percent for me."

The Aleuts and I waited in silence. Soon enough, the waitress returned and poured us four coffees, and we sipped at them until she returned again, with four plates of food. Eggs, bacon, toast, hash brown potatoes. It's amazing how much food you can buy for so little money.

Grateful, we feasted.

NOON

I said farewell to the Aleuts and walked toward the pawnshop. I heard later that the Aleuts had waded into the saltwater near Dock 47 and disappeared. Some Indians swore they had walked on the water and headed north. Other Indians saw the Aleuts drown. I don't know what happened to them.

I looked for the pawnshop and couldn't find it. I swear it wasn't in the place where it had been before. I walked twenty or thirty blocks looking for the pawnshop, turned corners and bisected intersections, and looked up its name in the phone books and asked people walking past me if they'd ever heard of it. But that pawnshop seemed to have sailed away like a ghost ship. I wanted to cry. And just when I'd given up, when I turned one last corner and thought I might die if I didn't find that pawnshop, there it was, in a space I swear it hadn't occupied a few minutes ago.

I walked inside and greeted the pawnbroker, who looked a little younger than he had before.

"It's you," he said.

"Yes, it's me," I said.

"Jackson Jackson."

"That is my name."

"Where are your friends?"

"They went traveling. But it's O.K. Indians are everywhere."

"Do you have the money?"

"How much do you need again?" I asked, and hoped the price had changed.

"Nine hundred and ninety-nine dollars."

It was still the same price. Of course, it was the same price. Why would it change?

"I don't have that," I said.

"What do you have?"

"Five dollars."

I set the crumpled Lincoln on the countertop. The pawnbroker studied it.

"Is that the same five dollars from yesterday?"

"No, it's different."

He thought about the possibilities.

"Did you work hard for this money?" he asked.

"Yes," I said.

He closed his eyes and thought harder about the possibilities. Then he stepped into the back room and returned with my grandmother's regalia.

"Take it," he said, and held it out to me.

"I don't have the money."

"I don't want your money."

"But I wanted to win it."

"You did win it. Now take it before I change my mind."

Do you know how many good men live in this world? Too many to count!

I took my grandmother's regalia and walked outside. I knew that solitary yellow bead was part of me. I knew I was that yellow bead in part. Outside, I wrapped myself in my grandmother's regalia and breathed her in. I stepped off the sidewalk and into the intersection. Pedestrians stopped. Cars stopped. The city stopped. They all watched me dance with my grandmother. I was my grandmother, dancing.

My Kid's Dog

RON HANSEN

My kid's dog died.

Sparky.

I hated that dog.

The feeling was mutual.

We got off on the wrong foot. Whining in his pen those first nights. My squirt gun in his face and him blinking from the water. And then the holes in the yard. The so-called accidents in the house. His nose snuffling into my Brooks Brothers trousers. Him slurping my fine Pilsner beer or sneaking bites of my Dagwood sandwich when I feel asleep on the sofa. Also his inability to fetch, to take a joke, to find the humor in sudden air horns. To be dandled, roughhoused, or teased. And then the growling, the skulking, the snapping at my ankles, the hiding from me under the house, and literally thousands of abject refusals to obey. Like, *Who the hell are you?*

You'd have thought he was a cat. When pushed to the brink I shouted, "I'll cut your face off and show it to you," and the small-brained mammal just stared at me.

But with the kids or my wife little Foo-Foo was a changeling, conning them with the tail, the prance, the peppiness, the soft chocolate eyes, the sloppy expressions of love, the easy tricks that if I performed I'd get no credit for.

Oh, we understood each other all right. I was on to him.

And then, at age ten, and none too soon, he kicked the bucket. You'd think that would be it. End of story. But no, he had to get even.

Those who have tears, prepare to shed them.

I was futzing with the hinges on the front-yard gate on a Saturday afternoon, my tattersall shirtsleeves rolled up and mind off in Oklahoma, when I noticed Fido in the California shade, snoozing, but for once a little wistful too, and far more serene than he usually was in my offensive presence. I tried to surprise him with my standard patriarchal shout, but it was no go, so I walked over and prodded the little guy with my wingtip. Nothing doing. And not so much as a flutter in his oddly abstracted face. Surely this was the big sleep, I thought.

She who must be obeyed was at the mall, provisioning, so I was safe from objection or inquiry on that account. I then made an inventory of my progeny: Buzz in the collegiate East, in the realm of heart-attack tuitions, Zack in the netherworld of the surf shop, Suzy, my last kid, on her bike and somewhere with her cousin. Were I to bury Rover with due haste and dispatch I could forestall the waterworks, even convince them that he'd signed up with the circus, run afoul of Cruella De Vil—anything but died.

I got a green tarpaulin from the garage and laid it out on the front lawn where I hesitated before using my shoe to roll Spot into his funeral shroud, then dragged him back into the victory garden where summer's dying zucchini plants were in riot. With trusty spade I dug his burial place, heaped earth atop him, tamped it down with satisfying *whumps.*

I was feeling good about myself, heroic, as if, miraculously, compassion and charity had invaded not only my bones but my sinewy muscle tissues. I fixed myself a tall glass of gin and tonic and watched the first quarter of the USC football game.

And then pangs of conscience assailed me. Hadn't my investigation of said demise of Precious been rather cursory? Wouldn't I, myself, closely cross-examine a suspect whose emotions were clouded, whose nefarious wishes were well established, whose veterinary skills were without credential? The innocence of my childhood had been spoiled with the tales of Edgar Allan Poe, so it was not difficult to conjure images of Scruffy clawing through tarpaulin and earth as he fought for one last gasp of air, air that others could more profitably use.

I marched out to the garden with aforementioned spade and with great lumbar strain exhumed our darling lapdog. Considering the circumstances, he seemed none the worse for wear, but I did detect a marked disinclination to respirate, which I took as a sign either of his inveterate stubbornness or of his having reached the Stygian shore. The latter seemed more likely. I heard in my fuddled head a line from *The Wild Bunch* when a critically injured gunman begs his outlaw gang to "finish it." And in the healing spirit of Hippocrates I lifted high the shovel and whanged it down on Harvey's head.

To my relief, not a whimper issued from him. I was confident he was defunct.

With care I shrouded and buried him again, committing earth to earth and dust to dust and so on, and with spritelike step conveyed myself to the kitchen where I made another gin and tonic and, in semiprone position, settled into the game's third quarter, the fabled Trojan running attack grinding out, it would seem, another win.

I was shocked awake by the impertinence of a ringing telephone, which I, with due caution, answered. It was my wife's friend Vicki inquiring about the pooch, for it was her assertion that Snip had fancied a taste of her son's upper calf and without invitation or permission to do so had partaken of same within the last twenty-four hours. Even while I was wondering what toxicity lurked in the child's leg and to what extent the poison was culpably responsible for our adored pet's actionable extinction, a loss we would feel for our lifetimes, Vicki insisted that I have the dog checked out by a vet to ascertain if he had rabies.

Cause of death: rabies? It seemed unlikely. Notwithstanding his surliness, there'd been no Cujoesque frothing or lunging at car windows; but my familiarity with torts has made me both careful and rather unctuous in confrontation with a plaintiff, and so I assured the complainant that I would accede to her request.

Off to the back yard again, my pace that of a woebegone trudge, and with my implement of agriculture I displaced the slack and loosened earth. This was getting old. With an accusatory tone I said, "You're doing this on purpose, aren't you," and I took his silence as a plea of nolo contendere.

My plan, of course, was to employ the Oldsmobile 88 to transport my burden to the canine's autopsy at Dr. Romo's office just a half mile away. However, upon settling into its plush front seat, it came to my attention that Zack—he who is but a sojourner on this earth—had not thought to replenish the fuel he'd used up on his trip to the Hollywood Bowl last night. The vehicle was not in a condition of plenitude. Would not ferry us farther than a block.

With Buster lying in the altogether on the driveway, not yet unsightly but no calendar page, I went into the house and found an old leather suitcase in the attic, then stuffed the mutt into the larger flapped compartment before hefting him on his final journey to those veterinary rooms he always shivered in.

I am, as I may have implied, a man of depth, perspicacity, and nearly Olympian strength, but I found myself hauling my heavy and lifeless cargo to Dr. Romo's with a pronounced lack of vigor and resolve. The September afternoon was hot, the Pasadena streets were vacant, the entire world seemed to have found entertainment and surcease in ways that I had not. I was, in a word, in a sweaty snit, and after many panting and pain-filled stops, my spine in Quasimodo configuration and my right arm gradually inching longer than my left, it was all I could do not to heave the suitcase containing Wonderdog into a haulaway behind the Chinese restaurant.

But during our joint ordeal I had developed a grudging affection for our pet; he who'd been so quick to defend my kith and kin against the noise of passing trucks, who took loud notice of the squirrels outside, who held fast in the foyer, hackles raised, fearlessly barking, whenever company arrived at the front door. With him I seemed calm, masterful, and uneccentric, the Superior Man that the *I Ching* talks so much about. Without him, I thought, I would be otherwise.

I put down the suitcase to shake the ache from my fingers and subtract affliction from my back, and it was then that my final indignity came. An angel of mercy spied my plight, braked his ancient Cadillac, and got out, his facial piercings and tattoos and shoot-the-marbles eyes belying the kindness and decency of his heart as he asked, "Can I help you with that suitcase?"

"I can handle it."

"Are you sure?"

"I'm just two blocks away."

"What the heck's in it?" he asked.

And for some reason I said, "A family heirloom."

"Wow!" he said. "Why don't you put it in my trunk and I'll help you with it? I got nothin' better to do."

Well, I did not just fall off the turnip truck. I would have been, in other circumstances, suspicious. But I was all too aware of the weight and worthlessness of my cumbrance, and so I granted his specified offer, hoisting the deceased into the Seville and slamming down the trunk lid. And, in evidence of our fallen state, my Samaritan immediately took off without me, jeering and peeling rubber and speeding west toward Los Angeles.

I could only lift my hand in a languid wave. *So long, old sport.*

Our world being the location of penance and recrimination, it was only right that my last kid should pedal up to me on her bike just then and ask, "Daddy, what are you doing here?"

Waving to a guy, I thought, *who's about to become an undertaker.*

And then I confessed. Sparky's sudden death, the burial, not the exhumation and execution attempt, but the imputation of rabies and my arduous efforts to acquit his reputation with a pilgrimage to the vet's.

Suzy took it in with sangfroid for a little while, but then the lip quivered and tears spilled from her gorgeous eyes, and as I held her close she begged me to get her another dog just like Sparky. And that was Sparky's final revenge, for I said, "Okay, honey. Another dog, just like him."

◆

Everything That Rises Must Converge

FLANNERY O'CONNOR

Her doctor had told Julian's mother that she must lose twenty pounds on account of her blood pressure, so on Wednesday nights Julian had to take her downtown on the bus for a reducing class at the Y. The reducing class was designed for working girls over fifty, who weighed from 165 to 200 pounds. His mother was one of the slimmer ones, but she said ladies did not tell their age or weight. She would not ride the buses by herself at night since they had been integrated, and because the reducing class was one of her few pleasures, necessary for her health, and *free*, she said Julian could at least put himself out to take her, considering all she did for him. Julian did not like to consider all she did for him, but every Wednesday night he braced himself and took her.

She was almost ready to go, standing before the hall mirror, putting on her hat, while he, his hands behind him, appeared pinned to the door frame, waiting like Saint Sebastian for the arrows to begin piercing him. The hat was new and had cost her seven dollars and a half. She kept saying, "Maybe I shouldn't have paid that for it. No, I shouldn't have. I'll take it off and return it tomorrow. I shouldn't have bought it."

Julian raised his eyes to heaven. "Yes, you should have bought it," he said. "Put it on and let's go." It was a hideous hat. A purple velvet flap came down on one side of it and stood up on the other; the rest of it was green and looked like a cushion with the stuffing out. He decided it was less comical than jaunty and pathetic. Everything that gave her pleasure was small and depressed him.

She lifted the hat one more time and set it down slowly on top of her head. Two wings of gray hair protruded on either side of her florid face, but her eyes, sky-blue, were as innocent and untouched by experience as they must have been when she was ten. Were it not that she was a widow who had struggled fiercely to feed and clothe and put him through school and who was supporting him still, "until he got on his feet," she might have been a little girl that he had to take to town.

"It's all right, it's all right," he said. "Let's go." He opened the door himself and started down the walk to get her going. The sky was a dying violet and the houses stood out darkly against it, bulbous liver-colored monstrosities of a uniform ugliness though no two were alike. Since this had been a fashionable neighborhood forty years ago, his mother persisted in thinking they did well to have an apartment in it. Each house had a narrow collar of dirt around it in which sat, usually, a grubby child. Julian walked with his hands in his pockets, his head down and thrust forward and his eyes glazed with the determination to make himself completely numb during the time he would be sacrificed to her pleasure.

The door closed and he turned to find the dumpy figure, surmounted by the atrocious hat, coming toward him. "Well," she said, "you only live once and paying a little more for it, I at least won't meet myself coming and going."

"Some day I'll start making money," Julian said gloomily—he knew he never would—"and you can have one of those jokes whenever you take the fit." But first they would move. He visualized a place where the nearest neighbors would be three miles away on either side.

"I think you're doing fine," she said, drawing on her gloves. "You've only been out of school a year. Rome wasn't built in a day."

She was one of the few members of the Y reducing class who arrived in hat and gloves and who had a son who had been to college. "It takes time," she said, "and the world is in such a mess. This hat looked better on me than any of the others, though when she brought it out I said, 'Take that thing back. I wouldn't have it on my head,' and she said, 'Now wait till you see it on,' and when she put it on me, I said, 'We-ull,' and she said, 'If you ask me, that hat does something for you and you do something for the hat, and besides,' she said, 'with that hat, you won't meet yourself coming and going.'"

Julian thought he could have stood his lot better if she had been selfish, if she had been an old hag who drank and screamed at him. He walked along, saturated in depression, as if in the midst of his martyrdom he had lost his faith. Catching sight of his long, hopeless, irritated face, she stopped suddenly with a grief-stricken look, and pulled back on his arm. "Wait on me," she said. "I'm going back to the house and take this thing off and tomorrow I'm going to return it, I was out of my head. I can pay the gas bill with the seven-fifty."

He caught her arm in a vicious grip. "You are not going to take it back," he said. "I like it."

"Well," she said, "I don't think I ought..."

"Shut up and enjoy it," he muttered, more depressed than ever.

"With the world in the mess it's in," she said, "it's a wonder we can enjoy anything. I tell you, the bottom rail is on the top."

Julian sighed.

"Of course," she said, "if you know who you are, you can go anywhere." She said this every time he took her to the reducing class. "Most of them in it are not our kind of people," she said, "but I can be gracious to anybody. I know who I am."

"They don't give a damn for your graciousness," Julian said savagely. "Knowing who you are is good for one generation only. You haven't the foggiest idea where you stand now or who you are."

She stopped and allowed her eyes to flash at him. "I most certainly do know who I am," she said, "and if you don't know who you are, I'm ashamed of you."

"Oh hell," Julian said.

"Your great-grandfather was a former governor of this state," she said. "Your grandfather was a prosperous landowner. Your grandmother was a Godhigh."

"Will you look around you," he said tensely, "and see where you are now?" and he swept his arm jerkily out to indicate the neighborhood, which the growing darkness at least made less dingy.

"You remain what you are," she said, "Your great-grandfather had a plantation and two hundred slaves."

"There are no more slaves," he said irritably.

"They were better off when they were," she said. He groaned to see that she was off on that topic. She rolled onto it every few days like a train on an open track. He knew every stop, every junction, every swamp along the way, and knew the exact point at which her conclusion would roll majestically into the station: "It's ridiculous. It's simply not realistic. They should rise, yes, but on their own side of the fence."

"Let's skip it," Julian said.

"The ones I feel sorry for," she said, "are the ones that are half white. They're tragic."

"Will you skip it?"

"Suppose we were half white. We would certainly have mixed feelings."

"I have mixed feelings now," he groaned.

"Well let's talk about something pleasant," she said. "I remember going to Grandpa's when I was a little girl. Then the house had double stairways that went up to what was really the second floor—all the cooking was done on the first. I used to like to stay down in the kitchen on account of the way the walls smelled. I would sit with my nose pressed against the plaster and take deep breaths. Actually the place belonged to the Godhighs but your grandfather Chestny paid the mortgage and saved it for them. They were in reduced circumstances," she said, "but reduced or not, they never forgot who they were."

"Doubtless that decayed mansion reminded them," Julian muttered. He never spoke of it without contempt or thought of it without longing. He had seen it once when he was a child before it had been sold. The double stairways had rotted and been torn down. Negroes were living in it. But it remained in his mind as his mother had known it. It appeared in his dreams regularly. He would stand on the wide porch, listening to the rustle of oak leaves, then wander through the high-ceilinged hall into the parlor that opened onto it and gaze at the worn rugs and faded draperies. It occurred to him that it was he, not she, who could have appreciated it. He preferred its threadbare elegance to anything he could name and it was because of it that all the neighborhoods they had lived in had been a torment to him—whereas she had hardly known the difference. She called her insensitivity "being adjustable."

"And I remember the old darky who was my nurse, Caroline. There was no better person in the world. I've always had a great respect for my colored friends," she said. "I'd do anything in the world for them and they'd..."

"Will you for God's sake get off that subject?" Julian said. When he got on a bus by himself, he made it a point to sit down beside a Negro, in reparation as it were for his mother's sins.

"You're mighty touchy tonight," she said. "Do you feel all right?"

"Yes I feel all right," he said. "Now lay off."

She pursed her lips. "Well, you certainly are in a vile humor," she observed. "I just won't speak to you at all."

They had reached the bus stop. There was no bus in sight and Julian, his hands still jammed in his pockets and his head thrust forward, scowled down the empty street. The frustration of having to wait on the bus as well as ride on it began to creep up his neck like a hot hand. The presence of his mother was borne in upon him as she gave a pained sigh. He looked at her bleakly. She was holding herself very erect under the preposterous hat, wearing it like a banner of her imaginary dignity. There was in him an evil urge to break her spirit. He suddenly unloosened his tie and pulled it off and put it in his pocket.

She stiffened. "Why must you look like *that* when you take me to town?" she said. "Why must you deliberately embarrass me?"

"If you'll never learn where you are," he said, "you can at least learn where I am."

"You look like a—thug," she said.

"Then I must be one," he murmured.

"I'll just go home," she said. "I will not bother you. If you can't do a little thing like that for me..."

Rolling his eyes upward, he put his tie back on. "Restored to my class," he muttered. He thrust his face toward her and hissed, "True culture is in the mind, the *mind*," he said, and tapped his head, "the mind."

"It's in the heart," she said, "and in how you do things and how you do things is because of who you *are*."

"Nobody in the damn bus cares who you are."

"I care who I am," she said icily.

The lighted bus appeared on top of the next hill and as it approached, they moved out into the street to meet it. He put his hand under her elbow and hoisted her up on the creaking step. She entered with a little smile, as if she were going into a drawing room where everyone had been waiting for her. While he put in the tokens, she sat down on one of the broad front seats for three which faced the aisle. A thin woman with protruding teeth and long yellow hair was sitting on the end of it. His mother moved up beside her and left room for Julian beside herself. He sat down and looked at the floor across the aisle where a pair of thin feet in red and white canvas sandals were planted.

His mother immediately began a general conversation meant to attract anyone who felt like talking, "Can it get any hotter?" she said and removed from her purse a folding fan, black with a Japanese scene on it, which she began to flutter before her.

"I reckon it might could," the woman with the protruding teeth said, "but I know for a fact my apartment couldn't get no hotter."

"It must get the afternoon sun," his mother said. She sat forward and looked up and down the bus. It was half filled. Everybody was white. "I see we have the bus to ourselves," she said. Julian cringed.

"For a change," said the woman across the aisle, the owner of the red and white canvas sandals. "I come on one the other day and they were thick as fleas—up front and all through."

"The world is in a mess everywhere," his mother said. "I don't know how we've let it get in this fix."

"What gets my goat is all those boys from good families stealing automobile tires," the woman with the protruding teeth said. "I told my boy, I said you may not be rich but you been raised right and if I ever catch you in any such mess, they can send you on to the reformatory. Be exactly where you belong."

"Training tells," his mother said. "Is your boy in high school?"

"Ninth grade," the woman said.

"My son just finished college last year. He wants to write but he's selling typewriters until he gets started," his mother said.

The woman leaned forward and peered at Julian. He threw her such a malevolent look that she subsided against the seat. On the floor across the aisle there was an abandoned newspaper. He got up and got it and opened it out in front of him. His mother discreetly continued the conversation in a lower tone but the woman across the aisle said in a loud voice, "Well that's nice. Selling typewriters is close to writing. He can go right from one to the other."

"I tell him," his mother said, "that Rome wasn't built in a day."

Behind the newspaper Julian was withdrawing into the inner compartment of his mind where he spent most of his time. This was a kind of mental bubble in which he established himself when he could not bear to be a part of what was going on around him. From it he could see out and judge but in it he was safe from any kind of penetration from without. It was the only place where he felt free of the general idiocy of his fellows. His mother had never entered it but from it he could see her with absolute clarity.

The old lady was clever enough and he thought that if she had started from any of the right premises, more might have been expected of her. She lived according to the laws of her own fantasy world, outside of which he had never seen her set foot. The law of it was to sacrifice herself for him after she had first created the necessity to do so by making a mess of things. If he had permitted her sacrifices, it was only because her lack of foresight had made them necessary. All of her life had been a struggle to act like a Chestny without the Chestny goods, and to give him everything she thought a Chestny ought to have; but since, said she, it was fun to struggle, why complain? And when you had won, as she had won, what fun to look back on the hard times? He could not forgive her that she had enjoyed the struggle and that she thought *she* had won.

What she meant when she said she had won was that she had brought him up successfully and had sent him to college and that he had turned out so well—good looking (her teeth had gone unfilled so that his could be straightened), intelligent (he realized he was too intelligent to be a success), and with a future ahead of him (there was of course no future ahead of him). She excused his gloominess on the grounds that he was still growing up and his radical ideas on his lack of practical experience. She said he didn't yet know a thing about "life," that he hadn't even entered the real world—when already he was as disenchanted with it as a man of fifty.

The further irony of all this was that in spite of her, he had turned out so well. In spite of going to only a third-rate college, he had, on his own initiative, come out with a first-rate education; in spite of growing up dominated by a small mind, he had ended up with a large one; in spite of all her foolish views, he was free of prejudice and unafraid to face facts. Most miraculous of all, instead of being blinded by love for her as she was for him, he had cut himself emotionally free of her and could see her with complete objectivity. He was not dominated by his mother.

The bus stopped with a sudden jerk and shook him from his meditation. A woman from the back lurched forward with little steps and barely escaped falling in his newspaper as she righted herself. She got off and a large Negro got on. Julian kept his paper lowered to watch. It gave him a certain satisfaction to see injustice in daily operation. It confirmed his view that with a few exceptions there was no one worth knowing within a radius of three hundred miles. The Negro was well dressed and carried a briefcase. He looked around and then sat down on the other end of the seat where the woman with the red and white canvas sandals was sitting. He immediately unfolded a newspaper and obscured himself behind it. Julian's mother's elbow at once prodded insistently into his ribs. "Now you see why I won't ride on these buses by myself," she whispered.

The woman with the red and white canvas sandals had risen at the same time the Negro sat down and had gone further back in the bus and taken the seat of the woman who had got off. His mother leaned forward and cast her an approving look.

Julian rose, crossed the aisle, and sat down in the place of the woman with the canvas sandals. From this position, he looked serenely across at his mother. Her face had turned an angry red. He stared at her, making his eyes the eyes of a stranger. He felt his tension suddenly lift as if he had openly declared war on her.

He would have liked to get in conversation with the Negro and to talk with him about art or politics or any subject that would be above the comprehension of those around them, but the man remained entrenched behind his paper. He was either ignoring the change of seating or had never noticed it. There was no way for Julian to convey his sympathy.

His mother kept her eyes fixed reproachfully on his face. The woman with the protruding teeth was looking at him avidly as if he were a type of monster new to her.

"Do you have a light?" he asked the Negro.

Without looking away from his paper, the man reached in his pocket and handed him a packet of matches.

"Thanks," Julian said. For a moment he held the matches foolishly. A NO SMOKING sign looked down upon him from over the door. This alone would not have deterred him; he had no cigarettes. He had quit smoking some months before because he could not afford it. "Sorry," he muttered and handed back the matches. The Negro lowered the paper and gave him an annoyed look. He took the matches and raised the paper again.

His mother continued to gaze at him but she did not take advantage of his momentary discomfort. Her eyes retained their battered look. Her face seemed to be unnaturally red, as if her blood pressure had risen. Julian allowed no glimmer of sympathy to show on his face. Having got the advantage, he wanted desperately to keep it and carry it through. He would have liked to teach her a lesson that would last her a while, but there seemed no way to continue the point. The Negro refused to come out from behind his paper.

Julian folded his arms and looked stolidly before him, facing her but as if he did not see her, as if he had ceased to recognize her existence. He visualized a scene in which, the bus having reached their stop, he would remain in his seat and when she said, "Aren't you going to get off?" he would look at her as at a stranger who had rashly addressed him. The corner they got off on was usually deserted, but it was well lighted and it would not hurt her to walk by herself the four blocks to the Y. He decided to wait until the time came and then decide whether or not he would let her get off by herself. He would have to be at the Y at ten to bring her back, but he could leave her wondering if he was going to show up. There was no reason for her to think she could always depend on him.

He retired again into the high-ceilinged room sparsely settled with large pieces of antique furniture. His soul expanded momentarily but then he became aware of his mother across from him and the vision shriveled. He studied her coldly. Her feet in little pumps dangled like a child's and did not quite reach the floor. She was training on him an exaggerated look of reproach. He felt completely detached from her. At that moment he could with pleasure have slapped her as he would have slapped a particularly obnoxious child in his charge.

He began to imagine various unlikely ways by which he could teach her a lesson. He might make friends with some distinguished Negro professor or lawyer and bring him home to spend the evening. He would be entirely justified but her blood pressure would rise to 300. He could not push her to the extent of making her have a stroke, and moreover, he had never been successful at making any Negro friends. He had tried to strike up an acquaintance on the bus with some of the better types, with ones that looked like professors or ministers or lawyers. One morning he had sat down next to a distinguished-looking dark brown man who had answered his questions with a sonorous solemnity but who had turned out to be an undertaker. Another day he had sat down beside a cigar-smoking Negro with a diamond ring on his finger, but after a few stilted pleasantries, the Negro had rung the buzzer and risen, slipping two lottery tickets into Julian's hand as he climbed over him to leave.

He imagined his mother lying desperately ill and his being able to secure only a Negro doctor for her. He toyed with that idea for a few minutes and then dropped it for a momentary vision of himself participating as a sympathizer in a sit-in demonstration. This was possible but he did not linger with it. Instead, he approached the ultimate horror. He brought home a beautiful suspiciously Negroid woman. Prepare yourself, he said. There is nothing you can do about it. This is the woman I've chosen. She's intelligent, dignified, even good, and she's suffered and she hasn't thought it *fun*. Now persecute us, go ahead and persecute us. Drive her out of here, but remember, you're driving me too. His eyes were narrowed and through the indignation he had generated, he saw his mother across the aisle, purple-faced, shrunken to the dwarf-like proportions of her moral nature, sitting like a mummy beneath the ridiculous banner of her hat.

He was tilted out of his fantasy again as the bus stopped. The door opened with a sucking hiss and out of the dark a large, gaily dressed, sullen-looking colored woman got on with a little boy. The child, who might have been four, had on a short plaid suit and a Tyrolean hat with a blue feather in it. Julian hoped that he would sit down beside him and that the woman would push in beside his mother. He could think of no better arrangement.

As she waited for her tokens, the woman was surveying the seating possibilities—he hoped with the idea of sitting where she was least wanted. There was something familiar-looking about her but Julian could not place what it was. She was a giant of a woman. Her face was set not only to meet opposition but to seek it out. The downward tilt of her large lower lip was like a warning sign: DON'T TAMPER WITH ME. Her bulging figure was encased in a green crepe dress and her feet overflowed in red shoes. She had on a hideous hat. A purple velvet flap came down on one side of it and stood up on the other; the rest of it was green and looked like a cushion with the stuffing out. She carried a mammoth red pocketbook that bulged throughout as if it were stuffed with rocks.

To Julian's disappointment, the little boy climbed up on the empty seat beside his mother. His mother lumped all children, black and white, into the common category, "cute," and she thought little Negroes were on the whole cuter than little white children. She smiled at the little boy as he climbed on the seat.

Meanwhile the woman was bearing down upon the empty seat beside Julian. To his annoyance, she squeezed herself into it. He saw his mother's face change as the woman settled herself next to him and he realized with satisfaction that this was more objectionable to her than it was to him. Her face seemed almost gray and there was a look of dull recognition in her eyes, as if suddenly she had sickened at some awful confrontation. Julian saw that it was because she and the woman had, in a sense, swapped sons. Though his mother would not realize the symbolic significance of this, she would feel it. His amusement showed plainly on his face.

The woman next to him muttered something unintelligible to herself. He was conscious of a kind of bristling next to him, muted growling like that of an angry cat. He could not see anything but the red pocketbook upright on the bulging green thighs. He visualized the woman as she had stood waiting for her tokens—the ponderous figure, rising from the red shoes upward over the solid hips, the mammoth bosom, the haughty face, to the green and purple hat.

His eyes widened.

The vision of the two hats, identical, broke upon him with the radiance of a brilliant sunrise. His face was suddenly lit with joy. He could not believe that Fate had thrust upon his mother such a lesson. He gave a loud chuckle so that she would look at him and see that he saw. She turned her eyes on him slowly. The blue in them seemed to have turned a bruised purple. For a moment he had an uncomfortable sense of her innocence, but it lasted only a second before principle rescued him. Justice entitled him to laugh. His grin hardened until it said to her as plainly as if he were saying aloud: Your punishment exactly fits your pettiness. This should teach you a permanent lesson.

Her eyes shifted to the woman. She seemed unable to bear looking at him and to find the woman preferable. He became conscious again of the bristling presence at his side. The woman was rumbling like a volcano about to become active. His mother's mouth began to twitch slightly at one corner. With a sinking heart, he saw incipient signs of recovery on her face and realized that this was going to strike her suddenly as funny and was going to be no lesson at all. She kept her eyes on the woman and an amused smile came over her face as if the woman were a monkey that had stolen her hat. The little Negro was looking up at her with large fascinated eyes. He had been trying to attract her attention for some time.

"Carver!" the woman said suddenly. "Come heah!"

When he saw that the spotlight was on him at last, Carver drew his feet up and turned himself toward Julian's mother and giggled.

"Carver!" the woman said. "You heah me? Come heah!"

Carver slid down from the seat but remained squatting with his back against the base of it, his head turned slyly around toward Julian's mother, who was smiling at him. The woman reached a hand across the aisle and snatched him to her. He righted himself and hung backwards on her knees, grinning at Julian's mother. "Isn't he cute?" Julian's mother said to the woman with the protruding teeth.

"I reckon he is," the woman said without conviction.

The Negress yanked him upright but he eased out of her grip and shot across the aisle and scrambled, giggling wildly, onto the seat beside his love.

"I think he likes me," Julian's mother said, and smiled at the woman. It was the smile she used when she was being particularly gracious to an inferior. Julian saw everything lost. The lesson had rolled off her like rain on a roof.

The woman stood up and yanked the little boy off the seat as if she were snatching him from contagion. Julian could feel the rage in her at having no weapon like his mother's smile. She gave the child a sharp slap across his leg. He howled once and then thrust his head into her stomach and kicked his feet against her shins. "Behave," she said vehemently.

The bus stopped and the Negro who had been reading the newspaper got off. The woman moved over and set the little boy down with a thump between herself and Julian. She held him firmly by the knee. In a moment he put his hands in front of his face and peeped at Julian's mother through his fingers.

"I see yooooooooo!" she said and put her hand in front of her face and peeped at him.

The woman slapped his hand down. "Quit yo' foolishness," she said, "before I knock the living Jesus out of you!"

Julian was thankful that the next stop was theirs. He reached up and pulled the cord. The woman reached up and pulled it at the same time.

Oh my God, he thought. He had the terrible intuition that when they got off the bus together, his mother would open her purse and give the little boy a nickel. The gesture would be as natural to her as breathing. The bus stopped and the woman got up and lunged to the front, dragging the child, who wished to stay on, after her. Julian and his mother got up and followed. As they neared the door, Julian tried to relieve her of her pocketbook.

"No," she murmured, "I want to give the little boy a nickel."

"No!" Julian hissed. "No!"

She smiled down at the child and opened her bag. The bus door opened and the woman picked him up by the arm and descended with him, hanging at her hip. Once in the street she set him down and shook him.

Julian's mother had to close her purse while she got down the bus step but as soon as her feet were on the ground, she opened it again and began to rummage inside. "I can't find but a penny," she whispered, "but it looks like a new one."

"Don't do it!" Julian said fiercely between his teeth. There was a streetlight on the corner and she hurried to get under it so that she could better see into her pocketbook. The woman was heading off rapidly down the street with the child still hanging backward on her hand.

"Oh little boy!" Julian's mother called and took a few quick steps and caught up with them just beyond the lamppost. "Here's a bright new penny for you," and she held out the coin, which shone bronze in the dim light.

The huge woman turned and for a moment stood, her shoulders lifted and her face frozen with frustrated rage, and stared at Julian's mother. Then all at once she seemed to explode like a piece of machinery that had been given one ounce of pressure too much. Julian saw the black fist swing out with the red pocketbook. He shut his eyes and cringed as he heard the woman shout, "He don't take nobody's pennies!" When he opened his eyes, the woman was disappearing down the street with the little boy staring wide-eyed over her shoulder. Julian's mother was sitting on the sidewalk.

"I told you not to do that," Julian said angrily. "I told you not to do that!"

He stood over her for a minute, gritting his teeth. Her legs were stretched out in front of her and her hat was on her lap. He squatted down and looked her in the face. It was totally expressionless. "You got exactly what you deserved," he said. "Now get up."

He picked up her pocketbook and put what had fallen out back in it. He picked the hat up off her lap. The penny caught his eye on the sidewalk and he picked that up and let it drop before her eyes into the purse. Then he stood up and leaned over and held his hands out to pull her up. She remained immobile. He sighed. Rising above them on either side were black apartment buildings, marked with irregular rectangles of light. At the end of the block a man came out of a door and walked off in the opposite direction. "All right," he said, "suppose somebody happens by and wants to know why you're sitting on the sidewalk?"

She took the hand and, breathing hard, pulled heavily up on it and then stood for a moment, swaying slightly as if the spots of light in the darkness were circling around her. Her eyes, shadowed and confused, finally settled on his face. He did not try to conceal his irritation. "I hope this teaches you a lesson," he said. She leaned forward and her eyes raked his face. She seemed trying to determine his identity. Then, as if she found nothing familiar about him, she started off with a headlong movement in the wrong direction.

"Aren't you going on to the Y?" he asked.

"Home," she muttered.

"Well, are we walking?"

For answer she kept going. Julian followed along, his hands behind him. He saw no reason to let the lesson she had had go without backing it up with an explanation of its meaning. She might as well be made to understand what had happened to her. "Don't think that was just an uppity Negro woman," he said. "That was the whole colored race which will no longer take your condescending pennies. That was your black double. She can wear the same hat as you, and to be sure," he added gratuitously (because he thought it was funny), "it looked better on her than it did on you. What all this means," he said, "is that the old world is gone. The old manners are obsolete and your graciousness is not worth a damn." He thought bitterly of the house that had been lost for him. "You aren't who you think you are," he said.

She continued to plow ahead, paying no attention to him. Her hair had come undone on one side. She dropped her pocketbook and took no notice. He stooped and picked it up and handed it to her but she did not take it.

"You needn't act as if the world had come to an end," he said, "because it hasn't. From now on you've got to live in a new world and face a few realities for a change. Buck up," he said, "it won't kill you."

She was breathing fast.

"Let's wait on the bus," he said.

"Home," she said thickly.

"I hate to see you behave like this," he said. "Just like a child. I should be able to expect more of you." He decided to stop where he was and make her stop and wait for a bus. "I'm not going any farther," he said, stopping. "We're going on the bus."

She continued to go on as if she had not heard him. He took a few steps and caught her arm and stopped her. He looked into her face and caught his breath. He was looking into a face he had never seen before. "Tell Grandpa to come get me," she said.

He stared, stricken.

"Tell Caroline to come get me," she said.

Stunned, he let her go and she lurched forward again, walking as if one leg were shorter than the other. A tide of darkness seemed to be sweeping her from him. "Mother!" he cried. "Darling, sweetheart, wait!" Crumpling, she fell to the pavement. He dashed forward and fell at her side, crying, "Mamma, Mamma!" He turned her over. Her face was fiercely distorted. One eye, large and staring, moved slightly to the left as if it had become unmoored. The other remained fixed on him, raked his face again, found nothing and closed.

"Wait here, wait here!" he cried and jumped up and began to run for help toward a cluster of lights he saw in the distance ahead of him. "Help, help!" he shouted, but his voice was thin, scarcely a thread of sound. The lights drifted farther away the faster he ran and his feet moved numbly as if they carried him nowhere. The tide of darkness seemed to sweep him back to her, postponing from moment to moment his entry into the world of guilt and sorrow.

◩ ◩ ◩

Writing Exercises

1. Write a short story on a three-by-five card or the back of a postcard. Notice that if you're going to manage a conflict, crisis, and resolution in this small space, you'll have to introduce the conflict immediately.

2. For this exercise, you will create what Jerome Stern calls the "Bear at the Door" scene. In this scene, your character must have an external problem. ("Honey, there's a bear at the door.") The problem should be significant. ("Honey, it's huge.") The problem should be pressing. ("Honey, I think it's trying to get in.") And the problem should force your character to act. ("Honey, do something!") Your character should have an internal conflict that affects her/his ability to deal with this problem—the bear within him/herself.

   a. Come up with a list of external conflicts, avoiding the overly dramatic or overly mundane. Choose the most intriguing one.

   b. Write a scene that places a character in the middle of the external conflict. Complicate the situation with the character's internal needs and desires.

3. For each character in one of your stories-in-progress, list all the predictable actions each could take to keep the plot moving. Now try mixing up the characters and the actions and see if you come up with a more interesting and surprising plot.

4. Robert Olen Butler wrote a collection of short stories, *Tabloid Dreams*, that was inspired by headlines and articles in supermarket tabloids (e.g., "Jealous Husband Returns in Form of Parrot"). Buy a tabloid magazine of your own. Find the silliest story in it. Use it as the jumping off point for a short, serious story.

5. Imagine an intriguing circumstance, or think of something puzzling you witnessed, heard, or read about in the newspaper. The circumstance should have no obvious explanation. (See page 11, "The Incongruity," about three women, one with a baby stroller, at a supermarket pay phone very late at night.)

   Write three very brief stories (200 words), each offering a different explanation for the same circumstance. Each story should have different characters and a different plot. Consider that in each story this same circumstance may function within the story in different ways: In one story, it may be the opening scene; in another, it might appear at the end.

6. Imagine some deceit growing out of control. Your character "borrowed" something without asking, and now it's lost or broken; the babysitter was distracted on the phone, and now one of the kids is missing; a character told a lie that seemed harmless. The little lie is now big; it has come back to haunt him.

   Now crank things up another notch: The lost item is irreplaceable; the missing child has a medical condition, etc. How might this trouble be related to the character's desire? She was desperate to impress others; he was fixated on getting into medical school. Take the situation and go with it.

7. Every student should come to class with what he or she considers to be a good first line for a story—either invented or lifted from somewhere. Students can write these lines on the board, discuss them, and then vote on one line for the entire class to use. Everyone will begin a story using the same line. After writing for a short period of time, students may stop and read their exercises aloud in order to see how different people have used the line differently and in what various directions the stories have gone and might go.

8

CALL ME ISHMAEL
Point of View

+ *Who Speaks?*

+ *To Whom?*

+ *In What Form?*

+ *At What Distance?*

+ *Consistency: A Final Caution*

Point of view is the most complex element of fiction. We can label and analyze it in a number of different ways, but however we describe it, point of view ultimately concerns the relationship among writer, characters, and reader.

The first thing to do is to set aside the common use of the phrase "point of view" as synonymous with "opinion," as in *It's my point of view that they all ought to be shot.* Rather than thinking of point of view as an opinion or belief, begin instead with the more literal synonym of "vantage point." *Who* is standing *where* to watch the scene?

Since we are dealing with words on a page, these questions might be better translated as: *Who speaks? To whom? In what form? At what distance from the action?*

Who Speaks?

The primary point-of-view decision that you as author must make before you can set down the first sentence of the story is *person.* This is the simplest and crudest subdivision that must be made in deciding who speaks. The story can be told

- *in the third person* (she walked out into the harsh sunlight),
- *in the second person* (you walked out into the harsh sunlight),
- or *in the first person* (I walked out into the harsh sunlight).

From the reader's perspective, third- and second-person stories are told by an author; first-person stories, by the character acting as "I."

THIRD PERSON

Third-person point of view, in which the author is telling the story, can be subdivided again according to the degree of knowledge the author assumes.

Omniscience. The *omniscient author* has total knowledge and tells us directly what we are supposed to think. As omniscient author you are God. You can

1. objectively report the action of the story;
2. go into the mind of any character;
3. interpret for us that character's appearance, speech, actions, and thoughts, even if the character cannot do so;
4. move freely in time or space to give us a panoramic, telescopic, microscopic, or historical view; tell us what has happened elsewhere or in the past or what will happen in the future; and
5. provide general reflections, judgments, and truths.

In all these aspects, we will accept what the omniscient author tells us. If you tell us that Ruth is a good woman, that Jeremy doesn't really understand his own motives, that the moon is going to explode in four hours, and that everybody will be better off for it, we will believe you. Here is a paragraph that blatantly exhibits all five of these areas of knowledge.

(1) Joe glared at the screaming baby. (2) Frightened by his scowl, the baby gulped and screamed louder. I hate that thing, Joe thought. (3) But it was not really hatred that he felt. (4) Only two years ago he himself had screamed like that. (5) Children can't tell hatred from fear.

This illustration is awkwardly compressed, but authors well in control of their craft can move easily from one area of knowledge to another. In the first scene of *War and Peace*, Tolstoy describes Anna Scherer.

To be an enthusiast had become her social vocation, and sometimes even when she did not feel like it, she became enthusiastic in order not to disappoint the expectations of those who knew her. The subdued smile which, though it did not suit her faded features, always played around her lips, expressed as in a spoiled child, a continual consciousness of her charming defect, which she neither wished, nor could, nor considered it necessary to correct.

In two sentences Tolstoy tells us what is in Anna's mind, what the expectations of her acquaintances are, what she looks like, what suits her, what she can and cannot do; and he offers a general reflection on spoiled children.

The omniscient voice is the voice of the classical epic ("And Meleager, far-off, knew nothing of this, but felt his vitals burning with fever"), of the Bible ("And all the people departed, every man to his house; and David returned to bless his house") and of most nineteenth-century novels ("Tito put out his hand to help him, and so strangely quick are men's souls that in this moment, when he began to feel that his atonement was accepted, he had a darting thought of the irksome efforts it entailed"). But it is one of the manifestations of modern literature's movement downward in class from heroic to common characters, from external action to the psychological action of the mind, that authors of realistic fiction have largely avoided the godlike stance of the omniscient author and have chosen to restrict themselves to fewer areas of knowledge.

Limited Omniscience.　　The *limited omniscient* viewpoint is one in which the author may move with some, but not all, of the omniscient author's freedom. The most commonly used form of the limited omniscient point of view is one in which the author can see events objectively and also grants himself or herself access to the mind of one character, but *not* to the minds of the others, nor to any explicit powers of judgment. Limited omniscience is particularly useful for the short story because it very quickly establishes the point-of-view character or *means of perception*. The short story is so compressed a form that there is rarely time or space to develop more than one consciousness. Staying with external observation and one character's thoughts helps control the focus and avoid awkward point-of-view shifts. A further advantage of limited omniscience is that it mimics our individual experience of life, that is, our own inability to penetrate the minds and motivations of others, which can lead to the kinds of conflicts or struggles for connection that inspire much fiction.

Limited omniscience is also frequently used for the novel, as in Gail Godwin's *The Odd Woman*.

It was ten o'clock on the evening of the same day, and the permanent residents of the household on the mountain were restored to routines and sobriety. Jane, on the other hand, sat by herself in the kitchen, a glass of Scotch before her on the cleanly wiped table, going deeper and deeper into a mood she could recognize only as unfamiliar. She could not describe it; it was both frightening and satisfying. It was like letting go and being taken somewhere. She tried to trace it back. When, exactly, had it started?

It is clear here that the author has limited her omniscience. She is not going to tell us the ultimate truth about Jane's soul, nor is she going to define for us the unfamiliar mood that the character herself cannot define. The author has the facts at her disposal, and she has Jane's thoughts, and that is all.

The advantage of the limited omniscient voice is immediacy. Here, because we are not allowed to know more than Jane does about her own thoughts and feelings, we grope *with* her toward understanding. In the process, a contract has been made between the author and the reader, and this contract must not now be broken. If at this point the author should step in and answer Jane's question "When, exactly, had it started?" with "Jane was never to remember this, but in fact it had started one afternoon when she was two years old," we would feel it as an abrupt and uncalled-for *authorial intrusion*. Nevertheless, within the limits the author has set herself, there is fluidity and a range of possibilities.

The Objective Author.   As an objective author, you restrict your knowledge to the external facts that might be observed by a human witness; to the senses of sight, sound, smell, taste, and touch. In the story "Hills Like White Elephants," Ernest Hemingway reports what is said and done by a quarreling couple, both without any direct revelation of the characters' thoughts and without comment.

> The American and the girl with him sat at a table in the shade, outside the building. It was very hot and the express from Barcelona would come in forty minutes. It stopped at this junction for two minutes and went on to Madrid.
> "What should we drink?" the girl asked. She had taken off her hat and put it on the table.
> "It's pretty hot," the man said.
> "Let's drink beer."
> "Dos cervezas," the man said into the curtain.
> "Big ones?" a woman asked from the doorway.
> "Yes. Two big ones."
> The woman brought two glasses of beer and two felt pads. She put the felt pads and the beer glasses on the table and looked at the man and the girl. The girl was looking off at the line of hills. They were white in the sun and the country was brown and dry.

In the course of this story we learn, entirely by inference, that the girl is pregnant and that she feels herself coerced by the man into having an abortion. Neither pregnancy nor abortion is ever mentioned. The narrative remains clipped, austere, and external. What does Hemingway gain by this pretense of objective reporting? The reader is allowed to discover what is

304 CALL ME ISHMAEL

really happening. The characters avoid the subject, prevaricate, and pretend, but they betray their real meanings and feelings through gestures, repetitions, and slips of the tongue. The reader, focus directed by the author, learns by inference, as in life, so that we finally have the pleasure of knowing the characters better than they know themselves.

SECOND PERSON

First- and third-person points of view are most common in literature; the second person remains an idiosyncratic and experimental form, but it is worth mentioning because several contemporary authors have been attracted to its possibilities.

Lorrie Moore's story "How to Become a Writer" illustrates how a reader is made into a character through second person.

> First, try to be something, anything, else. A movie star/astronaut. A movie star/missionary. A movie star/kindergarten teacher. President of the World. Fail miserably. It is best if you fail at an early age—say, fourteen. Early, critical disillusionment is necessary so that at fifteen you can write long haiku sentences about thwarted desire. It is a pond, a cherry blossom, a wind brushing against sparrow wing leaving for mountain. Count the syllables. Show it to your mom.

Here the author assigns you, the reader, specific characteristics and reactions, and thereby—assuming that you go along with her characterization of you—pulls you deeper and more intimately into the story.

Some writers choose second person to depict trauma, as its slight sense of detachment mutes possible melodrama and mirrors the sense of shock; others may use it to make a highly individual experience feel more universal.

The second person is the basic mode of the story *only when a character* is referred to as *you*. When one character addresses "you" in letter or monologue, that narrative is still told by the "I" character. When an omniscient author addresses the reader as *you* (*You will remember that John Doderring was left dangling on the cliff at Dover*), this is called "direct address" and does not alter the basic third-person mode of the piece. Only when "you" becomes an actor in the drama, so designated by the author, is the story or novel written in second person.

Unlike third or first person, second person draws attention to itself, and it can also be difficult to maintain—it's easy to slip back into third or first person. Also, some readers may resist second person because they don't identify with the character they are supposed to be in the story. (*You go into a bar. You get very, very drunk.*) It is unlikely that the second person will ever become a major mode of narration as the first and third person are, but for precisely that reason you may find it an attractive experiment.

FIRST PERSON

A story is told in the first person when one of its characters relates the story's action and events. The term "narrator" is sometimes loosely used to refer to any teller of a tale, but strictly speaking a story has a narrator only when it is told in the first person by one of the characters. This character may be the protagonist, the *I* telling *my* story, in which case that character is a *central narrator* (as in "Who's Irish?" at the end of this chapter); or the character may be telling a story about someone else, in which case he or she is a *peripheral narrator*.

In either case it's important to indicate early which kind of narrator we have so that we know who the story's protagonist is, as in the first paragraph of Alan Sillitoe's "The Loneliness of the Long-Distance Runner."

> As soon as I got to Borstal they made me a long-distance cross-country runner. I suppose they thought I was just the build for it because I was long and skinny for my age (and still am) and in any case I didn't mind it much, to tell you the truth, because running had always been made much of in our family, especially running away from the police.

The focus here is immediately thrown on the *I* of the story, and we expect that *I* to be the central character whose desires and decisions impel the action.

But from the opening lines of Amy Bloom's "Silver Water," it is the sister, Rose, who is brought alive through the description of her marvelous singing voice, while the narrator, Violet, is established as an observer and protector of her subject.

> My sister's voice was like mountain water in a silver pitcher, the clear, blue beauty of it cools you and lifts you up beyond your heat, beyond your body. After we went to see *La Traviata*, when she was fourteen and I was twelve, she elbowed me in the parking lot and said, "Check this out." And she opened her mouth unnaturally wide and her voice came out, so crystalline and bright, that all the departing operagoers stood frozen by their cars, unable to take out their keys or open their doors until she had finished and then they cheered like hell.
>
> That's what I like to remember and that's the story I told to all of her therapists. I wanted them to know her, to know that who they saw was not all there was to see.

The central narrator is always, as the term implies, at the center of the action; the peripheral narrator may be in virtually any position that is not the center. He or she may be the second most important character in the story, (as in the Amy Bloom story above) or may appear to be a bystander for much of the story. It is even possible to make the first-person narrator plural, as William Faulkner does in "A Rose for Emily" or as June Spence does in "Missing Women" (which is included at the end of this chapter). In these two examples the story is told by a narrator identified only as one of "us," the people of the town in which the action has taken place.

That a narrator may be either central or peripheral, that a character may tell either his or her own story or someone else's, is both commonly assumed and obviously logical. But the author and editor Rust Hills, in his book *Writing in General and the Short Story in Particular*, takes interesting and persuasive exception to this idea. When point of view fails, Hills argues, it is always because the perception we are using for the course of the story is different from that of the character who is moved or changed by the action. Even when a narrator seems to be a peripheral observer and the story is "about" someone else, in fact it is the narrator who is changed, and must be, in order for us to be satisfied by our emotional identification with him or her.

> This, I believe, is what will always be the case in successful fiction: that either the character moved by the action will be the point-of-view character, or else the point-of-view character will *become* the character moved by the action. Call it Hills' Law.

Obviously, this view does not mean that we have to throw out the useful fictional device of the peripheral narrator. Hills uses the familiar example of *The Great Gatsby* to illustrate his meaning. Nick Carroway as a peripheral narrator observes and tells the story of Jay Gatsby, but by the end of the book it is Nick's life that has been changed by what he has observed.

Anton Chekhov (as paraphrased by Tobias Wolff) cautioned, "The narrator cannot escape the *consequences* of the story he is telling. If he does, it's not a story. It's an anecdote, a tale, or something else."

Central or peripheral, a first-person narrator is a character, so it's vital to remember that she or he has all the limitations of a human being and cannot be omniscient. The narrator is confined to reporting what she or he could realistically know. More than that, although the narrator may certainly interpret actions, deliver dictums, and predict the future, these remain the fallible opinions of a human being; we are not bound to accept them as we are bound to accept the interpretations, truths, and predictions of the omniscient author. You may want us to accept the narrator's word, and then the most difficult part of your task, and the touchstone of your story's success, will be to convince us to trust and believe the narrator. On the other hand, it may be an important part of your purpose that we should reject the narrator's opinions and form our own. If the answer to *Who speaks?* is *a child, a bigot, a jealous lover, an animal, a schizophrenic, a murderer, a liar*, the implications may be that the narrator speaks with limitations we do not necessarily share. To the extent that the narrator displays and betrays such limitations, she or he is an *unreliable narrator*.

Here is a woman, imperious and sour, who tells her own story.

> I have always, always, tried to do right and help people. It's a part of my community duty and my duty to God. But I can tell you right now, you don't never gets no thanks for it! . . .

Use to be a big ole fat sloppy woman live cross the street went to my church. She had a different man in her house with her every month! She got mad at me for tellin the minister on her about all them men! Now, I'm doin my duty and she got mad! I told her somebody had to be the pillar of the community and if it had to be me, so be it! She said I was the pill of the community and a lotta other things, but I told the minister that too and pretty soon she was movin away. Good! I like a clean community!

J. California Cooper, "The Watcher"

We mistrust every judgment this woman makes, but we are also aware of an author we do trust, manipulating the narrator's tone to expose her. The outburst is fraught with ironies, but because the narrator is unaware of them, they are directed against herself. We can hear that interference is being dressed up as duty. When she brags in cliché, we agree that she's more of a pill than a pillar. When she appropriates biblical language—"so be it!"—we suspect that even the minister might agree. Punctuation itself, the self-righteous overuse of the exclamation point, suggests her inappropriate intensity. It occurs to us we'd probably like the look of that "big ole fat sloppy" neighbor; and we know for certain why that neighbor moved away.

In this case the narrator is wholly unreliable, and we're unlikely to accept any judgment she could make. But it is also possible for a narrator to be reliable in some areas of value and unreliable in others. Mark Twain's Huckleberry Finn is a famous case in point. Here Huck has decided to free his friend Jim, and he is astonished that Tom Sawyer is going along with the plan.

Here was a boy that was respectable, and well brung up; and had a character to lose; and folks at home that had characters; and he was bright and not leather-headed; and knowing and not ignorant; and not mean, but kind; and yet here he was, without any more pride, or rightness, or feeling, than to stoop to this business, and make himself a shame, and his family a shame, before everybody. I couldn't understand it, no way at all.

The extended irony in this excerpt is that slavery should be defended by the respectable, the bright, the knowing, the kind, and those of character. We reject Huck's assessment of Tom as well as the implied assessment of himself as worth so little that he has nothing to lose by freeing a slave. Huck's moral instincts are better than he himself can understand. (Notice, incidentally, how Huck's lack of education is communicated by word choice and syntax and how sparse the misspellings are.) So author and reader are in intellectual opposition to Huck the narrator, but morally identify with him. Similarly reliable "unreliable" narrators, whose distorted views reveal a strangely accurate portrait of the social institutions that confine them, include Chief Bromden, the narrator of Ken Kesey's *One Flew Over the Cuckoo's Nest*, and the "hysterical" wife and patient, forbidden to write, who relates Charlotte Perkins Gilman's 1892 story "The Yellow Wallpaper."

THE TRUTH IS NOT DISTORTED HERE, but rather a certain distortion is used to get at the truth.

FLANNERY O'CONNOR

The unreliable narrator—who has become one of the most popular characters in modern fiction—is far from a newcomer to literature and in fact predates fiction. Every drama contains characters who speak for themselves and present their own cases, and from whom we are partly or wholly distanced in one area of value or another. So we admire Oedipus's intellect but are exasperated by his lack of intuition, we identify with Othello's morality but mistrust his logic, we trust Mr. Spock's brain but not his heart, we count on Bridget Jones's wit, as revealed in her diary, but not her judgment. As these examples suggest, the unreliable narrator often presents us with an example of consistent inconsistency and always presents us with dramatic irony, because we always "know" more than he or she does about the characters, the events, and the significance of both.

THERE SHOULD BE THE ILLUSION that it's the character's point of view, when in fact it isn't; it's really the narrator who is there but who doesn't make herself...known in that role....What I really want is that intimacy in which the reader is under the impression that he isn't really reading this; that he is participating in it as he goes along.

TONI MORRISON

To Whom?

In choosing a point of view, the author implies an identity not only for the teller of the tale, but also for the intended audience. To whom is the story being told?

THE READER

Most fiction is addressed to a literary convention, "the reader." When we open a book, we tacitly accept our role as a member of this unspecified audience. After all, the most common assumption of the tale-teller, whether omniscient author or narrating character, is that the reader is an open and amenable Everyman, and that the telling needs no justification.

ANOTHER CHARACTER

More specifically, the story may be told to *another character*, or *characters*, in which case we as readers "overhear" it; the teller of the tale does not acknowledge us even by implication.

In the *epistolary* novel or story, the narrative consists entirely of letters written from one character to another, or between characters. The recipient of the letter may be a stranger or a close friend or relative, like the near-annual readers of *The Christmas Letters*, by Lee Smith.

> First, my apologies for not writing a Christmas letter last year (for not returning calls, for not returning letters, etc.). The fact is, for a long time I couldn't do anything. Not a damn thing. Nothing. I was shell-shocked, immobilized. This was followed by a period when I did *too many things*. Marybeth, who has been through it, wrote to me about this time, saying, "Don't make any big decisions"—very good advice, and I wish I'd followed it. Instead, I agreed to a separation agreement, then to a quick no-fault divorce, then to Sandy's plan of selling the house P.D.Q. I just wanted everything *over with*—the way you feel that sudden irresistible urge to clean out your closet sometimes.

Or the convention of the story may be that of a monologue, spoken aloud by one character to another.

> May I, *monsieur*, offer my services without running the risk of intruding? I fear you may not be able to make yourself understood by the worthy ape who presides over the fate of this establishment. In fact, he speaks nothing but Dutch. Unless you authorize me to plead your case, he will not guess that you want gin.
>
> Albert Camus, *The Fall*

Again, the possible variations are infinite: The narrator may speak in intimate confessional to a friend or lover, or may present his case to a jury or a mob; she may be writing a highly technical report of the welfare situation, designed to hide her emotions; he may be pouring out his heart in a love letter he knows (and we know) he will never send.

In any of these cases, the convention employed is the opposite of that employed in a story told to "the reader." The listener as well as the teller is involved in the action; the assumption is not that we readers are there but that we are not. We are eavesdroppers, with all the ambiguous intimacy that position implies.

THE SELF

An even greater intimacy is implied if the character's story is as secret as a diary or as private as a mind, addressed to *the self* and not intended to be heard by anyone inside or outside the action.

In a *diary* or *journal*, the convention is that the thoughts are written but not expected to be read by anyone except the writer.

> Tuesday 3 January
> 9 A.M. Ugh. Cannot face thought of going to work. Only thing which makes it tolerable is thought of seeing Daniel again, but even that is inadvisable since I am fat, have spot on chin, and desire only to sit on cushion eating chocolate and watching Xmas specials. It seems wrong and unfair that Christmas, with its stressful and unmanageable financial and emotional challenges, should first be forced upon one wholly against one's will, then rudely snatched away just when one is starting to get into it.
>
> Helen Fielding, *Bridget Jones's Diary*

The protagonist here is clearly using her diary to vent her feelings and does not intend it to be read by anyone else. Still, she has deliberately externalized her secret thoughts in a journal.

INTERIOR MONOLOGUE

Because the author has the power to enter a character's mind, the reader also has the power to eavesdrop on that character's thoughts. Overheard thoughts are generally of two kinds, of which the more common is *interior monologue*, the convention being that we follow that character's thoughts in their sequence.

> I must organize myself. I must, as they say, pull myself together, dump this cat from my lap, stir—yes, resolve, move, do. But do what? My will is like the rosy dustlike light in this room: soft, diffuse, and gently comforting. It lets me do...anything...nothing. My ears hear what they happen to; I eat what's put before me; my eyes see what blunders into them; my thoughts are not thoughts, they are dreams. I'm empty or I'm full... depending; and I cannot choose. I sink my claws in Tick's fur and scratch the bones of his back until his rear rises amorously. Mr. Tick, I murmur, I must organize myself, I must pull myself together. And Mr. Tick rolls over on his belly, all ooze.
>
> William H. Gass, "In the Heart of the Heart of the Country"

This interior monologue ranges, as human thoughts do, from sense impression to self-admonishment, from cat to light to eyes and ears, from specific to general and back again. But the logical connections between these things are all provided; the mind "thinks" logically and grammatically as if the character were trying to express himself.

STREAM OF CONSCIOUSNESS

Stream of consciousness acknowledges the fact that the human mind does not operate with the order and clarity of the monologue just quoted. Even what little we know of its operations makes clear that it skips, elides, makes and breaks images, leaps faster and further than any mere sentence can suggest. Any mind at any moment is simultaneously accomplishing dozens of tasks that cannot be conveyed simultaneously. As you read this sentence, part of your mind is following the sense of it; part of your mind is directing your hand to hold the book open; part of it is twisting your spine into a more comfortable position; part of it is still lingering on the last interesting image of this text, Mr. Tick rolling over on his belly, which reminds you of a cat you had once that was also *all ooze*, which reminds you that you're nearly out of milk and have to finish this chapter before the store closes—and so forth.

In *Ulysses*, James Joyce tried to catch the speed and multiplicity of the mind with the technique that has come to be known as stream of consciousness. The device is difficult and in many ways thankless: Since the speed of thought is so much faster than that of writing or speaking, and stream of consciousness tries to suggest the process as well as the content of the mind, *it requires a much more—not less—rigorous selection and arrangement* than ordinary grammar requires. But Joyce and a very few other writers have handled stream of consciousness as an ebullient and exciting way of capturing the mind.

> Yes because he never did a thing like that before as ask to get his breakfast in bed with a couple of eggs since the City Arms hotel when he used to be pretending to be laid up with a sick voice doing his highness to make himself interesting to that old faggot Mrs. Riordan that he thought he had a great leg of and she never left us a farthing all for masses for herself...
>
> James Joyce, *Ulysses*

The preceding two examples, of interior monologue and stream of consciousness, respectively, are written in the first person, so that we overhear the minds of narrator characters. We may also overhear the thoughts of the characters through the third-person omniscient and limited omniscient authors, as in John Edgar Wideman's *tour de force* story "The Tambourine Lady." Here, Wideman succeeds in the challenging fusion of third-person narrative and stream of consciousness, so that although the answer to the question "who speaks?" is technically "the author," nevertheless we are aware of the point-of-view character speaking to herself in rapid-fire associative thought:

> ...She thinks about how long it takes to get to the end of your prayers, how the world might be over and gone while you are still saying the words to yourself. Words her mama taught her, words her mama said her mother had taught her so somebody would always be saying them world without end amen. So God would not forget his children...

In What Form?

The form of the story also contributes to the overall point of view. That form may announce itself as a generalized *story*, either *written* or *spoken*; or it may suggest *reportage, confessional, interior monologue,* or *stream of consciousness*; or it may be overtly identified as *monologue, oratory, journal,* or *diary*. This list is not exhaustive; you can tell your story in the form of a catalog or a television commercial as long as you can also contrive to give it the form of a story.

Form is important to point of view because the form in which a story is told indicates the degree of self-consciousness on the part of the teller. This will in turn affect the language chosen, the intimacy of the relationship, and the honesty of the telling. An account that purports to be a character's thought will imply more spontaneity than a spoken one, which in turn will seem more spontaneous than one deliberately written down. A narrator writing a letter to his grandmother may be less honest than he is when he tells the same facts aloud to his friend.

Certain relationships established by the narrative between teller and audience make certain forms more likely than others, but almost any combination of answers is possible to the questions: *Who speaks? To whom? In what form?* If you are speaking as an omniscient author to the literary convention of "the reader," we may assume that you are using the convention of "written story" as your form. But you might say:

> Wait, step over here a minute. What's this in the corner, stuffed down between the bedpost and the wall?

If you do this, you slip at least momentarily into the different convention of the spoken word—the effect is that we are drawn more immediately into the scene—and the point of view of the whole is slightly altered. A central narrator might be thinking, and therefore "talking to herself," while actually angrily addressing her thoughts to another character. Conversely, one character might be writing a letter to another but letting the conscious act of writing deteriorate into a betrayal of his own secret thoughts. Any complexities such as these will alter and inform the total point of view.

At What Distance?

As with the chemist at her microscope and the lookout in his tower, fictional point of view always involves the *distance*, close or far, of the perceiver from the thing perceived. *Authorial distance*, sometimes called *psychic distance*, is the degree to which we as readers feel on the one hand intimacy and identification with, or on the other hand detachment and alienation from, the characters.

When desired, a sense of distance may be increased through the use of abstract nouns, summary, typicality, and apparent objectivity. Such techniques, which in other contexts might be seen as writing flaws, are employed in the following passage purposely to detach readers from characters.

> It started in the backyards. At first the men concentrated on heat and smoke, and on dangerous thrusts with long forks. Their wives gave them aprons in railroad stripes, with slogans on the front—*Hot Stuff, The Boss*—to spur them on. Then it began to get mixed up who should do the dishes, and you can't fall back on paper plates forever, and around that time the wives got tired of making butterscotch brownies and jello salads with grated carrots in them and wanted to make money instead, and one thing led to another.

> Margaret Atwood, "Simmering"

Conversely, you can achieve closeness and sympathy with concrete detail, scene, a character's thoughts, and so forth.

> She dreams she does not already have three children. A squeeze around the flowers in her hands chokes off three and four and five years of breath. Instantly she is ashamed and frightened in her superstition. She looks for the first time at the preacher, forces humility into her eyes, as if she believes he is, in fact, a man of God. She can imagine God, a small black boy, timidly pulling the preacher's coattail.

> Alice Walker, "Roselily"

Or a combination of techniques may make us feel simultaneously sympathetic and detached—a frequent effect of comedy—as in this example:

> I'm a dishwasher in a restaurant. I'm not trying to impress anybody. I'm not bragging. It's just what I do. It's not the glamorous job people make it out to be. Sure, you make a lot of dough and everybody looks up to you and respects you, but then again there's a lot of responsibility. It weighs on you. It wears on you. Everybody wants to be a dishwasher these days, I guess, but they've got an idealistic view of it.

> Robert McBrearty, "The Dishwasher"

As author you may ask us to identify completely with one character and to-tally condemn another. One character may judge another harshly while you as author suggest that we should qualify that judgment. If there is also a narrator, that narrator may think himself morally superior while behind his back you make sure that we will think him morally deficient.

The one relationship in which there must not be any distance, however, is between author and reader.

It is a frustrating experience for many beginning (and established) authors to find that although they meant the protagonist to appear sensitive, their readers find him self-pitying; although the author meant her to be witty, the readers find her vulgar. When this happens there is a failure of authorial or psychic distance: The author did not have sufficient perspective on the character to convince us to share his or her judgment. I recall one class in which a student author had written, with excellent use of image and scene, the story of a young man who fell in love with an exceptionally beautiful young woman, and whose feelings turned to revulsion when he found out she had had a mastectomy. The most vocal feminist in the class loved this story, which she described as "the exposé of a skuzz-wort." This was not, from the author's point of view, a successful reading of his story. He had meant for the young man in the story to be seen as a sympathetic character.

WHEN WRITERS ARE SELF-CONSCIOUS about themselves as writers they often keep a great distance from their characters, sounding as if they were writing encyclopedia entries instead of stories. Their hesitancy about physical and psychological intimacy can be a barrier to vital fiction.

Conversely, a narration that makes readers hear the characters' heavy breathing and smell their emotional anguish diminishes distance. Readers feel so close to the characters that, for those magical moments, they *become* those characters.

JEROME STERN

A writer may also create either distance or closeness through the use of time, space, tone, and irony. A story that happened long ago in a far away land, told by a detached narrator, won't feel the same as one happening in present tense, told by one of the characters. A story's tone and use of irony are also indications of how the reader should view the characters and their situations.

Point of View

WHO SPEAKS?

The Author	*The Author*	*A Character*
In: Third Person	In: Second Person	In: First Person
Editorial Omniscient	"You" as Character	Central Narrator
Limited Omniscient	"You" as Reader-	Peripheral Narrator
Objective	Turned-Character	

To Whom?

The Reader	Another Character or Characters	The Self

In What Form?

Story, Monologue,
Letter, Journal,
Interior Monologue,
Stream of Conscious-
ness, etc.

At What Distance?

Complete Identification		Complete Opposition

Choosing and *controlling* the psychic distance that best suits a given story is one of the most elusive challenges a writer faces. The good news for novice writers feeling overwhelmed by all these considerations is that point-of-view choices, like plot and theme, are seldom calculated and preplanned. Rather, point of view tends to evolve organically as a story develops, and you can usually trust intuition to guide you through several drafts. It is when a story is well underway that analysis of its specific point-of-view issues be-comes most useful, and the feedback of other workshop members may be of particular value.

Consistency: A Final Caution

In establishing the story's point of view, you make your own rules, but having made them, you must stick to them. Your position as a writer is analogous to that of a poet who may choose whether to write free verse or a ballad stanza. If the poet chooses the stanza, then he or she is obliged to rhyme. Beginning writers of prose fiction are often tempted to shift viewpoint when it is both unnecessary and disruptive for readers.

> Leo's neck flushed against the prickly weave of his uniform collar. He concentrated on his buttons and tried not to look into the face of the bandmaster, who, however, was more amused than angry.

This is an awkward point-of-view shift because, having felt Leo's embarrassment with him, we are suddenly asked to leap into the bandmaster's feelings. The shift can be corrected by moving instead from Leo's mind to an observation that he might make.

> Leo's neck flushed against the prickly weave of his uniform collar. He concentrated on his buttons and tried not to look into the face of the bandmaster, who, however, was astonishingly smiling.

The rewrite is easier to follow because we remain with Leo's mind as he observes that the bandmaster is not angry. It further serves the purpose of implying that Leo fails to concentrate on his buttons, and so intensifies his confusion.

Apart from the use of significant detail, there is no more important skill for a writer of fiction to grasp than this: the control of point of view. Sometimes it may be hard simply to recognize that your narrative has leapt from one point of view to another—often, in workshop, students are troubled by a point-of-view shift in someone else's story but can't spot one in their own. In other cases there's a healthy desire to explore every possibility in a scene, and a mistaken sense that this can't be done without changing point of view. Indeed, no writing rule is so frequently broken to such original and inventive effect as *consistency in point of view*, as several stories in this volume attest. Yet the general rule of consistency holds, and a writer shows his amateurism in the failure to stick to a single point of view. Once established, point of view constitutes a contract between author and reader, and it will be difficult to break the contract gracefully. If you have restricted yourself to the mind of James Lordly for five pages, as he observes the actions of Mrs. Grumms and her cats, you will violate the contract by suddenly dipping into Mrs. Grumms's mind to let us know what she thinks of James Lordly. We are likely to feel misused, and likely to cancel the contract altogether, if you then suddenly give us the thoughts of the cats.

◈

Missing Women

JUNE SPENCE

Three women have vanished, a mother, her teenage daughter, and the daughter's friend—purses and cars left behind, TV on, door unlocked. The daughter had plans to spend the day at the lake with friends and never showed. The phone has rung and rung all morning, unanswered.

Puzzled friends walk through the interrupted house, sweep up broken glass from a porch light before calling the police. Broom bristles, shoe soles, finger pads smearing, tamping down, obscuring possibilities. Neighbors come forward, vague. It was late, they say. A green van, a white truck seen in the area, trolling. A man with longish brown hair, army jacket, slight to medium build. Down by the train tracks, panties. A single canvas sneaker.

Details are not clues. What happened? Police conjecture an intruder or intruders intended only to deal with the mother, to rob or to rape. The girls' arrival was unexpected. Panicking, the perpetrator(s) abducted all three. Haste should have made the abductor(s) sloppy, dribbling evidence all the way to some lair. But little is found: a single drop of blood in the foyer, but it belongs to a friend—she nicked her finger while sweeping glass. We're aghast at all the friends who tidied up. No alarm in broken glass? Those purses; women don't leave their purses.

There is truth and there is rumor. The missing daughter, Vicki, has not been particularly close to the missing friend, Adelle, since junior high. They went in different directions—the stocky, glossy Vicki somewhat of a party girl, her hair bleached yellow-white against iodine skin; Adelle the more academic and wholesomely cheerleaderish one, willowy and fine-boned. Graduation party nostalgia brought them back together that night, where they let bygones be bygones, forgiving the small betrayals. Adelle called home to say she'd be spending the night at Vicki's, the first time in almost four years. Her shiny compact car blocks the driveway to show she made it as far as that.

In her abandoned purse is medicine Adelle must take every day. Early on, this is what worries her parents most. They circle the town doggedly, their station wagon filled with fliers, her face emblazoned on their sweatshirts. *Please. If you know anything, anything at all.* In a video they lend to the TV stations, she is modeling gauzy, diaphanous wedding gowns for a local dressmaker. With her skirts and hair swirling, her perfect pearly teeth, we feel that she is innocent and doomed.

Of the missing mother Kay and daughter Vicki, we are not so sure. Their estranged husband/father cannot immediately be located. Vicki once had a restraining order against her ex-boyfriend, and he is taken in for questioning. He is at first sullen and uncooperative with investigators. With grim confidence we await his confession, but he foils us: a punched timecard and security video corroborate his third-shift presence in the chicken-parts processing plant that night. The husband/father likewise disappoints. He is not on the lam but simply lives out of state. Someone calls him and he comes, and the son/brother too. They are briefly suspected, then cleared. But there is another shady matter. Kay ran a beauty parlor with increasingly disreputable ties. Some say she laundered money for drug dealers and got greedy, funneling too large a share for herself. The police deny all that, but we note her expensive tastes, the leather in her daughter's wardrobe, and conclude the worst.

Still, each of the three might have her own reasons for wanting to disappear. Kay had maxed out her credit cards and was falling behind in her mortgage payments. Was Vicki pregnant? Some say police found an unopened urine-test kit in her bureau. Adelle the consummate perfectionist was failing precalculus. Running off might have been easier to contemplate as a group: the girls plotting new looks in better towns; Kay mulling the practical details of bus tickets and low-profile jobs. We cannot rule out anything, but the strongest current is foul play, not the gentle fantasy of escape that we all have entertained.

Seventy-two hours pass without a trace, and the search kicks into high gear. Divers slick in neoprene suits bob the shallow lake as if for apples, rake the algaed muck along the bottom. City workers sonar the reservoir. The waters yield nothing, but the surrounding woods still swarm promisingly with hunters and hounds. We admire those who have volunteered to don orange caps and peer through binoculars, their dogs fanning out ahead and weaving through trees, loyal noses snuffling the ground. We admire the highway patrolmen in their thin summer khakis, poised in the roadside gravel, persistent but polite at the roadblocks checking licenses. The churchwomen bring pies and fried chicken and cold cans of soda to everyone tired and hungry from searching, and we admire them too.

All of us admirable, the way we rally together. We say, "We." We say, "Our community," "Our women," basking in the evidence of so many heroes lured out by tragedy: storefronts papered by high school kids with fliers provided free by local print shops, reward donations quietly accruing, information streaming through the phone lines, the cards and letters of commiseration. Surely this abundance of goodwill, mercy, and selfless volunteerism will prevail over the darker elements that abide here. For there are certain haggard people on the street, there are certain pockets of immigrants who will not master our grammar, whose children are insolent and fearless. There are people who look and sound uncannily like the rest of us, but if you shine a light in their crawlspaces, you might find the difference. Any might have stared with longing and hatred into the bright windows of pretty blondes.

There are leads. A reporter gets an anonymous call about a box, hidden in the park, containing information about the missing women. The caller will not disclose the nature of this information, will not linger on the line. Police are dispatched to the park, locate said box nestled amid gazebo shrubbery, examine it for explosives, dust it for prints, pry it open to find: a map, hastily sketched, of a floor plan. A park official recognizes the U shape of the building, the tiny hexagonal kitchen and bathroom appendages flanking individual units. Police coverage on the apartment building. Excited tenants cluster in the halls as rooms are searched. Nothing. Wild goose chase, read the headlines. Police vexed by fruitless search. Again Adelle's parents appear on television.

Their anguish chastens other would-be pranksters, but was it just a prankster? Someone who could snatch three women away without a trace might then goad the searchers. No person of authority will come right out and say so, but there it is. We feel it, huddled indoors, or venturing out in twos and threes.

A Waffle Hut waitress comes forward. She is fairly certain she served the three women omelets, french toast, and coffee around two a.m. on the day of the disappearance. They seemed quietly anxious, not like the raucous post-bar crowd she usually waits on around that time. The cheerleader type asked for boysenberry syrup and, told there was none, sank into a sullen lassitude.

A SuperDairy QuikMart clerk comes forward. Around two that same morning, a woman resembling the missing mother burst into the store, asked if he had seen two teenage girls, and stormed out when he said he hadn't. She sometimes bought cigarettes there, and milk in single-serving containers.

The graduation party attendees are questioned further. The girls were spotted leaving the party together at one, two, and three A.M. The hostess thought she heard them arguing in the bathroom, something about a borrowed necklace. The hostess's parents said both girls were polite and charming but seemed troubled. The hostess's boyfriend saw them hugging on the lawn. Others said the lawn embrace was a brawl; Vicki had Adelle in a chokehold. Or Adelle held Vicki while she vomited malt liquor onto the zinnias. Unless it wasn't those two at all. The salutatorian has his doubts. Around one-thirty, he says, he was sitting alone on the back patio. He had turned down a joint only to have the smoke blown into his ear, leaving him giddy and fretful and confused. He is going to Yale in the fall, and the prospect was then lying heavily on his mind. Now he feels relief and a delightful anticipation of leaving, but that night he brooded while the full moon silhouetted two figures dancing together on the lawn. The salutatorian watched in darkness two moving bodies he could identify as female by their shapes, the pitch of the laughter. It's possible they kissed or only whispered. He is pale and stammering in recall. Police seize his journals but return them the next day, almost dejected. His nervous intelligence seemed so promising—a budding sociopath?—but his journals hold only the sex-obsessed ramblings of run-of-the-mill adolescence: "May 5—Would absolutely rut Bethany R. given half a chance. Tits like grapefruit, and she smells like bubble-gum-flavored suntan lotion and sex."

The time is ripe for confessions, so people start to confess, as if in fits of misguided volunteerism. Some march right into the police station or the newspaper editor's office. Some hold press conferences. A man calling himself a freelance private eye and soldier of fortune says he helped the women conceal their identities and relocate, to where he is forbidden to disclose, but rest assured they are alive and well, enjoying lucrative careers in finance. A youth generally regarded as troubled leads police and reporters to an empty culvert, an empty railcar, and on a hike through acres of empty field. A woman claiming to be one of the missing women comes forward but will not specify which one she is—she resembles none—and is vague about the other two, saying only that they ditched her. Her parents persuade her to recant. A group calling itself the Urban Tide says they have taken the women hostage in belated protest of the U.S. invasion of Grenada.[1] They are revealed to be performance artists living off college fellowships. They say their intention was to "tweak the media and thereby tweak collective perceptions." There is talk of dismantling the university's theater arts program altogether, which is hotly debated until the diversion of Vicki's ex-boyfriend's appearance in a television interview.

He reaffirms his innocence and describes their first date: they had agreed to meet at the football game. She had not permitted him to kiss her that night. The first thing he admired about her was how she blew smoke rings "like she was forty years old or something." They dated for two years and got pre-engaged. She loved redhots and for him to knead her shoulders after a long day of school and sweeping up her mother's shop. The restraining order grew out of a misunderstanding, he explains. He was a jealous guy, he admits. She could be sort of a flirt, but no more than that, he is careful to emphasize. No speaking ill of the missing. He has grown up a lot since then, he swears, and his former

[1]The United States invaded Grenada, a small island in the southern Caribbean, in October 1983 to eliminate a Marxist regime that had allied itself with Castro's Cuba. (JHP)

guidance counselor agrees in a pre-taped clip. What's next for this wrongly accused young fellow who has stolen all our hearts? He's studying for his General Equivalency Diploma and plans to enter technical school. Weekends he fishes with Dad and brothers.

Lovely Adelle had (*has?* we must be careful with what tenses imply) no boyfriend. She seemed unapproachable, schoolmates say. Boys were intimidated by her height and her perfect smile. She carried herself as if maybe she thought she was a little better than everyone else. We detect the trace of a smirk in her wedding-dress video. Her parents start to seem a little *too* perfect in their televised worry, forever circling the town, meeting with the police chief, presiding over candlelight vigils. We can't help but wonder: don't they have to work? The friendly wood panels on their station wagon begin to come across as less than sincere. When Adelle's face appears alone on a billboard and a separate award fund is established from her college savings, we say they are elitist. Someone rents a billboard featuring only the faces of the other two, and passers through unfamiliar with the case think they are unrelated disappearances.

The paper still presents them as a united front, the Missing Women, and prints their photos side by side in equal rectangles. The rectangles have shrunk, though, and are relegated to the B section, except on Sundays, when a summary appears on the front page featuring the best of the tip cards and the psychic *du jour*. In the absence of verifiable fact, reporters track the psychics' emanations and contribute wispy, artful meditations on the nature of truth. One suggests that the women never existed at all except as modern local archetypes: Kay the divorced mom, Vicki the short-skirted slattern, Adelle the model child from a better neighborhood. Cruise any strip mall in town, muses the reporter, and you will see several of their ilk. Subscriptions to the paper take a nosedive until the reporter resigns and a larger-format, full-color TV schedule is introduced.

How we are holding up: Summer presses on, August flares. As the phones' ringing wanes, crime-line volunteers drop off reluctantly, like rose petals. Friends and relatives of the missing women who have flocked here must return to their towns, jobs, more immediate families. There is no such thing as indefinite leave unless you are the missing women. Fliers in windows start to flap at the edges, tape losing its tack. Still, church attendance remains up. Moonlight strolls are kept to a minimum. Locksmiths can't install deadbolts quickly enough. Neighborhoods stay illuminated by floodlights and seething with attack dogs. Psychologists from the university advise us, in these prolonged times of stress, to be absolutely forthright with one another and to get plenty of rest and light to moderate exercise. Sixty-four percent of residents polled believe there will be more disappearances. Seventy-nine percent say the missing women are dead. Eleven percent believe the supernatural was involved. Two percent suggest they know something about the disappearance that the rest of us don't, and they aren't telling. The poll has a two percent margin of error.

Our police chief is often spotted raking a hand through his thin, whitening hair, loosening his collar. He has gained thirty pounds. We worry that the ordeal will force him into early retirement. For the most part we appreciate what he has done for the town, keeping both the leftist fringe and the religious zealots at bay to preserve our moderate sensibilities. Whereas our mayor is perceived to be an ineffectual weasel, the apprehended drunk drivers, college rowdies, neo-Nazis, drug dealers, and other riffraff can attest that our police chief has kept the peace. But even he cannot collar this invisible threat, this thief who whisks our women into the night, leaving only their plaintive, flat faces pressed against yellowing planes of paper, asking everyone: *Have you seen us?*

August simmering down, the newspaper finally succumbs to investigative inertia. No news is no news; they've been carrying the missing women for weeks now without a new development. Journalism must prevail; the women's photos are sponged from the B pages. Without the newspaper's resolve, we let the fair distract us, then a strike at the chicken-parts processing plant, then the college students' return to town. There's talk of rebuilding the stadium. We have our hands full.

The mayor orates, finally. This tragedy has torn at the heart of our community, he says. We are shocked, saddened, and bewildered, he says. Grappling for clues. Desperate for answers. Neighbor pitted against neighbor in suspicion and fear. We are momentarily stirred by the drama of his speech, but he is voicing sentiments of weeks ago. A belated coda. We've gotten on with it. That's his problem; no finger on the pulse. He's slow to evaluate, even slower to act. We resent his jowly, bow-tied demeanor. He proposes a monument in the square, a small gas torch that will stay lit, eternally vigilant, until the women return. Donations trickle in, guiltily.

From this, the newspaper enjoys a brief second wind of missing-women coverage. After the press conference, there are additional quotes to be gleaned from the mayor, the locally available friends and family of the missing, and the major contributors to the gas torch. There is even a statement from the fire marshal attesting to the relative safety of the proposed monument. The newspaper's cartoonist, known for her acid social commentary, draws bums and bag ladies toasting skewered rats over the torch's flame—to call attention to the downtown homeless. This is generally derided as tasteless, and the editor prints what amounts to an apology under CORRECTIONS, saying the paper "regrets the error." The cartoonist resigns under pressure and files suit. She donates part of her settlement to the torch fund, part to the soup kitchen. There will be other occasional flare-ups. Adelle's parents will reemerge woefully from time to time, but in retrospect we will see that it was here the story's last traces turned to ash.

And what of the missing women? They do turn up, but only in dreams. We're at a party, and though the dream seems intended only to air private anxieties (we find ourselves naked in a room full of people), there are the three of them, lingering over the bean dip. Or we walk into an alcove filled with light and see Adelle in her wedding dress, spinning, spinning, her face aging with each rotation, the smile lined and straining, G forces undulating her cheeks. Or from the reception area of her beauty shop we watch Kay cutting hair that drops in soft heaps, the yellow-blond hair of her daughter, black at the root. Or the girls are wearing graduation caps and robes and clutching scrolls. The scrolls are not diplomas but maps of their whereabouts. They offer us a peek, but when we lean in to look, they pull away, snickering with teenage disdain, and vanish. Or, in the one we don't speak of, we are running down a familiar forest path, hunted, and we sense them beneath the pads of our feet, planted deep in the dark, green woods, bones cooling, and we wake, knowing they've been here all along.

◈

Who's Irish?

GISH JEN

In China, people say mixed children are supposed to be smart, and definitely my granddaughter Sophie is smart. But Sophie is wild, Sophie is not like my daughter Natalie, or like me. I am work hard my whole life, and fierce besides. My husband always used to say he is afraid of me, and in our restaurant, busboys and cooks all afraid of me too. Even the gang members come for protection money, they try to talk to my husband. When I am there, they stay away. If they come by mistake, they pretend they are come to eat. They hide behind the menu, they order a lot of food. They talk about their mothers. Oh, my mother have some arthritis, need to take herbal medicine, they say. Oh, my mother getting old, her hair all white now.

I say, Your mother's hair used to be white, but since she dye it, it become black again. Why don't you go home once in a while and take a look? I tell them, Confucius say a filial son knows what color his mother's hair is.

My daughter is fierce too, she is vice president in the bank now. Her new house is big enough for everybody to have their own room, including me. But Sophie take after Natalie's husband's family, their name is Shea, Irish. I always thought Irish people are like Chinese people, work so hard on the railroad, but now I know why the Chinese beat the Irish. Of course, not all Irish are like the Shea family, of course not. My daughter tell me I should not say Irish this, Irish that.

How do you like it when people say the Chinese this, the Chinese that, she say.

You know, the British call the Irish heathen, just like they call the Chinese, she say.

You think the Opium War was bad, how would you like to live right next door to the British, she say.

And that is that. My daughter have a funny habit when she win an argument, she take a sip of something and look away, so the other person is not embarrassed. So I am not embarrassed. I do not call anybody anything either. I just happen to mention about the Shea family, an interesting fact: four brothers in the family, and not one of them work. The mother, Bess, have a job before she got sick, she was executive secretary in a big company. She is handle everything for a big shot, you would be surprised how complicated her job is, not just type this, type that. Now she is a nice woman with a clean house. But her boys, every one of them is on welfare, or so-called severance pay, or so-called disability pay. Something. They say they cannot find work, this is not the economy of the fifties, but I say, Even the black people doing better these days, some of them live so fancy, you'd be surprised. Why the Shea family have so much trouble? They are white people, they speak English. When I come to this country, I have no money and do not speak English. But my husband and I own our restaurant before he die. Free and clear, no mortgage. Of course. I understand I am just lucky, come from a country where the food is popular all over the world. I understand it is not the Shea family's fault they come from a country where everything is boiled. Still, I say.

She's right, we should broaden our horizons, say one brother, Jim, at Thanksgiving. Forget about the car business. Think about egg rolls.

Pad thai, say another brother, Mike. I'm going to make my fortune in pad thai. It's going to be the new pizza.

I say, You people too picky about what you sell. Selling egg rolls not good enough for you, but at least my husband and I can say, We made it. What can you say? Tell me. What can you say?

Everybody chew their tough turkey.

I especially cannot understand my daughter's husband John, who has no job but cannot take care of Sophie either. Because he is a man, he say, and that's the end of the sentence.

Plain boiled food, plain boiled thinking. Even his name is plain boiled: John. Maybe because I grew up with black bean sauce and hoisin sauce and garlic sauce, I always feel something is missing when my son-in-law talk.

But, okay: so my son-in-law can be man, I am baby-sitter. Six hours a day, same as the old sitter, crazy Amy, who quit. This is not so easy, now that I am sixty-eight, Chinese age almost seventy. Still, I try. In China, daughter take care of mother. Here it is the other way around. Mother help daughter, mother ask, Anything else I can do? Otherwise daughter complain mother is not supportive. I tell daughter, We do not have this word in Chinese, *supportive*. But my daughter too busy to listen, she has to go to meeting, she has to write memo while her husband go to the gym to be a man. My daughter say otherwise he will be depressed. Seems like all his life he has this trouble, depression.

No one wants to hire someone who is depressed, she say. It is important for him to keep his spirits up.

Beautiful wife, beautiful daughter, beautiful house, oven can clean itself automatically. No money left over, because only one income, but lucky enough, got the baby-sitter for free. If John lived in China, he would be very happy. But he is not happy. Even at the gym things go wrong. One day, he pull a muscle. Another day, weight room too crowded. Always something.

Until finally, hooray, he has a job. Then he feel pressure.

I need to concentrate, he say. I need to focus.

He is going to work for insurance company. Salesman job. A paycheck, he say, and at least he will wear clothes instead of gym shorts. My daughter buy him some special candy bars from the health-food store. They say THINK! on them, and are supposed to help John think.

John is a good-looking boy, you have to say that, especially now that he shave so you can see his face.

I am an old man in a young man's game, say John.

I will need a new suit, say John.

This time I am not going to shoot myself in the foot, say John.

Good, I say.

She means to be supportive, my daughter say. Don't start the send her back to China thing, because we can't.

Sophie is three years old American age, but already I see her nice Chinese side swallowed up by her wild Shea side. She looks like mostly Chinese. Beautiful black hair, beautiful black eyes. Nose perfect size, not so flat looks like something fell down, not so large looks like some big deal got stuck in wrong face. Everything just right, only her skin is a brown surprise to John's family. So brown, they say. Even John say it. She never goes in the sun, still she is that color, he say. Brown. They say. Nothing the matter with brown. They are just surprised. So brown. Nattie is not that brown, they say. They say, It seems like Sophie should be a color in between Nattie and John. Seems funny, a girl named Sophie Shea be brown. But she is brown, maybe her name should be

Sophie Brown. She never go in the sun, still she is that color, they say. Nothing the matter with brown. They are just surprised.

The Shea family talk is like this sometimes, going around and around like a Christmas-tree train.

Maybe John is not her father, I say one day, to stop the train. And sure enough, train wreck. None of the brothers ever say the word *brown* to me again.

Instead, John's mother, Bess, say, I hope you are not offended.

She say, I did my best on those boys. But raising four boys with no father is no picnic.

You have a beautiful family, I say.

I'm getting old, she say.

You deserve a rest, I say. Too many boys make you old.

I never had a daughter, she say. You have a daughter.

I have a daughter, I say. Chinese people don't think a daughter is so great, but you're right. I have a daughter.

I was never against the marriage, you know, she say. I never thought John was marrying down. I always thought Nattie was just as good as white.

I was never against the marriage either, I say. I just wonder if they look at the whole problem.

Of course you pointed out the problem, you are a mother, she say. And now we both have a granddaughter. A little brown granddaughter, she is so precious to me.

I laugh. A little brown granddaughter, I say. To tell you the truth, I don't know how she came out so brown.

We laugh some more. These days Bess need a walker to walk. She take so many pills, she need two glasses of water to get them all down. Her favorite TV show is about bloopers, and she love her bird feeder. All day long, she can watch that bird feeder, like a cat.

I can't wait for her to grow up, Bess say. I could use some female company.

Too many boys, I say.

Boys are fine, she say. But they do surround you after a while.

You should take a break, come live with us, I say. Lots of girls at our house.

Be careful what you offer, say Bess with a wink. Where I come from, people mean for you to move in when they say a thing like that.

Nothing the matter with Sophie's outside, that's the truth. It is inside that she is like not any Chinese girl I ever see. We go to the park, and this is what she does. She stand up in the stroller. She take off all her clothes and throw them in the fountain.

Sophie! I say. Stop!

But she just laugh like a crazy person. Before I take over as baby-sitter, Sophie has that crazy-person sitter, Amy the guitar player. My daughter thought this Amy very creative—another word we do not talk about in China. In China, we talk about whether we have difficulty or no difficulty. We talk about whether life is bitter or not bitter. In America, all day long, people talk about creative. Never mind that I cannot even look at this Amy, with her shirt so short that her belly button showing. This Amy think Sophie should love her body. So when Sophie take off her diaper, Amy laugh. When Sophie run around naked, Amy say she wouldn't want to wear a diaper either. When Sophie go *shu-shu* in her lap, Amy laugh and say there are no germs in pee. When Sophie take off her shoes, Amy say bare feet is best, even the pediatrician say so. That is why Sophie now walk around with no shoes like a beggar child. Also why Sophie love to take off her clothes.

Turn around! say the boys in the park. Let's see that ass!

Of course, Sophie does not understand. Sophie clap her hands, I am the only one to say, No! This is not a game.

It has nothing to do with John's family, my daughter say. Amy was too permissive, that's all.

But I think if Sophie was not wild inside, she would not take off her shoes and clothes to begin with.

You never take off your clothes when you were little. I say, All my Chinese friends had babies, I never saw one of them act wild like that.

Look, my daughter say. I have a big presentation tomorrow.

John and my daughter agree Sophie is a problem, but they don't know what to do.

You spank her, she'll stop, I say another day.

But they say, Oh no.

In America, parents not supposed to spank the child.

It gives them low self-esteem, my daughter say. And that leads to problems later, as I happen to know.

My daughter never have big presentation the next day when the subject of spanking come up.

I don't want you to touch Sophie, she say. No spanking, period.

Don't tell me what to do, I say.

I'm not telling you what to do, say my daughter. I'm telling you how I feel.

I am not your servant, I say. Don't you dare talk to me like that.

My daughter have another funny habit when she lose an argument. She spread out all her fingers and look at them, as if she like to make sure they are still there.

My daughter is fierce like me, but she and John think it is better to explain to Sophie that clothes are a good idea. This is not so hard in the cold weather. In the warm weather, it is very hard.

Use your words, my daughter say. That's what we tell Sophie. How about if you set a good example.

As if good example mean anything to Sophie. I am so fierce, the gang members who used to come to the restaurant all afraid of me, but Sophie is not afraid.

I say, Sophie, if you take off your clothes, no snack.

I say, Sophie, if you take off your clothes, no lunch.

I say, Sophie, if you take off your clothes, no park.

Pretty soon we are stay home all day, and by the end of six hours she still did not have one thing to eat. You never saw a child stubborn like that.

I'm hungry! She cry when my daughter come home.

What's the matter, doesn't your grandmother feed you? My daughter laugh.

No! Sophie say. She doesn't feed me anything!

My daughter laugh again. Here you go, she say.

She say to John, Sophie must be growing.

Growing like a weed, I say.

Still Sophie take off her clothes, until one day I spank her. Not too hard, but she cry, and when I tell her if she doesn't put her clothes back on I'll spank her again, she put her clothes back on. Then I tell her she is good girl, and give her some food to eat. The next day we go to the park and, like a nice Chinese girl, she does not take off her clothes.

She stop taking off her clothes, I report. Finally!

How did you do it? my daughter ask.

After twenty-eight years experience with you, I guess I learn something, I say.

It must have been a phase, John say, and his voice is suddenly like an expert.

His voice is like an expert about everything these days, now that he carry a leather briefcase, and wear shiny shoes, and can go shopping for a new car. On the company, he say. The company will pay for it, but he will be able to drive it whenever he want.

A free car, he say. How do you like that.

It's good to see you in the saddle again, my daughter say. Some of your family patterns are scary.

At least I don't drink, he say. He say, and I'm not the only one with scary family patterns.

That's for sure, say my daughter.

***

Everyone is happy. Even I am happy, because there is more trouble with Sophie, but now I think I can help her Chinese side fight against her wild side. I teach her to eat food with fork or spoon or chopsticks, she cannot just grab into the middle of a bowl of noodles. I teach her not to play with garbage cans. Sometimes I spank her, but not too often, and not too hard.

Still, there are problems. Sophie like to climb everything. If there is a railing, she is never next to it. Always she is on top of it. Also, Sophie like to hit the mommies of her friends. She learn this from her playground best friend, Sinbad, who is four. Sinbad wear army clothes every day and like to ambush his mommy. He is the one who dug a big hole under the play structure, a foxhole he call it, all by himself. Very hardworking. Now he wait in the foxhole with a shovel full of wet sand. When his mommy come, he throw it right at her.

Oh, it's all right, his mommy say. You can't get rid of war games, it's part of their imaginative play. All the boys go through it.

Also, he like to kick his mommy, and one day he tell Sophie to kick his mommy too.

I wish this story is not true.

Kick her, kick her! Sinbad say.

Sophie kick her. A little kick, as if she just so happened was swinging her little leg and didn't realize that big mommy leg was in the way. Still I spank Sophie and make Sophie say sorry, and what does the mommy say?

Really, it's all right, she say. It didn't hurt.

After that, Sophie learn she can attack mommies in the playground, and some will say, Stop, but others will say, Oh, she didn't mean it, especially if they realize Sophie will be punished.

* * *

This is how, one day, bigger trouble come. The bigger trouble start when Sophie hide in the foxhole with that shovel full of sand. She wait, and when I come look for her, she throw it at me. All over my nice clean clothes.

Did you ever see a Chinese girl act this way!

Sophie! I say. Come out of there, say you're sorry.

But she does not come out. Instead, she laugh. Naaah, naah-na, naaanaaa, she say.

I am not exaggerate: millions of children in China, not one act like this.

Sophie! I say. Now! Come out now!

But she know she is in big trouble. She know if she come out, what will happen next. So she does not come out. I am sixty-eight, Chinese age almost seventy, how can I crawl under there to catch her? Impossible. So I yell, yell, yell, and what happen? Nothing. A Chinese mother would help, but American mothers, they look at you, they shake their head, they go home. And, of course, a Chinese child would give up, but not Sophie.

I hate you! she yell. I hate you, Meanie!

Meanie is my new name these days.

Long time this goes on, long long time. The foxhole is deep, you cannot see too much, you don't know where is the bottom. You cannot hear too much either. If she does not yell, you cannot even know she is still there or not. After a while, getting cold out, getting dark out. No one left in the playground, only us.

Sophie, I say. How did you become stubborn like this? I am go home without you now.

I try to use a stick, chase her out of there, and once or twice I hit her, but still she does not come out. So finally I leave. I go outside the gate.

Bye-bye! I say. I'm go home now.

But still she does not come out and does not come out. Now it is dinnertime, the sky is black. I think I should maybe go get help, but how can I leave a little girl by herself in the playground? A bad man could come. A rat could come. I go back in to see what is happen to Sophie. What if she have a shovel and is making a tunnel to escape?

Sophie! I say.

No answer.

Sophie!

I don't know if she is alive. I don't know if she is fall asleep down there. If she is crying, I cannot hear her.

So I take the stick and poke.

Sophie! I say. I promise I no hit you. If you come out, I give you a lollipop.

No answer. By now I worried. What to do, what to do, what to do? I poke some more, even harder, so that I am poking and poking when my daughter and John suddenly appear.

What are you doing? What is going on? say my daughter.

Put down that stick! say my daughter.

You are crazy! say my daughter.

John wiggle under the structure, into the foxhole, to rescue Sophie.

She fell asleep, say John the expert. She's okay. That is one big hole.

Now Sophie is crying and crying.

Sophie, my daughter say, hugging her. Are you okay, peanut? Are you okay?

She's just scared, say John.

Are you okay? I say too. I don't know what happen, I say.

She's okay, say John. He is not like my daughter, full of questions. He is full of answers until we get home and can see by the lamplight.

Will you look at her? he yell then. What the hell happened?

Bruises all over her brown skin, and a swollen-up eye.

You are crazy! say my daughter. Look at what you did! You are crazy!

I try very hard, I say.

How could you use a stick? I told you to use your words!

She is hard to handle, I say.

She's three years old! You cannot use a stick! say my daughter.

She is not like any Chinese girl I ever saw, I say.

I brush some sand off my clothes. Sophie's clothes are dirty too, but at least she has her clothes on.

Has she done this before? ask my daughter. Has she hit you before?

She hits me all the time, Sophie say, eating ice cream.

Your family, say John.

Believe me, say my daughter.

A daughter I have, a beautiful daughter. I took care of her when she could not hold her head up. I took care of her before she could argue with me, when she was a little girl with two pigtails, one of them always crooked. I took care of her when we have to escape from China, I took care of her when suddenly we live in a country with cars everywhere, if you are not careful your little girl get run over. When my husband die, I promise him I will keep the family together, even though it was just two of us, hardly a family at all.

But now my daughter take me around to look at apartments. After all, I can cook, I can clean, there's no reason I cannot live by myself, all I need is a telephone. Of course, she is sorry. Sometimes she cry, I am the one to say everything will be okay. She say she have no choice, she doesn't want to end up divorced. I say divorce is terrible, I don't know who invented this terrible idea. Instead of live with a telephone, though, surprise, I come to live with Bess. Imagine that. Bess make an offer and, sure enough, where she come from, people mean for you to move in when they say things like that. A crazy idea, go to live with someone else's family, but she like to have some female company, not like my daughter, who does not believe in company. These days when my daughter visit, she does not bring Sophie. Bess say we should give Nattie time, we will see Sophie again soon. But seems like my daughter have more presentation than ever before, every time she come she have to leave.

I have a family to support, she say, and her voice is heavy, as if soaking wet. I have a young daughter and a depressed husband and no one to turn to.

When she say no one to turn to, she mean me.

These days my beautiful daughter is so tired she can just sit there in a chair and fall asleep. John lost his job again, already, but still they rather hire a baby-sitter than ask me to help, even they can't afford it. Of course, the new baby-sitter is much younger, can run around. I don't know if Sophie these days is wild or not wild. She call me Meanie, but she like to kiss me too, sometimes. I remember that every time I see a child on TV. Sophie like to grab my hair, a fistful in each hand, and then kiss me smack on the nose. I never see any other child kiss that way.

The satellite TV has so many channels, more channels than I can count, including a Chinese channel from the Mainland and a Chinese channel from Taiwan, but most of the time I watch bloopers with Bess.

Also, I watch the bird feeder—so many, many kinds of birds come. The Shea sons hang around all the time, asking when will I go home, but Bess tell them, Get lost.

She's permanent resident, say Bess. She isn't going anywhere.

Then she wink at me, and switch the channel with the remote control.

Of course, I shouldn't say Irish this, Irish that, especially now I am become honorary Irish myself, according to Bess. Me! Who's Irish? I say, and she laugh. All the same, if I could mention one thing about some of the Irish, not all of them of course, I like to mention this: Their talk just stick. I don't know how Bess Shea learn to use her words, but sometimes I hear what she say a long time later. *Permanent resident. Not going anywhere.* Over and over I hear it, the voice of Bess.

◈

Reply All

ROBIN HEMLEY

To: Poetry Association of the Western Suburbs Listserve
From: Lisa Drago-Harse
Subject: Next Meeting
Date: July 17th

Hi all,

I wanted to confirm that our next meeting will be held in the Sir Francis Drake Room at the Bensonville Hampton Inn on August 3rd. Minutes from our last meeting and an agenda for the next meeting will follow shortly.

Peace and Poetry,
Lisa Drago-Harse
Secretary/PAWS

To: Poetry Association of the Western Suburbs Listserve
From: Michael Stroud
Re: Re: Next Meeting
Date: July 17th

Dearest Lisa,

First of all, I LOVE your mole and don't find it unsightly in the least! There is absolutely no reason for you to be ashamed of it (though it might be a good idea to have it checked out). But please don't remove it! Heaven forbid, my darling! As I recall, I gave you considerable pleasure when I sucked and licked it like a nipple. A nipple it is in size and shape, if not placement. That no one else knows your mole's position on your body (other than your benighted husband, poor limp Richard, that Son(net) of a Bitch as you call him) is more the pity (if Marvell had known such a mole, he undoubtedly would have added an extra stanza to his poem). But my coy mistress is not SO terribly coy as all that, if I remember correctly (and how could I forget!) You were not at all what I had expected in bed—not that I had any expectations at all. When you started massaging my crotch with your foot underneath the table in the Sir Francis Drake Room, I was at first shocked. For a moment, I thought perhaps the unseen massager was none other than our esteemed president, the redoubtable Darcy McFee, (makeup and wardrobe courtesy of Yoda). Is that terrible of me? I have nothing personal against her, really, except for her execrable taste in poetry, and the fact that you should be president, not she. And her breath. And that habit of pulling her nose when she speaks and that absolutely horrific expression of hers, Twee. As in, "I find his poetry just so twee." What does twee mean and why does she keep inflicting it upon us! So imagine my horror when I felt this foot in my crotch and I stared across the table at the two of you—she twitching like a slug that's had salt poured on it and you immobile except for your Mont Blanc pen taking down the minutes. Ah, to think that the taking down of minutes could be such an erotic activity, but in your capable hands, it is. To think that mere hours later, it would be my Mont Blanc you'd grasp so firmly, guiding me into the lyrical book of your body. But initially, I thought the worst, that it was Darcy, not you. My only consolation was the idea that at least I had her on a sexual harassment suit, her being my boss after all at Roosevelt. Another reason, I thought it was her and not you was because I know you're married and she isn't and I knew that Richard is a member of our esteemed organization, too (and he was in the room, seated beside you no less!). It was only that sly smile in your eyes that tipped me off. I, too, love the danger that illicit public sex brings, as long as it's kept under the table, so to speak. And yes, maybe someday we can make love on that very same table in the Sir Francis Drake Room, my darling. But I must ask you, sweetheart, where did you learn that amazing trick. I have seen people wiggle their ears before, but never that! What amazing talent and such a pity that this is not something you bring out at parties or poetry readings to awe the dumb masses! Would Darcy find that too twee? I think not! Thinking of you now makes me so hot. I want to nibble you. I want to live in your panties. I want to write a series of odes to you equal in number to every lucky taste bud on my tongue, every nerve ending (no, not endings but beginnings!) on my body that live in rapture of your every pore. No, not poor, but rich. I am rich. I make metaphors of your muscles, of your thighs, of the fecund wetness bursting with your being and effulgence. I must swallow now. I must breathe. I must take my leave, my darling, and go now to relieve myself of my private thoughts of you and you alone.

With undying love and erotic daydreams,

Mikey

P.S. Do you think you could get away for an evening next week? Could you be called away from Richard for an emergency meeting of the Public Relations Committee?

To: PAWS Listserve
From: Darcy McFee
Re: Re: Re: Next Meeting
Date: July 17th

I am traveling now and will not be answering e-mails until I return on July 21st.

Thanks!

Darcy

To: PAWS Listserve
From: Sam Fulgram, Jr.
Re: Re: Re: Re: Next Meeting
Date: July 17th

Whoa boy! Do you realize you just sent out your love note to the entire Poetry Association of the Western Suburbs listserve?

Cheers,
Sam

P.S. That mole? You've got my imagination running wild. As long as the entire organization knows about it now, would you mind divulging its location? I'd sleep better at night knowing it.

To: PAWS Listserve
From: Betsy Midchester
Re: Re: Re: Re: Re: Next Meeting
Date July 17th

Hi all,

Well! That last message from "Mikey" Stroud certainly made my day. I thought at first the message was addressed to me. As I had no memory of placing my foot in Mike's crotch, I naturally assumed that I needed an adjustment of my medication so that I wouldn't forget such episodes in the future. Now I see it's simply Michael ("Down Boy") Stroud and our esteemed Secretary of the Galloping Mont Blaaaaanc who need the medication adjustments. Thanks, in any case, for a much needed lift in an otherwise humdrum day.

Betsy Midchester
Treasurer/PAWS

To: PAWS Listserve
From: Lisa Drago-Harse
Re: Re: Re: Re: Re: Re: Next Meeting
Date: July 17th

This is a nightmare. I'm not quite sure what to say except that life is unpredictable and often irreversible. While I do not wish to go into details or make excuses for the above e-mail from Michael Stroud, I would like to clarify one thing: that was not my foot in your crotch Michael. But your belief that it was my foot in your crotch explains a few things concerning your subsequent behavior toward me that were, up until this moment, a mystery.

LDH

To: PAWS Listserve
From: Michael Stroud
Re: Re: Re: Re: Re: Re: Re: Next Meeting
Date: July 17th

I'm

To: PAWS Listserve
From: Michael Stroud
Re: Re: Re: Re: Re: Re: Re: Re: Next Meeting
Date: July 17th

I hit the send button by mistake before I was ready. This isn't my day, to say the least! I'm sorry!!!! I'd like to apologize to the entire PAWS community, and also to Lisa's husband Richard and to Darcy. And to you, Lisa. I don't mean to make excuses for myself, but I would like to say that I've been under a tremendous amount of pressure of late, at school, at home, and I am nothing if not vulnerable and flawed. All I can say is that in poetry I find some solace for the petty actions of others and the sometimes monstrous actions of which I'm all too capable. As déclassé as Truth and Beauty are these days, it is in such expressions as those of Matthew Arnold, Keats, Byron, and Shelly to whom I look for my meager draught of the Divine. And sometimes, I must admit, I seek in the affection of my fellow poetry lovers, the divinity which I myself lack. I ask you all to blame me, not Lisa for what has happened.

But if not your foot, Lisa, then whose?

Michael Stroud

To: PAWS Listserve
From: Greg Rudolfsky
Re: Re: Re: Re: Re: Re: Re: Re: Re: RESPECT
Date: July 17th

Just a little bit, Just a little bit.
Sock it to me, sock it to me, sock it to me, sock it to me, sock it to me, sock it to me, sock it to me, sock it to me, RESPECT, Just a little bit, just a little bit...

To: PAWS Listserve
From: Samantha M. Poulsen, RN
Subject: Fecund Poets
Date: July 17th

I do not care whose foot is in whose crotch, but I think it's insulting and idiotic that so-called educated people would use such phrases as, "the fecund wetness bursting with your being and effulgence." And officers of the PAWS at that!

To: PAWS Listserve
From: Richard Harse
Re: Fecund Poets
Date: July 17th

I would like to tender my resignation in the Poets of the Western Suburbs, as I will be tendering my resignation in several other areas of my life. I only belonged to PAWS in any case because of my wife's interest in poetry. I wanted to share her interests, but clearly not all of them.

To: PAWS
From: Darcy McFee
Re: Fecund Poets
Date: July 22nd

Well, it seems that our little organization has been busy in my absence. I have over 300 new messages in my e-mail account, all, it seems from my fellow poetry lovers! I haven't yet had a chance to read your exchanges, but I will soon. In the meantime, I wanted to convey some exciting news. This weekend, while attending a workshop at Wright State in Dayton, I ran into the former Poet Laureate, Billy Collins, who has agreed to be our special guest at our annual Poetry Bash in Oak Park. He said he's heard quite a lot about our organization in recent days and that our board had achieved near legendary status in the poetry community. I knew this would make you as proud as it makes me.

To: PAWS Listserve
From: Darcy McFee
Subject: Twee
Date: July 24th

So this is how it is. Upon reading the 300 e-mails that collected in my inbox over the weekend, my mind is a riot of emotions. I have not slept for nearly 48 hours. Never before have I been so insulted. Yet, I also know that I am, at least in part, to blame. Had I not stuck my foot in Michael Stroud's crotch, none of this would have happened. Twitching like a slug that's had salt poured on it? That hurts, Michael. It really does. I didn't realize you were so shallow. But in reading your collective e-mails, I see that at least half our membership has a decidedly sadistic bent. In any case, it was not your crotch, I aimed for, Michael, but the crotch of our Vice-President, Amir Bathshiri, with whom I have long been intimately acquainted, both of us having lost our spouses several years ago. If the seating arrangements in the Sir Francis Drake Room were any less cramped, none of these misunderstandings would have occurred. Of course, I never would have tried to fondle you, Michael. In the first place, you are the most boring, tedious person I have met in my life, and believe me, as Chair of the English Dept. at Roosevelt, I have met my share of boring, tedious people. You recite poetry with all the grace of a highway sign that cautions one to beware of falling rocks. In fact, I would rather make love to a falling rock. But enough! I know that it is my errant foot to blame. Amir and I have talked this over and have decided to withdraw from PAWS as well as from academia. Early retirement calls, Michael and Lisa, and I will give neither of you a thought as I walk along the beach hand in hand with Amir in the months and years to come, listening to the mermaids singing each to each.

Yes, Michael, I find you and your crotch and your paramour the very essence of Twee.

To: PAWS Listserve
From: Betsy Midchester/Treasurer
Subject: New Elections
Date: July 30th

Please note that the agenda for our next meeting has changed. We will spend most of the meeting on new elections to be held for the positions of President, Vice-President and Secretary of our organization. Note, too, that we will no longer be meeting in the Sir Francis Drake Room of the Bensonville Hampton Inn. Instead, we will be meeting in the cafeteria of Enchanted Gardens Residence for Seniors in Glen Ellyn. The change in venue was planned well in advance of recent events, so members should not read anything into this (though if any organization's members are skilled at reading between the lines, it should be ours). Please think about whom you would like to nominate for these important positions in our organization. And in the meantime, please remember to always be conscious and considerate of your audience.

Peace and poetry,
Betsy Midchester
Treasurer and Acting President/PAWS

Writing Exercises

1. Part 1: In the first-person or third-person limited omniscient, write a scene where your character hears the sound of someone trying to break into the house. Your character is home alone (although it may not be her house), vulnerable in some way: in the bath, or in bed, or trapped in a windowless room. The scene should begin with the first hint of danger and it should end the moment before your narrator actually sees the intruder. Your goal here is to imagine in a convincing way your narrator's emotions and perceptions, and to create as much suspense as possible.

   Part 2: Write the same scene from the perspective of the intruder. This might be a random break-in by a common burglar, or maybe the intruder's story is more complex. Consider your intruder's expectations: Does he expect the home to be empty? If not, who does he think might be there? Consider whether or not your intruder knows (or thinks he knows) the occupant of the house. In this scene, the reader should identify with the intruder, and again, your goal is to create suspense.

2. Write five openings to a story, each from a different authorial distance. The first version should be written from a great distance. With each version you should lessen the authorial distance, so that by the fifth version we immediately feel close to the character. It may help to use filmmaking as an analogy: Your first version should be like a panoramic establishing shot, and your fifth version an extreme close-up. For instance:
   a. It was the blizzard of 1972, the worst storm Boston had experienced in a decade. A young woman, holding her coat closed over her pregnant stomach, struggled down Broad Street.
   b. Jennifer Meyers clutched her coat and prayed she wouldn't slip on a patch of ice.
   c. Jenny waddled down the snowy sidewalk and imagined how silly she must look: a pregnant woman staggering around in a blizzard.
   d. How Jenny wished she were back inside her little apartment, at one with her futon couch, an afghan pulled up to her chin, watching *Days of Our Lives*.
   e. What was she thinking? Trudging through a blinding storm to the Circle K just for a pint of Chunky Monkey? Pregnancy cravings were one thing, but this was ridiculous.

Now write the opening paragraph of your story. Start at a great distance, but steadily reduce the psychic distance with each sentence, so that by the final sentence of the paragraph the reader feels extremely close to the character.

3. Select a tense situation such as an auto accident, a potentially violent encounter, or a disintegrating love affair, and describe it four times from four different points of view:
   a. first person
   b. third-person *limited* omniscient
   c. third-person objective
   d. third-person omniscient
   Which point of view works best for this material, and why?

4. Choose a significant incident from a child's life (your own or invented). First, write a scene from the point of view of the child in first-person present tense. Try to capture a child's perceptions, vocabulary, and syntax. Now rewrite the scene in first-person past tense from the perspective of the same character as an adult. In this version, your character will not only possess an adult's perception of the event, but will also be able to recall his own childish reaction to it. Try to convey how your character feels about his child-self through his tone (affectionate, amused, nostalgic, embarrassed, mocking, ironic and detached, etc.). What do you gain/lose with the two different points of view?

5 Write a gossipy letter from the point of view of one family member who passes scathing judgments on another, but let readers know that the speaker really loves or envies the other (an unreliable narrator). Alternatively, have the speaker loudly praise the other family member, but let readers hear harsh criticism implied.

6. Write down a false statement about yourself, such as "I have a pet snake." Keep going, elaborating on the false statement, allowing the "I" character to develop. You are beginning to create a narrator who is not like you, which will give you more imaginative freedom than you might feel when writing about yourself as the "I" narrator.

7. Imagine a character who is your complete opposite in some specific way. For example, if you hate country music, take on the "I" voice of someone who is, among other things, a country music fan. Now choose an action (walking to school, eating in a café, making a sale to a customer), and write a scene in which your "opposite I" character is performing that action. Make the character sympathetic and intriguing. Don't announce that he or she is a country music lover, but allow the detail and dialogue in the scene to gradually reveal this to the reader.

9

PLAY IT AGAIN, SAM
Revision

"Talent is a long patience," Anton Chekhov remarked, an acknowledgment that the creative process is not all inventive, and extends far beyond the first heated rush. Partly corrective, critical, nutritive, and fostering, revision is a matter of rendering a story the best that it can be. William C. Knott, in *The Craft of Fiction*, cogently observes that "anyone can write—and almost everyone you meet these days is writing. However, only the writers know how to rewrite. It is this ability alone that turns the amateur into a pro."

While the focus of this chapter is the overall revision of stories and the best use of readers' feedback, the methods of shaping, enriching, and enlivening stories discussed throughout this book implicitly concern the revision of fiction, element by element. We have already visited the process of revision through the discussion of the story workshop in the preface (a discussion that will continue here); in the Chapter 4 review "Character: A Summary"; and in the Chapter 6 section "Revising Summary and Scene."

Re-Vision

Revising is a process more dreaded than dreadful. The resistance to rewriting is, if anything, greater than the resistance to beginning in the first place. Yet the chances are that once you have committed yourself to a first draft, you'll be unable to leave it in an unfinished and unsatisfying state. You'll be *unhappy* until it's right. Making it right will involve a second commitment, to seeing the story fresh and creating it again with the advantage of this "re-vision." Alice Munro, in the introduction to her *Selected Stories*, describes the risk, the readiness, and the reward.

> ...The story, in the first draft, has put on rough but adequate clothes, it is "finished" and might be thought to need no more than a lot of technical adjustments, some tightening here and expanding there, and the slipping in of some telling dialogue and chopping away of flabby modifiers. It's then, in fact, that the story is in the greatest danger of losing its life, of appearing so hopelessly misbegotten that my only relief comes from abandoning it. It doesn't do enough. It does what I intended, but it turns out that my intention was all wrong.... I go around glum and preoccupied, trying to think of ways to fix the problem. Usually the right way pops up in the middle of this.
>
> A big relief. Renewed energy. Resurrection.
>
> Except that it isn't the right way. Maybe a way *to* the right way. Now I write pages and pages I'll have to discard. New angles are introduced, minor characters brought center stage, lively and satisfying scenes are written, and it's all a mistake. Out they go. But by this time I'm on the track, there's no backing out. I know so much more than I did, I know what I want to happen and where I want to end up and I just have to keep trying till I find the best way of getting there.

To find the best way of getting there, you may have to "see again" more than once. The process of revision involves external and internal insight. You'll need your conscious critic, your creative instinct, and readers you trust. You may need each of them several times, not necessarily in that order. A story gets better not just by polishing and refurbishing, not by improving a word choice here and an image there, but by taking risks with the structure, reenvisioning, being open to new meaning itself. "In the first draft is the talent," said French poet Paul Valery, "in the second is the art."

Worry It and Walk Away

To write your first draft, you banished the internal critic. Now make the critic welcome. Revision is work, but the strange thing is that you may find you can concentrate on the work for much longer than you could play at freedrafting. It has occurred to me that writing a first draft is very like tennis or softball—I have to be psyched for it. Energy level up, alert, on my toes. A few hours is all I can manage, and at the end of it I'm wiped out. Revision is like careful carpentry, and if I'm under a deadline or just determined to get this thing crafted and polished, I can be good for twelve hours of it.

The first round of rewrites is probably a matter of letting your misgivings surface. Focus for a while on what seems awkward, overlong, undeveloped, flat, or flowery. Tinker. Tighten. Sharpen. More important at this stage than finishing any given page or phrase is that you're getting to know your story in order to open it to new possibilities. You will also get tired of it; you may feel stuck.

Then put it away. Don't look at it for a matter of days or weeks—until you feel fresh on the project. In addition to getting some distance on your story, you're mailing it to your unconscious, not consciously working out the flaws but temporarily letting them go. Rollo May, in *The Courage to Create*, describes what frequently happens next:

> Everyone uses from time to time such expressions as, "a thought pops up," an idea comes "from the blue" or "dawns" or "comes as though out of a dream," or "it suddenly hit me." These are various ways of describing a common experience: the breakthrough of ideas from some depth below the level of awareness.

It is my experience that such realizations occur over and over again in the course of writing a short story or novel. Often I will believe that because I know who my characters are and what happens to them, I know what my story is about—and often I find I'm wrong, or that my understanding is shallow or incomplete.

In the first draft of one novel, for instance, I opened with the sentence, "It took a hundred and twelve bottles of champagne to see the young Poindexters off to Arizona." A page later one character whispered to another that the young Mr. Poindexter in question had "consumption." I worked on this book for a year (taking my characters off to Arizona where they dealt with the desert heat, lack of water, alcoholism, loss of religion, and the development of mining interests and the building trade) before I saw the connection between "consumption" and "champagne." When I understood that simple link, I understood the overarching theme—surely latent in the idea from the moment it had taken hold of me—between tuberculosis, spiritual thirst, consumerism, and addiction, all issues of "consumption."

"... THE FIRST IMPULSE IN WRITING IS TO FLOOD IT OUT, let as much run freely as you possibly can. Then to take a walk or go to the bank...and come back in a day or six months later. To read it with a cold eye and say, "This is good. This is not. That sentence works. This is magical. This is crummy." You have to maintain your critical sensibility and not just assume, because it was an extraordinary dream for you, that it will be a dream for other people. Because people need maps to your dreams.

ALAN GURGANUS

It might seem dismaying that you should see what your story is about only after you have written it. Try it; you'll like it. Nothing is more exhilarating than the discovery that a complex pattern has lain in your mind ready to unfold.

Note that in the early stages of revision, both the worrying and the walking away are necessary. Perhaps it is bafflement itself that plunges us to the unconscious space where the answer lies.

Criticism and the Story Workshop

Once you have thought your story through, drafted it, and worked on it to the best of your ability, someone else's eyes can help to refresh the vision of your own. Wise professionals rely on the help of an agent or editor at this juncture (although even the wisest still smart at censure); anyone can rely on the help of friends, family, or classmates in a story workshop. The trick to making good use of criticism is to be utterly selfish about it. Be greedy for it. Take it all in. Ultimately you are the laborer, the arbiter, and the boss in any dispute about your story, so you can afford to consider any problem and any solution. Most of us feel not only committed to what we have put on the page, but also defensive on its behalf—wanting, really, to be told only that it is a work of genius or, failing that, to find out that we have gotten away with it. Therefore, the first exigency of revision is that you learn to hear, absorb, and accept criticism.

"Revising is like cutting your own hair," says novelist Robert Stone, for while you may sense the need for improvement, it's hard to get right what you can never entirely see for yourself. This is the major advantage of a workshop—your fellow writers may not be able to tell you how to style the material in the way that best suits the story, but they can at least hold up the mirror and see from a more distanced perspective. (If you are just beginning the practice of group critiques, you may wish to look back at the description of common workshop procedures in Chapter 1.)

How can you assimilate so many opinions, let alone choose what is useful? First, give special consideration to the comments of those two or three workshop members with whose responses you have generally agreed before. However, the best—or at any rate the most useful—criticism, John L'Heureux suggests, simply points out what you had already sensed for yourself but had hoped to get away with. Or as Flannery O'Connor put it, with typical bluntness, in fiction "you can do anything you can get away with, but nobody has ever gotten away with much."

It used to be popular to speak of "constructive criticism" and "destructive criticism," but these are misleading terms suggesting that positive suggestions are useful and negative criticism useless. In practice the opposite is usually the case. You're likely to find that the most constructive thing a reader can do is say *I don't believe this, I don't like this, I don't understand this*, pointing to precisely the passages that made you uneasy. This kind of laying-the-finger-on-the-trouble-spot produces an inward groan, but it's also satisfying; you know just where to go to work. Often the most destructive thing a reader can do is offer you a positive suggestion—*Why don't you have him crash the car?*—that is irrelevant to your vision of the story. Be suspicious of praise that is too extravagant, of blame that is too general. If your impulse is to defend the story or yourself, still the impulse. Behave as if bad advice were good advice, and give it serious consideration. You can reject it after you have explored it for anything of use it may offer.

> ...THE WRITING WORKSHOP FINALLY IS THE ONE PLACE where you can be sure you and your work are taken seriously, where your writing intentions are honored, where even in a mean-spirited comment you can divine—if you wish—the truth about your writing, its strengths and its weaknesses. It is a place where you are surrounded by people whose chief interest is also yours, where the talk is never anything but writing and writing well and writing better....It is where you somehow pick up the notion that what you're doing is a good and noble thing, and though you may not write as well as you'd like, it is enough and will suffice.
>
> JOHN L'HEUREUX

Workshop members often voice sharply divided responses to a manuscript, a situation that may confuse and frustrate the author. Algonquin Books of Chapel Hill editor Duncan Murrell advises workshop writers to pay close attention to the parts of their work that make readers stumble, but to disregard most of the solutions those readers suggest. Give a flawed story to ten good readers and they'll accurately find the flawed passages before offering ten wildly varying explanations and a handful of contradictory solutions. Good readers have a gut level understanding that something's wrong in a story, but they're often unclear about what it is, or what to do about it. Yet once pointed to the weak sections, authors almost always come up with better solutions than anything a reader or an editor can offer; they know the story and the characters better. The trick is to bite your lip when readers tell you how to fix your story, while noting the passages that need repair.

Indeed, while the author may or may not benefit from peer suggestions, everyone else in the workshop does because the practice of thinking through and articulating responses to a story's challenges eventually makes all participants more objective critics of their own work. You will notice that the more specific the criticism you offer—or receive—the more useful it proves and the less it stings; similarly, the more specific the praise of "what works," the more likely it is to reinforce good habits—and to be believed. After a semester's experience of workshopping, you'll find that you can critique a story within your own imagination, knowing who would say what, with whom you would agree, and telling yourself what you already know to be true.

Within a day or two of the workshop, novelist, playwright, and teacher Michelle Carter advises that the author try to "re-hear criticism," that is, to assess what it is readers are responding to, which may not be apparent from the suggested "fix." For example, if a number of readers suggest changing the story's point of view from third person to first, Carter might reinterpret that to mean that the narrator seems overly remote from the characters—not that first-person narration is literally a better choice, but that readers want a more immediate experience of the main character's emotional dilemma.

A second example would be wanting "to know more about Character X." This doesn't necessarily mean sprinkling on some facts and history; but rather that the reader may want a greater understanding of the character's motivations or a closer rendering of crucial moments.

Additionally, Carter cautions, be tough with yourself, even when you realize that criticism is based on a misreading. Rarely is misinterpretation solely the mistake of the reader: Ask what awkwardness of writing or false emphasis might have led to that skewed reading. Novelist Wally Lamb reinforces this point: "Often I think we let the writer get away with too much. If the writing is unclear, we'll read it a second time and make it clear to ourselves and then let the writer off the hook, when, in fact, the writing has to stand for itself.... You want to work on the writing until it is good enough that the writer doesn't have to be in the room explaining and interpreting."

Kenneth Atchity, in *A Writer's Time*, advises compulsory "vacations" at crucial points in the revising process, in order to let the criticism cook until you feel ready, impatient, to get back to writing. So once again, walk away, and when you feel that you have acquired enough distance from the story to see it anew, go back to work. Make notes of your plans, large and small. Talk to yourself in your journal about what you want to accomplish and where you think you have failed. Let your imagination play with new images or passages of dialogue. Always keep a copy (and/or a document on disk) of the story as it is so that you can go back to the original, and then be ruthless with another copy. Eudora Welty advised cutting sections apart and pinning them back together so that they can be easily rearranged. I like to use the whole surface of the kitchen table as a cut-and-paste board. Some people can keep the story in their heads and do their rearranging directly onto the computer screen—which in any case has made the putting-back-together process less tedious than retyping.

Asking the Big Question: What Have I Written?

In a piece of literary criticism, your goal is to say as clearly and directly as possible what you mean. In fiction, your goal is to make people and make them do things and, ideally, never to "say what you mean" at all. Theoretically, an outline can never harm a paper for a literature class: This is what I have to say, and I'll say it through points A, B, and C. But if a writer sets out to write a story to illustrate an idea, the fiction will almost inevitably be thin. Even if you begin with an outline, as many writers do, it will be an outline of the action and not of your "points." You may not know the meaning of the story until the characters begin to tell you what it is. You'll begin with an image of a person or a situation that seems vaguely to embody something important, and you'll learn as you go what that something is. Likewise, what you mean will emerge in the reading experience and take place in the reader's mind, "not," as the narrator says of Marlow's tales in *Heart of Darkness*, "inside like a kernel but outside, enveloping the tale which brought it out."

Early on in the revision process, you may find yourself impelled by, under pressure of, or interested primarily in your theme. It will seem that you have set yourself this lonely, austere, and tortuous task because you do have something to say. Therefore, attempting to articulate the theme of your story is something you'll want to do when you're preparing to revise, so as to direct your revision work toward exploring your understanding of the theme.

At this point you will, and you should, begin to let the sorting-comparing-cataloging neocortex of your brain go to work on the stuff of your story. Rather than "putting in a theme," you'll be looking back to see what you've already, mostly subconsciously, been doing all along. John Gardner describes the process in *The Art of Fiction*.

Theme, it should be noticed, is not imposed on the story but evoked from
within it—initially an intuitive but finally an intellectual act on the part
of the writer. The writer muses on the story idea to determine what it is
in it that has attracted him, why it seems to him worth telling. Having
determined...what interests him—and what chiefly concerns the major
character...he toys with various ways of telling his story, thinks about
what has been said before about [his theme], broods on every image that
occurs to him, turning it over and over, puzzling it, hunting for connections, trying to figure out—before he writes, while he writes, and in the
process of repeated revisions—what it is he really thinks.... Only when
he thinks about a story in this way does he achieve not just an alternative
reality or, loosely, an imitation of nature, but true, firm art—fiction as
serious thought.

So, theme is what your story is about. But that is not enough, because a story
may be "about" a dying Samurai or a quarreling couple or two kids on a tram-
poline, and those would not be the themes of those stories. A story is also
"about" an abstraction, and if the story is significant, that abstraction may be
very large; yet thousands of stories are about love, other thousands about
death, and still other thousands about both love and death, and to say this is
to say little about the theme of any of them.

We might better understand theme if we ask questions like: What does the
story have to say about the idea or abstraction that seems to be contained in it?
What attitudes or judgments does it imply? Above all, how do the elements of
fiction contribute to our experience of those ideas and attitudes in the story?

How Fictional Elements Contribute to Theme

Whatever the idea and attitudes that underlie the theme of a story, that story
will bring them into the realm of experience through its particular and unique
pattern. Theme involves emotion, logic, and judgment, all three—but the
pattern that forms the particular experience of that theme is made up of every
element of fiction this book has discussed: the arrangement, shape, and flow of
the action, as performed by the characters, realized in their details, seen in
their atmosphere, from a unique point of view, through the imagery and the
rhythm of the language.

This book, for example, contains at least eight stories that may be said to
have what used to be called "the generation gap" as a major theme: "Everything
That Rises Must Converge," "Big Me," "A Visit of Charity," "Fiesta, 1980," "My
Kid's Dog," "Mrs. Dutta Writes a Letter," "Following the Notes," and "Who's
Irish?" Some of these are written from the point of view of a member of the older
generation, some from the point of view of the younger. In some, conflict is
resolved by bridging the gap; in others, it is not. The characters are variously
poor, middle-class, rural, urban, male, female, adolescent, middle-aged, old,

Asian, Indian, white. The imagery variously evokes food, landscape, religion, music, cars, dogs, sex, child abuse, and death. It is in the different uses of the elements of fiction that each story makes unique what it has to say about, and what attitude it takes toward, the idea of "the generation gap."

The process of discovering the theme of your story—worrying it until its theme reveals itself, connections occur, images recur, a pattern emerges—is more conscious than readers know, beginning writers want to accept, or established writers are willing to admit. It has become a popular—cliché— stance for writers to claim that they haven't the faintest idea what they meant in their writing. *Don't ask me; read the book. If I knew what it meant, I wouldn't have written it. It means what it says.* When an author makes such a response, it is well to remember that an author is a professional liar. What he or she means is not that there are no themes, ideas, or meanings in the work but that these are not separable from the pattern of fictional experience in which they are embodied. It also means that, having done the difficult writerly job, the writer is now unwilling also to do the critic's work. But beginning critics also resist. Students irritated by the analysis of literature often ask, "How do you know she did that on purpose? How do you know it didn't just happen to come out that way?" The answer is that you don't. But what is on the page is on the page. An author no less than a reader or critic can see an emerging pattern, and the author has both the possibility and the obligation of manipulating it. When you have put something on the page, you have two possibilities, and only two: You may cut it or you are commit- ted to it. Gail Godwin asks:

> But what about the other truths you lost by telling it that way?
> Ah, my friend, this is my question too. The choice is always a killing one. One option must die so that another may live. I do little murders in my workroom every day.

In the unified pattern of a fiction there is something to which the name of "magic" may be given, where one empty word is placed upon another and tapped with a third, and a flaming scarf or a long-eared hope is pulled out of the tall black heart. The most magical thing about this magic is that once the trick is explained, it is not explained, and the better you understand how it works, the better it will work again.

Finally, through revision, through deciding what to cut and what to commit to, you will, or at least might, arrive at a story that is of a piece, a story that is organic, a story that cannot be reduced to theme, but that embodies one.

Revision Questions

As you plan the revision and as you rewrite, you will know (and your critics will tell you) what problems are unique to your story. There are also general, almost universal, pitfalls that you can avoid if you ask yourself the following questions:

Is there unnecessary summary? Remember that it is a common impulse to try to cover too much ground. Tell your story in the fewest possible scenes; cut down on summary and unnecessary flashback. These dissipate energy and lead you to tell rather than show.

Why should the reader turn from the first page to the second? Is the language fresh? Are the characters alive? Does the first sentence, paragraph, page introduce real tension? If it doesn't, you have probably begun at the wrong place. If you are unable to find a way to introduce tension on the first page, you may have to question whether you have a story after all.

Is it original? Almost every writer thinks first, in some way or other, of the familiar, the usual, the given. This character is a stereotype, that emotion is too easy, that phrase is a cliché. First-draft laziness is inevitable, but it is also a way of being dishonest. A good writer will comb the work for clichés and labor to find the exact, the honest, and the fresh.

Is it clear? Although ambiguity and mystery provide some of our most profound pleasures in literature, beginning writers are often unable to distinguish between mystery and muddle, ambiguity and sloppiness. You may want your character to be rich with contradiction, but we still want to know whether that character is male or female, black or white, old or young. We need to be oriented on the simplest level of reality before we can share your imaginative world. Where are we? When are we? Who are they? How do things look? What time of day or night is it? What's the weather? What's happening?

Is it self-conscious? Probably the most famous piece of advice to the rewriter is William Faulkner's "kill all your darlings." When you are carried away with the purple of your prose, the music of your alliteration, the hilarity of your wit, the profundity of your insights, then the chances are that you are having a better time writing than the reader will have reading. No reader will forgive you, and no reader should. Just tell the story. The style will follow of itself if you just tell the story.

Where is it too long? Most of us, and even the best of us, write too long. We are so anxious to explain every nuance, cover every possible aspect of character, action, and setting that we forget the necessity of stringent selection. In fiction, and especially in the short story, we want sharpness, economy, and vivid, telling detail. More than necessary is too much. I have been helped in my own tendency to tell all by a friend who went through a copy of one of my novels, drawing a line through the last sentence of about every third paragraph. Then in the margin he wrote, again and again, "Hit it, and get out." That's good advice for anyone.

Where is it undeveloped in character, action, imagery, theme? In any first, second, or third draft of a manuscript there are likely to be necessary passages sketched, skipped, or skeletal. What information is missing, what actions are incomplete, what motives obscure, what images inexact? Where does the action occur too abruptly so that it loses its emotional force? Is the crisis presented as a scene?

Where is it too general? Originality, economy, and clarity can all be achieved through the judicious use of significant detail. Learn to spot general, vague, and fuzzy terms. Be suspicious of yourself anytime you see nouns like *someone* and *everything*, adjectives like *huge* and *handsome*, adverbs like *very* and *really*. Seek instead a particular thing, a particular size, an exact degree.

Although the dread of "starting over" is a real and understandable one, the chances are that the rewards of revising will startlingly outweigh the pains. Sometimes a character who is dead on the page will come to life through the addition of a few sentences or significant details. Sometimes a turgid or tedious paragraph can become sharp with a few judicious cuts. Sometimes dropping page one and putting page seven where page three used to be can provide the skeleton of an otherwise limp story. And sometimes, often, perhaps always, the difference between an amateur rough cut and a publishable story is in the struggle at the rewriting stage.

Further Suggestions for Revision

- If you have been writing your story on a computer, retype at least one full draft, making both planned and spontaneous changes as you go. The computer's abilities can tempt us to a "fix-it" approach to revision, but jumping in and out of the text to correct problems can result in a revision that reads like patchwork. Rather, the effect of even small changes should ripple through the story, and this is more likely to happen if the writer reenters the story as a whole by literally rewriting it from start to finish.

- Screenwriter Stephen Fischer emphasizes that "writing is not a monolithic process, just as cooking is not a monolithic process. You don't just go in the kitchen and cook—you do a number of very specific things that you focus on one at a time—you peel garlic, you dice garlic, you saute onions—these are separate processes. You don't go into a kitchen and flap your arms and just cook—and in the same way, you don't 'just write.'"

  To put this analogy into practice, write two or three revisions of a story draft, focusing on a different issue each time. For example, you might zero in on the motivations of a character whose behavior and dialogue don't yet ring true; or you might simply focus on using setting to reflect emotion or threading physical activity through dialogue scenes. Focusing on a single goal lets you concentrate your efforts—yet other developments will naturally occur in response to the single-focus changes.

- In an interview in *Conversations on Writing Fiction*, novelist and teacher Jane Smiley says she asks her student writers to confront their own sets of "evasions," the counterproductive "rituals which don't actually allow them to spend time with or become engaged with their chosen themes or characters." For example, many people find conflict hard to handle in real life and therefore avoid it, often for good reason. Yet many of us sidestep conflict in our fiction too, even knowing its necessity in driving a character toward a defining crisis. If this sounds like an evasion you've experienced, take a look back at places in the story where explosive scenes *should* happen—places where characters ought to confront or defend. Are these, in fact, all-out scenes? Or do your characters neatly sidestep the conflict and retreat to their private thoughts? Does another character too conveniently knock at the door?

Taking refuge in the making of metaphors, however vivid, rather than clearly depicting what *is*, may be another form of evasion, perhaps reflecting a writer's lack of confidence in the interest of his or her material.

Spiraling off into the weird and random may reflect a similar lack of confidence or indecision; overly clever, bantering dialogue that strains to entertain may reflect a desire to dazzle, while avoiding the harder search for dialogue that is both realistic and revealing.

Evasions may be easier to observe in others' work at first, so you might want to ask a trusted workshop friend to help you recognize the evasions in your own stories. As you revise and encounter points of resistance—those places where you hesitate to probe further or describe more specifically—ask yourself, Is this right for the story or is it simply my comfortable habit?

...YOU GENERALLY START OUT WITH SOME OVERALL IDEA that you can see fairly clearly, as if you were standing on a dock and looking at a ship on the ocean. At first you can see the entire ship, but then as you begin work you're in the boiler room and you can't see the ship anymore....What you really want in an editor is someone who's still on the dock, who can say, Hi, I'm looking at your ship, and it's missing a bow, the front mast is crooked, and it looks to me as if your propellers are going to have to be fixed.

MICHAEL CRICHTON

Examples of the Revision Process

When reading a polished, published story, it can be difficult to imagine that it once was any other way—difficult to realize that the author made both choices and unplanned connections, difficult to envision the story's history. After all, by the point of publication the writer has likely heeded critic Annie Dillard's admonition: "Process is nothing; erase your tracks. The path is not the work."

Yet a glimpse of these earlier "tracks" may reveal the paths writers forged to final versions of their stories, and this may in turn inspire you to a more thorough reenvisioning of your own work. What follows are authors' accounts of the revision process.

In her book-length essay *The Writing Life*, Annie Dillard uses the metaphor of knocking out "a bearing wall" for the revising writer's sacrifice of the very aspect of the story that inspired its writing. Strange as it sounds, this is an experience familiar to many accomplished writers: "The part you must jettison," says Dillard, "is not only the best-written part; it is also, oddly, that part which was to have been the very point. It is the original key passage, the passage on which the rest was to hang, and from which you yourself drew the courage to begin."

Joyce Carol Oates describes this phenomenon—and more—in her essay "Smooth Talk: Short Story into Film." Readers of "Where Are You Going, Where Have You Been?" one of the most famous American stories of the late twentieth century, may be surprised to learn that the author's initial impulse to write the story disappeared in the drafting process. Recounts Oates:

> Some years ago in the American Southwest, there surfaced a tabloid psychopath known as "The Pied Piper of Tucson." I have forgotten his name, but his specialty was the seduction and occasional murder of teen-aged girls. He may or may not have had actual accomplices, but his bizarre activities were known among a circle of teenagers in the Tucson area; for some reason they kept his secret, deliberately did not inform parents or police. It was this fact, not the fact of the mass murderer himself, that struck me at the time. And this was a pre-Manson time, early or mid-1960s.
>
> The Pied Piper mimicked teenagers in their talk, dress, and behavior, but he was not a teenager—he was a man in his early thirties. Rather short, he stuffed rags in his leather boots to give himself height. (And sometimes walked unsteadily as a consequence: did none among his admiring constituency notice?) He charmed his victims as charismatic psychopaths have always charmed their victims, to the bewilderment of others who fancy themselves free of all lunatic attractions. The Pied Piper of Tucson: a trashy dream, a tabloid archetype, sheer artifice, comedy, cartoon—surrounded, however improbably, and finally tragically, by real people. You think that, if you look twice, he won't be there. But there he is.
>
> I don't remember any longer where I first read about this Pied Piper—very likely in *Life* Magazine. I do recall deliberately not reading the full article because I didn't want to be distracted by too much detail. It was not after all the mass murderer himself who intrigued me, but the disturbing fact that a number of teenagers—from "good" families—aided and abetted his crimes. This is the sort of thing authorities and responsible citizens invariably call "inexplicable" because they can't find explanations for it. *They* would not have fallen under this maniac's spell, after all.
>
> An early draft of my short story, "Where Are You Going, Where Have You Been?" —from which the film *Smooth Talk* was adapted by Joyce

Chopra and Tom Cole—had the rather too explicit title "Death and the Maiden." It was cast in a mode of fiction to which I am still partial—indeed, every third or fourth story of mine is probably in this mode—"realistic allegory," it might be called. It is Hawthornean, romantic, shading into parable. Like the medieval German engraving from which my title was taken, the story was minutely detailed yet clearly an allegory of the fatal attractions of death (or the devil). An innocent young girl is seduced by way of her own vanity; she mistakes death for erotic romance of a particularly American/trashy sort.

In subsequent drafts the story changed its tone, its focus, its language, its title. It became "Where Are You Going, Where Have You Been?" Written at a time when the author was intrigued by the music of Bob Dylan, particularly the hauntingly elegiac song "It's All Over Now, Baby Blue," it was dedicated to Bob Dylan. The charismatic mass murderer drops into the background and his innocent victim, a fifteen-year-old, moves into the foreground. She becomes the true protagonist of the tale, courting and being courted by her fate, a self-styled 1950s pop figure, alternately absurd and winning. There is no suggestion in the published story that "Arnold Friend" has seduced and murdered other young girls, or even that he necessarily intends to murder Connie. Is his interest "merely" sexual? (Nor is there anything about the complicity of other teenagers. I saved that yet more provocative note for a current story, "Testimony.") Connie is shallow, vain, silly, hopeful, doomed—but capable nonetheless of an unexpected gesture of heroism at the story's end.

Annie Dillard concludes the section of her essay "The Writing Life" by suggesting that a writer may save the abandoned idea for another story: "So it is that a writer writes many books. In each book, he intended several urgent and vivid points, many of which he sacrificed as the book's form hardened.... The writer returns to these materials, these passionate subjects, as to unfinished business, for they are his life's work."

What follows are an essay by author Ron Carlson on the writing of his story "Keith" an early draft of the story, and the story as it finally appeared.

Notes on "Keith"

RON CARLSON

The first signal from the real world for the story "Keith": I saw a woman in the hospital. I was in the University of Utah Hospital visiting a friend, and walking along the fifth floor corridor, the glassed part which offers a view of the whole valley below, I passed a young woman who was coming the other way dressed in pajamas and a robe. She was walking very slowly, little stab steps, and she had one hand at the throat of the robe, holding it together. She was very beautiful there moving like that on a floor where only dire things transpired. We were alone for a moment in that strange daylight and then gone and I never saw her again.

But I thought about her, trying to make sense of her youth and her beauty and the implications of her being in that serious place in her bedclothes.

I was teaching in a high school at the time, as a visiting writer, and the hundred people I dealt with every day were young and healthy and full of energy and foolish wisdom, and of course being around such people and reading their stories proves soon enough that their worries are real and that they are young and old at once. My wife and I taught in a boarding school for ten years, long enough to see that high school is a little world with all the allegiances and betrayals any small planet needs. There's a good deal of drama every day in a high school. And it was there I made this odd connection: the young woman I saw wasn't gravely ill, she was simply on a lark. She'd come up to the hospital, changed into her pajamas and was walking around. It was a kind of theater; I saw ten examples of it every day at school. And then—logically— I had the other thought: that would be a great date. You go to the hospital with your girlfriend, change into your pajamas and walk around. It might seem oddly out of context, but to a fiction writer working in a high school who was bothered by a woman he'd seen, it made real good sense. So many times as a writer, you ask "what if?" and then follow the premise as it connects to others.

Many years before I saw the woman in the hospital, while I was teaching high school English in Connecticut, I had taught a story which stayed with me for some reason. The story was "How Beautiful with Shoes," (and I can't find the story or the author's name now) and it was set in the thirties, I think, and it was about the night that an escaped inmate from an insane asylum changes the life of a rural farm girl. Two worlds collide, you could say: he's crazy, incandescent, poetic, doomed. She's stolid, prosaic, asleep. The idea took hold of me. There's a moment in that story when after her rescue from a long night with the lunatic, her fiancé—a sturdy farmhand—comes up and embraces her and she tells him something like: Oh, just go away. Leave me alone. It's the first time she's stood up to him. I loved that and pay tribute to it in "Keith."

When I started writing "Keith," I named the girl Barbara Peterson because I wanted it to be a "standard" name and I wanted her to be a standard success in high school, a type. (Also, Barbara Peterson is the name of one of my friends—one, coincidentally, who definitely breaks type.) I find that many times in my stories I start with a person who could be a stereotype, a generic character unit, and then work to earn them credibility, personhood. I did it with homeless people in a story called, "The Governor's Ball," and I did it with DeRay who starts as a biker in "DeRay" and proves himself a kind of rocket scientist. All I wanted my Barbara Peterson in the story to be was a person from the "right" world who meets someone who shows her other possibilities.

I pinched the name Zetterstrom from a fine friend of mine in Connecticut, a wonderful photographer, because the name is not typical and it starts with a Z.

The first hint that Keith might be sick emerged with the writing of the story. I was kind of playing with that option until Barbara's friend Dana said, "Bald kids in high school who don't have earrings have got cancer." Then it tipped for me, and that informed the rest of the story with that notion—that he had a life-threatening disease. The idea that he was doomed came from "How Beautiful with Shoes." The madman in that story was also fated for trouble, and I wanted Keith to be speaking from an edge, an extreme time. Being there has caused him to speak out, and it colors what he says and how he says it. There was some ambiguity in early drafts that he might be acting at being sick for the purpose of tricking, seducing Barbara, but that vanished when I found my final scene in the airport. Their frank exchange in this good-bye scene nailed both characters for me. It is an important moment for Barbara because she gets to climb into personhood, take charge, announce an agenda for her own. I knew all along that she wasn't in the story to be a backboard or counterpoint for Keith. If the story was going to be any good, she'd have to be a full person too. What she tells him there by the boarding gate lets me feel that she's arrived, that in fact she's always been in there, measuring things as well as Keith has.

The airport setting was a bit of a surprise and I found it by looking back through the story at the other sets he'd chosen for their "non-dates." The public picnic, the thrift stores, the restaurant, the hospital. The airport as theatre felt simply like a natural extension for Keith, something he would choose.

He was such a pleasure to write. In each moment I simply conjured what would be the thing that would most challenge the expected response and I let him do or say that. He makes that statement about sulfur. He writes her that note. In their discussion about his truck, he tells Barbara to try riding the school bus—as a kind of adventure. No ordinary high school kid would ever associate himself with that kind of remark. And that's what I was after: the non-ordinary.

I have a long personal history with thrift shops, which I won't go into here, except to say I'm always arrested by the bowling balls (most weight for your dollar anywhere) and the trophies, and I've bought more than a few. And there actually used to be a motorcycle hill climbing contest called The Widowmaker Hill Climb in south Salt Lake near where I lived. Having my characters find that big trophy was fun because it felt like a real moment and that's all I'm ever after is a real moment. I didn't see the connection to scooters at the time and I certainly didn't see that the icon of the trophy would become so important in allowing me to close the story quickly in a single paragraph with just the implication I'd hoped for. I didn't see the trophy (big as it was) coming back into the story until I was typing that page.

"Keith" was a story I had in the drawer a long time before I made the final decisions about it and trimmed it up. I'm glad I did. I write from part to whole, staying as specific as I can as I go along in order to create an inventory that might tell me where to go next. "Keith" turned out to be a simple story of moments that speak of a world where wit and a sense of humor might have a chance against the forces of convention.

OH KEITH

They were lab partners. It was that simple, how they met. She was the Barbara Peterson, President of half the school offices and Queen of the rest. He was Keith Zetterstrom, a character, an oddball, a Z. His name was called last. The spring of their senior year at their equipment drawer she spoke to him for the first time in all their grades together: "Are you my lab partner?"

He spread the gear on the counter for the inventory and looked at her. "Yes, I am," he said. "I haven't lied to you this far, and I'm not going to start now."

After school Barbara Peterson met her boyfriend ~~Brian~~ *Don* Woodworth in the parking lot. They had twin red scooters because Don had given her one at Christmas. "That guy," Barbara said, pointing to where Keith stood in the bus line, "Is my lab partner."

"Who is he?" Brian said.

Keith was the window, wallpaper, woodwork. He'd been there for years and they'd never seen him. This was complicated because for years he was short and then he grew tall. And then he grew a long black slash of hair and now he had a crewcut. He was hard to see, hard to fix in one's vision.

The experiments in Chemistry that spring concerned states of matter, and Barbara and Keith worked well together, quietly and

Carlson   Oh Keith   2

methodically testing the elements.

    "You're Barbara Peterson," he said finally as they waited
for a beaker to boil. "We were on the same kickball team in
fourth grade and I stood behind you in the sixth grade Christmas
play. I was a Russian soldier."

    Barbara Peterson did not know what to say to these things.
She couldn't remember the sixth grade play...and fourth grade?
So she said, "What are you doing after graduation?"

    "The sky's the limit," he said. "And you are going off to
Brown University."

    "How did you know that?"

    "The list has been posted for weeks."

    "Oh. Right. Well, I may go to Brown and I may stay here
and go to the University with my boyfriend."

    Their mixture boiled and Keith poured some off into a
cooling tray. "So what do you do?" he asked her.

    Barbara eyed him. She was used to classmates having
curiosity about her, and she had developed a pleasant
condescension, but Keith had her off guard.

    "What do you mean?"

    "On a date with ~~Brian~~ Don, your boyfriend. What do you do?"

    "Lots of things. We play miniature golf."

    "You go on your scooters and play miniature golf."

    "Yes."

action >   "Is there a windmill?"

    "Yes there's a windmill. Why do you ask? What are you

Carlson   Oh Keith   3

getting at?"

    "Who wins? The golf."

    "Brian," Barbara said. "He does."

(***)

    Barbara showed the note to Trish, her best friend.

<u>REASONS YOU SHOULD GO WITH ME</u>

    A.   You are my lab partner.

    B.   Just to see. (You too, even the accomplished
        Barbara Peterson, contain the same
        restless germ of curiosity that
        all humanity possess, a trait that has led us
        the complacency of our cells into the
        bright world where we invented the
        game of bowling, among other things.

    C.   It's not a "date."

    "Great," Trish said. "No teenage beauty is complete without

a night out with a bald oddball. And I don't think he's going to

ravish you against your will, that is. Go for it. We'll tell

Brian that you're staying at my house."

(***)

    Keith drove a Chevy pickup, forest green, and when Barbara

climbed in, she asked, "Why don't you drive this to school?"

    "There's a bus. I love the bus. Have you ever been on

one?"

    "Not a school bus."

    "Oh, try it," he said. "Try it. It's so big and it doesn't

drop you off right at your house."

Carlson   Oh Keith   4

"You ~~are an oddball.~~ we weird." "You are an oddball."

"Why? Oh, does the bus go right to your house? Come on, does it? But you've got to admit they're big and that yellow paint job? Show me that on any other vehicle, I dare you. Fasten your seat belt, let's go."

The evening went like this: Keith turned onto Bloomfield, the broad business avenue that stretched from near the airport all the way back to the university. "I want you to point out your least favorite building on this street," he told her. You get two chances. We'll head out west and then come all the way back. Now concentrate."

"So we're not going bowling?"

"No, we're saving that. I thought we'd just get a little something to eat. But look, keep your eyes peeled, any places you can't stand?" By the time they reached the airport, Barbara had pointed out four places she thought were ugly. When they turned around, Keith added: "Now, your final choice please. And not ~~just~~ someplace you ~~kind of~~ just don't like. We're looking for genuine aversion."

They made one more complete circuit of the route before Barbara selected a four story metal building near downtown, with a simple crude marquee above the main doors that read: INSURANCE.

"Excellent," Keith said as he swung the pickup to the curb. He hopped out and began unloading his truck. "This is truly ugly. The architect here is now serving time."

Carlson   Oh Keith   5

"This is where my father used to work."

Keith paused, his arms full of equipment. "When..."

"When he divorced my mom. His office was right up there."
She pointed. "He's gone now: Denver. God, I hate driving by
this place."

"Good," Keith said with renewed conviction. "Come over here
and sit down. Have a Coke."

Barbara sat in a chaise lounge that Keith had set on the
floodlit front lawn next to a folding table. He handed her a
Coke. "We're eating here?"

"Yes, Miss," he said, toting over the cooler and the little
propane stove. "It's rustic but traditional: cheese omelets and
hash brown potatoes. Sliced tomatoes for a salad with choice of
dressing, and -- for dessert -- ice cream. On the way home, of
course." Keith poured some oil into the frying pan. "There is
nothing like a meal to alter the chemistry of a place."

On the way home, they did indeed stop for ice cream and
Barbara asked him: "Wasn't your hair long last year, like in
your face and down like this?" She swept her hand past his eye.

"It was."

"Why is it short now?"

Keith ran his hand back over his head. "For the 880. I'm
going to run the eight-eighty for track."

Barbara looked at him over her ice cream. "I didn't know
you were on the track team."

"I'm running the 880," he said, nodding. "I'm not going to

start lying to you now."

***

It was a weird week for Barbara. She actually did feel
different about the Insurance building as she drove her scooter
by it on the way to school. When Trish found out about dinner,
she said, "That was you! I saw your spread as we headed down to
Barney's. You were like camped out, right. What did Don say?"

Barbara stared Trish down: "Don't start. There is
something about this Keith."

"Right. But, hey, I've known a lot of boys who cook and
they were some of the slickest. High School Confidential says:
'There are three million seductions and only one goal.'"

"You cynic."

"Cynicism is a sign of good mental health."

***

In chemistry, it was sulfur. Liquid, solid, and gas. The
hallways of the chemistry annex smelled like rotten eggs and
jokes abounded. Barbara winced through the white wispy smoke as
Keith stirred the melting sulfur nuggets.

"This is awful," Barbara said.

"This is wonderful," Keith said. "This is the exact smell
of human beings raised to one hundred degrees centigrade. That
is what greets you in Hell. It is a totally organic odor,-
perhaps the world's ultimate natural odor."

Barbara looked at her lab partner, her mouth, which she
remembered to never let gape open, open. "My lab partner is a

certifiable..."

"Your lab partner wants to meet you tonight at seven
o'clock."

"Keith," she said, taking the stir stick from him and
prodding the nodules of undissolved sulfur. "I go with B~~ri~~an. I
have a boyfriend."

"Good. Good." he said. "Now tell me something I don't
know. Listen: I want to pick you up at seven. This isn't a
date. This isn't dinner. This is errands. I'm serious.
Necessary errands for your friends."

Barbara Peterson rolled her eyes.

"I'll have you home by nine, young Mr. B~~ri~~an can come by on
his scooter then. I mean it." Keith leaned toward her, the
streams of baking acrid sulfur rising past his face. "I'm not
~~going to start~~ lying to you ~~now~~."

*****

When she got to the truck that night, Keith asked her, "What
did you tell B~~ri~~an?"

"I told him I had errands at my aunt's and to come by at ten
for a little while."

"That's awfully late on a school night."

"Keith!"

"I mean, why didn't you tell him you'd be with me for two
hours." He looked at her. "I have trouble lending credibility
to a relationship that is almost one year old and one in which
one of the members has given another an actual full-size, road-

worthy motor vehicle, and yet it remains a relationship in which
one of the members lies to the other when she plans to spend two
hours with her lab partner, a person with whom she has inhaled
the very vapors of hell."

"Stop the truck, Keith. I'm getting out."

"And miss bowling? And miss the search for bowling balls?"

Half an hour later they were in Veteran's Thrift, reading
the bowling balls. They'd already bought five at Desert Industry
Thrift Shops and the Salvation Army store. Keith's rule was it
had to be less than two dollars. They already had "Patty" for
Trish, Betsy and Kim for two more of Barbara's friends, an
initialled ball B.R. for Brian even though his last name was
Woodworth,("Puzzle him," Keith said. "Make him guess."), and
WALT for their chemistry teacher, Mr. Walter Miles. They found
three more in the bins in Veteran's thrift, one marked SKIP, one
marked COSMO, ("A must," Keith said), and a brilliant green ball,
run deeply with hypnotic swirls which had no name at all.

Barbara was touring the wide shelves of used appliances,
toys, and kitchen utensils. "Where do they get all this stuff?"

"You've never been in a second-hand store before, have you?"

"No. Look at all this stuff. This is a quarter?" She held
up a large plastic tray with the Beatles pictures on it.

"That," Keith said, taking it from her and placing it in the
cart with their bowling balls, "Came from the home of a fan of
the first magnitude,"Oh, it's a sad story. It's enough to say
that this is here tonight because of Yoko Ono." Keith's

attention was taken by a large trophy, standing among the dozen
other trophies on the top shelf. "Whoa," he said, pulling it
down. The golden trophy was over three feet tall: six columns,
ascending from a white marble base to a silver obelisk, framed by
two embossed silver wreaths, and topped by a silver woman on a
rearing motorcycle. The inscription on the base read:
WIDOWMAKER HILL CLIMB -- FIRST PLACE 1987. Keith held it out to *rename*
show Barbara, like a man holding a huge bottle of aspirin in a
television commercial. "But this is another story altogether."
He placed it reverently in the basket.

"What is the story?"

"No time. You've got to get back and meet Brian, a person
who doesn't know where you are." Keith led her to the check out.
He was quiet all the way to the truck. He placed the balls
carefully in the cardboard boxes in the truck bed and then set
the huge trophy between them on the seat.

"What is the deal with this trophy -- you don't know where
it came from."

Keith put a finger to his lips: "Shhhh," and started the
truck and headed to Barbara's house. After several blocks of
silence, Barbara folded her arms. "It's a tragic, tragic story,"
he said in a low voice. "I mean, this girl was a golden girl, an
angel; the light in everybody's life."

"Do I want to hear this tragic story?"

"She was a wonder. Straight A's, with an A plus in
chemistry. The girl could do no wrong." Keith looked at

Carlson   Oh Keith   10

Barbara.   "And then she got involved with motorcycles."

      "Is this her on top of the trophy?"

      "The very girl." Keith nodded grimly. "Oh, it started
innocently enough with a little red motor scooter, a toy really,
and she could be seen running errands for the Ladies' Society and
other charities every Saturday and Sunday when she wasn't home
studying." Keith turned to Barbara, moving the trophy forward so he
could see look at her. "I should add here that her fine academic standing
got her into Brown University, where she was going that fateful
fall," Keith laid the trophy back. "When her thirst for speed
grew and grew, breaking over her good common sense like a tidal
wave, sending her into the arms of a 350 cc Harley Davidson, one
the most powerful two wheel vehicles in the history of mankind."
They turned onto Barbara's street.

        She said, "And she entered the Widowmaker Hill Climb."

      "She had to, didn't she. Her obsession had no other
outlet." Keith said, pulling over in front of her house. "And
look, here's Brian."

      Brian was, in fact, leaning against his scooter in her
driveway.

      "Oh great."

      "He's early," Keith said, waving at Brian. "Have fun. And
one last thing, partner. I'll pick you up at four to deliver
these bowling balls."

      "Four?"

      "Four a.m. Brian will be gone, won't he?"

Carlson   Oh Keith   11

"Keith!"

"It's not a date. It's an errand. We've got to finish this
program, right?"

Barbara looked over at Brian and quickly back at Keith as
she opened the truck door. "O.K., but meet me at the corner.
There," she pointed, "by the postbox."

***

She was there. The streets of the suburbs were dark and
quiet, everything in its place, sleeping, but Barbara Peterson
stood in the humming lamplight, hugging her elbows. It was
eerily quiet and she could hear Keith coming for two or three
blocks before he turned onto her street. He had the heater on in
the truck and when she climbed in he handed her a blue cardigan
which she quickly buttoned up. "Whoa," she said, rubbing her
hands over the air vent. "Four a.m. Now this is weird out
here."

"Yeah," Keith said. "Four o'clock makes it a different
planet. I recommend it. But bring a sweater." He looked at
her. "You look real sleepy," he said. "It becomes you. This is
the face you ought to bring to school."

Barbara looked at Keith and smiled. "No make up, O.K. It's
four a.m." His face did look - tired and in the pale dash
lights, with his short, short hair he looked more like a ~~young~~
child, a little boy. "What do we do?"

"We give each of these babies," Keith nodded back at the
bowling balls in the truck bed, "a new home."

They delivered the balls, placing them carefully on the porches of their friends, including Trish and Brian, and then - they spent half an hour finding Mr. Miles' house, which was across town, a tan split-level. Keith handed Barbara the ball marked "WALT" and made her walk it up to the front porch. When she returned to the truck, Keith said, "Years from now you'll be able to say, 'When I was seventeen I put a bowling ball on my chemistry's teacher's front porch.'"

"His name was Walt," Barbara added.

At five-thirty, as the first gray light rose, Barbara Peterson and Keith walked into Jewel's Cafe carrying the last two balls: the green beauty and COSMO. Jewel's was the oldest cafe in the city, an all night diner full of mailmen. "So," Barbara said, as they slid into one of the huge maroon booths, "Who gets these last two?" She was radiant now, fully awake, and energized by the new day.

Keith pointed at the backs of all the mailmen sitting at the counter. "This is the U.S. Postal System stoking up. It is in here, in this hallowed hall, that your mailman gets the stamina to carry many pounds of love letters to your door. This place is one of the sources."

The waitress appeared and they ordered Round-the-World omelettes, hash browns, juice, milk, coffee, and wheat muffins, and Barbara ate with gusto, looking up half way through. "So, where next?" She saw his plate. "Hey, you're not eating."

Keith looked odd, his face milky, his eyes gray. "This food

Carlson   Oh Keith   13

is full of the exact amino acids to have a certifiably

fluorescent day," he said. "I'll get around to it."

But he never did. He pushed his plate to the side and

turned the place mat over and began to write on it.

"Are you feeling all right?" Barbara said.

"I'm O.K."

She tilted her head at him skeptically.

"Hey. I'm O.K. I haven't lied to you this far. Why would

I start now? You know I'm O.K., don't you? Well? Don't you

think I'm O.K.?"

She looked at him and said quietly: "You're O.K."

He showed her the note he had written:

> Dear Waitress: My girlfriend and I are from
> rival families -- different sides of the
> tracks, races, creeds, colors, and zip codes,
> and if they found out we had been out bowling
> all night, they would banish us to prison
> schools on separate planets. Please, please
> find a good home for our only bowling balls.
> Our enormous sadness is only mitigated by the
> fact that we know you'll take care of them.
>   With sweet sorrow ----COSMO

In the truck, Barbara said, "Mitigated?"

"Always leave them something to look up."

"You're sick aren't you?" she said.

"You look good in that sweater," he said. When she started

to remove it, he added, "Don't. I'll get it after class, in

just," he looked at his watch, "Two hours and twenty minutes."

***

Carlson   Oh Keith   14

But he wasn't there. He wasn't there all week. The class
did experiments with oxidation and Mr. Miles spent two days
explaining and diagramming rust. On Friday, Mr. Miles worked
with Barbara on the experiments and she asked him what was wrong
with Keith. "I'm not sure," her teacher told her. "But I think
he's on medication."

Barbara had a tennis match on Tuesday afternoon at school
and Brian picked her up and drove her home. Usually he came in
for an hour on these school days, but for the first time she
begged off, claiming homework, kissing him on the cheek and
running into her house. But on Friday, during her away match at
Viewmont, she felt odd again. She knew Brian was in the stands.
When she walked off the court after the match it was nearly dark
and Brian was waiting. She gave Trish her rackets and Barbara
climbed on Brian's scooter without a word. "You weren't that
bad," he said. "Viewmont always has a good team."

"Brian, let's just go home."

"You want to stop at Swenson's, get something to eat?"

"No."

So Brian started his scooter and drove them home. Barbara
could tell by the way he was driving that he was mad, and it
confused her: she felt strangely glad about it. She didn't want
to invite him in, let him grope her on the couch. She held on as
he took the corners too fast and slipped through the stop signs,
but all the way home she didn't put her chin on his shoulder.
She didn't know what was going on, but she felt fairly sure that

Carlson   Oh Keith   15

it was her fault.

At her house, she got the scene she'd been expecting. "Just
what is the matter with you?" Brian said. For some reason when
he'd gone to kiss her, she averted his face. Her heart burned
with pleasure and shame. She was going to make up a lie about
tennis, but then just said, "Oh Brian. Just leave me alone for a
while, will you. Just go home."

Inside, she couldn't settle down. She didn't shower or
change clothes. She sat in the dark of her room for a while and
then using only the tiny spot of her desk lamp she copied her
chemistry notes for the week and called Trish.

It was midnight when Trish picked her up quietly by the
mailbox on the corner. Trish was smoking one of her Marlboros
and blowing smoke into the windshield. She said," High School
Confidential, Part Five: Young Barbara Peterson, still in her
foxy tennis clothes, and her old friend Trish meet again late at
night, cruise the Strip, pick up two strong young men with
tattoos and are never seen alive again. Is that it? Count me
in."

"Teenage Adventure, Part Two."

"And that is?"

"Two sultry babes, one in tennis clothes who has just been a
royal bitch to her boyfriend for no reason, drive to 1147
Fairmont to drop off the week's chemistry notes."

"That would be Keith Zetterstrom's address," I'd guess."
Trish said.

Carlson   Oh Keith   16

"He's my lab partner."

"Of course he is," Trish said.

"He missed all last week. Mr. Miles told me that Keith's on
medication."

"Oh my god!" Trish let go of the steering wheel for a
second and then clamped it tight. "He's got cancer. That's that
scary hairdo. He's sick."

"No he doesn't. I checked the college lists. He's going to
Dickinson."

"Not for long, honey. I should have known this." Trish
inhaled and blew smoke thoughtfully out of the side of her mouth.
"Bald kids in high school without earrings have got cancer."

***

Keith was in class the following Monday for the chemistry
exam: sulfur and rust. After class, Barbara Peterson took him by
the arm and led him to her locker. "Thanks for the notes,
partner. They were fluorescent. I aced the quiz."

"You were sick last week."

"Last week," he pondered. "Oh, you mean because I wasn't in
school. What do you do, come every day? I couldn't do that; it
would take the something special I feel for this place all away.
I like to come time to time and keep the dew on the rose, so to
speak."

"I know what's the matter with you."

"Good for you, Barbara Peterson. And I know what's the
matter with you too; sounds like a promising relationship."

Carlson   Oh Keith   17

Barbara pulled his folded sweater from the locker and handed
it to him. As she did, Brian came up and said to them both: "Oh
I see." He started to walk away.

"Brian," Keith said. "Listen. You don't see. I'm not a
threat to you. Look at me. How could I be a threat to you. How
could I do something great that you couldn't do? Think about
it." Brian stood, his eyes narrowed. Keith went on: "Barbara's
not stupid. What am I going to do, trick her? Force her to do
something? Look at me. I'm her lab partner in chemistry.
Relax." Keith went to Brian and took his hand, shook it. "I'm
certainly no threat to you, Brian Woodworth."

Brian stood for a moment longer until Barbara said, "I'll
see you at lunch," and then he backed and disappeared down the
hall. When he was gone, Barbara said, "<u>Are</u> you tricking me?"

"I don't know. Something's going on. I'm a little
confused."

"You're confused. Who are you? Where have you been, Keith
Zetterstrom? I've been going to school with you all these years
and I've never even seen you and then we're delivering bowling
balls together and now you're sick. Where were you last year?
What are you doing? What are you going to do next year?"

"This year I'm going to die. Last year I got a C in Spanish
with Mrs. Whitehead. It was gruesome. This year I'm going to
die." Keith took her wrist. "But not before I run the 880."

Barbara took a sharp breath through her nose and quietly
began to cry.

Carlson   Oh Keith   18

"Oh, let's not," Keith said, pushing a handkerchief into her
hand. "Here. Think of this." He moved her back against the
wall, out of the students passing by. "If I hadn't found out
that I was sick, I would have never spoken to you. I went all
those years sitting in the back and then I had to get sick to
start talking. Now that's something, isn't it? Besides, I've
got a plan. Can you do this? I'll pick you up at nine. Listen:
bring your pajamas and a robe."

Barbara looked at him over the handkerchief.

"Hey. Trust me. You were the one who was crying. I'll see
you at nine o'clock. This will cheer you up."

*** →

The hospital was on the hill and Keith parked in the
furthest corner of the vast parking lot, one hundred yards from
the nearest car. Beneath them in the dark night, the city teemed
and shimmered, a million lights.

"It looks like a city on another planet," Barbara Peterson
said, as she stepped out of the truck.

"It does, indeed." Keith said, grabbing his bag. "Now if
we only knew if we were taking off or coming in for a landing."

"If we only knew why we were up in the hospital parking lot
with our pajamas in our gym bags, -- that would be a start."

"I'm going to cheer you up. I said I would and I'm going to
keep my word. I'm going to take you in that building," Keith
pointed at the huge hospital, lit like an ocean liner in the
night, "and buy you a package of gum."

Carlson   Oh Keith   19

They changed clothes in the fifth floor restrooms and met in
the hallway, in pajamas and robes, and stuffed their street
cloths into Barbara's tennis bag.

"Oh, I feel better already," Barbara said.

"Now take my arm like this," Keith moved next to her and
placed her hand above his elbow, "And look down like this." He
put his chin on his chest. Barbara tried it. "No, not such a
sad face, more serious, be strong. Good. Now walk just like
this, little stab steps, real slow."

They started down the hallway, creeping along one side.
"How far is it?" Barbara said. People passed them quietly in
groups of two or three. It was the end of visiting hours. "A
hundred yards to the elevators and down three floors then out a
hundred more. Keep your face down."

"Are people looking at us?"

"Well, yes. They've never seen a braver couple. And
they've never seen such fluorescent pajamas. What are those
little deals, lambs?"

They continued along the windows, through the lobby and down
the elevator, in which they stood side by side, their four hands
clasped together, while they were looking at their tennis shoes.
The other people in the car gave them room out of respect. The
main hall was worse, thick with people, everyone going five miles
an hour faster than Barbara and Keith who shuffled along
whispering.

"In the gift shop, finally, they parted the waters. The

small room was crowded, but the people stepped aside and Keith
and Barbara stood right at the counter. "A package of chewing
gum, please," Keith said.

"Which kind?" said the Candy Striper.

"Anything sugarless. My sister and I want our teeth to last
forever."

***

They ran to the truck, leaping and swinging their arms.
Keith threw the bag containing their clothes into the truck bed
and climbed in the cab. It was when Barbara climbed in,
laughing, and Keith said, "Come on, face the facts: you feel
better! You're cured!" And she slid across the seat meaning to
hug him and it turned on both of them and they kissed. She   *ph*
pulled him to her side and they kissed again, one of her arms
around his neck and one of her hands on his face. They fell into
a spin there in the cab of the truck, eyes closed, holding onto
each other in their pajamas, her robe open, their heads against
the back seat, kissing. Barbara shifted and Keith sat up; the
look they exchanged held. Below them the city's lights flickered
in a simmering network. Barbara put her hand carefully on the
top of Keith's bald scalp. She pulled him forward and they
kissed. Then Keith sat up and blinked, saying, "Why would we do
this? Why would two people use their faces this way?"

Barbara Peterson whispered: "Don't you want to?"

Keith sat straighter and adjusted his robe. "Want to? Want
to? Oh, sure, I want to, but...I'm a kid. I'm only seventeen

Carlson   Oh Keith   21

and a half years old. I'm too young for this. It's different
for you with your husband and twelve kids. I'm just a little
holiday for you. But me, I'm too young for this."

She smiled at him and touched the end of his nose. "Or too
old?"

"Well, yes. I'm too old too. That's it... You, you've got
your whole life ahead of you, poor child. Me, I'm already
leaving three generations of Zetterstroms all across the
continent. Why I'm old enough to be your grandfather, your
father..."

"Oh Keith. You are not."

"Well, I'm old enough to be your...brother! How does that
sound? Isn't that alarming enough."

"Oh Keith," Barbara said again hugging his head to her
chest. "You bozo."

-"Absolute, fluorescent bozo,

"You absolute, fluorescent bozo."

***

The day of the track meet, Keith and Barbara cleaned out
their equipment locker in chemistry and waited for Mr. Miles to
check them out. They would graduate in three days. "Are you
coming to the race?" Keith asked her. "I've been practicing my
false start."

"Are you sure you want to do this? Do you feel like it?"

"No. Not at all. Eight hundred and eighty yards. Come on,
that's gotta hurt."

Carlson   Oh Keith   22

"You don't have to."

Keith looked at her. "Barbara. Yes I do. First, I told
you I was going to; second, I've been training -- remember when I
ran across the parking lot the other night? And third, I'm so
full of chemicals from this treatment that if they make me a
urine test, there'll be a fire. Come on, be there. This is one
of the last uses I have for this great body. Besides," he took
her hand under the table, "I won't be at graduation. Isn't that
strange? I'm going to a clinic. In Minnesota. Tomorrow."

Keith did not look good in his track suit. The jersey
bagged off his skinny chest ridiculously. There were only a
hundred or so spectators. Barbara and Trish waved at him when
they arrived, and he winked at them as the 880 runners took their
starting places. When the runners were settled and the started
raised his gun, Keith blasted off the blocks, pulling the other
five boys twenty yards down the track. He walked back to his
place rubbing his bald head and he said to the starter. "I'm
sorry. That's my moment of glory. Now, whatever else happens,
keep the track open and let me finish this damn thing."

When the gun did fire, the six runners bunched and fell into
line, Keith at the rear. Each step left him further behind, and
by the first back stretch he was all alone, his short pained
steps a crawl compared to the lithe pace of the other runners.
They lapped him before he'd run the first four-forty and they all
finished before he began his second lap. "Wait here," he told

Carlson   Oh Keith   23

the starter as he limped through the line, "I'll be back."

It was a long lap. Keith kept his head down and swung his
arms as if willing his legs to carry him forward, but his pace
only diminished. He was sick in the last turn, spitting up
quickly onto the infield grass, wiping his mouth and continuing.
He finished in a modified walk, his face gray and translucent,
and he wandered down a hundred yards and sat alone on the
infield.

By the time Barbara and Trish had walked across to him, he
was lying on his back, and he looked up into their faces and
smiled. "That second lap is so boring," he said. "I mean, I saw
it all the first time. They've got to change the course before I
try this again."

Trisha and Barbara looked at each other and then Trish said,
"You go ahead and kiss him, he's too sweaty for me." Barbara
fell to her knees and kissed his forehead.

"And this shirt, talk about wind resistance." He sat up (*when*)
"Hey, Barbara Peterson, I'm glad I knew you."

(***)

That evening at twilight, as Keith was washing his truck, he
saw Barbara Peterson pull up in her mother's Buick. He was
wiping down the chrome and she came walking up. "Looks good," she   ⌐
said.

"Where's your scooter?"

"It has been returned." She moved in front of Keith,
blocking the hubcap he was wiping. "When do you leave?"

— How should this story end?

"Seven in the morning. Is that what this is, goodbye? You want to have a final scene?"

"No. I drove over to see you, Keith. It goes like this. I love you."

Keith moved around Barbara to the back bumper, started to polish it, then just lowered the tailgate and sat down. "If it's a final scene you want, how about this: You better call Brian and get your scooter back. Tell him it was a trick. I tricked you." He stood up and continued, "You think I wanted to go alone. Come on, get real. It was a joke. I wanted to give Barbara Peterson a whirl. I was selfish, O.K.? I just cranked you around a little. Wake up. That's all I've got to say." Keith balled up his polish rag and threw it into the truck. "How was it?"

"Oh, Keith, it was pretty good, really, pretty good. But I don't believe a fluorescent word of it. You were there. You meant every minute. So did I."

She took his shirt and kissed him. He put his arm around her neck. "I remember you." She started to cry. "This is O.K.. I get to cry. You're my lab partner." She kissed him again and whispered the next; "I love you." Then she left.

***

Simply put, that was the last time Barbara Peterson saw Keith Zetterstrom. She received two postcards from Minneapolis, and then that fall when she arrived in Providence for her freshman year at Brown, there was one package waiting for her, a

Carlson   Oh Keith   25

large trophy topped by a girl on a motorcycle. She had seen it
before. She kept it in her dorm window where it was visible four
stories from the ground and she told her roommates that it meant
a lot to her, that it represented a lot of fun and hard work but
her goal had been to win the Widowmaker Hill Climb, and once she
had done that, she sold her bikes and gave up her motorcycles
forever.

— Lying /tricking

— trophies

◈

Keith

RON CARLSON

They were lab partners. It was that simple, how they met. She was *the* Barbara Anderson, president of half the school offices and queen of the rest. He was Keith Zetterstrom, a character, an oddball, a *Z*. His name was called last. The spring of their senior year at their equipment drawer she spoke to him for the first time in all their grades together: "Are you my lab partner?"

He spread the gear on the counter for the inventory and looked at her. "Yes, I am," he said. "I haven't lied to you this far, and I'm not going to start now."

After school Barbara Anderson met her boyfriend, Brian Woodworth, in the parking lot. They had twin red scooters because Brian had given her one at Christmas. "That guy," Barbara said, pointing to where Keith stood in the bus line, "is my lab partner."

"Who is he?" Brian said.

Keith was the window, wallpaper, woodwork. He'd been there for years and they'd never seen him. This was complicated because for years he was short and then he grew tall. And then he grew a long black slash of hair and now he had a crewcut. He was hard to see, hard to fix in one's vision.

The experiments in chemistry that spring concerned states of matter, and Barbara and Keith worked well together, quietly and methodically testing the elements.

"You're Barbara Anderson," he said finally as they waited for a beaker to boil. "We were on the same kickball team in fourth grade and I stood behind you in the sixth-grade Christmas play. I was a Russian soldier."

Barbara Anderson did not know what to say to these things. She couldn't remember the six-grade play...and fourth grade? So she said, "What are you doing after graduation?"

"The sky's the limit," he said. "And you are going off to Brown University."

"How did you know that?"

"The list has been posted for weeks."

"Oh, right. Well, I may go to Brown and I may stay here and go to the university with my boyfriend."

Their mixture boiled and Keith poured some off into a cooling tray. "So what do you do?" he asked her.

Barbara eyed him. She was used to classmates having curiosity about her, and she had developed a pleasant condescension, but Keith had her off guard.

"What do you mean?"

"On a date with Brian, your boyfriend. What do you do?"

"Lots of things. We play miniature golf."

"You go on your scooters and play miniature golf."

"Yes."

"Is there a windmill?"

"Yes, there's a windmill. Why do you ask? What are you getting at?"

"Who wins? The golf."

"Brian," Barbara said. "He does."

Barbara showed the note to Trish, her best friend.

Reasons You Should Go with Me

A. *You are my lab partner.*

B. *Just to see. (You too, even Barbara Anderson, contain the same restless germ of curiosity that all humanity possesses, a trait that has led us out of the complacency of our dark caves into the bright world where we invented bowling—among other things.)*

C. *It's not a "date."*

"Great," Trish said. "We certainly believe this! But, girl, who wants to graduate without a night out with a bald whatever. And I don't think he's going to ravish you—against your will, that is. Go for it. We'll tell Brian that you're staying at my house."

Keith drove a Chevy pickup, forest-green, and when Barbara climbed in, she asked, "Why don't you drive this to school?"

"There's a bus. I love the bus. Have you ever been on one?"

"Not a school bus."

"Oh, try it," he said. "Try it. It's so big and it doesn't drop you off right at your house."

"You're weird."

"Why? Oh, does the bus go right to your house? Come on, does it? But you've got to admit they're big, and that yellow paint job? Show me that somewhere else, I dare you. Fasten your seat belt, let's go."

The evening went like this: Keith turned onto Bloomfield, the broad business avenue that stretched from near the airport all the way back to the university, and he told her, "I want you to point out your least favorite building on this street."

"So we're not going bowling?"

"No, we're saving that. I thought we'd just get a little something to eat. So, keep your eyes open. Any places you can't stand?" By the time they reached the airport, Barbara had pointed out four she thought were ugly. When they turned around, Keith added: "Now, your final choice, please. And not someplace you just don't like. We're looking for genuine aversion."

Barbara selected a five-story metal building near downtown, with a simple marquee above the main doors that read INSURANCE.

"Excellent," Keith said as he swung the pickup to the curb. He began unloading his truck. "This is truly garish. The architect here is now serving time."

"This is where my father used to work."

Keith paused, his arms full of equipment. "When..."

"When he divorced my mom. His office was right up there," She pointed. "I hate driving by this place."

"Good," Keith said with renewed conviction. "Come over here and sit down. Have a Coke."

Barbara sat in a chaise lounge that Keith had set on the floodlit front lawn next to a folding table. He handed her a Coke. "We're eating here?"

"Yes, Miss," he said, toting over the cooler and the little propane stove. "It's rustic but traditional: cheese omelets and hash brown potatoes. Sliced tomatoes for a salad with choice of dressing, and—for dessert—ice cream. On the way home, of course." Keith poured some oil into the frying pan. "There is nothing like a meal to alter the chemistry of a place."

On the way home, they did indeed stop for ice cream, and Barbara asked him: "Wasn't your hair long last year, like in your face and down like this?" She swept her hand past his eye.

"It was."

"Why is it so short now?"

Keith ran his hand back over his head. "Seasonal cut. Summer's a coming in. I want to lead the way."

It was an odd week for Barbara. She actually did feel different about the insurance building as she drove her scooter by it on the way to school. When Trish found out about dinner, she said, "That was you! I saw your spread as we headed down to Barney's. You were like camped out, right?"

Wonder spread on Barbara's face as she thought it over. "Yeah, it was cool. He cooked."

"Right. But please, I've known a lot of guys who cook and they were some of the slickest. *High School Confidential* says: 'There are three million seductions and only one goal.'"

"You're a cynic."

"Cynicism is a useful survival skill."

In chemistry, it was sulfur. Liquid, solid, and gas. The hallways of the chemistry annex smelled like rotten eggs and jokes abounded. Barbara winced through the white wispy smoke as Keith stirred the melting sulfur nuggets.

"This is awful," Barbara said.

"This is wonderful," Keith said. "This is the exact smell that greets sinners at the gates of hell. They think it's awful; here we get to enjoy it for free."

Barbara looked at him. "My lab partner is a certifiable..."

"Your lab partner will meet you tonight at seven o'clock."

"Keith," she said, taking the stir stick from him and prodding the undissolved sulfur, "I'm dating Brian. Remember?"

"Good for you," he said. "Now tell me something I don't know. Listen: I'll pick you up at seven. This isn't a date. This isn't dinner. This is errands. I'm serious. Necessary errands—for your friends."

Barbara Anderson rolled her eyes.

"You'll be home by nine. Young Mr. Brian can scoot by then. I mean it." Keith leaned toward her, the streams of baking acrid sulfur rising past his face. "I'm not lying to you."

When she got to the truck that night, Keith asked her, "What did you tell Brian?"

"I told him I had errands at my aunt's and to come by at ten for a little while."

"That's awfully late on a school night."

"Keith."

"I mean, why didn't you tell him you'd be with me for two hours?" He looked at her. "I have trouble lending credibility to a relationship that is almost one year old and one in which one of the members has given another an actual full-size, roadworthy motor vehicle, and yet it remains a relationship in which one of the members lies to the other when she plans to spend two hours with her lab partner, a person with whom she has inhaled the very vapors of hell."

"Stop the truck, Keith. I'm getting out."

"And miss bowling? And miss the search for bowling balls?"

Half an hour later they were in Veteran's Thrift, reading the bowling balls. They'd already bought five at Desert Industry Thrift Shops and the Salvation Army store. Keith's rule was it had to be less than two dollars. They already had PATTY for Trish, BETSY and KIM for two more of Barbara's friends, an initialled ball B.R. for Brian even though his last name was Woodworth ("Puzzle him," Keith said. "Make him guess"), and WALT for their chemistry teacher, Mr. Walter Miles. They found three more in the bins in Veteran's Thrift, one marked SKIP, one marked COSMO ("A must," Keith said), and a brilliant green ball, run deeply with hypnotic swirls, which had no name at all.

Barbara was touring the wide shelves of used appliances, toys, and kitchen utensils. "Where do they get all this stuff?"

"You've never been in a secondhand store before, have you?"

"No. Look at all this stuff. This is a quarter?" She held up a large plastic tray with the Beatles' pictures on it.

"That," Keith said, taking it from her and placing it in the cart with their bowling balls, "came from the home of a fan of the first magnitude. Oh, it's a sad story. It's enough to say that this is here tonight because of

Yoko Ono." Keith's attention was taken by a large trophy, standing among the dozen other trophies on the top shelf. "Whoa," he said, pulling it down. It was huge, over three feet tall: six golden columns, ascending from a white marble base to a silver obelisk, framed by two embossed silver wreaths, and topped by a silver woman on a rearing motocycle. The inscription on the base read: WIDOWMAKER HILL CLIMB—FIRST PLACE 1987. Keith held it out to show Barbara, like a man holding a huge bottle of aspirin in a television commercial. "But this is another story altogether." He placed it reverently in the basket.

"And that would be?"

"No time. You've got to get back and meet Brian, a person who doesn't know where you are." Keith led her to the checkout. He was quiet all the way to the truck. He placed the balls carefully in the cardboard boxes in the truck bed and then set the huge trophy between them on the seat.

"You don't know where this trophy came from."

Keith put a finger to his lips—"*Shhhh*"—and started the truck and headed to Barbara's house. After several blocks of silence, Barbara folded her arms. "It's a tragic, tragic story," he said in a low voice. "I mean, this girl was a golden girl, an angel, the light in everybody's life."

"Do I want to hear this tragic story?"

"She was a wonder. Straight A's, with an A plus in chemistry. The girl could do no wrong. And then," Keith looked at Barbara, "she got involved with motorcycles."

"Is this her on top of the trophy?"

"The very girl." Keith nodded grimly. "Oh, it started innocently enough with a little red motor scooter, a toy really, and she could be seen running errands for the Ladies' Society and other charities every Saturday and Sunday when she wasn't home studying." Keith turned to Barbara, moving the trophy forward so he could see her. "I should add here that her fine academic standing got her into Brown University, where she was going that fateful fall." Keith laid the trophy back. "When her thirst for speed grew and grew, breaking over her good common sense like a tidal wave, sending her into the arms of a twelve-hundred-cc Harley-Davidson, one of the most powerful two-wheeled vehicles in the history of mankind." They turned onto Barbara's street, and suddenly Barbara ducked, her head against Keith's knee.

"Drive by," she whispered. "Just keep going."

"What?" Keith said. "If I do that Brian won't see you." Keith could see Brian leaning against his scooter in the driveway. "Is that guy always early?"

Keith turned the next corner, and Barbara sat up and opened her door. "I'll go down the alley."

"Cool," Keith said. "So you sneak down the alley to meet your boyfriend? Pretty sexy."

She gave him a look.

"Okay, have fun. But there's one last thing, partner. I'll pick you up at four to deliver these bowling balls."

"Four?"

"Four A.M. Brian will be gone, won't he?"

"Keith."

"It's not a date. We've got to finish this program, right?"

Barbara looked over at Brian and quickly back at Keith as she opened the truck door. "Okay, but meet me at the corner. There," she pointed, "by the postbox."

She was there. The streets of the suburbs were dark and quiet, everything in its place, sleeping, but Barbara Anderson stood in the humming lamplight, hugging her elbows. It was eerily quiet and she could hear Keith coming for two or three blocks before he turned onto her street. He had the heater on in the truck, and when she climbed in he handed her a blue cardigan, which she quickly buttoned up. "Four A.M.," she said, rubbing her hands over the air vent. "Now this is weird out here."

"Yeah," Keith said. "Four o'clock makes it a different planet. I recommend it. But bring a sweater." He looked at her. "You look real sleepy," he said. "You look good. This is the face you ought to bring to school."

Barbara looked at Keith and smiled. "No makeup, okay? It's four A.M." His face looked tired, and in the pale dash lights, with his short, short hair he looked more like a child, a little boy. "What do we do?"

"We give each of these babies," Keith nodded back at the bowling balls in the truck bed, "a new home."

They delivered the balls, placing them carefully on the porches of their friends, including Trish and Brian, and then they spent half an hour finding Mr. Miles's house, which was across town, a tan split-level. Keith handed Barbara the ball marked WALT and made her walk it up to the front porch. When she returned to the truck, Keith said, "Years from now you'll be able to say, 'When I was seventeen I put a bowling ball on my chemistry's teacher's front porch.'"

"His name was Walt," Barbara added.

At five-thirty, as the first gray light rose, Barbara Anderson and Keith walked into Jewel's Café carrying the last two balls: the green beauty and COSMO. Jewel's was the oldest café in the city, an all-night diner full of mailmen. "So," Barbara said, as they slid into one of the huge maroon booths, "who gets these last two?" She was radiant now, fully awake, and energized by the new day.

The waitress appeared and they ordered Round-the-World omelettes, hash browns, juice, milk, coffee, and wheat muffins, and Barbara ate with gusto, looking up halfway through. "So, where next?" She saw his plate. "Hey, you're not eating."

Keith looked odd, his face milky, his eyes gray. "This food is full of the exact amino acids to have a certifiably chemical day," he said. "I'll get around to it."

But he never did. He pushed his plate to the side and turned the place mat over and began to write on it.

"Are you feeling all right?" Barbara said.

"I'm okay."

She tilted her head at him skeptically.

"Hey. I'm okay. I haven't lied to you this far. Why would I start now? You know I'm okay, don't you? Well? Don't you think I'm okay?"

She looked at him and said quietly: "You're okay."

He showed her the note he had written:

Dear Waitress: My girlfriend and I are from rival families—different sides of the tracks, races, creeds, colors, and zip codes, and if they found out we had been out bowling all night, they would banish us to prison schools on separate planets. Please, please find a good home for our only bowling balls. Our enormous sadness is only mitigated by the fact that we know you'll take care of them.

With sweet sorrow—COSMO

In the truck, Barbara said, "Mitigated?"

"Always leave them something to look up."

"You're sick, aren't you?" she said.

"You look good in that sweater," he said. When she started to remove it, he added, "Don't. I'll get it after class, in just," he looked at his watch, "two hours and twenty minutes."

But he wasn't there. He wasn't there all week. The class did experiments with oxidation and Mr. Miles spent two days explaining and diagramming rust. On Friday, Mr. Miles worked with Barbara on the experiments and she asked him what was wrong with Keith. "I'm not sure," her teacher told her. "But I think he's on medication."

Barbara had a tennis match on Tuesday afternoon at school, and Brian picked her up and drove her home. Usually he came in for an hour or so on these school days and they made out a little and raided the fridge, but for the first time she begged off, claiming homework, kissing him on the cheek and running into her house. But on Friday, during her away match at Viewmont, she felt odd again. She knew Brian was in the stands. When she walked off the court after the match it was nearly dark and Brian was waiting. She gave Trish her rackets and Barbara climbed on Brian's scooter without a word. "You weren't that bad," he said. "Viewmont always has a good team."

"Brian, let's just go home."

"You want to stop at Swenson's, get something to eat?"

"No."

So Brian started his scooter and drove them home. Barbara could tell by the way he was driving that he was mad, and it confused her: she felt strangely glad about it. She didn't want to invite him in, let him grope her on the couch. She held on as he took the corners too fast and slipped through the stop signs, but all the way home she didn't put her chin on his shoulder.

At her house, she got the scene she'd been expecting. "Just what is the matter with you?" Brian said. For some reason when he'd gone to kiss her, she'd averted her face. Her heart burned with pleasure and shame. She was going to make up a lie about tennis, but then just said, "Oh Brian. Just leave me alone for a while, will you? Just go home."

Inside, she couldn't settle down. She didn't shower or change clothes. She sat in the dark of her room for a while and then, using only the tiny spot of her desk lamp, she copied her chemistry notes for the week and called Trish.

It was midnight when Trish picked her up quietly by the mailbox on the corner. Trish was smoking one of her Marlboros and blowing smoke into the windshield. She said, *"High School Confidential*, Part Five: Young Barbara Anderson, still in her foxy tennis clothes, and her old friend Trish meet again at midnight, cruise the Strip, pick up two young men with tattoos, and are never seen alive again. Is that it? Count me in."

"Not quite. It goes like this: two sultry babes, one of whom has just been a royal bitch to her boyfriend for no reason, drive to 1147 Fairmont to drop off the week's chemistry notes."

"That would be Keith Zetterstrom's address, I'd guess," Trish said

"He's my lab partner."

"Of course he is," Trish said.

"He missed all last week. Mr. Miles told me that Keith's on medication."

"Oh my god!" Trish clamped the steering wheel. "He's got cancer. That's that scary hairdo. He's sick."

"No he doesn't. I checked the college lists. He's going to Dickinson."

"Not for long, honey. I should have known this." Trish inhaled and blew smoke thoughtfully out of the side of her mouth. "Bald kids in high school without earrings have got cancer."

Keith was in class the following Monday for the chemistry exam: sulfur and rust. After class, Barbara Anderson took him by the arm and led him to her locker. "Thanks for the notes, partner," he said. "They were absolutely chemical. I aced the quiz."

"You were sick last week."

"Last week." He pondered. "Oh, you mean because I wasn't here. What do you do, come every day? I just couldn't; it would take away the something special I feel for this place. I like to come from time to time and keep the dew on the rose, so to speak."

"I know what's the matter with you."

"Good for you, Barbara Anderson. And I know what's the matter with you too; sounds like a promising relationship."

Barbara pulled his folded sweater from the locker and handed it to him. As she did, Brian came up and said to them both: "Oh, I see." He started to walk away.

"Brian," Keith said, "Listen. You don't see. I'm not a threat to you. How could I be a threat to you? Think about it." Brian stood, his eyes narrowed. Keith went on: "Barbara's not stupid. What am I going to do, trick her? I'm her lab partner in chemistry. Relax." Keith went to Brian and took his hand, shook it. "I'm serious, Woodworth."

Brian stood for a moment longer until Barbara said, "I'll see you at lunch," and then he backed and disappeared down the hall. When he was gone, Barbara said, "*Are* you tricking me?"

"I don't know. Something's going on. I'm a little confused."

"You're confused. Who are you? Where have you been, Keith Zetterstrom? I've been going to school with you all these years and I've never even seen you and then we're delivering bowling balls together and now you're sick. Where were you last year? What are you doing? What are you going to do next year?"

"Last year I got a C in Spanish with Mrs. Whitehead. It was gruesome. This year is somewhat worse, with a few exceptions, and all in all, I'd say the sky is the limit." Keith took her wrist. "Quote me on that."

Barbara took a sharp breath through her nose and quietly began to cry.

"Oh, let's not," Keith said, pushing a handkerchief into her hand. "Here. Think of this." He moved her back against the wall, out of the way of students passing by. "If I was having a good year, I might never have spoken to you. Extreme times require extreme solutions. I went all those years sitting in the back and then I had to get sick to start talking. Now that's something, isn't it? Besides, I've got a plan. I'll pick you up at nine. Listen: bring your pajamas and a robe."

Barbara looked at him over the handkerchief.

"Hey. Trust me. You were the one who was crying. I'll see you at nine o'clock. This will cheer you up."

The hospital was on the hill, and Keith parked in the farthest corner of the vast parking lot, one hundred yards from the nearest car. Beneath them in the dark night, the city teemed and shimmered, a million lights.

"It looks like a city on another planet," Barbara Anderson said as she stepped out of the truck.

"It does, indeed," Keith said, grabbing his bag. "Now if we only knew if the residents are friendly." He took her arm. "And now I'm going to cheer you up. I'm going to take you in that building," Keith pointed at the huge hospital, lit like an ocean liner in the night, "and buy you a package of gum."

They changed clothes in the fifth-floor restrooms and met in the hallway, in pajamas and robes, and stuffed their street clothes into Barbara's tennis bag.

"Oh, I feel better already," Barbara said.

"Now take my arm like this," Keith moved next to her and placed her hand above his elbow, "and look down like this." He put his chin on his chest. Barbara tried it. "No, not such a sad face, more serious, be strong. Good. Now walk just like this, little stab steps, real slow."

They started down the hallway, creeping along one side. "How far is it?" Barbara said. People passed them walking quietly in groups of two or three. It was the end of visiting hours. "A hundred yards to the elevators and down three floors, then out a hundred more. Keep your face down."

"Are people looking at us?"

"Well, yes. They've never seen a braver couple. And they've never seen such chemical pajamas. What are those little deals, lambs?"

They continued along the windows, through the lobby and down the elevator, in which they stood side by side, their four hands clasped together, while they were looking at their tennis shoes. The other people in the car gave them room out of respect. The main hall was worse, thick with people, everyone going five miles an hour faster than Barbara and Keith, who shuffled along whispering.

In the gift shop, finally, they parted the waters. The small room was crowded, but the people stepped aside and Keith and Barbara stood right at the counter. "A package of chewing gum, please," Keith said.

"Which kind?" said the candy striper.

"Sugarless. My sister and I want our teeth to last forever."

They ran to the truck, leaping and swinging their arms. Keith threw the bag containing their clothes into the truck bed and climbed into the cab. Barbara climbed in, laughing, and Keith said, "Come on, face the facts: you feel better! You're cured!" And she slid across the seat meaning to hug him but it changed for both of them and they kissed. She pulled him to her side and they kissed again, one of her arms around his neck and one of her hands on his face. They fell into a spin there in the truck, eyes closed, holding on to each other in their pajamas, her robe open, their heads against the backseat, kissing. Barbara shifted and Keith sat up; the look they exchanged held. Below them the city's lights flickered. Barbara cupped her hand carefully on the top of Keith's bald scalp. She pulled him forward and they kissed. When she looked in his eyes again she knew what was going to happen, and it was a powerful feeling that gave her strange new certainty as she went for his mouth again.

There were other moments that surfaced in the truck in the night above the ancient city. Something Keith did, his hand reminded her of Brian, and then that thought vanished as they were beyond Brian in a moment. Later, well beyond even her notions of what to do and what not to do, lathered and breathing as if in toil, she heard herself say, "Yes." She said that several times.

She looked for Keith everywhere, catching glimpses of his head, his shoulder, in the hallways. In chemistry they didn't talk; there were final reports, no need to work together. Finally, three days before graduation, they stood side by side cleaning out their chemistry equipment locker, waiting for Mr. Miles to check them off. Keith's manner was what? Easy, too confident, too neutral. He seemed to take up too much space in the room. She hated the way he kept his face blank and open, as if fishing for the first remark. She held off, feeling the restraint as a physical pang. Mr. Miles inventoried their cupboard and asked for their keys. He had a large ring of thirty or forty of the thin brass keys. Keith handed his to Mr. Miles and then Barbara Anderson found her key in the side of her purse and handed it to the teacher. She hated relinquishing the key; it was the only thing she had that meant she would see Keith, and now with it gone something opened in her and it hurt in a way she'd never hurt before. Keith turned to her and seeing something in her face, shrugged and said, "The end of chemistry as we know it. Which isn't really very well."

"Who are you?" Barbara said, her voice a kind of surprise to her. "You're so glib. Such a little actor." Mr. Miles looked up from his check sheet and several students turned toward them. Barbara was speaking loudly; she couldn't help it. "What are you doing to me? If you ask me this is a pretty chickenshit good-bye." Everyone was looking at her. Then her face would not work at all, the tears coming from some hot place, and Barbara Anderson walked from the room.

Keith hadn't moved. Mr. Miles looked at Keith, alarmed. Keith whispered: "Don't worry, Mr. Miles. She was addressing her remarks to me."

There was one more scene. The night before graduation, while her classmates met in the bright, noisy gym for the yearbook-signing party, Barbara drove out to the airport and met Keith where he said he'd be: at the last gate, H-17. There on an empty stretch of maroon carpet in front of three large banks of seats full of travelers, he was waiting. He handed her a pretty green canvas valise and an empty paper ticket sleeve.

"You can't even talk as yourself," she said. "You always need a setting. Now we're pretending I'm going somewhere?"

He looked serious tonight, weary. There were gray shadows under his eyes. "You wanted a goodbye scene," he said. "I tried not to do this."

"It's all a joke," she said. "You joke all the time."

"You know what my counselor said?" He smiled thinly as if glad to give her this point. "He said that this is a phase, that I'll stop joking soon." Their eyes met and the look held again. "Come here," he said. She stepped close to him. He put his hand on her elbow. "You want a farewell speech. Okay, here you go. You better call Brian and get your scooter back. Tell him I tricked you. Wake up, lady. Get real. I just wanted to see if I could give Barbara Anderson a whirl. And I did. It was selfish, okay? I just screwed you around a little. You said it yourself: it was a joke. That's my speech. How was it?"

"You didn't screw me around, Keith. You didn't give me a whirl." Barbara moved his hand and then put her arms around his neck so she could speak in his ear. She could see some of the people watching them. "You made love to me, Keith. It wasn't a joke. You made love to me and I met you tonight to say—good for you. Extreme times require extreme solutions." She was whispering as they stood alone on that carpet in their embrace. "I wondered how it was going to happen, but you were a surprise. Way to go. What did you think? That I wanted to go off to college an eighteen-year-old virgin? That pajama bit was great; I'll remember it." Now people were deplaning, entering the gate area and streaming around the young couple. Barbara felt Keith begin to tremble, and she closed her eyes. "It wasn't a joke. There's this: I made love to you too. You were there, remember? I'm glad for it." She pulled back slightly and found his lips. For a moment she was keenly aware of the public scene they were making, but that disappeared and they twisted tighter and were just there, kissing. She had dropped the valise and when the mock ticket slipped from her fingers behind his neck, a young woman in a business suit knelt and retrieved it and tapped Barbara on the hand. Barbara clutched the ticket and dropped her head to Keith's chest.

"I remember," he said. "My memory is aces."

"Tell me, Keith," she said. "What are these people thinking? Make something up."

"No need. They've got it right. That's why we came out here. They think we're saying goodbye."

Simply put, that was the last time Barbara Anderson saw Keith Zetterstrom. That fall when she arrived in Providence for her freshman year at Brown, there was one package waiting for her, a large trophy topped by a girl on a motorcycle. She had seen it before. She kept it in her dorm window, where it was visible four stories from the ground, and she told her roommates that it meant a lot to her, that it represented a lot of fun and hard work but her goal had been to win the Widowmaker Hill Climb, and once she had done that, she sold her bikes and gave up her motorcycles forever.

◧ ◧ ◧

Writing Exercises

1. Do a word count of one of your stories. Suppose that it has been accepted for publication, but the magazine has one condition: You must cut it by twenty-five percent. Figure out your word count goal and edit toward it. Be both aggressive and picky. Cut any expendable scenes or paragraphs, but also wring out every extraneous word and phrase. Cut beyond the twenty-five percent if it feels right to do so.

2. Photocopy a published story you like and highlight the direct dialogue in one color and all indirect discourse or summarized dialogue in another color. Do the same for your most recent story. Compare the two. Are your most important lines in direct dialogue or summarized? (Generally, these should be direct.) Is information or idle chatter direct or summarized? (Generally, these should be summarized.) Revise to make sure that the most important moments are in direct dialogue.

3. For his novel *A Farewell to Arms*, Ernest Hemingway wrote thirty-nine endings before finding the one he decided was best. For one of your stories, write three different endings, each one showing, in some way, how your main character has been changed by the action in the story. Think about what is resolved and what is left unresolved with each ending. Then ask yourself what really needs to happen, emotionally, to your character by the end. In each ending, have the main character's emotional needs truly been addressed, or have you simply tied up some loose ends the reader doesn't care about?

4. Write three new openings to one of your stories. Each one should be at least a few paragraphs long. In each opening, start from a different moment in the story—maybe even at the very end. (Richard Ford's story "Great Falls" opens with these two sentences: "This is not a happy story. I warn you.") What possibilities are created by these new openings?

5. Select one of your stories that is causing you trouble. Print out a hard copy and cut it into scenes, summary, and flashbacks. Number each piece in the order in which it appears. Then lay these pieces out on a table or floor and see what you've got. How many scenes are there? Is every scene necessary? Can some be combined, deleted, or summarized? Are important scenes buried in sections of summary? Are there missing scenes? Is the material from the past in the right places? Try rearranging the sequence of events. Experiment. Move beyond fiddling with sentences to this kind of reenvisioning and rearranging.

6. Choose one of your stories that seems low in tension and try to pump up every conflict you find and add new ones. Don't be afraid to be ridiculous; you can always back off later. Throw more and bigger obstacles in your character's way. Let this revision sit for a day or two; then go back and see how much of what you've added does in fact work.

7. Look back through some of the stories you've read in this book and ask what, exactly, the main character wants in each story. Then look at some of your own stories and ask yourself the same question. If you don't have an answer, or if the answer is vague or rambling, you probably don't yet know either your character or his story.

8. Take one of your stories that isn't quite working yet and explore the main character by writing from that character's point of view. You might have her write out a diary entry, an e-mail, a dream, a letter, or even a short autobiography. Don't worry about whether or not what you write will actually fit into the story. It might, but it might not. In either case, you'll probably learn something important about your character and her story.

9. You may have written a story that is too tidy, one that needs to be messed up a bit. Take a story of yours with a very "final" ending—one in which a relationship ends, someone dies, success is achieved, a moral is revealed, or the like. Now rewrite the opening, briefly announcing the story's final outcome (i.e., "This was a few months before Ted left me, our last Christmas as a married couple"). Now reexamine your story. How does giving away the ending affect it? Is the reader still motivated to read through to the end? Revise your story so it remains compelling even though you may well decide to return your ending to its original place.

10. Each year in the back of the *Best American Short Stories* and *O. Henry Prize Stories*, the winning authors write a paragraph or two in which they discuss the genesis of their stories. Take a look at some of these, and then try it yourself. After your story has been workshopped, but before you've started the next draft, write a "contributor's note" similar to those in the back of the *Best American* or *O. Henry*. How did the story first occur to you? What intrigued you about it? How did the story evolve? Which of your plans changed, and why? What do you hope that readers will think the story is "about"? Read these contributors' notes aloud in class. Do they help you articulate the dramatic and thematic elements you wish to address in the revision process? Does your note illuminate the story or is it merely an explanation of what should be in the story, but hasn't yet made it there?

11. Spend about half an hour writing a scene that involves a conflict between two characters. Make a copy of what you write. Send the other

copy home with a class member so he or she can write on it, making critical comments and suggestions. Keep the other copy for yourself, and take it home and rewrite it. When you get your reader's copy back, compare your impulses with those of your reader. Now, let everything sit for another day, so that you can "forgive" your reader and let yourself accept some of his or her ideas. On the day after that, rewrite the scene once more, incorporating the most intriguing of your reader's suggestions.

APPENDIX

KINDS OF FICTION

What follows is a discussion of some kinds of fiction likely to be found in current books and magazines, which are also the kinds of contemporary narrative most likely to show up in a workshop. This is not by any means a comprehensive list, nor does it deal with the forms that represent the history of narrative—myth, tale, fable, allegory, and so forth—some of which are mentioned elsewhere in this book.

Mainstream refers to fiction that deals with subject matter with a broad appeal—situations and emotions common to and of interest to large numbers of readers in the culture for which it is intended. Mainstream fiction is **literary fiction** if its appeal is also lodged in the original, interesting, and illuminating use of the language; the term also implies a degree of care in the psychological exploration of its characters, and an attempt to shed light on the human condition. All of the stories in this volume fall under the general category of literary fiction.

Literary fiction differs from **genre fiction** fundamentally in the fact that the former is character-driven, the latter plot-driven. There is a strong tendency—though it is not a binding rule—of genre fiction to imply that life is fair, and to let the hero or heroine, after great struggle, win out in the end; and of literary fiction to posit that life is not fair, that triumph is partial, happiness tentative, and that the heroine and hero are subject to mortality. Literary fiction also strives to reveal its meaning through the creation of unexpected or unusual characters, through patterns of action and turns of event that will surprise the reader. Genre fiction, on the other hand, tends to develop character stereotypes and set patterns of action that become part of the expectation, the demand, and the pleasure of the readers of that genre.

Readers of the **romance** genre, for example, will expect a plucky-but-down-on-her-luck heroine, a handsome and mysterious hero with some dark secret (usually a dark-haired woman) in his background, a large house, some woods (through which the heroine will at some point flee in scanty clothing), and an eventual happy ending with the heroine in the hero's arms. These elements can be seen in embryo in the literary fiction of the Brontë sisters; by now, in the dozens of Harlequin and Silhouette romances on the supermarket rack, they have become **formulaic,** and the language is similar from book to book.

Like romance, most genres have developed from a kind of fiction that was at one time mainstream and represented a major social problem or concern. Early romance, for example, dealt with the serious question of how a woman was to satisfy the need for both stability and love in married life, how to be both independent and secure in a society with rigid sexual rules. The **detective story** evolved simultaneously with widespread and intense interest in science, an optimistic expectation that violence and mystery could be rationally explained. The **western** dealt with the ambivalence felt by large numbers of westward-traveling Euro-Americans about the civilizing of the wilderness, the desire to rid the West of its brutality, the fear that "taming" it would also destroy its promise of solitude and freedom. **Science fiction,** the most recently developed and still developing genre, similarly deals with ambivalence about technology, the near-miraculous accomplishments of the human race through science, the dangers to human feeling, soul, and environment. The surge in popularity of **fantasy fiction** can probably be attributed to nostalgia for a time even more free of technological accomplishment and threat, since fantasy employs a medieval setting and solves problems through magic, whereas science fiction is set in the future and solves problems through intelligence and technology. It is relevant that science fiction usually deals with some problem that can be seen to have a counterpart in the contemporary culture (space travel, international or interplanetary intrigue, mechanical replacement of body parts, genetic manipulation), whereas the plots of fantasies tend to deal with obsolete or archaic traumas—wicked overlords, demon interlopers, and so forth. Because of this contemporary concern, science fiction seems capable at this point in history of a deployment much more varied and original than other genres, and more often engages the attention of writers (and filmmakers) with literary intentions and ambitions. Among such writers are Octavia Butler, William Gibson, J. B. Ballard, Ray Bradbury, Ursula K. Le Guin, Philip K. Dick, and Doris Lessing.

In any case, the many other genres, including but not confined to **adventure, spy, horror,** and **thriller,** each have their own set of conventions of character, language, and events. Note again that the very naming of these kinds of fiction implies a narrowing; unlike mainstream fiction, they appeal to a particular range of interest.

Many—perhaps most—teachers of fiction writing do not accept manuscripts in genre, and I believe there's good reason for this, which is that whereas writing literary fiction can teach you how to write good genre fiction, writing genre fiction does not teach you how to write good literary fiction—does not, in effect, teach you "how to write," by which I mean how to be original and meaningful in words. Further, dealing in the conventions and hackneyed phrases of romance, horror, fantasy, and so forth, can operate as a form of personal denial, using writing as a means of avoiding rather than uncovering your real concerns. It may be fine to offer readers an escape through fiction, but it isn't a way to educate yourself as a writer, and it's also fair to say that escape does not represent the goal of a liberal education, which is to pursue, inquire, seek, and extend knowledge of whatever subject is at hand, fiction no less than science.

Partly because many college teachers of creative writing do not welcome genre fiction in the classroom, there has developed a notion of a "workshop story" that is realistic, sensitive, and small. I have never known a teacher who solicited such stories, or any particular sort of story. Leaps of imagination, originality, and genuine experimentation are in my experience welcome to both instructors and students. But it is true that often what seems wild and crazy to the student writer has occurred to others before. Stories set in dreams, outer space, game shows, heaven and hell, may seem strange and wonderful by comparison with daily life, but they are familiar as "experiments" and likely to be less startling to their readers than the author expects, whereas extreme focus on what the author has experienced may seem striking and fresh. **Realism**—the attempt to render an authentic picture of life, in such a way that the reader identifies with one or more characters—is a fair starting point for the pursuit of literary fiction. The writer's attempt at verisimilitude is comparable to the scientific method of observation and verification. Realism is also a convention, and not the only way to begin to write; but like the drawing of still life in the study of painting, it can impart skills that will be useful in more sophisticated efforts whether they are realistic or not. Many of the stories in this book are realistic; "Tandolfo the Great," "Mrs. Dutta Writes a Letter," and "Keith," for example, might be seen as attempts to reveal in recognizable detail the drama of ordinary life.

Experimental fiction is always possible, however. It's more difficult by far to describe what is experimental in fiction than what is cliché, because by definition the experimental is the thing that nobody expects or predicts. There are, however, a number of kinds of experiment that have come to be recognized as subsets of literary fiction, and a few of these are worth mentioning.

Magic realism uses the techniques and devices of realism—verisimilitude, ordinary lives and settings, familiar psychology—and introduces events of impossible or fantastic nature, never leaving the tone and techniques of realism. Whereas fantasy will attempt to bedazzle its readers with the amazing quality of the magic, magic realism works in the opposite direction, to convince the reader that the extraordinary occurs in the context and the guise of the ordinary. David Lodge, in *The Art of Fiction,* interestingly points out that the practitioners of magic realism tend to have lived through some sort of historical upheaval—a political coup or terror, a literal war or gender war. Flight, he points out, is a central image in this fiction, because the defiance of gravity represents a persistent "human dream of the impossible." Colombian novelist Gabriel García Márquez is a foremost practitioner of magic realism, and his novel *One Hundred Years of Solitude* is the best-known example of the genre. Interested readers might also look for *Labyrinths* by Jorge Luis Borges, who is often considered the father of this experimental mode.

Metafiction takes as its subject matter the writing of fiction, calls attention to its own techniques, and insists that what is happening is that a story is being written and read. Often the writing of the story is used as a metaphor for some other human struggle or endeavor.

Minimalism (also called miniaturism) refers to a flat, spare, and subdued style of writing, characterized by an accumulation of (sometimes apparently random) detail that gives an impression of benumbed emotion. The point of view tends to be objective or near-objective, the events accumulating toward a tense, disturbing—and inconclusive—conclusion.

The short-short story or **sudden fiction** is a fiction under 2,000 words; **microfictions** is a term sometimes used to distinguish stories under 250 words. Such pieces, according to Nancy Huddleston Packer, "push to the limit the basic elements of all short stories—compression, suggestion, and change. They combine the intensity and lyricism of a poem with the dramatic impact and movement of a short story—these stories are so compressed, they explode." In a short-short story, change is often subtle, taking form as a moment of surprise or a shift in perception.

It's always comforting to have a good reference book on hand when an unfamiliar literary term comes up. Two I recommend are *The Fiction Dictionary* by Laurie Henry (Cincinnati: Story Press, 1995) and *The Bedford Glossary of Critical and Literary Terms*, 3rd ed., by Ross Murfin and Supryia M. Ray (Boston and New York: Bedford Books, 2008).

Credits

Sherman Alexie. "What You Pawn I Will Redeem" from *Ten Little Indians* by Sherman Alexie, published by Secker & Warburg. Copyright © 2003 by Sherman Alexie. Used by permission of Grove/Atlantic, Inc. and The Random House Group Ltd.

Yehuda Amichai. Three lines from "We Did It" from *Songs of Jerusalem and Myself* by Yehuda Amichai and translated by Harold Schimmel. Copyright © 1973 by Yehuda Amichai. English Translation copyright © 1973 by Harold Schimmel. Reprinted by permission of HarperCollins Publishers.

Richard Bausch. "Tandolfo the Great" from *The Stories of Richard Bausch* by Richard Bausch. Copyright © 1992 by Richard Bausch. Reprinted by permission of HarperCollins Publishers.

Ron Carlson. "Early Draft of 'Oh Keith'" by Ron Carlson. Copyright © by Ron Carlson. Reprinted by permission of Brandt & Hochman Literary Agents, Inc. All rights reserved.

Ron Carlson. "Keith" from *A Kind of Flying: Selected Stories* by Ron Carlson. Copyright © 2003, 1997, 1992, 1987 by Ron Carlson. Used by permission of W. W. Norton & Company, Inc.

Ron Carlson. "Keith," copyright © 1993 by Ron Carlson. Originally appeared in *Tell* magazine, also appeared in *A Kind of Flying: Selected Stories* by Ron Carlson. Reprinted by permission of Brandt & Hochman Literary Agents, Inc. All rights reserved.

Ron Carlson. "Notes on Keith" by Ron Carlson. Copyright © 1997 by Ron Carlson. Reprinted by permission of Brandt & Hochman Literary Agents, Inc. All rights reserved.

Dan Chaon. "Big Me" from *Among the Missing* by Dan Chaon. Copyright © 2001 by Dan Chaon. Used by permission of Ballantine Books, a division of Random House, Inc.

Junot Diaz. "Fiesta 1980" from *Drown* by Junot Diaz. Copyright © 1996 by Junot Diaz. Used by permission of Riverhead Books, an imprint of Penguin Group (USA) Inc.

Junot Diaz. "Fiesta 1980" from *Drown* by Junot Diaz. Copyright © 1996 by Junot Diaz. Used by permission of Faber and Faber (UK) Inc.

Chitra Banerjee Divakaruni. "Mrs. Dutta Writes a Letter" from *The Unknown Errors of Our Lives* by Chitra Banerjee Divakaruni. Copyright © 2001 by Chitra Banerjee Divakaruni. Used by permission of Doubleday, a division of Random House, Inc. Copyright © 1998 by Chitra Divakaruni. First published in *The Atlantic Monthly*. Reprinted by permission of the author and the Sandra Dijkstra Literary Agency.

Stuart Dybek. "We Didn't" from *I Sailed with Magellan* by Stuart Dybek. Copyright © 2003 by Stuart Dybek. Reprinted by permission of Farrar, Straus and Giroux, LLC

Pia Z. Erhardt. "Following the Notes" by Pia Z. Ehrhardt. Reprinted by permission of author.

Teolinda Gersão. "The Red Fox Fur Coat" by Teolinda Gersão. Reprinted by permission of the author.

John Gould. "Feelers" from *Kilter* by John Gould. Copyright © 2005 by John Gould. Reprinted by permission of Other Press LLC.

John Gould. "Feelers" from *Kilter* by John Gould. Copyright © 2005 by John Gould. Reprinted by permission of Turnstone Press LLC.

John Gould. "Feelers" from *Kilter* by John Gould. Copyright © 2005 by John Gould. Reprinted by permission of The Cooke Agency.

Ron Hansen. "My Kid's Dog" by Ron Hansen. Copyright by Ron Hansen. Reprinted by permission of SLL/Sterling Lord Literistic, Inc.

Robin Hemley. "Reply All" from *Sudden Fiction* by Robin Hemley. Copyright © 2007 by Robin Hemley. Reprinted by permission of International Creative Management, Inc.

Gish Jen. "Who's Irish?" by Gish Jen. Copyright © 1998 by Gish Jen. First published in *The New Yorker*. Reprinted with permission by Melanie Jackson Agency, LLC.

Jill McCorkle. "Hominids" from *Creatures of Habit* by Jill McCorkle. Copyright © 2001 by Jill McCorkle. Reprinted by permission of Algonquin Books of Chapel Hill and Darhansoff, Verrill, Feldman Literary Agents. All rights reserved.

Joyce Carol Oates. Excerpt from "'Where Are You Going, Where Have You Been?' Smooth Talk: Short Story Into Film" from *(Woman) Writer: Occasions and Opportunities* by Joyce Carol Oates. Copyright © 1988 by The Ontario Review. Used by permission of Dutton, a division of Penguin Group (USA) Inc. and John Hawkins Associates, Inc.

Flannery O'Connor. "Everything That Rises Must Converge" from *The Complete Stories* by

Index

403